D1234433

NOTE: The legend under the diagram on page 46 should read

- - - - - - - - - CITY BOUNDARY

VICTOR GRUEN

THE HEART OF OUR CITIES

THE URBAN CRISIS: DIAGNOSIS AND CURE

SIMON AND SCHUSTER NEW YORK • 1964

PUBLISHED BY SIMON AND SCHUSTER, INC.
ROCKEFELLER CENTER, 630 FIFTH AVENUE
NEW YORK 20, N.Y.

FIRST PRINTING

LIBRARY OF CONGRESS CATALOG CARD NUMBER: 64-13607
MANUFACTURED IN THE UNITED STATES OF AMERICA

DESIGNED BY EDITH FOWLER

TO LAZETTE

Whose sudden death, in July 1962, robbed me not only of a beloved and most wonderful wife but also of one who gave inspiration to all my work, including this book

Contents

Introduction

Planning a Book on Planning

WHAT BETTER OPPORTUNITY could there be for planning a book on planning than a leisurely ocean voyage? I did this some years ago aboard the *Leonardo da Vinci,* flagship of the Italian Line, as it cut its path through the Atlantic toward Europe. Here, midway between the bustling North American continent with its busy and oftentimes dizzy activity, with its sprawling cities of comparatively recent vintage, and old Europe which, though once again prosperous, remains more sedate in its ways; midway between my active work as an environmental architect and a holiday period; midway between daily routine and relaxations, I started the task.

A big ship is a good place to think about the fate of our cities. Carrying 1,255 passengers and nearly as many crew members, this beautiful vessel with its truly functional design is a city in itself, one which is carefully planned to the last detail to function and operate in order to offer comfort and convenience. On it are solved daily problems of administration, of housing, of food storage and preparation, of health, of entertainment, of social functions. This city has its own shops, hospitals, and its own power station.

It is one of the rare cities that do not have internal traffic problems. There is some public transportation in the form of elevators that whisk people and goods up and down between the eight decks, but it is free of the problems which private transportation in the form of automobiles poses in other human settlements.

It is a pedestrian island swimming across the water. Its temporary citizens make fullest use of the opportunities offered by the restfulness of the environment. They promenade and amble. They sit around in deck chairs reading or conversing.

The *Leonardo da Vinci* is an extremely compact city. Even its most luxurious staterooms are comparatively small, and thus all citizens live close to each other. Maybe this explains why social contacts are so easily made and why in a matter of days a civic spirit of the community develops.

Leisurely travel aboard a ship makes me contemplative (in contrast to the speedy trip on a jet plane, which just makes me impatient). And thus, midway between the American and European continents I thought about cities I have experienced in my adult life, which is divided about equally between stays in Europe and the United States. I thought of the city in which I was born and where I lived until I was thirty-five years old—Vienna, a place of intense urban character, saturated with history and tradition, a city in which revolutions and counterrevolutions were discussed in the coffeehouses and executed on the boulevards. In Vienna they refer to the compact amassment of buildings which make up this extremely compact settlement as "*das Haeusermeer*," or "ocean of houses." It presents a most dramatic contrast to the lovely wreath of forests and meadows, the Vienna Woods, which surrounds it—where weekend after weekend I used to hike in summer, ski in winter.

My thoughts turned to the many cities and towns that had become meaningful to me as a child and as a young man, which I have revisited again and again during the last twelve years: Hamburg, the city where my mother was born and where we used to spend our summers, a city that embraces a lovely lake, the Alster; Berlin, where I visited my cousins almost every year, and which used to intimidate me with its bustling life; Budapest, a city that has been fashioned by the Danube as it winds between monumental buildings—a brilliant example of urban design; Prague and Salzburg, both cities in which the hills form an integral part of cityscape; Venice, which has preserved its magic undisturbed by motor noises and where architectural beauty counts for more than it does anywhere else because one can contemplate it on foot; Aix-en-Provence, where the shadows of gigantic trees are so deep that one receives the illusion of walking under water; Paris, with its strong contrasts of majestic boulevards and narrow streets, of brilliant life and quiet intimacy; and all those other cities like London and Rome, Stockholm and Copenhagen, each of which, with its strong individuality, has impressed itself on my mind.

And then my thoughts wandered in the opposite direction. I remembered the day in July, 1938, when, traveling as a refugee on another ship, the *Staatendam,* I got my first glimpse of the mountain peaks of Manhattan. I thought of Los Angeles, where my children were born and raised, where our main office is located and where I have spent about half my time since 1940—a place I do not think of in terms of a city at all but rather in terms of the gardens and houses I myself have inhabited and those of my friends and acquaintances, and of the highways that connect them and to which the buildings of the city seem to be only incidental. I thought of Detroit, where I lived for many months, working on my first big architectural assignment; of Boston, Philadelphia and San Francisco, which always seem to me to have the most in common with European cities; and of the dozens of large and medium-sized cities and towns which, in contrast, seem to have little individuality, congealing in my memory into one picture: Main Street, U.S.A.

The trip on the *Leonardo da Vinci* proved in another way a good inspiration for this book. Along the walls of the public rooms are exhibited drawings and models of the work of the great man for whom this city afloat was named—designs for flying machines, for war machines, sketches for paintings and, most interesting to me, architectural and city planning concepts in which Leonardo da Vinci approximately five hundred years ago proposed cities in which human functions are strictly separated from purely utilitarian ones, cities in which the basement levels are used for cars and carriages, the ground level reserved for walking only. One of the schemes shows a city with underground canals where all transportation is taken care of by boat. The surface land then is devoted to pedestrian streets, plazas and lanes surrounded by arcaded or colonnaded buildings.

Sections through Leonardo da Vinci's ideal city. All vehicular traffic moves through underground tunnels. The surface space between colonnaded buildings is reserved for pedestrians only.

Leonardo da Vinci's variation on his theme. Here traffic moves on boats and barges on lower levels; people on foot move through colonnades on ground level.

One of the serious problems we encounter in the planning of our environment is that hundreds of specialists seem to approach it from varying points of departure over divergent avenues of procedure. The men of the Renaissance did not have this problem. How would one classify Leonardo da Vinci? As an architect? A city planner? An engineer? A sculptor? An industrial designer? A graphic designer? A transportation expert? He had no title, no license, no academic degree.

In planning this book I decided that I had to try to break through the divisions and barriers which specialization has put up. I propose to deal with the planning of the man-made, man-influenced environment from an over-all point of view. Under the term *planning* I understand an activity (not necessarily executed by professionals) which projects experiences of the past into the foreseeable future and has the aim of creating that amount of order necessary to make possible the fullest extent of individual expression.

In discussing the planning of the man-made and man-influenced environment, I shall concentrate on the urban environment and, specifically, on the essence of urbia: the core of the city, which I shall call its "heart."

Geographically, I shall concentrate on the heart of the cities of the United States, which, because of the stormy technological and demographic development, seem to be the ones most immediately threatened in the Western world.

Thematically, I shall concentrate on action necessary to end the urban crisis and to bring about the renaissance of the city.

Historically, I shall concentrate on the present and the foreseeable future.

In contrast to the areas of emphasis, which are chosen with deliberation, the areas of de-emphasis are forced upon me by lack of space and the need to concentrate on what, in my opinion, not only is most essential but has not been sufficiently covered by others. This need for restraint is not foreign to an architect who, if he wishes his structures to become a reality, must limit the scope of every project. Such restraint on my part is made easier by the fact that certain areas, of great importance to the planning of cities, have been dealt with excellently in the works of others. Thus, I feel I can exclude, without too much danger, statistical information dealing with population growth, sociological changes, housing supply, etc., since excellent data are available in books and periodicals dealing with research on cities and their metropolitan areas.

The shortcomings of our cities have been dealt with by professional writers, historians, and critics of high academic standing—those to whom New York's autocratic anti-planner, Robert Moses, refers as "ivory tower planners and counselors of despair." Though I do not share Mr. Moses' hostile attitude toward those who are thinkers rather than doers, I do not intend to deal with urban problems from either a purely critical or a purely historical point of view. Lewis Mumford's book *The City in History,* for example, is a thorough, scholarly work on the development of urban life since the beginning of mankind. Mr. Mumford states that in order to deal with the problems of today, we need a "long running start in history." In his book, the largest space is devoted to that long running start, and it would be my hope to begin where he leaves off: with the action needed at present to secure the better cities of the future.

An excellent critical appraisal of certain parts of the urban environment is contained in Jane Jacobs' book, *The Death and Life of Great American Cities.* Mrs. Jacobs devotes her study to residential sections with a special flavor, as found in some of the older cities; sections like Greenwich Village in New York, some parts of Boston, Philadelphia, and Chicago. Some, though by no means all, of the results of her critical appraisal are applicable to urbia generally; so, too, are some of her findings and recommendations.

Another part of today's metropolis is critically and effectively dealt with in *A Crack in the Picture Window,* the book by John C. Keats, which specifically debunks the suburban myth.

Many other books and articles have appeared in the last twenty years which deal with the essential backdrop either historically, critically or sociologically. I shall mention those I am familiar with in the reading list at the end of this book, hoping thus to assist those of my readers who may wish to explore further in this all-important field of human existence.

Though many of the experiences, ideas and concepts expressed in this book are based on those of theorists, planners, architects and philosophers past and present, and though many have been developed specifically in cooperation with the partners, associates and staff members of Victor Gruen Associates, I am speaking in this book for myself alone. In doing so I am acting not from a selfish desire to take credit for the concepts and ideas expressed but because it would be unfair to expect those of my co-workers who may not agree with everything I have to say to share the responsibility. For this reason, too, when it comes to the explanation and description of projects that I regard as contributions toward the solution of the urban crisis, I shall utilize in the main those with which I am most thoroughly familiar, which will necessarily have to be those in which I have actively participated or cooperated within the framework of my professional activities. In doing so, I trust I shall not be misunderstood as either having no respect for the work of others or wanting to blow my own horn. It is simply that, having easier access to the background and planning material, as well as the most intimate knowledge about the virtues and shortcomings, of work that has originated from our offices, I am persuaded to utilize it for examples and illustration.

My own position as the writer of a book is a peculiar one. I have no business writing a book because writing is not my business; and yet I believe that a book about the city, if it is to be constructive, can best be written by one who has fought, and is fighting actively, for a better man-made environment. The battle line is not exactly the most peaceful place in which to write contemplatively. This worried me for a long time, until I realized that I have been writing this book over the last fifteen years and that many parts of it were actually suggested by those who, at citizens' meetings, public hearings, or in personal interviews, expressed their reactions to various features of projects which we presented. This book was born in animated discussions around the drafting tables, on endless walks through dozens of cities, during lively conversations with my co-workers, during subway rushes and traffic jams, long before I ever set pen to paper.

One of the troubles of our era is specialization, leading to a condition in which people working in a special field within the over-all environment do not understand each other's language, or even try to. There is a further division of specialists into "thinkers" and "doers," with the thinkers often having lost contact with reality, and the doers bustling about, devoting neither time nor interest to reflection.

The reshaping of the man-made environment cannot even be approached by compartmentalization. Planning is a coordinating activity that embraces hundreds of the so-called specialties, guiding them into a single entity that transcends them all. I would like to think that this book may form a bridge between the thinkers, theoreticians, contemplators on the one hand, and the doers and practitioners on the other. Each is important to the other, and both are vital to the end result. For I have faith in the old English proverb that states, "Great thoughts reduced to practice become great actions."

Planning is not an activity reserved for a special profession. It is everybody's business. To contemplate what we are going to do in the foreseeable future is an activity that may be, and generally is, exercised by everyone: the housewife who plans her meals, the businessman who plans for expansion, the family that plans a vacation, the man who plans for retirement. Whatever our walk of life, we are all planners. Therefore, this book addresses itself to all who live in a city, work in a city, who sometimes enjoy it and often hate it. In our increasingly urbanized society, that is the vast majority of the population.

I shall regard this book as a failure unless it is understood not only by those who are professionally active but by all those who are involved.

Whether or not we are going to make progress in the betterment of urban environment and at what speed we will be able to proceed depends on the fullest and most widespread understanding of the problems and extent of the crisis, and on a realization of the potentials for progress.

Because I am convinced of the need for the broadest participation, I have tried to write this book not in the jargon of the planners, the secret shorthand writing of the small circle who make their living by planning, designing and building the city, but in a language understandable to all whose lives are bound up in that of the city.

The bringing about of order is one of the main characteristics of the activity of planning. In planning a book about planning, it thus behooves me to organize the contents. I have therefore divided the book into three main parts and each of the parts into chapters. The first part, "The City," attempts to define the term, describe the city's purpose, meaning and content. The second part, "The Anti-City," deals with the symptoms of degeneration which together form the phenomenon we sometimes call the urban crisis. The third part, "The Counterattack," traces the efforts, already under way or projected, to restore the functions and the enjoyableness of the city.

Thus I have attempted to contain elements of the over-all material within specific boundaries: parts and chapters. But just as, in the planning of the human environment, orderliness is only the fertile ground from which variety and diversification sprout, the formal pattern of the chapters and parts is occasionally modified by the inclusion of thoughts and asides which, though they may seem to be digressions, are essential to the consideration of the diversity of human needs. The reader therefore, I hope, will excuse overlappings and discussion of apparently extraneous matters, side trips and excursions which may not fit into a strict discipline but which can hardly be avoided if planning is considered not as a technical practice but as an activity concerned with human needs and individual freedom.

As I proceeded to outline the plan, I finally asked myself, "Why am I writing this book?" The answer is that I believe I have something of significance to contribute.

The contribution I hope to make is based on deep convictions which, in turn, have evolved out of the experiences of my life, which is a tale of many cities: a tale of living in cities, working in cities, and being active in trying to improve the urban environment.

These convictions are:

> Though we live in a time of urban crisis, there is such an overpowering need for the values of urbanism that the crisis will be overcome.

After a long period of lethargy in consciously shaping our environment, strong feelings about the impact of a desirable environment on our health and economy are spreading.

Most of the facts that make up the urban crisis are the direct result of a man-made mess. I am convinced that man-made disorder can be straightened out by man.

The renaissance of urbia is not only necessary but possible. In the last decades we have learned much with regard to methods and approaches toward the aim.

The renaissance of urbia is, in fact, already under way.

PART ONE

THE CITY

The cities—their needs, their future, their financing—these are the great unspoken, overlooked, underplayed problems of our times.

—JOHN F. KENNEDY,
President of the
United States of America,
1962

Our society will never be great until our cities are great. In the next forty years we must rebuild the entire urban United States. . . . There is the decay of the centers and the despoiling of the suburbs. There is not enough housing for our people or transportation for our traffic. Open land is vanishing and old landmarks are violated. . . . A few years ago we were concerned about the ugly American. Today we must act to prevent an ugly America.

—LYNDON B. JOHNSON,
President of the
United States of America,
1964

What Makes a City?

"But ah, Paris! He who has not stopped in admiration of your dark passageways, before your glimpses of light, in your blind alleys deep and silent, he who has not heard your murmur between midnight and two in the morning, does not know your true poetry nor your strange and vast antitheses."

—Honoré de Balzac,
Ferragus, Chef des Dévorants

That an urban crisis engulfing most parts of the civilized world exists is obvious to everybody who lives and works in urban conglomerations. The feeling of frustration in dealing with life in urbia is so strong that there are some who would like to abandon the city altogether.

The idea of the city has always had its enemies. There have always been those who characterized the city as a cesspool of human vices, as the breeding ground of social evils, and there are many who argue and feel that cities generally should be destroyed as the Lord destroyed Sodom and Gomorrah for their licentious way of life, and Babylon for its voluptuousness and iniquitous behavior. But, although the city has numerous enemies, it seems, like a cat, to have nine lives. It is said that several successive cities have stood on the approximate site of Delhi, India. Think of Rome, burned, sacked and destroyed time and again, yet still flourishing today, larger than ever. Think of the destruction of cities in Europe and Japan during World War II, some of them, like Coventry and Warsaw, with the outspoken intention of wiping them off the face of the globe forever, and note that every single one of them has been built up and is again brimming with urban life. Think of Hiroshima and Nagasaki, demolished, it seemed, forever by that most terrible of weapons, the atomic bomb; yet built up again, stone by stone; living and functioning once more in spite of the terror and the suffering experienced by those who survived the holocaust.

Today's urban crisis, however, is brought on by dangers much more deadly than the ones of the past. What the sword and fire, what earthquakes and floods, what artillery, bombs and even atom bombs could not manage—the killing of the city, of urban life, and urbane culture—may be brought about by creeping anti-urbanitis, aided and abetted by those seemingly harmless "advantages" that modern science and modern technology have put at our disposal.

If one considers the population data which statisticians furnish us so generously, it would appear that the golden age of the city has arrived. Census figures reveal that urbanization of the United States has taken place at a tremendous rate. In 1790, 5.1 per cent of the population were considered urbanites; fifty years later, in 1840, it was 10.8 per cent; another fifty years later, in 1890, 35.1 per cent; in 1940, 56.5 per cent. The 1960 census classified 63.1 per cent of our population as urbanites. The 212 standard metropolitan statistical areas, as established in the 1960 census, contained 63 per cent of the 1960 population, whereas they held only 59 per cent of the population in 1950. These standard metropolitan statistical areas captured 84 per cent of the total national population increase. Sociologists tell us that we live in the epoch of greatest urbanization. An ever-decreasing number of people is required for the growing of our food, the mining of our raw materials and those other activities that take place outside urban conglomerations, with the result that rural populations wander off into urbanized areas. Growing birth rates all over the world, together with improved health care which is extending the average life expectancy, have caused drastic population increases, so dramatic indeed that we refer to this trend as a population explosion. As a result of this explosion new masses of mankind are concentrated in urbanized areas.

With few exceptions, this phenomenon is to be found in countries the world over. It is of concern to the so-called Western world: Western Europe, the North American continent and Australia; it expresses itself in the Communist world; and in the underdeveloped countries of Asia, Africa and South America. An ever-increasing portion of an increasing human population becomes urbanized.

And yet the manner in which those areas where humanity is concentrated to the highest degree (which, for lack of a better word, we call urban areas) develop is one that threatens the ruination of the city as mankind has known it throughout history. Lewis Mumford, in his book *The City in*

History, has given a long list of reasons for the founding and functioning of cities. But whatever the reasons, they have functioned throughout the ages in specific ways and for specific purposes. One of the primary purposes is to bring together many people so that, through direct communication with each other, they may exchange goods and ideas without undue loss of energy and time.

A well-functioning city gives each inhabitant a free choice between sociability and privacy, affording him the opportunity to express his human gregariousness in meeting with others, but also the chance to disappear, if that is his desire, in the anonymity of its huge organization. The city acts as a mixing ground of races and nations, of the rich and the poor, the powerful and the helpless. In earlier days, it offered protection from wild beasts and human enemies. Today it is still giving protection from natural elements and from the harshness of climatic conditions. Because it has always been confronted with the necessity of making possible the living together of multitudes of people in close quarters, it was forced to develop laws, sanitary measures and social arrangements of the highest order. It has been, therefore, the cradle of civic virtues, medical progress, social legislation. As a result of the city's manifold activities, and because of the city dweller's need to compete with his co-urbanites, the city has sharpened the wits and intellects of its inhabitants. Progress, that subconscious striving toward unknown aims, which appears to be one of the most deep-seated instincts of the human race, would have been impossible without the city.

Why is it, then, that in the light of the dynamically growing urban population of the world we are concerned about the fate of our cities to such an extent that we hear, in every language of the civilized world, consistent talk of an urban crisis? Paradoxically, this crisis is felt most in those countries which have become urbanized to the highest degree. While felt and registered most intensely in the United States, it exists as well in other highly industrialized countries like Japan, England and most nations of Western Europe. It is also beginning to be experienced on a minor scale in every other part of the globe. The symptoms of this disease known as the urban crisis are generally the following: a spreading of the intensively inhabited area in an amorphous manner reaching dozens of miles in all directions from the formerly established city centers; and simultaneously with this cancerous growth caused by urban fallout, a shrinking and drying up of those central areas which, in the established sense of the word "city," represented its urban and urbane values. And with this new type of growth pattern, which converts urbia into amorphia, there appear ugly side issues and plagues, which threaten to destroy those advantages for which cities have functioned, for which they have been loved and enjoyed. Growing time-consuming distances, congestion of traffic ways, deadly dangers which confront inhabitants as they travel from one part of the urban conglomeration to the other, hamper or even destroy the possibilities for intimate human communication, for the exchange of goods and ideas. They are bringing about segregational tendencies by dividing human activity areas and by herding sociological, national and racial groups into separated areas. An increasing reliance is being placed on secondary, indirect means of communication, such as the telephone, radio and television; meetings between man and man, woman and woman, man and woman, friend and friend, and simple chance meetings of one human being with another are growing increasingly rare.

Thus, all the talk one hears about the progress of urbanization in the United States and other parts of the world, the increasing number of urbanites, is actually to be taken with several grains of salt. If we understand the term "urbia" to mean basically the same as the term "city," then we are indeed not faced with urban growth but rather with urban shrinkage. Quite typically, the cities of the United States are losing population, and this loss is most acute in the most highly citified areas and least apparent in the outlying suburbanized areas within the city's boundaries. The population growth occurs in vast amorphous regions stretching around the cities in a wide circle or arc, areas to which we refer as "metropolitan regions."*

If we were to call the inhabitants of these areas "regionites," then we could state correctly that the rural *and* urban population of the United States is shrinking but that the number of regionites is increasing at an impressive rate. Regionites are a new type of creature. They are neither countryfolk nor cityfolk. They are not even suburbanites who, though living in peripheral areas of the city, still have a close communication with the life of the urban community. Regionites lead detached lives in detached houses and are connected with the city only by the umbilical cord by which they receive their nourishment from its creativity.

What is a city? Is it a place like Manhattan, Paris, Rome, or Vienna, where there is still recognizable a concentrated, teeming, dynamic expression of urbanism? Or is it a place like Los Angeles, which has been called "seventeen suburbs in search of a city"? Is it a place like Oakland, California, of which Gertrude Stein once said, when she was asked how she liked it there: "There? There is no there there."? Or is it a place like Venice, which, although it has little industry, is enjoyed by its inhabitants and by millions

* According to the United States Department of Commerce census, December 14, 1963: In the 1950s, in the United States as a whole, metropolitan areas received a net in-migration of more than 8,000,000 persons, while incorporated city areas had a net out-migration of about 5,500,000 persons.

of visitors every year? Must it be a big place like metropolitan New York with 16,000,000 inhabitants, or can it be as small as Salzburg, the jewel of Austrian cities, with truly citified life and about 100,000 population? Does it become a city just by the act of being incorporated, or must it offer social, cultural, recreational and political consciousness to its inhabitants?

The city is the sum total of countless features and places, of nooks and

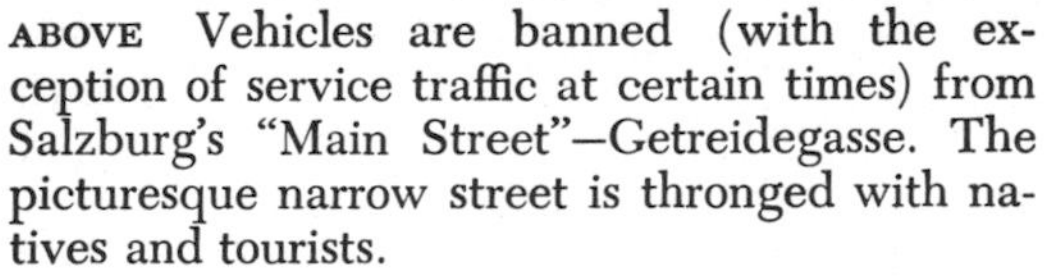

ABOVE Vehicles are banned (with the exception of service traffic at certain times) from Salzburg's "Main Street"—Getreidegasse. The picturesque narrow street is thronged with natives and tourists.

ABOVE RIGHT The weather is no better in Paris than in many a city of the United States, yet the desire to participate in "urban life" is so overpowering that thousands fill the sidewalk cafés and sidewalk bistros from morning to night, year in and year out.

RIGHT The few urban amenities U.S. cities did possess have fallen prey to traffic. Gone are the town squares with their band shells and their promenading music lovers. This picture shows Tompkins Square in New York as it appeared in 1891.

crannies, of vast spaces and intimate spots, an admixture of the public and private domain, of rooms for work and rooms for living, of rooms for trade, where money and wares change hands, and rooms where music and drama lift the soul, of churches and night spots, of landmarks expressing the spirit of the community, and homes for the comfort of the individual.

It is the fountains and flower beds, the trees shading streets and boulevards, the sculptures and monuments, the rest benches placed in thousands of spots. The city is the little merchants who make their living on the streets,

In Paris, narrow streets of great informality contrast with formal plazas and squares like the Place Vendôme which, in spite of its architectural uniformity—or maybe because of it—is delightful.

the vendors of balloons and pretzels, of newspapers, chestnuts, ice cream, flowers, lottery tickets and souvenirs. And the city, of course, is also the buildings. Decisive for the city's qualities is the relationship of these buildings to each other and, most important of all, to the spaces created between them.

The city is the countless cafés and sidewalk cafés of Vienna, from the ornate ones for the well-to-do to the little ones called *Tchochs,* where a person with little money may spend hours over a cup of coffee and a newspaper; it is the beer gardens and *Weinstuben* in German-speaking countries, the *bistros* and cafés of France, the *espressos* of Italy, and the pubs and tearooms of England. (The city is not the drive-ins, which are antisocial and anti-city.)

The city is the crowded sidewalks, the covered galleries of Italy, the arcades and colonnades, and the people on them and in them, some bustling, some walking for pleasure (*spazieren gehen,* they call it in Vienna), some engaged in the age-old tradition of the *corso* or the promenade. (The highway, however, is not the city. It tears people from people instead of bringing them together.) The city is the parks: the tiny green spots with benches,

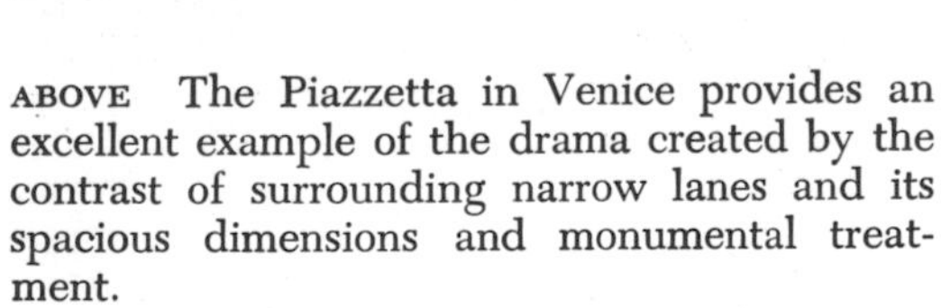

ABOVE The Piazzetta in Venice provides an excellent example of the drama created by the contrast of surrounding narrow lanes and its spacious dimensions and monumental treatment.

ABOVE RIGHT Venice, a city in which separation of human activities from mechanical functions still exists, has been able to hold on to the type of enjoyment destroyed in other places by the automobile. St. Mark's Square shows crowds listening to concerts provided by competing orchestras in various cafés. One could wager that the majority of the listeners are U.S. citizens.

RIGHT A bridge can become the continuation of a bustling market lane on both banks. The Rialto Bridge in Venice, spanning the Grand Canal, does so by the arrangement of shops on the bridge itself.

the middle-sized ones that interrupt rhythmically the sea of stone and brick, the big ones that act as lungs and recreational places. It is the skaters in the park on a frosty night and the spectators looking down on Rockefeller Center's jewel-like rink. The city is the elderly lady who strikes up a conversation with the elderly gent sitting next to her on the bench in Central Park, and later marries him; the six-year-old boy who asks another, "Do you want to play with me?" and later becomes his lifelong friend; the young man who offers a seat in the streetcar to the young girl, and becomes engaged to her two weeks later; the gentleman who asks for permission to sit at a sidewalk café with another, and ends up writing a book with him; the businessmen who strike up a conversation in a bar and later go into partnership; the millions of chance meetings that turn out to be the important events of a lifetime.

The city is the community of soul and spirit rising from an audience in a theater or at the opera, or from those attending services in a church. The city is the daily chat with the *Fleischhauer* in Vienna, or the *charcutier* in

LEFT The pastoral quality of huge Central Park in Manhattan not only provides rest and recreation but also dynamic counterpoint to the city's dynamism. New York's skyscrapers look most alluring through the lacework of tree branches.

RIGHT True cities make the most of their natural advantages: their hills and their ocean, river and lake fronts. Along the beach of the city of Nice, France, one can swim, sunbathe, promenade, eat and drink.

Paris, or the greengrocer in London, or the flowerseller on the boulevard. But it is also the yell that rises in unison from thousands of throats when the ball is hit in Yankee Stadium.

The city is also the excursion into its surroundings, picnics in the forests, the meadows and the farmlands, trips to the villages, the beaches, and the lakes, the enjoyment of meals in terrace cafés or restaurants. It is the viewing of the city from high above, from surrounding hills or observation towers, or from the tops of high buildings in its midst. It is the pointing with pride to visitors from out of town, and the proof of one's knowledge of all the things that make the city tick.

The city inspires awe and suffering, pride and love, all of which find expression in books and poems, in music and song.

The city for some is loneliness at times, and a social whirl at other times. In the city there is the struggle for power and for wealth, but also the striving for knowledge, for self-expression; there is love and there is hate, because the city is a mirror of everything human.

A real city is full of life, with ever-changing moods and patterns: the morning mood, the bustling day, the softness of evening and the mysteries of night, the city on workdays so different from the city on Sundays and holidays. In contrast are America's "downtown" areas, those part-time ghost towns, spawned by the one-sided and one-track development of many of our city cores, which are busy eight hours a day on weekdays and deadly silent and unpopulated in the evening, during the night, on Saturdays and Sundays.

Some diary notes I made on a trip from Naples along the spine of Italy toward Florence illustrate the all-time vivacity of Italian cities, large or small: metropolitan Naples, medium-sized Perugia, the small Benevento and L'Aquila, or tiny ones like Todi. Life goes on in these places endlessly, vigorously and interestingly, although with different emphasis, depending on the time of the day, and the day of the week.

Arriving in Perugia, a city of 100,000, around six o'clock of a weekday evening, we found the main avenue, the Corso Vanucci, closed to all automobile traffic for two or three hours, but brimming with milling crowds in which smartly dressed young people predominated. It was the *corso:* not a parade or a special event of any sort; merely the act of participating with one's fellow citizens in urban life. Participation in the *corso* entails walking up and down the broad street, meeting and greeting friends and acquaintances, talking things over, standing around in groups and discussing politics, sitting along the sidewalks in outdoor cafés, drinking an *apéritif* or an *espresso,* admiring the floodlighted public buildings and the playing fountains, enjoying the garlands of lights strung along the boulevards, the flags flying in the breeze, and the general feeling of being immersed in festivity. In every city we passed, something special was going on, and quite obviously it had not been arranged especially for us. In Naples we attended a large church festival, with hundreds of little temporary sales booths along the sidewalks, with bands of music, flags and lights. Whenever we passed through a city on Sunday, it appeared even livelier than on weekdays because of the people arriving from the surrounding countryside to participate in city life. Each of these cities seemed to have its own specialty, to be guarding its unique quality, striving to accentuate its own flavor by every means available. The specialty might be some food or candy, local ceramics, handicraft, certain types of pastry, or a distinctive wine. This is true not only for those cities that are tourist centers, but for those that are bypassed by the tourist traffic as well. Even the smallest cities proudly boast of beautiful parks; even towns of 25,000 inhabitants manage to convey a genuinely urbane atmosphere. Street lighting is not merely utilitarian, but splendid and glamorous. Public gardens are not merely tended, but furnished with luxuriant floral displays, impressive fountains, comfortable benches, and thus become not only feasts for the eye but welcome resting places. Large cities like Paris or Vienna, it is true, empty out to a certain degree during the hot summer months, but those are the months when the tourists take over. The lull in the world of art and culture is extremely short. The theater and concert season slows down in July and August, but otherwise things are always in full swing.

What makes a city a city? It certainly is not size. I know of villages in the United States with over 100,000 inhabitants, and, on the other hand, I know towns of 5,000 souls which convey the unmistakable imprint of urbia. It is certainly not the wealth of the population, nor its high living standard. Naples, with its very low standard of private life, is most certainly a city in the true sense of the word.

If one were to try to reduce to three the qualities or characteristics that make a city, they might be:

1) Compactness

2) Intensity of public life

3) A small-grained pattern in which all types of human activities are intermingled in close proximity.

In the sound city there must be a balance between the pleasures and comforts of private life, and the values which only the public phases of life can offer. We in the United States have upset this balance in favor of private life. We proudly assert that our living standards are the highest in the world. But this is true only of the standards of private life, which have been raised at the cost, and to the detriment, of public life.

In Italian cities, where sun and tempers are hot, shady, airy arcades open to pedestrians only form lively centers of urban activity.

STREET SCENE IN PARIS

STREET SCENE IN NEW YORK

A HUMILIATING CONTRAST

Historically, the cities of the U.S.A., growing rapidly, neglected the creation of urban quality in their early stages. *Harper's Weekly*, in 1881, criticized New York by printing two contrasting drawings with this original caption.

A chance conversation I recently had in Boston may illustrate this better than any theoretical discussion.

In Boston there is a Freedom Trail. It is marked carefully by appropriate signs. In following it one can relive the dramatic events of our national history. There comes a point on the Freedom Trail, however, where the main traffic artery, a many-laned freeway, has to be crossed. This is a point at which one has to choose between Freedom and life. But if one is heroic, as my wife and I were when we followed the Freedom Trail, one takes one's life into one's hands, and reaches, on the other side of the traffic stream, an area where Paul Revere's house is located; a section, now mostly populated by immigrants from Italy, with a quiet, urbane Mediterranean character. People sit around on benches and on stoops and, in their little "hole in the wall" places, sell goods and refreshments along the narrow streets. We walked into an *espresso,* so completely Italian that it could have been in Rome, even to the Italian newspapers hanging along the wall on those typical bamboo holders, with people sitting around speaking Italian and sipping their *espressos.* We immediately got into a conversation with a group including the owner, who, we learned, had just arrived from Naples a few weeks earlier. We asked him how he liked America and specifically how he liked Boston. He drew his face into thoughtful lines, and replied that he was "not so sure." He was torn in his feelings. He admired and enjoyed the comforts of his new home, the fact that he had a modern bathroom and a kitchen with a gas stove, which were princely in comparison with his Naples place in which he had only a shower that dribbled slowly because the plumbing was faulty. "But," he said, "when I took a shower in my little flat in Naples, and dressed myself carefully to go out, I knew what it was for. I mixed with people in the beautiful parks with the handsome fountains and masses of colorful flowers. I sat around with my friends, and I had endless good talks over a bottle of wine. In Boston I get bathed and dressed much faster. But then I do not know where to go. I wonder," he said, "whether there could not be a city where one could have both." If we could answer that question, we might find the solution to the problem of the urban crisis.

If we feel that cities are worthwhile human inventions, that they establish strongholds of national health and wealth, that without them urban culture—and, therefore, culture as such—cannot exist, as I feel so strongly, what can we do to stop their destruction, their transformation into Amorphia? What can we do to promote the reorganization of our time-tested cities as well as the founding and building of new ones, in our age of rapidly advancing science and technology? The answer to these questions can be found only if we are willing to understand and apply the science of planning.

2 Planning—Waste or Wisdom?

Paradise and hell can be had in this world.

—Yiddish Proverb

I borrowed the title of this chapter from a discussion, published in the newspaper *The National Observer* between Mrs. Jane Jacobs, a writer, and Mr. Robert Moses, who refers to himself as a planner. The fact that Mr. Moses felt that planning was wisdom, while Mrs. Jacobs felt it was waste, holds little significance for me because both were speaking of a specific type of planning, different from the activity and terminology that I wish to employ. They were referring to certain mechanics, to tools and methods of the practitioner which, although necessary in the specific application of the planning process, must be regarded as subservient to the main function of what I may term "creative planning."

Planning is as old as mankind and of divine origin. Let me quote briefly from the Book of Genesis (the italics are mine):

> In the beginning God created the heaven and the earth.
>
> And the earth was *without form* and void; and darkness was upon the face of the deep. And the Spirit of God moved upon the face of the waters.

> And God said, Let there be light; and there was light;
> . . . and *God separated the light from the darkness.* . . .
> And God said, Let there be a firmament in the midst of the waters, and let it separate the waters from the waters.
> And God made the firmament, and *separated the waters which were under the firmament from the waters which were above the firmament.* . . .
> And God said, Let there be lights in the firmament of the heaven to *separate the day from the night.* . . .

The story of Genesis contains all the elementary tasks of the planning profession. From the very beginning of time, we find the urge to *separate* disparate functions from one another, and to organize them into a meaningful pattern of greatest diversity.

In the beginning was chaos; and the very act of Creation was the conversion of chaos into meaningful order. Out of everlasting, monotonous fog and dusk, the Lord created the wonder of morning, the day, the evening, and then the night, with the sun lending its brilliance to the day, the moon and stars sparkling in the night sky. The Lord *separated* the water from the dry land, and heaven from earth, and on the earth He created mountains and valleys, oceans and continents. He made animals to live in the water and on the ground and in the air; and finally He created man and woman. And when He rested and observed what He had created, He saw that it was good.

Whether one is a believer, taking the Bible literally and asserting that God shaped man in His image, or whether one takes a more liberal outlook and considers the Bible as a beautiful story—believing conversely that man created God as the ideal of his own image—the fact remains that creation, or planning—the making of order out of chaos—appears to man as a most worthy goal.

The separating of elements from each other, endowing each with specific characteristics, defining boundaries between them, the achievement of infinite variety within organic order, whether regarded as divine inspiration or as the highest expression of human aspiration, is accepted in every religion and every philosophic belief as the ultimate achievement.

In spite of this, since the beginning of human history mankind has been busy undoing the divine work; blurring the clean edges of the borders He set up; leveling the differences; watering down characteristics and, in an unholy conspiracy with the powers of evil, nullifying the six days of creative labor and recreating chaos where there was order. Man has, in his perverseness, tried to make day out of night, to create bodies of water where there was dry land and, in a reversal of the usual procedure, to make molehills out of mountains.

For thousands of years of human history, man's struggle to undo the high order of variety met with scant success. Earthquakes, floods and storms, volcanic eruptions and other geological upheavals corrected the situation, reminding him not to tinker with the "divine" order. But nowadays, feeling uppish because of the great and growing size of the human membership roll, we are more hell-bent than ever, especially where we are assembled in large groups, to undo the perfection and rhythm of the act of Creation and re-establish shapelessness, formlessness—in short, chaos.

The concept of hell exists in nearly every religion. There seems to be universal agreement that it is a highly unenjoyable place for sinners in retirement, who suffer there from inescapable sameness. They are further punished by the fact that they are exposed thoroughly to the company of a sociologically undifferentiated group consisting only of devils. There is neither night nor day, neither culture nor artistic pursuits (as opposed to heaven where there are at least such diversions as choral singing or harp playing); only an endless infernal boredom.

Humanity today is using the power of its vast numbers, its scientific and technological "progress," to convert its cities and metropolitan regions into hell on earth. Where once there was an infinite variety of hills and mountains, valleys and forests, streams and lakes, satisfying both the eye and the spirit, an even, cancerous growth of man-made uniformity is being spread. Vast areas are robbed of every last tree, every bush and flower, and covered with an inescapable sameness. Fumes and smoke pervade the day and darken it, while millions of lights illuminate the night. Because we have learned to shrink distances by air travel and by our elaborate means of communication, we are slowly succeeding in wiping out the differences that once existed between individual cities on the various continents, and one man-made hell begins to look like another. Our power to resist natural elements has grown infinitely in the last hundred years; our wisdom in utilizing this power for man's enjoyment has not kept pace.

The human population on this planet is increasing dynamically. We tend more and more to concentrate in already heavily populated areas because modern technology demands such concentration. But unless we learn the true meaning of planning, which is the injection of diversity and variety into a meaningful organic pattern, we will succeed in making our cities unlivable, unworkable places of infernal sameness, plagued by boredom and discomfort—a fate which human fantasy once imagined to be the punishment for those who had sinned against God and man.

The French, with a twinkle in their eyes, say, "*Vive la différence,*" referring mainly to the difference between the sexes. An important difference, indeed. Without it life would be, to say the least, dull, and mankind would die out. But *Vive la différence* should be the slogan for all expressions of life, and for the planning of our cities. *Vive la différence* between the new and the old, between the clustered-together buildings in which we work and live, the closely knit city and the openness of the surrounding landscape and countryside, between man-made or man-influenced and natural environment.

What is planning? When we relate planning to the shape of the man-made and man-influenced environment, we find that three main types are being practiced.

The first, which we may refer to as *laissez-faire* planning, actually is not planning at all. Its advocates—and many thoughtful people must be counted among them—feel that things should be permitted to grow freely as individual wishes, needs and requirements bring them about, with only the most essential policing measures to prevent "criminal" actions in which one individual or group of individuals seriously endangers others. In defense of their attitude, they point to the fact that the powerful United States, with the highest living standard on earth, was created by pioneering individuals, and that any action going beyond the most essential policing methods would be an interference with personal freedom. They also point to the fact that some of the old European cities which we most admire grew without a master plan, and that much of their charm and architectural value is the result of this non-directed free growth.

The second type of planning we might refer to as *autocratic* planning. It is the method that was employed in the past by monarchs and other autocratic rulers; a method which, for example, created the beautiful wide boulevards of Paris, the grand palaces of the Renaissance and baroque periods, and in our own time has been employed by the modern dictators, by Hitler and Mussolini, by Franco, by Stalin, by various Communist states and certain autocratic Latin American governments. It is the method by which large portions of cities can be rebuilt practically overnight, and by which whole new cities like Brasilia can be created in a few years. Autocratic planning, however, is by no means restricted to those countries which are governed by dictators; in many a city in the United States, strong-willed men have pushed through pompous projects for political gain. Some of our monumental but dreary "civic centers," "cultural centers," and "centers for the performing arts" isolate higher urban functions into ghettos, creating sterility within them and impoverishing the remainder of the city outside their boundaries. Some powerful government agencies, run by specialists whose views are shielded by blinders from everything outside their departments, have cut communities to ribbons with highways and freeways. Others have misinterpreted the aims of urban renewal legislation by demolishing whole districts and by replacing lively environments, which could have been rehabilitated, with sterile, inhuman and poorly planned projects.

And then there is a third type, that I will call *democratic planning*, which, although its implementation is the most difficult, most complex and most time-consuming, is, in my view, the only one that holds out real hope for us.

Those who advocate *laissez-faire* planning deny the existence of historic development. Pioneering days in the United States, and, indeed, in every other part of the world, are irretrievably gone. Independence has been replaced, as the late President Kennedy said, by interdependence. Modern means of communication have shrunk the world, and a shot fired in Korea has repercussions in every American town. Our country has been developed from the Atlantic to the Pacific, and the only "new frontiers" toward which we can strive lie in the direction of planning for better national and international conditions. Our national house, once inhabited by a few who could indulge in the vanishing luxury of living and acting as they pleased without unduly disturbing their neighbors, has filled up and will get even more crowded in the near future.

In the process of *laissez-faire* planning we have, of course, always taken the way of least resistance. We have concentrated urban development in those areas where basic conditions were most favorable, along the East Coast and the West Coast and in the Great Lakes region in the Midwest. Those millions of acres which for climatic or geologic reasons are more difficult, though not impossible, to urbanize, we have, in the process of *laissez-faire* planning, simply neglected.

Those who point to beautiful old cities that have grown without planning must be made to realize that restraints of another type explain their virtues. The need for moving close together was dictated to them not by planning ordinances, but by the threat of enemy attack. Take, for example, the nearly perfect plan of my native town of Vienna. Its inner city, with its small-grained, endless variety of buildings, streets and squares, was once ringed by fortifications. Outside the inner fortification walls stretched, on all sides, a broad area on which nothing could be built, the so-called Glacis, left free of structures so that one could shoot unhindered at the approaching enemy. Beyond the Glacis grew other communities. (These communities, interestingly, are called *Vorstädte*, literally, "before-cities," expressing the idea that these are places one reaches, when coming from the outside, in anticipation of one's arrival in the big city; implying something quite different from our word "suburb," which rather seems to indicate substandard quality.) They in turn were surrounded by a second fortification wall, and it was only in the

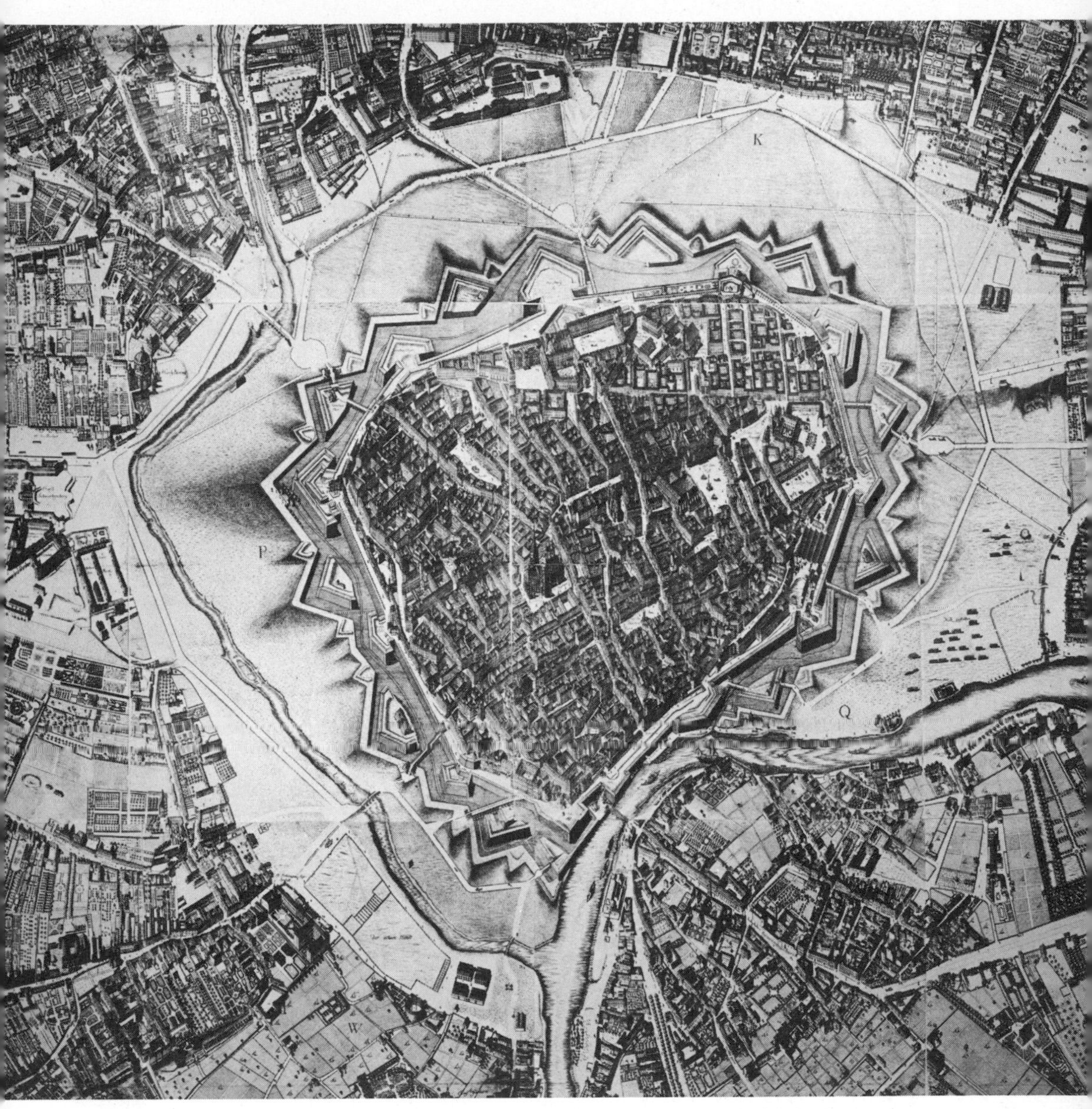

Professor Roland Rainer, author of the Master Plan for Vienna (published 1963) comments: "In this bird's-eye view, drawn by Daniel Hubers in 1766, the Vienna of the Baroque nearly represents the modern concept of an organized metropolis. Around the center city are grouped the units of satellite towns, separated from the center by the broad green area of the Glacis. Other 'green belts' separate the satellite towns from each other. Here we see a functionally clearly organized yet lively, nature-connected urban organism."

nineteenth century that other satellite towns grew outside these fortifications. Their spread, however, was halted by the desire of the monarch and the aristocracy for spacious hunting grounds in the forests, hills and meadows that surround the city in a wide arc. As the city became a modern metropolis in the second half of the nineteenth century, as the need for fortification ceased, and as the power of autocratic monarchs was broken, planning did set in, and it was only thanks to planning that the elements of the urban organism, which had been based on stringent needs of the population and on the wishes and desires of the landed gentry, were converted into lasting assets of the city. The inner fortifications surrounding the old town, together with the vacant area of the Glacis, were converted into a pair of concentric roads: the unique Ringstrasse with its broad, tree-lined promenades, parks, private and public buildings of all types; and a secondary ring road called Lastenstrasse, a service road for the hauling of goods. Between those two roads wide-open spaces, parks and plazas were created. The second outlying fortification was converted into an outer ring called the Gürtel or belt, forming not only an excellent distributary road with a rapid-transit system, but also, because of its tree-lined boulevards and parks, a recreation area and a clear division between the inner and outer districts. The former hunting grounds, finally, were declared a permanently protected nature park, in which only agricultural activities, vine growing, and facilities for recreational uses are permitted. They now form the much-sung-about Vienna Woods, an easily accessible area for all Viennese citizens, offering for their *Ausflüge,* or excursions, virgin woods, meadows, hills and mountains. Only beyond this broad ring of nature park does further metropolitan growth take place in the form of satellite towns and villages.

Similar acts of conscious planning, which take advantage of city patterns that originally stemmed from the need to guarantee the continued life of the city and its residents against enemy attack, can be observed in many European cities, large and small.

The order and logic that prevail in the city of older origin are derived also from a number of restraints imposed upon them by the technological conditions of the period, the restricted availability of materials, and existence of regional traditions, some of which still endure despite the intense exchange of knowledge and techniques that we enjoy—and suffer under—today. Because building technology had not produced the know-how to build safely higher than five or six stories, there is a unity of building heights. Because only a limited number of building materials was available, and a small number of building methods known, there is harmony, created by the predominant use of brick, stone, wood or stucco, depending on the particular region. Only for a few exceptional buildings were rare materials used and special feats of building technique achieved. Thus landmarks such as towering cathedrals, majestic palaces and city halls form effective accents within the orderly, even appearance of older cityscape.

Today, being deprived of these natural reasons of restraint, we must achieve through planning that measure of harmony which formerly was the result of necessity. *Laissez-faire* planning is a luxury we can no longer permit ourselves to indulge in. The interdependence of each structure with its neighbor, of each group of structures with its district, of each district with the city, of the city with its neighboring cities (which with it forms the metropolitan area), of one metropolitan area with the other, of all of them with the state, the nation, and indeed the world, has become so great that policing measures alone can no longer work.

The second type of planning, autocratic planning, could effectively regulate this interrelationship if it were guided and implemented by supermen. But inasmuch as men, including planners, are subject to the usual human shortcomings and, in an autocratic society especially, to the lust for power and intense desire for self-expression, the result of autocratic planning is usually deeply disappointing. It suffers from the lack of those balances which lie only within the rules of democracy, and the virtue of their swift accomplishment becomes their downfall. The results are made out of one mold, and that mold may be to the liking of the autocrat who created it, but it does not necessarily fit the varied and widely diversified needs of the individuals who make up the city.

The question is often asked: "Is planning possible in a democratic society, where every single step has to be negotiated, has to be subjected to public hearings, and very often has to be decided upon by vote?" Two issues are involved in this question: The first refers to creative planning for a democratic society, the second to the possibility of practical implementation of such planning.

Creative city planning in a democratic society can undoubtedly be successfully carried out, if one basic condition is met: We must know what our aims and goals are, what we want our cities and urban areas to look like, and why. We need an urban planning philosophy for the second half of the twentieth century. One of my purposes in writing this book is to arrive at the main tenets of such an urban planning philosophy, and I hope to lay the groundwork for this purpose in Parts One and Two of this book and start to erect the philosophical structure in Part Three.

The problem of implementing these planning efforts can be solved only through improved legislation and its effective administration. Inasmuch as laws and regulations are made by our democratically elected representatives, they will express the will of the people, if it will make itself heard, loud and clear.

Thus if planning in a democratic society, and its implementation, are to succeed, there will have to be creativity, leadership, perseverance and, above all, a consistent philosophy. Planning without these ingredients, piecemeal planning by specialists and special interests—whether they are called economists, real estate experts, traffic engineers, planning officials, zoning administrators, or redevelopment agencies—may indeed be waste. Planning based on philosophical thought and humanitarian principles with experienced and knowledgeable leadership, planning in which the specialists serve the whole (instead of running off in many directions, each with his own little specialty alone at heart)—such planning is not only wise; it is essential if we are to save our culture, which is an urban one.

3 Anatomy of the City

THOUGH THE WORD "anatomy" is primarily a medical term, it may be usefully applied in dissecting the "body urban" because, like everything nature has supplied us with, or what man in imitation of nature has produced, the body urban has certain characteristics of organic construction in common with the human organism.

Let us first investigate the component parts of this urban organism, and find out how they relate to their surroundings. The various elements of the human environment were once pretty clearly recognizable, and in some parts of the world they still are. There was cityscape, there was landscape, and there was nature, plain and unadulterated.

As cityscape we regarded the clearly defined area in which man-made structures were predominant.

As landscape we saw an environment in which nature was predominant, but which had been welded together with expressions of human activity into a harmonious unit. Landscape is a successful marriage of nature and human endeavor, areas in which man-made and naturally created elements cooperate successfully. Landscape is the rolling hills of Pennsylvania with their farmhouses; Alpine valleys and mountains with small villages strewn about; rural New England areas accented by the slim fingers of church steeples; a rocky seacoast with a fishing village; an Italian lake with colorful houses clinging to its steep shore.

And then there is nature, an environment untouched by human hand, either inaccessible or accessible only with some difficulty by footpath or primitive road. Nature exists today, in industrially developed countries, only where it is so hostile to human activities that it is permitted to remain undisturbed, or where it has been artifically protected by legislation as in the case of our state and national parks.

This is how simple it once was to arrive at a listing of the major environmental categories. Today, thanks to our untiring efforts to diminish differentiation, we have succeeded in wiping out wherever we possibly could these distinct and clearly recognizable environmental categories. Cityscape, for example, has been subdivided into numerous other categories, arranged in such a manner that they steadily interfere with each other. Within cityscape, we now have *technoscape,* an environment shaped predominantly

---

"Technoscape." Industrial area in Indiana.

by the complex apparatus of technology in both its respectable and less palatable forms. It is an area dotted with oil wells, refineries, high-voltage lines; with chimneys, conveyors, dump heaps; with mining towers and storage areas; with missile sites and auto cemeterics.

Then there is *transportationscape:* millions of square miles covered with the tinny surfaces of automobiles, the concrete bands of highways, freeways, expressways, parking lots, cloverleaves and their spaghettilike convulsions, all tastefully trimmed with traffic signs, billboards and dangling wires of power and communication lines. All those who defend billboards, and a powerful lobby in Washington is doing exactly that, have best been answered in a little poem by Ogden Nash:

I think that I shall never see
A billboard lovely as a tree.
Indeed, unless the billboards fall
I'll never see a tree at all.

"Transportationscape." Three-way interchange within an urban area—Los Angeles, California.

"Suburbscape." Air view of a portion of the city of Houston, Texas.

"Subcityscape." A major surburban highway: Ventura Boulevard in the city of Los Angeles, California.

Again, "Subcityscape." Auto junkyard located within a suburban area.

Transportationscape also includes the vast amount of arid land used in connection with airport runways and railroad yards.

There is *suburbscape* in its various manifestations, from plush settlements composed of mock historic mansions to the packed grounds of anonymous mass housing where dingbats* are lined up for inspection. Suburbia is the land of economic and racial segregation, with phony respectability and genuine boredom.

And we have *subcityscape*, a category covering probably more acreage than all the others combined, a cacophony of the worst elements of cityscape, technoscape, suburbscape and transportationscape—"the red-and-green-light districts" of our major metropolitan regions, clinging like leeches to roads and highways, and blocking out the view to whatever may be left of landscape; the shameful, inelegant entry into our cities and towns; the scourge of urbia. Subcityscape features gas stations, repair shops, shacks and shanties, used-car lots, billboards, dump heaps, roadside stands, highway stores, rubbish, dirt and trash. It grows like a weed in all directions, reaching into cityscape, raping suburbia, cluttering up the spaces between cities and towns, between one metropolitan area and another. Spreading its tentacles in all directions, it overgrows region, state and country. Subcityscape drags all other urban elements down to its lowest level, hampering their functioning, disrupting communications between them, and converting every attempt to reach landscape or nature from cityscape or suburbscape into a nightmare. Its existence is the most obvious indictment of *laissez-faire* planning, or non-planning.

This conflict between the various facets of man's urban environment, caused by the blitzkrieg of technology, which has devastated cityscape and is threatening landscape and even nature with ultimate destruction, makes the task of logically dissecting the urban organism and establishing the functions or diseases of its various organs infinitely complex. If, using the terminology of the medical practitioner, we attempt to label the various organs, we will find, in applying this analysis to certain urban regions of the United States, that there are cases where some of these organs do not exist any longer, or where their functions have so deteriorated and diminished in size and importance that a completely inorganic growth is apparent.

We will, for the moment, have to disregard these anomalies and concentrate on the normal, though suffering, body urban.

Every one of our cities, and even most of our larger towns today, must be considered an urban region, inhabitated by those who, in one way or

* "Dingbat" is an expression used widely on the West Coast of the United States to characterize the typical speculative builder's cheaply and hastily constructed house.

another, are dependent for their livelihood and for their life's expression on the conglomeration which we still call the city. The boundaries of the metropolitan region usually do not coincide with legally established city lines, but reach far beyond into areas that were once landscape or countryside. If we are to deal with the problem of urban areas theoretically, we will have to disregard the political boundaries and concentrate on those which determine the actual functioning of the city.

Inasmuch as a confusing multitude of expressions is now in use, I will try to establish a terminology that I shall use in the remainder of this book.

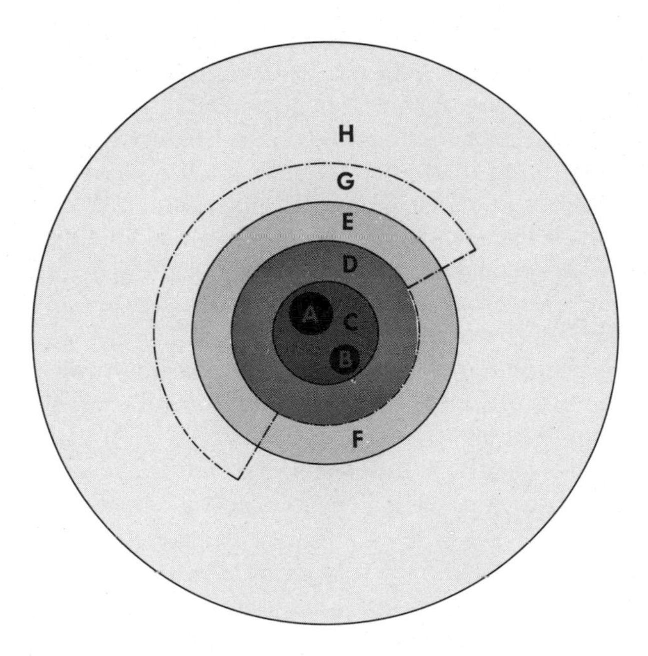

Schematic diagram of typical metropolitan region:
A. The Metropolitan Core
B. The Secondary Core
C. The Core Frame
D. The Core Fringe
E. The Urbanized Area Within City Boundaries
F. The Urbanized Area Outside City Boundaries
G. The Suburbanized Area Within City Boundaries
H. The Metropolitan Region

A. *The Metropolitan Core* (the core, for short)

This is the area on which, in this book, I intend to concentrate: the heart of the city. Expressions now in use refer to "downtown" or "CBD," which stands for "central business district." The word "downtown" is confusing. It originated in New York, where it referred only to the old city area around Wall Street, in contrast to "midtown" and "uptown." In some cities, the central section is on a higher elevation, and it seems illogical to call it "downtown." The expression "central business district" is not only illogical but plainly misleading. It implies that the heart of a city is meant to serve only business, and though this is unfortunately true for the central areas of some American cities, it seems to me by no means desirable. What we mean, then, by the term "metropolitan core" is the most highly urbanized area, which ideally should contain a complete range of the highest productive uses and most significant urban functions not only in the fields of business and civic administration, but also in cultural, recreational, social and spiritual activities as well, and residential quarters of high quality and density. Highest productivity should be understood in both the quantitative and qualitative sense. The core should provide not only the most but also the best, the rare and the unusual.

B. *Secondary Cores*

These are areas, to be found in some American cities, in which highly urbanized functions have developed at a point geographically removed and at some distance from the metropolitan core; thus, in many ways, competitive to it.

C. *The Core Frame*

This is an area of intensive development containing secondary urban functions, such as residential developments of high density, which are needed in immediate adjacency to the core.

D. *The Core Fringe*

This is an area containing facilities serving the metropolitan core and the secondary cores, but of lesser productivity and density than that occurring in the core frame.

E. *The Urbanized Area Within the City Boundaries*

This is an area occupied by multiple housing units (apartment houses), related local retail, cultural, civic facilities and other urban functions, and working places that are devoid of obnoxious characteristics (noise, smoke, poisonous fumes); this would include all types of light industry, laboratories, offices, etc.

F. *The Urbanized Area Outside the City Boundaries*

This is an area which, in character and use, is identical to that mentioned above but which, by some historical accident, happens to be located outside the geographical city line.

G. *The Suburbanized Area Within City Boundaries*

This is devoted mostly to single residential units (detached houses) and to a sprawling development for other functions.

H. *The Metropolitan Region*

This includes all areas located outside the city limits which depend, as far as employment and other activities of its inhabitants are concerned, more than 50 per cent on the economic vitality of the urbanized area within the city boundaries. Within this metropolitan region one usually finds unplanned patterns of residential subdivisions intermingled with languishing cores of former cities and towns, which have been pulverized in the magnetic field of the metropolis; industries of all types (including those with obnoxious characteristics), warehousing, retail facilities which occur either along highways in stringlike form or in organized shopping centers, and so on.

The relationship which the metropolitan core (as regards its size, population and intensity of activity) bears to the rest of the city, and which the city (with regard to its population and size) bears to the population and size of the metropolitan region, give some clues to the health and strength of the urban organism. For purposes of comparison, I have attempted to illustrate this relationship by listing the size and population figures for a number of cities. (In spite of thorough research, however, I found out that only an approximation was possible since all available census figures relate to other systems of terminology. I was completely unable to secure figures that would reflect the vitality of the core. For this purpose, I would have had to ascertain the number of core activity participants. That means the number of those people who, either by residing in the core or by visiting it at any and all times of the day or night in order to work there or to engage in other urban activities, create the heartbeat of the city. Thus the charts do not reveal the quality, intensity or attractive power of the cores but represent only a comparative listing of the size and population of the various areas. Yet they do highlight some significant differences.)

Let me attempt to relate these various parts of the metropolis in anatomical terms to their roles within the urban environment. I am referring to the core as the "heart" of the city.

The function of the human heart is to pump blood and send it coursing through the body in two circulation patterns: one reaching from the heart to the lungs and back; the other carrying the blood, which has been refreshed by oxygen from the lungs, to the tissues and cells of the entire organism.

Blood is the substance that brings the nutrients and energy necessary for the maintenance of life to every cell; another of its functions is to remove toxic substances from the cells. Without blood there would be no life, and without the functioning of the heart, which steadily pumps reoxygenated blood, the life-giving substance would not reach the cells and tissues. The human brain, being the most highly organized tissue, is most dependent on the steady supply of revitalized blood; deprived of it, it would stop functioning within minutes. Once the brain ceases to function, all activity must necessarily stop.

There are any number of disturbances that may beset the human heart. Cardiac output can be affected if, for example, the veins and arteries, which form the circulatory system, become congested. Disturbance in the blood pressure results, and the heart enlarges because of the strain under which it works. On the other hand, a loss of functioning tissue of the heart might take place, so that in spite of the fact that its actual size remains the same, its cardiac output will decrease.

Now let us see in what manner the role of the city's heart parallels that of the human organism. It, too, works as a pump, supplying the cells and tissues located throughout the metropolitan area with life-giving energy. Most of all, it supplies the brain of the city, represented by public and private leadership, by institutions of learning, by administration of all types which, in the urban body, have their seat in the metropolitan core. An urban heart whose cardiac output (in this case its urban vitality) has been reduced will cause circulatory difficulties, with the result that the necessary quantity of revitalized blood will be unable to reach the urban cells. Conversely, the sound functioning of the heart depends on the health of the circulatory system and the health of all cells and tissues. In the body urban this circulatory system is embodied in the veins and arteries of the communication apparatus, represented by mass transportation and individualized transportation for people and for goods; by telephone and telegraph lines; and by the postal system. This circulatory system moves the life stream—people, goods, messages and ideas—from the heart to all parts of the organism and back again. If stagnation or congestion sets in, if the arteries or veins harden, then the heart cannot function properly and serious diseases result, with the danger of coronary thrombosis always present. The diseases of the urban heart are analogous to those of the human organ. Though the core area may remain identical in size, portions of its tissue may

EXPLANATION OF SCHEMATIC DRAWING ON PAGE 51, COMPARING FIVE URBANIZED AREAS

Schematic drawing comparing five urbanized areas. The areas of the Metropolitan Region, the areas within the City Limits and the areas constituting the Metropolitan Core are indicated roughly by the size of the circles. For each of these three areas and in each of the five cases, figures denote the size of the area and the population within it. The figures are based on information from the U.S. Census. The terms used by the U.S. Census are not necessarily the most logical or the ones used by other statisticians. For example, the U.S. Census is based on the concept of the "Standard Metropolitan Statistical Area." This is usually smaller than the actual regional influence area of a metropolis. For example, in the case of New York, the U.S. Census considers an area of approximately two thousand square miles with a population of 10,700,000. The Regional Plan Association, on the other hand, states that the boundaries are wider and counts as regional population 16,139,000. Similar differences of opinion exist with regard to all other cities.

Size and population of the incorporated city area are indicated on these drawings as reflecting the latest figures. However, size and population of the core are highly influenced by divergences of statistical methods. The U.S. Census, for example, recognizes an area termed "Central Business District." This term omits not only secondary core areas but also some other areas which, according to other statistics, should logically be regarded as core areas. The differences are quite dramatic in the case of New York City, where the U.S. Census figures reflect only size and population of the area between Canal Street and 60th Street and between Third and Tenth Avenues. In order to arrive at a somewhat more realistic picture, I have used, in the case of New York's core, the figures established by the Regional Plan Association which include all of Manhattan up to 61st Street. These schematic drawings and charts should not be regarded as infallible material. Available statistics are outmoded to such a degree that it would be impossible to gather accurate, reliable material. Yet these illustrations and charts represent an approximation of the size and population of various types of urban areas and thus give a basis for analysis and offer comparison

At first sight, therefore, it is possible to conclude that a typical compact European city like Vienna not only is much smaller (as far as size of its region and incorporated area are concerned), but that the relationship between the incorporated area and the outlying metropolitan region (as far as size and population are concerned) is very different from the typical American city. Beyond that, the much greater role of the core in relation to the total urbanized area becomes evident.

In comparing American cities, it becomes apparent that great differences exist where compactness is concerned. New York, having an overall population nearly twice that of Los Angeles, has a considerably smaller region and a smaller incorporated city area. The core of New York City, on the other hand, is larger than that of Los Angeles and contains a much larger population.

If one compares Los Angeles and Chicago, it is interesting to note that though the incorporated area of Chicago is only half the size of that of Los Angeles, it contains about 50 per cent more population.

One of the most spread-out metropolitan areas is Dallas (not shown), the region of which, by size, is only a little smaller than that of Los Angeles, whereas its population is only one-sixth that of Los Angeles.

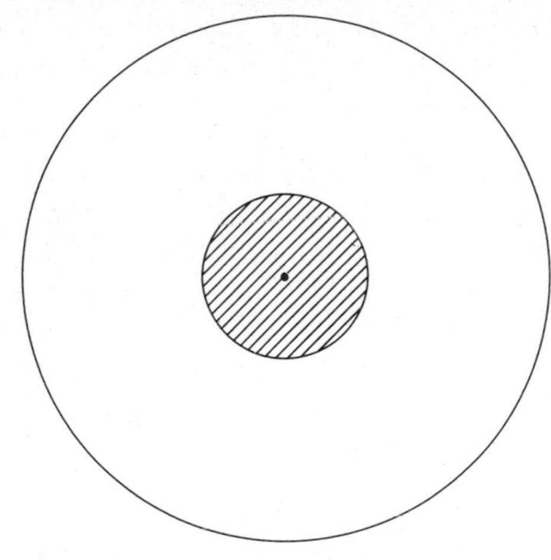

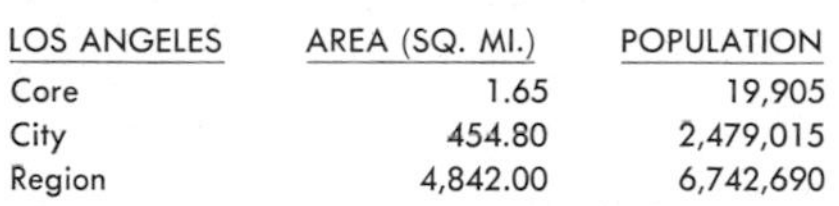

LOS ANGELES	AREA (SQ. MI.)	POPULATION
Core	1.65	19,905
City	454.80	2,479,015
Region	4,842.00	6,742,690

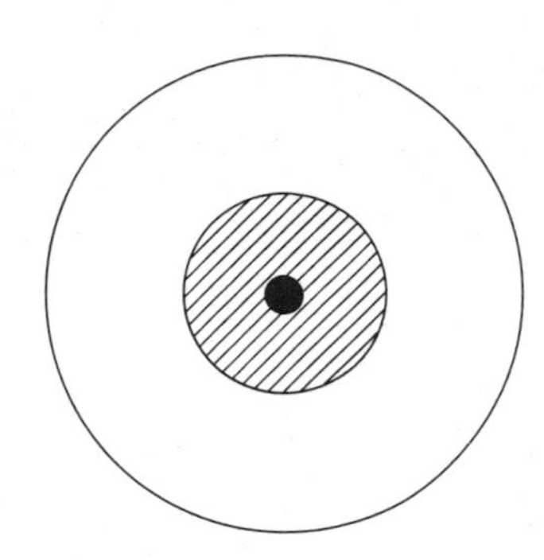

NEW YORK CITY	AREA (SQ. MI.)	POPULATION
Core	9.33	600,000
City	315.10	7,781,984
Region	2,149.00	10,694,633

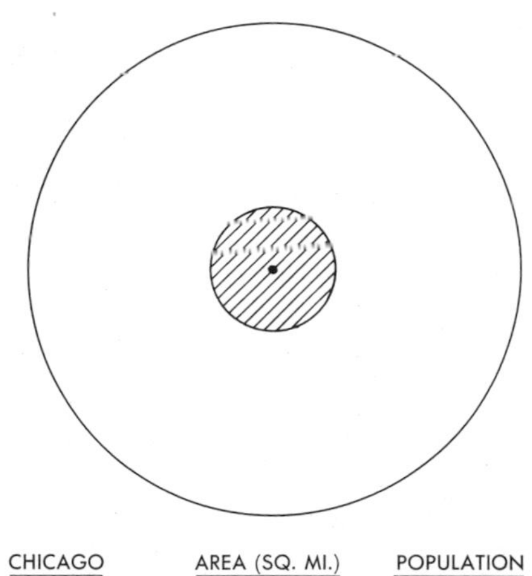

CHICAGO	AREA (SQ. MI.)	POPULATION
Core	1.51	4,337
City	224.20	3,550,404
Region	3,714.00	6,220,913

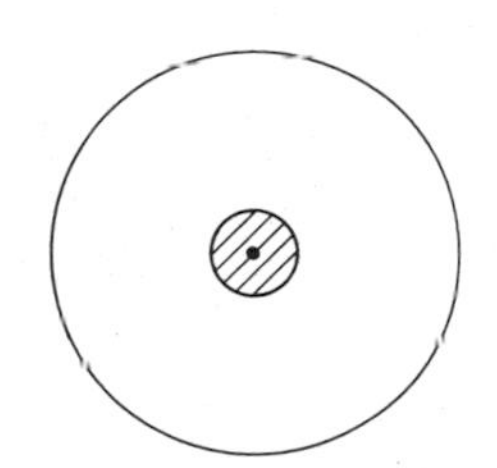

BOSTON	AREA (SQ. MI.)	POPULATION
Core	.95	5,361
City	47.80	697,197
Region	969.00	2,589,301

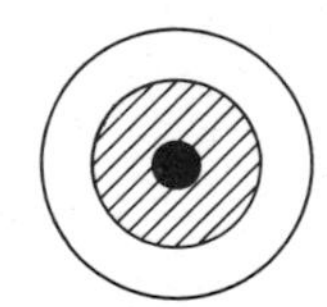

VIENNA	AREA (SQ. MI.)	POPULATION
Core	10.80	558,887
City	160.00	1,627,034
Region	359.00	1,990,000

dry up, in which case the cardiac output diminishes. Or poor functioning of the circulatory system may impede the work of the heart and reduce its cardiac output, thus impairing its health and vitality. This happens when the urban heart has to absorb on its surface large numbers of vehicles, some moving on its streets, others stored at curbs, in parking lots and in garages.

The city also has a digestive system in the form of markets, slaughterhouses, eating places, private kitchens, etc., depending for its functioning on the digestive tract, represented by railroads, trucks, harbors and airports.

The city's lungs are its parks and green areas, trees and flower beds, and nature reserves surrounding it but within the region.

Wherever the functions of any part of the urban organism are disturbed, the body urban falls prey to diseases similar to those affecting the human being. It can suffer from indigestion, from pains in the outlying limbs, from psychological disturbances like crime and juvenile delinquency; it can develop heart trouble of all sorts; it can become the victim of cancerous growth either in the outskirts or in the center. Any of these diseases will result in endless suffering to the community at large and to individuals, alike.

The urban patient, like the human one, visits the doctor. And like the human patient, afraid of being exposed to an operation or a difficult cure, he prefers the advice of quacks. Upon their prescription, he takes pleasant pink pills or aspirin, uses compresses or has a light massage, and goes home happy in the conviction that there is nothing organically wrong with him. The pink pills, aspirin, vitamins, and so on in this case consist of traffic regulations, signaling systems, parking lots, spot renewal, slum clearance, downtown promotional gimmicks, etc. They make the patient feel better for a day or so, but they have no effect whatsoever on the underlying organic diseases. Thus, more often than not, the patient becomes steadily worse, struggling, with ebbing strength, against death. Those who inhabit the sick urban organism try to escape the infected areas, becoming refugees from urban disease. They settle in the region, and promptly transfer the germs of the sickness to it.

The dissecting of an organism is never a pleasurable activity. Yet we have to engage in a most thorough examination of the patient if we want to diagnose the disease and attempt to find a cure.

4 Death or Transfiguration

L'avenir est la projection du passé, conditionnée par le présent. (*The future is the projection of the past, conditioned by the present.*)

—Georges Braque, *Sketchbook*,
Published in Paris, 1948

Death of the city or its transfiguration—these are, in my opinion, the two alternatives before us. To me the choice seems to be an easy one, and beyond that I believe that the forces working in favor of the city are so overwhelmingly strong that though a society may waver at times in its interest in the city, the desire and the need for cities will, in the end, always win out. Just consider the European cities which, with 6,000,000 houses completely or partially destroyed and 10,000,000 more damaged as a result of World War II bombings, rebuilt and rejuvenated themselves within a space of about ten years. Leo Grebler, commenting on this phenomenon in an article in the *American Journal of Sociology*, states, "In the rebuilding process no case of abandonment of a city is on record."

In spite of this optimistic forecast concerning the fate of cities, I will not deny that they are presently in a perilous situation and that there are strong forces working against the city on various levels and for various reasons.

There are first of all those persons who, by their indifference, impede any action directed toward the solving of the urban crisis. They would not shed a tear if the city were to die, some of them simply because they do not really know what a city is. There is a whole generation of Americans who have known the city only at its worst and who have not experienced the pleasures and advantages of true urban life. Their expectations and their demands on the city are extremely modest. In many instances the only inkling these people have that a city can be more than just a place in which to make one's living is gleaned from reading about true urbanism or from journeys to European cities. Since such travelers are in the minority, there is danger that the very longing for improvement might vanish, for the simple reason that one does not long for something of whose existence one is unaware.

There are also those who honestly feel that the city is no longer needed, that, having been given new tools for movement and communication by technology and science, we could just as well spread ourselves out all over the countryside, or, for that matter, onto the moon and the planets, utilizing the automobile, the jet liner and the rocket for transportation, and telephone, television and radio for communication with each other.

A case for extreme decentralization is made by E. A. Gutkind in his book *The Twilight of Cities*. His statements are to be taken seriously because he approaches his subject with great thoroughness. One also has the feeling, in reading his book, that it is with some regret that he recommends the dissolution of the city. The first part of his book is devoted to the history of cities through 180 generations. In the preface he refers to his book as one written by a "partially revised author," indicating, I gather, that in writing this work he has altered his position with regard to the city. One of his arguments against those who feel that cities could be improved, and against those who may be actively working on the task, is significant. He says, "If cities are 'improved' . . . they will attract more people." And, he adds, if more people "go to the 'improved' cities . . . the old vicious circle begins again and city renewal will become a new city deterioration." To give up the will to improve because one might succeed is of course a highly fatalistic and negative attitude. All worthwhile human endeavor is based on the desire for improvement. To abandon this desire just because it may create new problems would be a denial of all human purpose.

Mr. Gutkind says of his book, "Its principal thesis is the notion of a centerless region as the next phase in the evolution of environmental structure." He regards this, he says, as a radical solution and the only one possible, in contrast to those who "are convinced *that the basic fabric of our cities cannot be changed* and that redevelopment schemes and reforms will rejuvenate our urban environment."

Mr. Gutkind forgets the third possibility, to which my book is devoted: that of changing the basic fabric of our cities; what I prefer to call transfiguring them, and thus re-establishing the city on the basis of needs and conditions of our times. Mr. Gutkind acknowledges that economic and intellectual creativity depend on cooperation and mutually fructifying exchanges and that these prerequisites will continue to exist in the centerless region with its looser and more dispersed structure of settlement. All he wants to do, he states, is change the scale and enlarge the space within which these activities are carried on, in accordance with our greatly increased mobility. He concludes his book, which he describes as rather "abstract," with a program of action. Part of this action program is an opening and thinning out, and systematic dispersal. For some reason, he hopes to achieve by this dispersal a "genuine social and cultural proximity." The procedure in detail, according to Mr. Gutkind, involves the following:

"1. No slum areas are to be rebuilt. They are to be retained as open spaces or playgrounds, however small they may be.
"2. A central open space is to be developed by a gradual thinning out of the core area in every city.
"3. Only the absolutely essential functions of the administration and commerce are to be concentrated in a small but loosely laid out *Desk City* at the fringe of the central open space."

In other words, Mr. Gutkind proposes to do by intention what unfortunately we have done up to now by default. The results would be the same —sprawl and scatterization on the outside and nothingness in the center. It all comes back to the simile of the doughnut, with all the dough on the outside and the hole in the middle. Now, of course, Mr. Gutkind proposes a far superior development of the centerless region, with carefully planned land uses, highways that disappear in the landscape, open spaces separating parts of the region from each other, etc.—all noble aims for which effective legislation would be required, giving full control to governmental bodies over all types of land use. That the need for such controls exists is a point on which I fully agree with Mr. Gutkind; but I submit that once they are available, then there is no longer any need to abandon the city. And why, I ask, make a sacrifice when it is not needed?

Not only is the sacrifice unnecessary, but the proposal to bear it has little chance for acceptance. It seems highly doubtful that communication through mechanical gadgets can fulfill basic human instincts like love and gregariousness. Besides that, dispersal and scatterization are impractical—for the simple reason that we are running out of that irreplaceable resource, land, which would be devoured in an even more wasteful manner than it is today if Mr. Gutkind's proposals were followed. In the face of a population explosion which in the United States has brought about, within a hundred years, an increase from 20,000,000 to 180,000,000 people, and in the face of all the new activities characterized by conspicuous space consumption (like airfields for jet planes, horizontally spreading industrial plants, and the millions of acres of asphalt and concrete that make up the transportation media for automobiles, trucks and buses in the form of highways and freeways), we are running out of usable land for the growing of our food supply and for our recreational needs. As the supply of land shrinks, we will obviously have to move closer together—not farther apart. That is why Frank Lloyd Wright's scheme for Broadacre City appears historically unsound, and why utopian schemes based solely on adapting the human settlement to the automobile (like the Motopia study by G. A. Jellicoe) are not only utopian but misdirected.

Partial view of model of Frank Lloyd Wright's utopian Broadacre City, in which he attempted to provide agricultural land for every family; this forced him to adopt an excessively spread-out organizational pattern.

Besides those who sincerely propose abandoning the concept of the city, there are others who hinder action for the city's improvement: those, for example, who do not believe that a choice between death and transfiguration has to be made, because they do not notice, or do not want to notice, that an urban crisis actually exists.

Finally, there are many who long for better cities but feel that the existing ones are utterly hopeless and should be left to their tragic fate. Instead of sinking any more money or effort into them, they say, let us start to build new, shining, ideal cities in new locations. Now, there is no doubt that some new cities will have to be built to take care of the explosive growth of our urban population, but even with the greatest national effort we will be able to take care of only an insignificant percentage of urban newcomers in new,

A partial view of Motopia, the utopian concept which subordinates human activities in residences to the mechanized functions of traffic. The pattern of this utopian city is created by a number of multi-level highways and their circular intersections, which then form the roofs of buildings located beneath them.

favorably located urban organisms in the next forty years. And even if, by some miracle, we could today write off all our existing cities like bad investments, it is highly doubtful that this would be a gain. We would be losing not only the best and most logical sities for urban developments, and enormous human and economic values, but we would also lose the continuity of human experience that makes life worthwhile. If we cannot muster the strength and ingenuity to reorganize and rebuild our existing cities, then I seriously doubt the availability of sufficient wisdom and ability to create new ones that will be any better.

Thus I believe that transfiguration of our existing urban organisms is the only remaining alternative. I have chosen the term "transfiguration," which may sound strange to some, in order to indicate a change that is deep and fundamental. Transfiguration, in the sense in which I use it, means not just tearing down old structures and replacing them with new ones, not just redevelopment or rehabilitation or slum clearance, not just new highways or even new mass transportation; it means a change of urban pattern, a new order that can be superimposed over the existing one, transcending what we have inherited from the past with the spirit of the present and the immediate future. Transfiguration is the application of radical, meaningful measures necessary because of the enormous time lag that now exists between the rapidly moving developments in technology, science, sociology, and political patterns, and the backward, unadjusted urban organism. Transfiguration means overcoming the obsolescence that we have allowed to creep into urban arrangements and catching up emotionally, intellectually and spiritually with the discoveries and inventions made in our times.

Contemporary developments have been powerful enough to change our dictionary and our language. New words and phrases—like automation, atomic energy, television, jet propulsion, astronaut, intercontinental missile, supersonic speed and many more—have been added to our vocabulary. Sociological changes have added expressions like mass production, mass consumption, population explosion and suburbia. Our urban vocabulary has not been similarly enriched. We are still using the old terms—streets and roads and squares; streetcars, buses, subways. Maybe this stunted urban vocabulary signifies our impotence with regard to changes in city life, city patterns and urban culture.

Transfiguration of the city implies the finding of new ways and means, which will then express themselves in new urban terms and words.

I am aware of the fact that the problems are staggering. I know that thousands of planners and public administrators, sociologists and architects have tried sincerely and are inclined to give up in frustration. The mess is so great that they say it can no longer be undone. They observe that traffic congestion becomes worse as more highways are built, and they exclaim, "Traffic is like the weather. Everybody talks about it but nobody can do anything about it."

Yet traffic congestion and urban disorder are all man-made, and I submit that every mess man has made can be undone by men.

The first tool we need in order to attack the task is the fullest knowledge of the extent of urban disease. To what degree have we lost the city and been saddled instead with the "anti-city"? What are the characteristics of "anti-city"? To these diagnostic procedures I shall devote Part Two of this book.

PART TWO

THE ANTI-CITY

The misery and squalor which we people of civilization bear with so much complacency as a necessary part of the manufacturing system is just as necessary to the community at large as a proportionate amount of filth would be in the house of a rich man. If such a man were to allow the cinders to be raked all over his drawing-room, and a privy to be established in a corner of his dining-room, if he habitually made a dust and refuse heap of his beautiful garden, never washed his sheets or changed his table cloth and made his family sleep five in a bed, he surely would find himself in the claws of a commission de lunatico. *But such acts of miserly folly are just what our present society is doing daily under the compulsion of a supposed necessity, which is nothing short of madness. I beg you to bring your commission of lunacy against civilization without delay.*

—William Morris,
Useful Work Versus Useless Toil

5 Spread, Sprawl and Scatterization

You have never sufficiently foreseen how enormously rich and populous a nation you are going to be.

—JAMES BRYCE (British Ambassador to the United States, 1906–1913)

WHAT THE BRITISH AMBASSADOR said fifty years ago is even more true today. Population statistics forecast that by 1976, two hundred years after the Declaration of Independence, there will be in this country 55,000,000 more so-called urbanites than there are today. And unless planning on the broadest level and of the highest quality is utilized to prevent it, nearly all of them will live, as millions already do, in that never-never land which is neither city, town, village nor countryside, but something that punishes us by harboring the disadvantages of all known patterns of human habitation, while offering us the advantages of none; something which the Regional Plan Association of New York has called "Spread City," and which is referred to by others as urban sprawl, regional spread, or simply scatterization.

Advertisers use the circumlocution "the popular-priced spread" for margarine, which is urged on us as a replacement for the natural dairy product, butter (referred to obliquely as "the high-priced spread").

In developing vast urban regions we are using the popular-priced spread produced by the new technology. We are spreading it thinly, using one particular brand on one slice of land, another on the neighboring one. Every year we cover millions of acres of landscape and natural beauty indiscriminately with industrial, residential and mixed spread, using the same basic types in the east as in the west, and from the northern to the southern edge of the country. We are cutting down hills and filling in valleys; we are felling our trees; we devastate fields and meadows, desecrate ocean and lake beaches, and the banks of rivers and brooks, blanketing all with mass-produced sameness.

We have, of course, always had in our country active, articulate conservationists. President Theodore Roosevelt and Governor Pinchot of Pennsylvania are prominent historical figures that come to mind. Today also, great efforts of conservationists are noticeable. The Wilderness Bill is at the moment of writing being considered by Congress. However, the very fact that there always have been crusading conservationists who had a tough time selling their ideas, just as the Wilderness Bill today finds tough opposition, indicates how great is the power of the opposing desecrating forces and how serious the problem.

What makes that spread so popular? Having gained political democracy as the result of the Revolutionary War, we have been striving ever since toward the goal of complete economic democracy. Although economically we still have mountains and abysses, multimillionaires and the abjectly poor, the medium plateau of a vast and growing middle-class society fills, to an increasing degree, the area between economic peaks and valleys; and the flatness of the new middle class covers the land.

We have already pointed out, when discussing the charms of old European cities, that their compactness, their variety, their dynamism stem to a large degree from the sharp social differences which feudal systems created. The King's castle, surrounded by the huts of the serfs, created romantic contrast—although, one might add, not to the entire satisfaction of the serfs. Because, in our world, sociological differences are ebbing away, because those characteristic local features that resulted from a limited knowledge of construction techniques and the limited availability of materials have been eliminated, and because those marked differences from region to region which were the result of poor communications no longer exist, we must find new ways to express variety, the desire for which still exists as strongly as ever between individuals and between urban organisms of different size and function. We must learn how to vary the elements of urbanization, if we do not want to lose the rich differentiation in human experience that is the salt of the earth. If we do not succeed in accomplishing this, we shall lose the city forever, and with it will go urban culture. We shall lose, simultaneously, landscape and countryside, and will accept in

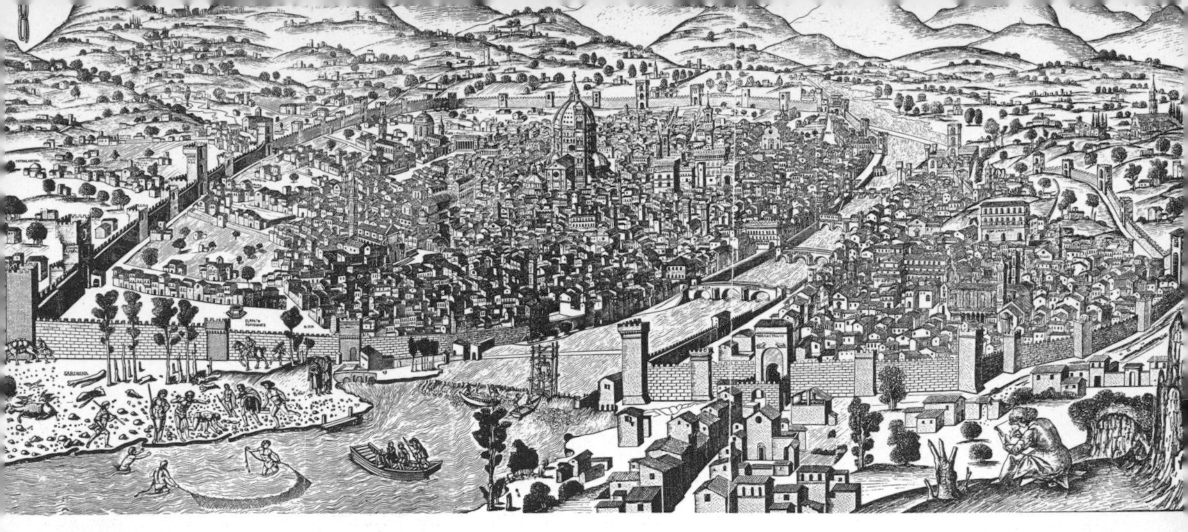

The city of Florence, Italy, around 1490. Inside the walls is the compact city, contrasting with the countryside surrounding it. Within the city there is dynamism and variety accentuated by landmark buildings serving political, administrative or spiritual functions. Outside the strongly accentuated urban nucleus and in sharp contrast to it is the area of rural activity, providing recreational green areas for the urban population within easy reach of everyone.

Aerial view of Los Angeles, California, illustrating effectively today's pattern of "anti-city" created by spread, sprawl and scatterization. A limited and defined urban pattern has ceased to exist, and as a result, variety and dynamism have disappeared. A centerless region without landmarks, stopped only by the hills in the background. (In the case of Los Angeles it even has spread over these hills and continues on the other side.) Vanished also are the rural areas, the countryside surrounding the urbanized region so that access to recreational and green areas has become extremely difficult for all.

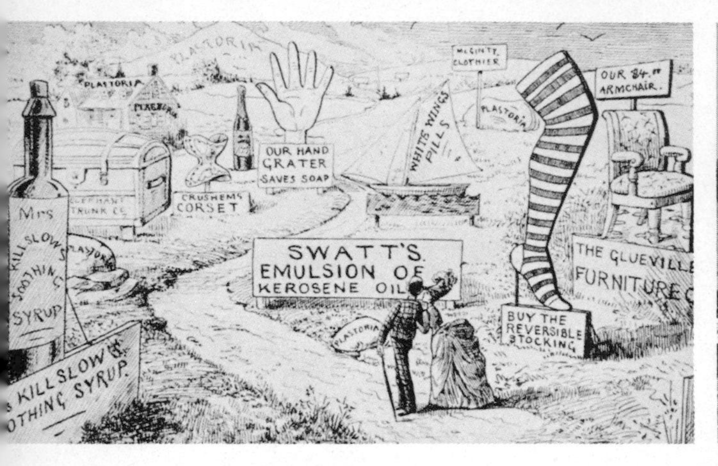

LEFT In 1891, the humorous magazine, *Life*, published a prophetic drawing captioned "An American Landscape of the Future." Inasmuch as the artist's drawing anteceded the arrival of the automobile, his fear was that most of the landscape might be blocked out by billboards and advertising for pedestrians like the strolling couple in the foreground.

RIGHT The prophecy of 1891 has become a fact half a century later. Gigantic billboards, the ones shown here in greater Los Angeles, effectively cut off any view of the landscape for the motorist.

---

trade for them that boring amorphous conglomeration which I term "anti-city."

Instead of the city with its rooted citizens, we will have urban sprawl with its drifting nomadic inhabitants. Instead of the city with transportation media to permit its citizens to reach their destinations, we will have urban spread containing only traffic with which inhabitants must battle. Instead of urbia with its points of attraction, we will have anti-city with its areas of distraction.

"Genuine, kosher Hungarian Goulash with Italian Spaghetti, Dixie style, served with French bread, $1.15" announces a sign in the shape of a moon rocket on a highway restaurant located in Southern California. The place is operated by a couple from Brooklyn, who were formerly White Russians. The miracles of our technological age have thrown them all together—White Russia, Brooklyn, France, Italy, Israel, Hungary, California—and combined them into one gigantic atomic goulash within the horrid chaos of anti-city.

Quite an achievement. But does it add anything to the enjoyment of life? Hungarian goulash may be good, kosher cooking may be good, Italian spaghetti may be good, but mixed up with each other, served on plastic dishes to those sitting in their automobiles listening to the blare of the newest jazz record, they taste flat and uninteresting.

Once upon a time the world was full of wonderful landscapes and beautiful stretches of nature, and spotted between them were cities, each one different from the other. We read about them in the reports of courageous adventurers who traveled by horse or by sailing vessel.

Today we can get everywhere, and fast. As a nation on wheels we can, at least theoretically, rush from place to place at a speed of a hundred miles an hour. We can jet anywhere on the globe on the installment plan. Short workweeks and paid vacations give us the time to do so, and improved economic conditions even give many of us the money. But the millions who look forward to the enjoyment of the gains for which they fought so long are betrayed. Hours of their free time are stolen by traffic jams. Their nerves are frayed by dangers on the highway, and when they finally, exhausted, reach the target of their drive, a beach or some spot of natural beauty, hundreds of others have gotten there earlier and have taken all available parking spaces; even if by luck one is found, the dream is tainted with beer cans and trash, studded with the elements of subcityscape. We have become a nation "all dressed up with no place to go."

Because we have devastated our own land, because we have filled its habitable areas with spread and sprawl and scatterization, we are now seeking new frontiers outside our planet, the moon and the stars, hoping that the Russians won't arrive there first.

But flight has never helped. One cannot run away from oneself. Let me relate a little story to illustrate what may be found in outer space.

According to "reliable information from usually well-informed sources" an expedition of American astronauts has already been to a faraway planet and has successfully returned to earth. The reason this historic event has not become public knowledge is that the information has been classified as top secret, since it might threaten our national economic security. I will therefore have to ask my readers to keep this story strictly confidential. This is what our astronauts found:

There is in existence a planet with a civilization similar to our own, but much further advanced. Unfortunately, when our astronauts reached the planet, they found that all human life had just become extinct. However, impressive amounts of printed information were found, from which it could be concluded that the planet is called Motorius and that the outer-space beings living there referred to themselves as Motorists. The planet Motorius is crisscrossed by an ingeniously engineered 86-lane expressway system,

A recent drawing in a Danish newspaper, speculating on what a view from a helicopter might be like if we continue to cover a good part of our globe's surface with asphalt, might prove just as prophetic as the cartoon shown in the illustration on page 66 drawn in 1891.

which intersects over cloverleaves eighteen stories high. The expressway network covers 92 per cent of the land area of the planet. The slivers of land remaining between the expressways were utilized for service stations that dispensed not only gasoline and oil but also a fuel for the upkeep of drivers and passengers of the automobiles, called Motrocal.

Before the final catastrophe on the star Motorius occurred, the expressways were constantly crowded with vehicles going slowly from one service station to another, where each stopped for a short time, and where the Motorists gave a short order in their native language, which sounded something like "Fill 'er up." This order applied not only to the machine but to the occupants inside as well. Due to their mechanical population explosion, the inhabitants of the star Motorius had to demolish all their buildings in order to have enough space for highways. They therefore lived, slept and procreated in their machines.

This wonderful and far-advanced civilization was destroyed—as a note in a diary found by the astronauts revealed—when a blowout occurred in one tire of one automobile. Unfortunately, the tire change was handled rather inefficiently and thus, within one hour, all traffic on the entire planet stopped. Death by starvation of the entire Motorian race was the tragic result.

Having read this sad account, you will now understand why this information was classified "top secret." News of this kind could have disastrous results on the progress of the national freeway program, on the employment situation in Detroit, on traffic improvements within our cities, and on garage construction projects.

Those of my readers who feel that there is a moral to the story may have a point. Some of them may have experienced the demolition of their houses, their schools, their churches, their places of work by onrushing bulldozers acting as shock troops for highway construction crews. Our increasing need for automobiles leads to the sacrifice of millions of acres of that irreplaceable national resource, land, to highways, roads and freeways. As these are completed, they promote the further spreading out of anti-city, and in turn an increased need for automobiles and roads. Robert Moses is quoted as having said, "It does not make any difference where one builds a freeway, it will fill up in any case." Thus, spread causes further spread, congestion causes further congestion, freeways bear new freeways, and anti-city begets more of its own malformed type.

So the story of the star Motorius not only has a moral, but might very well be prophetic. Urban sprawl is inescapably leading to "Autopia." Because of its loosely knit, wide-meshed pattern, it has had to do away with all types of transportation but one: the mechanical, individual container for the transportation of people, and its counterpart, the truck for the transport of goods. Its inhabitants are still outfitted with the lower limbs provided to the human species, but these are used differently than originally intended. In cars of older vintage they developed into a gas foot and a clutch foot. In cars with automatic shift, which no longer have a clutch, there is a danger that in the process of evolution one foot, having no further function, might completely disappear. Walking is a forgotten activity, and most of anti-city does not even provide sidewalks. In some of the better suburbs across the nation, people who walk are stopped by the police, being suspected of illegal and subversive activities. People who want to walk in spite of this attach themselves for this purpose to dogs, in which case the activity becomes legitimate.

Public transportation cannot for practical reasons be introduced in anti-city. Nowhere are there sufficiently large concentrations of people who would like to be transported together to specific destinations to make the planning or operating of public transportation possible. Los Angeles, which has within its city limits more freeways than many a state or nation, recently concluded that the transportation problem of their superspread city can no longer be solved, even by the most heroic effort of freeway construction. It was decided to study routes for a public rapid transportation system. Experts hired from New York started the preliminary planning work by the usual method of establishing points of origin (those points from which most people in outlying districts would want to begin their trips) and points of destination (those points to which they wish to travel). In Eastern cities, where the tendency to spread has not quite reached the breadth and depth that it has in Western ones, the experts usually find a few hundred spots of origin, one point of destination of greatest importance, namely, the core, and maybe half a dozen secondary points representing travel goals for large numbers of persons. Los Angeles confounded the New York experts completely. They were able to pinpoint about three hundred points of destination; some of these "points" were five miles long, and none of them seemed to possess sufficient power of attraction to qualify as a terminal for public transport lines.

I would like to ask those who doubt my statement that spread city must inevitably lead to Autopia to consider for a moment how many mechanized vehicles are put on the road by every single detached suburban residence. Besides the two or more cars of the owner and his family, there are the vehicles used by the maid, the cleaning woman, the laundress, the letter carrier, the newspaper delivery boy, the milkman, the gardener, the swimming pool attendant, the plumber, the electrician, the trash and garbage collector, the men who read the gas and electric meters, the television repairman, the tax assessor, the visitors, etc., etc. In our offices located in the suburb of Beverly Hills, we have to provide parking space for our two hundred employees, for partners, associates, designers, draftsmen, secretaries, office boys, cleaning women—and also, we trust, for clients. The University of California in Los Angeles has wrestled for years with the problem of providing sufficient space for its students' cars, and because the problem is a costly one to solve, it charges for the use of parking space. Paradoxically and significantly, the yearly fee for the parking of the student's car is higher than the tuition. Storage space for the jalopy costs more than the training of the mind.

To those who think scatterization is an exclusively Los Angeles or West Coast phenomenon, I recommend the reading of Bulletin No. 100, published in September, 1962, by the Regional Plan Association, entitled "Spread City," which deals with "projection of development trends and the issues they pose for the New York Metropolitan Region for the time space of 1960 to 1985." This report reflects the result of research and analysis, scientifically arrived at but not pretending to be either prediction or prescription. It states: "Regional Plan Association does not think that the events projected here will necessarily take place. Our function is to present the facts to be used by the region's citizens in guiding the metropolis to the rich future that its natural beauty, economic strength, historic greatness and cultural and intellectual leadership can provide—*if we do not continue to drift from these foundations.*" It then explains what is meant by "drift from these foundations," a drift in which we are presently engaged, and concludes that the Greater New York area is drifting into "spread city." If the drift goes on, it points out, then 6,500,000 new inhabitants of the region will about double the present built-up area, urbanizing over the next twenty-five years as much land as had been built up in the last three hundred years. "If this should happen," the report goes on, "it will not be a true city, because it lacks centers, nor a suburb, because it is not a satellite of the city, nor truly rural, because it is loosely covered with houses and urban facilities. People will be living and working too far from each other to use public transportation, or to walk the distances they want to go to, or even to car-pool. The cost of this spread city, especially for transportation, will be much higher than the cost of making full use of old cities and building at higher density with facilities better related. A declining percentage of population will have ready access to the cities. At the same time, a decreasing percentage will have easy access to the countryside. By spreading and scattering, rather than concentrating, jobs, goods, services and homes, we fail to build communities, and we have poor access to, and so less choice of, jobs, friends, recreation, goods, services, types of housing and modes of travel." It concludes: "The Region's new form, in sum, will give most of us neither the benefits of the city nor the pleasures of the countryside—*if present policy and trends continue*." (Italics are Regional Plan Association's.)

The manner in which scatterization automatically generates the need for travel—and that means more automobiles, more highways and more freeways—and thus creates unproductive, lost time is illustrated by data published by the Bureau of Census (*Place of Work and Means of Transportation to Work, 1960*):

> Of the 19.6 million workers living in the suburban ring of the 190 largest standard metropolitan statistical areas in 1960, about 50% worked in the ring, 33% commuted to the central cities,* and 5% went to jobs outside the standard metropolitan statistical area of residence.
>
> Of the 22.1 million workers living in the central cities, about 83% worked in the central cities,† 9% went to jobs in the outlying suburban ring, and 2% went to jobs beyond the standard metropolitan statistical area.

To what degree the metropolitan area of New York has already become "spread city" is evident if one studies the following figures:

The region comprised in the tri-state (i.e., New York, New Jersey, Connecticut) transportation area covers nearly 8,000 square miles, providing residence to 17,000,000 inhabitants. Of this, not quite one-half, namely

---

* That is, long distances away from the place of residence.

† That is, short travel distances.

8,000,000, live on 320 square miles within the incorporated area of New York City. In other words, about one-half of the regional population lives on one-twenty-fifth of the regional land area; the other half, or more, already lives in spread city. Moreover, spreading anti-city is filled not only with the bedroom towns that make up suburbia, but also, intertwined along the roads and highways which dissect it, with the expressions of subcityscape. It started with gas stations and restaurants needed by the traveler. But these were soon joined by shops, bars and eating places, until we find, on automatically self-congesting highways, something for everyone. Frozen custard, pizza pies, foot-long hot dogs, golf, baseball, shooting ranges, wild animals, snake pits, frontier villages, drive-in movies, drive-in banks, drive-in churches, steak palaces, gin mills, burlesque shows, discount houses, and so on. Like highway robbers in medieval times, and stagecoach bandits in the West when it was new, they aim to stop the traveler and get his money. And though they no longer do it by threatening him with a gun, their methods are no less vicious. They assault the senses and sensibilities of the inhabitants of anti-city with an orgy of ugliness and bad taste, with neon signs and garlands of naked electric bulbs, and with such expressions of ingenious originality as hot-dog stands in the form of gigantic stucco sausages, motels with minarets, and pizza stands featuring "The Leaning Tower of Pizza." The fact that entrepreneurs of such establishments are more often than not successful and that part of the public flocks to these places makes the crime no less heinous. They are ruining not only the human environment but also public taste.

The inhabitants of anti-city are not exactly happy with their lot. A Freudian giveaway of the fact that their dream wish is that of living in the country is to be found in the way they name their places. Shopping centers are referred to as villages, and everywhere one finds Town and Country markets, Town and Country shops, and Country Clubs. The industrial park is a place where there are no trees but places to park. The names of subdivisions refer to nonexistent lakes, woods, glens, dales, etc. Those who have fled from the congested city realize by now that they have gained nothing worthwhile. For their unfulfilled and unfulfillable dream, they have sacrificed all those things which are summarized in the term "urban culture." But they have not sacrificed them only for themselves; they are endangering, as we will see in later chapters, the city as a whole, and especially its heart.

6 Flight and Blight

THIS IS THE TALE of a group of happy picnickers who set out for a day of fun in the country. They formed a cavalcade of twenty vehicles, some of them containing only a couple, others holding family groups of four or five. They had sent ahead one man, in whose judgment they all had great confidence, as a researcher, so to speak, to find the best place for a picnic lunch and for a nice rest afterward. Our advance man drove for quite some time out of the city, through the spread of suburbia, until he had passed the last gas station and the last hot-dog stand, and had arrived at something that is hard to reach these days: unspoiled nature. Soon there appeared before his eyes the ideal picnic ground: a lush green meadow surrounded by forest, with a gurgling brook along one edge; colorful flowers dotting the ground, birds singing, and deer peering out shyly between the trees. He stopped, and gave the agreed-upon signal—three loud honks of his horn.

The picnickers arrived. They parked their cars in the meadow and unloaded them. Soon there appeared hundreds of cardboard boxes containing food, cans of beer, bottles of soft drinks, tablecloths and paper napkins, foam rubber mattresses and folding chairs; and bustling life unfolded. Some built fires for barbecues, others washed their cars, some had portable hi-fi radios with them, and one even produced a portable television set. Finally everybody settled down to the meal, but there arose certain problems: as groups formed, quarrels ensued as to who should sit with whom. There were some popular characters with whom everybody wanted to picnic; certain others who seemed forlorn and even avoided, who finally settled a little apart from the rest in a rather unhappy and hostile group.

In the middle of the meal, our advance man, the researcher, arose. "My friends," he said unexpectedly, "I am afraid I have done a bad job. When I came here, I thought this was a beautiful piece of landscape, but now, as I look around, I see I was utterly mistaken. It is dirty, disorderly, noisy. In fact, it is a disgusting place, full of trash, and I can't understand how I ever came to choose it. I must have been the victim of an illusion. I thought I saw flowers, but now I see there are none. I thought I heard birds, but now I hear only cheap music. I thought it would be a setting where we could find rest and peacefulness, but I see I was even wrong about that: it's a quarrelsome place. I apologize for my poor judgment. There must be better places around—let's go and look for them."

The picnickers all agreed. They packed up, and with great excitement and honking of horns they set out to find another beautiful, unspoiled spot of nature, and if they have not died in the meantime, they are still looking.

The shape, form and character of modern urbia have been created by sloppy picnickers. Technology has given us the wherewithal to move wherever we please, an unheard-of freedom of choice. We are, as a result, going around as urban nomadic tribes, desecrating and devastating every place on which we settle, creating blight with amazing rapidity, and then moving on to another picnic ground. We have founded cities along the shores

Landscape desecrated and devastated through the debris of technology.

of beautiful lakes and on the oceanfront, and have studded them with garbage dumps, industrial sites and parking lots. We have carelesssly strewn around the trash of our civilization and, horrified by our own sloppiness, have then moved out into the suburbs. We have lit our campfires: the smoke-belching chimneys of industrial plants, the smog-creating chemical plants; we have added to them the exhaust fumes of our cars, and when the stench became unbearable, we have moved on into better air, starting the same procedure all over again. We have divided ourselves into groups of picnickers, settling one group as far apart from the other as possible, and have thus succeeded in spreading the mess resulting from the picnics. We have brought along our own individual radios and portable television sets, and, to add to their competing sounds, we have created further racket with motors and sledgehammers and pneumatic drills, and the whining of jets, until we have all had to declare, "This is no picnic, let's go somewhere else."

And although we all are determined to stick together, partly because of the need to make a living by working with others and for others, and partly because we enjoy sociability, we are endlessly moving about, pulling up our tents and our roots, always looking for greener pastures, and always being frustrated in our search.

As we run out of hope and out of space, we take a second look at the places we left. We are disgusted with their appearance and character. We call them blighted, or we call them slums. We tear down everything that was built up in them by preceding generations, and we start from scratch with brand-new structures. But, sloppy picnickers that we are, we manage to desecrate the redeveloped areas in record time, and decide that we must start next door with similar efforts.

Flight and blight not only rhyme with each other; they are causally

Cityscape desecrated and "blighted" by neglect.

interrelated. Flight causes blight, and blight in turn causes new flight.

The typical old American city consists of the old core area, its heart, and the refugee camps of suburbia, exurbia and subcityscape which surround it. In the center one can still see some of the solid and attractive houses once inhabited by its citizens, although most of them have fallen prey to the bulldozer and the iron ball. Those that are left have changed their usage and occupancy. Those located along major roads have become mortuaries, restaurants, offices, churches, clubhouses; while those on minor streets have been converted into rooming houses and boardinghouses, or have been subdivided, with an eye to maximum income potential and with little thought or skill, into smaller and smaller apartments. Where the old houses have been demolished, they have given way to new roads or to gas stations, car repair shops, used-car lots, warehouses, office buildings, industrial plants, parking lots, trucking terminals, and a multitude of other structures or uses, many of them interfering violently with the usefulness of the remaining ones. Planners refer in their lingo to these areas, which were once the best residential and business sections of the city, as the "gray" areas. In the ring circling the gray area we find, in the typical American city, those structures which originally housed industries and services necessary for the life of the city core. With the quickly changing requirements for efficient industrial operation, they, too, have been deserted by their original occupants and have been either demolished or converted into warehouses, parking lots, small, economically unsound workshops, etc. Thus the gray belt of industry is created. Around this we find another ring, that of the old suburbs, target of the first wave of migration from the deteriorating core, which, plagued eventually by noise, traffic congestion and fumes, were finally abandoned by the original inhabitants, and taken over by those who, either for economic reasons or because of their racial or minority status, were excluded from the areas which then seemed most desirable, on the fringe of the city.

As we go beyond this last ring of older, unfashionable suburbs, it becomes increasingly difficult to analyze the structure of the urban organism. Historically the development of the area beyond this ring falls into the epoch of the automobile, when the rubber-wheeled vehicle became a means of mass transportation, and settlement and development were freed of bondage to railroad, streetcar, subway or bus lines—now no holds were barred. Under these free-for-all conditions, organized patterns could no longer develop. Older settlements, towns, villages, and even cities are engulfed by what we have described earlier as a "popular-priced spread," with industry, stores and the thousandfold expressions of free enterprise clinging to the tentacles of major arterial highways, and the sprawl of suburbia covering the spaces between.

Older development within the heart of the city, and within the gray area, might be compared to a ball of knitting wool, which grew as the population grew, by having new wool wound around the old ball. But in the automobile age the pieces of added wool, or new development, pull away from the original compact ball and instead of winding closely around the core, become a series of strings reaching out radially in all directions, growing in length by the knotting on of additional pieces until they are stopped by some natural barrier (perhaps a mountain, or the ocean) far away from the center. Along these strings (that is, roads and highways), starting from the central ball, creep the places of trade, of amusement and of work. The strings are utilized for two purposes, which unfortunately interfere with each other seriously. They act as guidelines for the various structures along their sides, but also as the means of communication between each of these structures and the original ball of wool. The buildings on both sides of the string steadily receive and emit people and vehicles. Thus friction is created between the flow of communications along the string, and those who move their vehicles in and out of the adjoining buildings, or who wish to cross the street, passing from one side of the string highway to the other. When this friction becomes intolerable, flight of enterprise takes place. What used to be Miracle Mile becomes a languishing strip, occupied by pawnshops, saloons and unsound marginal business enterprises. Sound enterprise moves on by adding a piece of string and establishing a new Miracle Mile. And so it goes, mile after mile in a steady process of flight and running away from itself. In its wake, this flight leaves a trail of commercial blight and commercial slums. A proud commercial structure, which, at its opening, was hailed as a most luxurious and functional merchandising emporium, has become, through flight, a deserted hag in a disreputable location a few years later.

If one wishes to observe and analyze on a small scale the reasons for blight and flight, one may find valuable clues in observing certain streets in older city centers such as New York, Boston, Philadelphia or Chicago. There are, for example, in Greenwich Village in New York where I live part of the time, two streets in close proximity, constructed in the same year and basically framed by the same type of building; yet one of these streets has remained a highly desirable, respectable residential area, while the other has deteriorated and is under consideration for slum clearance. In the first street,

"Help Keep Our City Clean" is the slogan painted on the overflowing trash container which proves not to be large enough to hold the trash which our "affluent" society creates.

buildings are carefully tended, steadily brought up to date, and the "best" people live there. In the second street, the houses are in ill repair, there is trash on the sidewalks, windows are broken, and one is warned not to pass through it at night. Its inhabitants are the poor, or the national or racial minorities: Italians, Spaniards, Negroes or Puerto Ricans. What are the events that brought about this contrasting development? They are manifold and, to start with, often insignificant. Street No. 1, the "good" street, has remained comparatively quiet and uncongested; street No. 2, because of some fluke within the over-all traffic movement pattern, became a preferred thoroughfare for trucks, automobiles and possibly buses. The "better" people, who wanted, in exchange for the money they were willing to spend, restfulness and quietude, moved from street No. 2 to street No. 1. The building owners of street No. 2 suffered for a while, but found a solution to their economic problems by converting their buildings into rooming houses and boardinghouses, or by subdividing them into small apartments. They could realize more money from their buildings than ever before by the simple device of filling them with more people; in other words, by overcrowding them. Once the owner of one of the buildings on Street No. 2 got this bright idea, a new chain of troubles was started. He moved in more people than the street could comfortably digest, people who, because they had less money and were forced to spend too much of the little they had for rent, had to wash their own laundry and hang it out of the windows or on the fire escape; people who, because of their great number, made more noise or created more disorder than the inhabitants of the adjoining buildings were willing to put up with. Thus, flight and blight were accelerated, soon spreading over the whole length of the street, and, in many cases, spilling over into adjoining areas.

Inasmuch as noise and all the other effects of this impregnation with mechanical traffic eventually spread until they disturb practically every single street of the city core, only a very few good residential streets are left in some cities, and none in others. Those original inhabitants who could afford it, and who were not restrained by the existence of national or racial prejudices from doing so, have moved out into suburbia, leaving the city core to a steadily diminishing population composed of those in lower and lower income groups, and to those national and racial minorities who have no other choice but to stay there. This conversion of residential areas of the city from the dwelling place of those living on a high and medium standard to one inhabited only by those who live there not by choice but through necessity, together with the flight of the economically stronger population to outlying areas, triggers a flight of retailing, cultural facilities, entertainment and most other urban functions.

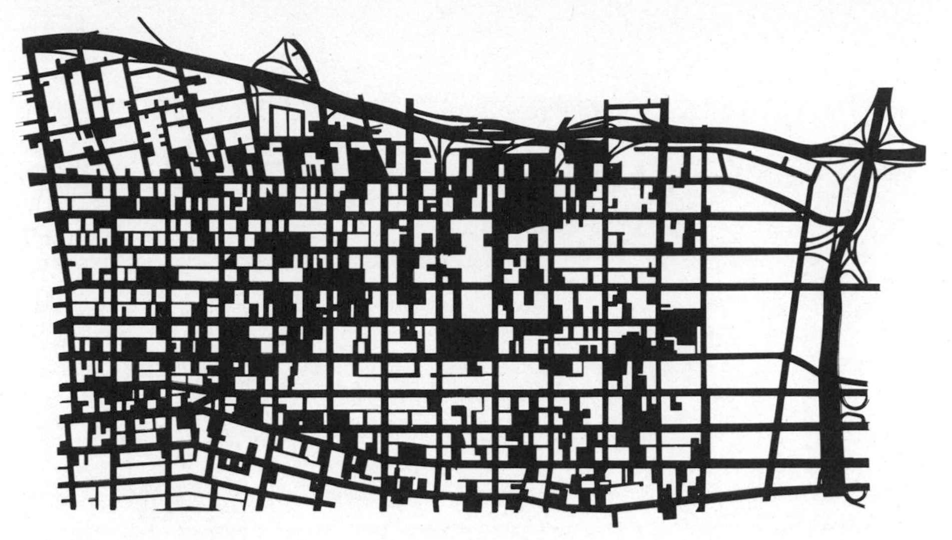

On this map of downtown Los Angeles are indicated in black those areas serving the automobile exclusively: streets, roads, freeways, garages, parking lots, gas stations, etc. They occupy two-thirds of the land area in the "heart of the city."

The merchant who finds that his paying clientele has been replaced by one with just enough money for the most basic needs of life moves as close as possible to the place where his former customers now live. The farther out they move, the farther he follows them. Theaters and churches, restaurants and hotels, art galleries and social clubs find that visitors are discouraged from weathering the long strenuous trips from their outlying residences into the unattractive city of the poor. They either close their doors forever, or they attempt to create substitutes in suburbia. Institutions employing white-collar workers find that they can get better employees at lower wages if they construct their office buildings in the outlying fringe of the region, where they can offer vast parking facilities but where, as a substitute for urban amenities, they are also forced to create, within their new office complexes, eating places, company stores, recreation facilities, etc.

As the centrifugal forces continue to operate, city centers of the poor, surrounded by outlying communities of the well-to-do, are created.

The city core of Los Angeles, for example, center of a region with 6,000,000 inhabitants, is not only small in size but void of true urban life as well. Two-thirds of the core area is devoted to the automobile: streets, roads, freeways and their appendages—garages, parking lots, gas stations, repair stations, car dealers' lots, and so on. Usage of the core for residences has almost completely disappeared. What remain in the heart of that mighty

Freeway pattern around Civic Center of Los Angeles, California.

metropolis are the structures serving public administration, the remnants of the original headquarters of banks and corporations (insignificant in comparison with their enormous branches); stores and shops selling cheap merchandise in neglected quarters to those who live in the adjoining gray area, who either are of low income or have minority status; one or two theaters, which open their doors for a few weeks of the year; one concert hall, which soon may close forever when the new music center, directly related to the freeway network, opens; and a park, which is the hangout of those unfortunate characters who cannot find their place in society, the bums. There are still the offices of those who have to work intimately with public administration: some lawyers, public notaries and engineers.

Tremendous efforts have been made, especially in the last few years, to pump new life into the heart of downtown Los Angeles. Freeways were built to make it more easily accessible from all sides, with the ironic result that they permit the motorized populace to bypass downtown more speedily than was the case before. A huge new residential development is projected for the Bunker Hill area, but up to now no developers have been found with the courage necessary to swim against the stream. Some new office buildings are the only visible result of the gigantic strife.

Real estate developments are advertised on tremendous billboards: a further extension of scatterization along Ventura Boulevard in Los Angeles. Stretches of natural beauty appear in name only. Thus Walnut Grove, for example, will contain everything but a grove.

The phenomena of flight and blight can be observed even more clearly in Los Angeles than in most other cities. What was glamorous Hollywood at the beginning of the century is now a depressing disappointment to the tourists, an area of economic and cultural blight. What was the famous Miracle Mile in the 1930s is now a poor excuse for the existence of a string of chain stores. Once-fashionable enclaves of the gray area, with palatial mansions, are now residential slums. The migratory character of the population is manifested by thousands of FOR SALE, FOR RENT, and OPEN FOR INSPECTION signs and by an impressive army of real estate agents. New developments, advertising the ultimate in luxurious living, or in prestige office headquarters, are destined to become the blighted areas of tomorrow. The stringlike tentacles of freeways and highways stretch farther and farther, until they meet with the tentacles of other cities—San Diego to the south and Santa Barbara to the north—stopped only by the Pacific Ocean to the west, and the mountains and the desert to the east. Thus flight has become increasingly difficult to accomplish as the years go by, and, slowly and hesitantly, politicians, administrators and planners are beginning to realize that an alternate route will have to be found.

The problems posed by nonending migration within urban areas are made significantly more complex by the problems of national migratory patterns. There is migration from rural areas, which, thanks to mechanized equipment and modern agricultural methods, no longer have to employ the masses of people once needed to raise our food. There is the migration from Puerto Rico into the cities of the East and the Middle West. And there is the rapidly increasing migration of the Negro population from areas of legalized or semilegalized discrimination in the South to those with only unofficial discrimination in the North and West.

New York, for example, has a net in-migration of 30,000 Puerto Ricans and 10,000 Negroes annually. Inasmuch as about 50,000 whites leave the city every year, city officials estimate that by 1970 New York will be 28 per cent Negro and Puerto Rican, and Manhattan, the heart of the city, will house a million Negroes and Puerto Ricans, more than half its total population.

Chicago's Negro population is increasing by 35,000 a year; white Chicagoans simultaneously move out at the rate of 15,000 a year.

Cleveland loses 3,000 members of the white race yearly, and gains 6,500 Negroes in the same period.

St. Louis's Negro population has increased from 12 per cent to 30 per cent of the total population since 1940.

Since new Negro immigrants from the South are often regarded with disfavor by the older Negro population, the latter are wont to move, where possible, to the suburbs. Similarly, immigration of the white low-income population from the South results in the flight of previous white inhabitants to the suburbs. This flight of older residents from cities when new ones arrive is not necessarily the result of prejudice but is just as likely to be brought about by discord resulting from different educational and cultural backgrounds and different living patterns.

Thus it must be admitted that some of the problems of flight and blight cannot be dealt with by city planning alone, but only through national effort and national legislation. The destructive phenomenon of physical compartmentalization, of ghetto formation, can be effectively eliminated only when its sociological motivations disappear. The sooner and the more completely we as a nation eliminate racial and ethnological discrimination and that stubbornly persisting paradox of abject poverty of a minority in an "affluent society," the sooner will we succeed in stopping flight and blight, those scourges of a healthy civilization.

7 The Tired Hearts of Our Cities

What is happening now is hardly more than what happened in Rome in the Dark Ages. Men tear down great works, and put up the best they can.

—Edgar Kaufmann, Jr.,
Harper's Magazine, May, 1960

In the chapter on the "Anatomy of the City" we observed that the urban organism, like the human one, has a heart, and that the health and vigor of the city's heart are as vital and essential to the continued health of the urban organism as the human heart is to man's existence. The one point of deviation in the pattern of similiarity is this: that the urban heart area is the seat of the urban brain and of the urban spirit, or the city's soul, as well.

The seriousness of urban disease in the United States, or what is referred to so often as the "urban crisis," can best be recognized if one examines the condition of the heart. One soon realizes that where the heart area of a city has been most seriously affected, the entire urban area has suffered the most. In a city where coronary disease is still well controlled, the over-all health of the urban organism is more satisfactory.

In previous chapters I have described spread, sprawl, and scatterization, flight and blight as some of the germs that infect and cause diseases of the urban heart. In this chapter we will take a closer look at the hearts of cities themselves, examining them thoroughly and trying to arrive at a diagnosis.

The use of language often gives interesting clues in the judgment of conditions. Motorists in the United States arriving within a metropolitan area from the outside will generally be guided by signs reading TO THE CENTRAL BUSINESS DISTRICT, OF TO MAIN STREET. The motorist entering a metropolitan area in Europe, on the other hand, will find signs that read TO THE CENTER, TO THE INNER CITY, or simply TO THE CITY. In this variation in language is expressed some of the trouble that besets the hearts of our cities.

It will be helpful in diagnosing the urban heart disease if we can first agree on what the characteristics of a normally functioning heart should be. The normal heart should have high *vitality*, or, to put it in medical terms, high cardiac output. Vitality will be at its highest when the primary functions, to which we also refer as human functions, can be carried out successfully and without strain. This, in turn, is possible only when secondary or *utilitarian* functions perform efficiently and without interfering with human activities. Utilitarian functions are, for example, the sewer system, electric and telephone cables, water and gas lines, and all means of mechanized transportation. In order for both human and utilitarian functions to work optimally, the distances they have to overcome should be as short as possible, and compactness of arrangement is therefore necessary. To achieve such compactness, the urban heart, like the human organ, should consist solely of working tissue of the highest order; it must be free of dead matter. We will hereafter speak of healthy tissue as "suitable uses" and dead matter as "unsuitable uses." A healthy pattern, created by a compact arrangement of suitable uses and optimal conditions for the carrying on of human functions—unmolested by utilitarian functions, no matter how efficiently they may work—will create the basis for intensive *core activities* such as working, dwelling, shopping, sightseeing, participating in civic, social, cultural, recreational and spiritual events. An urban heart with these healthy conditions will then attract great numbers of people whom we will call *activity participants*. In the long run, however, it will succeed in doing so only if it has those *superior environmental qualities* which affect positively the well-being, safety, comfort and pleasure of the activity participants. These would include safeguards of the individual's health; protection from wind, weather and physical hazards; shielding of the senses from distasteful sights, sounds and smells while, at the same time, affording opportunities for a varied and pleasurable sensory experience; and offering opportunities for rest and relaxation.

Now, let us assume that we have been able to create a city heart possessing all these criteria of good health. It would still not function if it were not within easy reach of those who wish to become activity participants. It must therefore have good *accessibility*—a term denoting ease of travel to and from the core, for people as well as for goods, from all land areas that make up the metropolitan region, and beyond that, from other cities and from the countryside, from the state, the nation and, in fact, the world. There must be a variety of *instruments of accessibility,* some effecting primarily the transportation of goods, others of people. One such instrument is *individualized transportation,* a term referring to comparatively small travel containers utilized by single individuals or by a small number of people (automobiles, taxicabs, motorcycles, bicycles) or for carrying a comparatively small quantity of goods (trucks of various sizes and types). Another instrument of accessibility is *mass transportation,* referring to transportation in much larger travel containers used by a considerable number of people at the same time, such as planes, railroad trains, rapid-transit trains, buses, conveyor systems and, for the transportation of goods, freight trains, trucks, etc. A healthy urban heart, then, is also one that offers easy accessibility through a composite of instruments balanced to work most beneficially. A significant part of easy accessibility is good *core terminal facilities,* well placed. These are the starting or terminal points for travel in and out of the core, and they match in diversity the variety of instruments of accessibility. There will be commuter train and other railroad terminals, bus terminals, terminals for individualized transportation (automobile storage facilities), freight terminals.

The surfaces on which the various instruments of accessibility move in order to reach the core terminal facilities we will term *accessibility media.* As far as individualized transportation is concerned, these media are the *core bound roads,* those which in the main are arranged radially, leading from the outlying areas toward the heart; and *distributary roads,* those which follow the basic pattern of concentric rings around the heart at various distances from it (often referred to, also, as ring roads or loop roads). To some extent mass transportation, as in the case of buses, uses the same media, but for the most part it utilizes media specifically reserved for it, like rail lines for trains, for rapid transit, and so on. Here, too, we find core-bound transportation media radially approaching the core from the outside, and distributary media following the pattern of concentric circles. A well-designed system of transportation media, balanced in quantity and quality to ensure the easiest accessibility, is another symptom of a healthy heart.

A large metropolitan area will have a core of proportionate size and will therefore require an adequate *core transportation system.* Transportation facilities within the core are: movement on foot, mass transportation specifically designed for suitability to short distances, possibly taxicabs, etc. A sign of good health in a large core area is a transportation system specifically adjusted to the needs of a compact area of great vitality—rather than a carbon copy, in reduced scale, of transportation systems designed to achieve easy accessibility to and from the outside.

Now, let us go back for a moment to the terms "suitable uses" and "unsuitable uses," which we discussed previously but which deserve further examination. As suitable uses, I regard those which represent the highest expression of urban activity, achieve high productivity in a comparatively small space and serve specialized needs, tasks and standards. In the field of public administration, for example, suitable uses within the core would be main seats of city, county and state government; central offices dealing with the health, welfare, housing and transportation of the citizens of the metropolitan area. In the realm of private enterprise, suitable uses would be main offices of corporations large and small, the facilities of banks and other financial institutions, and those of the retail and wholesale trades; the offices of those who are closely related to these enterprises through services of all types—advertising, publicity, etc.; in the professional field, lawyers and doctors, architects and engineers, economists and other experts; in the cultural field, theaters and concert halls, libraries and museums; as expressions of spiritual life, churches of all denominations and the seats of societies concerned with the nonmaterialistic life; in the educational field, higher institutions of learning. Then there are the suitable uses devoted to leisure and relaxation—restaurants, bars, movie theaters, nightclubs, cafés, and so on.

Unsuitable uses are those which create disturbances and nuisances, and those which are of low quality and low productivity in relation to the space they occupy. Such unsuitable uses are, for example, warehousing, storage, factories that create obnoxious noises or fumes, and plants which, because of their production methods, stretch in one-story structures over vast areas. Other unsuitable uses would of course be slaughterhouses, cemeteries, agriculture, etc.

A healthy city heart attracts and holds creative people—painters, sculptors, musicians, poets, actors and actresses, dancers, philosophers, architects, writers and planners (including those who criticize the city and would like to do away with it). It is a haven for those who find in its environment not only a source of income, but inspiration, too. It is a preferred place of residence for those who value intimate contact with urban features and for whom, whether they are wealthy, middle-class or poor, the city is a way of life. The healthy city heart is a place of infinite variety whose buildings and structures form, between them, spaces of differing size and character, narrow or broad, serene or dynamic, modest or monumental, contrasting with each other by virtue of varied treatment of pavement, landscaping and lighting. Sprinkled throughout the core are green areas ranging from tiny landscaped spots to good-sized parks. A healthy urban heart pulsates with life day and night, weekday and Sunday, spring, summer, fall and winter.

Now that I have attempted to give a clinical picture of the healthy urban heart, and now that we have developed a terminology to denote the signs of health, let us take a look at the actual condition of various cities. We have stated that compactness is one of the signs of health. It is significant that those two American cities whose hearts, at least at first glance, seem to be least affected—New York and San Francisco—are also the ones in which compactness of the heart area prevails to a large degree. In both these cases natural boundaries have prevented spread. The city core occupies in one case an island, in the other a peninsula, and bodies of water have called a halt to sprawl in both. Similarly, the core in Chicago has been protected from spreading by the geographic restraint applied by Lake Michigan and the Chicago River. Los Angeles, on the other hand, located in a tremendous basin with only the Pacific Ocean and the mountains, both at considerable distance from the city core, forming geographic boundaries, has lost its heart because of the lack of restraining forces.

Manhattan, New York's heart area and the largest and most important city core in the United States, is a very special case in many respects. The fact that it is still dynamic—and more important, the news-making, news-distributing center of the United States—contributes largely to the comparative unawareness on the part of the American public of the seriousness of the urban crisis.

Manhattanites, their ears filled with the din of construction machinery, their eyes adjusting to new zigs and zags in the skyline every year, cannot quite believe that there is such a thing as a critical disease of the heart of American cities; and since so much that is written on every subject, including urban problems, originates in Manhattan or at least is published there, the picture becomes distorted and the full impact of urban disease is not brought to national attention. But Manhattan is an atypical representation of American city cores. If it were to depend for its functioning solely on the New York metropolitan region, it would in all probability be just as seriously infected by anti urban bacilli as other city cores. But Manhattan, beyond its role as a metropolitan core, also happens to be the business capital of the United States and, to a large degree, of the free Western world. It also has become the political center of the world by virtue of the fact that it contains the headquarters of the United Nations; it is, as well, the financial center of the United States, with great influence on the rest of the free world. Because of this trinity of central roles it attracts millions of activity participants, not only from the region but from all the states of the Union and from the many nations of the world; and because of this it is the American city core in which a strong theatrical, musical, cultural, and art life is most in evidence.

Yet even Manhattan shows symptoms sufficiently divergent from the clinical picture we have drawn of a healthy city heart as to cause serious concern. There most certainly has been a loss in vitality as far as retail trade is concerned. In the Fourteenth Street area alone there has been a radical dying off of department stores and other merchandising enterprises. Gone from this area are Wanamaker's, Hecht's, Hearn's, Ohrbach's, and dozens of smaller stores that lived from the traffic the big ones generated. The retail trade area along America's classical shopping street, Fifth Avenue, is shrinking steadily, giving way to banks and other institutions. There is also a strong loss of vitality in the theatrical life. Of the sixty Broadway theaters that operated in the 1930s, only thirty are left.

Streets in Manhattan are overcrowded with automobiles, trucks and taxis, and from this one might conclude that the number of core activity participants has grown. Statistics reveal, however, that 300,000 fewer people visit Manhattan during a twenty-four-hour workday period today than did ten years ago. In addition to this, during the last ten years Manhattan has lost about 200,000 inhabitants, in spite of the fact that there was an in-migration of large numbers of economically or racially underprivileged inhabitants. The meaning behind these figures is that about half a million or more persons of middle-class status who contributed greatly to the vitality of the core as shoppers, theater-and-concert-goers, etc., have, as refugees, settled in suburbia. The puzzling fact that streets are overcongested, and become more so each year in spite of population decrease and participant decrease, is explained by the dramatic increase in individualized transportation instruments (automobiles) and an even more significant decrease in users of mass transportation. Inasmuch as mass transportation is still overcrowded in the so-called rush hours, morning and evening, but underutilized during the rest of the day or evening, it can be easily concluded that those core participants who come to Manhattan daily for the purpose of making a living have not decreased in number but possibly have even increased, and

The never-ending warfare between machines and human beings, creating heavy casualties on both sides, is illustrated by this street scene in Manhattan.

that the number of other core participants visiting Manhattan—for the purpose of shopping or participating in the multitude of other urban activities—has dramatically decreased. Manhattan, thus, is changing in character. It becomes a gigantic workshop, lopsidedly fulfilling only one part of its urban destiny; as far as the character of its population is concerned, it becomes a place for the few very rich and the many awfully poor. The sociological effects of this are serious. They are mistrust and fear, founded or unfounded, between citizen and citizen, between citizen and government. *The New York Times,* in an editorial of September 7, 1962, entitled "The Decay of New York," offers two disturbing reminders of the extent of social decay: "One was the decision to cancel the dedication of four rehabilitated buildings on West 49th Street, because an outbreak of violence was feared." The *Times* characterizes this as a confession that "the police could not guarantee the safety of Mayor Wagner and other ranking officers at a ceremony to be held in broad daylight in the heart of Manhattan's west side." The second reminder offered by the *Times* is "the announcement that 80 newly enrolled members of the Peace Corps were being assigned to a month of work in the city slums to prepare them for the privations and neglect they will find in the poverty-wracked districts of various cities in Colombia." The editorial closes with this admonition: "How many more such reminders does the city administration need to develop a sense of outrage? Our parks are no man's land after dark. Muggings throughout the city are commonplace."

So it would appear that Manhattan, too, in spite of its exceptional status, is beset by a serious heart condition, differing from the ailments of other cities in degree only, and a little harder to recognize because of the eye-catching, feverish activity in specialized fields, especially the construction of office and bank buildings.

Quite generally speaking, all American cities, large, small or middle-sized, show marked, though slightly varying, aberrations from the norm in the state of health of their hearts. Let me point out these aberrations by taking a clinical look at the hearts of various American cities, using as examples those I have had an opportunity to study through my work.

Cincinnati, Ohio

Located within a healthily growing region, the heart of Cincinnati should be relatively sound; yet figures reveal that its health has been undermined, and projections for the future demonstrate that unless presently existing centrifugal forces can be stopped, devitalization of the core is likely to progress at an accelerated pace in the next twenty years. One of the most reliable barometers for measuring the vitality of a city heart is the number of core participants. This figure is composed of the number of core residents plus the number of daily core visitors. Cincinnati had 11,500 core inhabitants in 1940, but by 1960 this figure had dwindled to 6,500. In 1945, 209,000 persons visited the city core during a typical twenty-four-hour working day; in 1960, only 171,000 did so. Cause and effect (and it is difficult to determine what is cause and what is effect) of this dwindling number of core participants are then expressed in other figures. In 1948 there were 1,054 retail establishments; in 1958 only 854. Buildings in usable condition for productive purposes in 1937 comprised a floor area of 28,600,000 square feet; in 1954, this figure was 28,000,000 square feet. The total assessed real property tax for the core as expressed in the percentage of the total assessment for the city was, in 1945, 21 per cent; in 1955, 17 per cent.

These dry statistics are reflected in the poor appearance and the lifelessness of the city core, in the numerous FOR RENT signs on stores and office buildings, in the large vacancy rate of hotel rooms, in a downgrading of the quality and character of the stores still doing business, in the closing of many theaters and movie houses, in the emptiness of streets at night and on holidays and Sundays (brought about by a sharp decrease in social and cultural activities), in the neglected appearance of buildings and stores and in a general deterioration of the environmental qualities.

A detailed analysis of the figure showing the decrease of core participants reveals that the number of people who visit the city core daily for the purpose of working has remained steady, and that the entire loss of 38,000 per day is made up of those who used to come to the core as shoppers and as participants in cultural, social and recreational activities.

We shall return to a discussion of Cincinnati in Part Three, when we shall describe the measures that have been recommended for the restoration of its vitality.

Detroit, Michigan

This city, too, lies within a growing metropolitan region—growing in space as well as in population. This growth, however, is not reflected in the heart. In spite of efforts to improve accessibility (and probably because these efforts were made in an unbalanced manner, being limited solely to the construction of arterial freeways for individualized transportation) and in spite of the construction of a new civic center along the riverfront, the core shows serious symptoms of devitalization. How unimportant the city center has become is revealed when one observes surface traffic patterns. In contrast to the accepted phenomenon of overcongestion within the city core, in

Detroit it is comparatively easy to get around by automobile in the core area; the difficulties arise as one approaches the suburban ring. An ambitious planning program of municipal garages has provided ample parking space in the core, but it has not been able to provide the activity participants who would use this space. There is always plenty of parking space available in Detroit, for the simple reason that there is no longer sufficient urban activity to fully utilize it. Rush-hour traffic on some of the Detroit freeways moves in the opposite direction from the usual movement pattern: heaviest in the morning hours, moving away from downtown, and in the evening hours in the direction of downtown. The explanation lies in the fact that automobile traffic on the freeways is not bound for downtown at all but moves from suburban residential areas into suburban industrial areas, bypassing the core entirely.

I have not been able to obtain exact figures that would trace the decline of core activity participants during the last twenty years, but judging from outward appearances, the decline must be a sharp one. There are large amounts of vacant office and retail store space. Of the four major department stores which the downtown area once contained, one large one has closed its doors completely; one has rented more than half its area for use by governmental offices, and the largest of the department stores (the J. L. Hudson Company) has lost business volume in its downtown location, though it has more than made up for this loss in outlying locations. Theaters are dark most of the year, and the number of good eating or entertainment places is, for a city the size of Detroit, alarmingly low—at least within the core area.

Milwaukee, Wisconsin

This city has been so concerned with the deterioration of its center that a few years ago it called a conference of national planners to investigate reasons and possible cures. The city administration furnished voluminous statistical information demonstrating that all the factors I discussed in the case of Cincinnati were present here in a much more advanced stage. The traffic department report revealed the usual steep upward curve of persons entering the core by individualized transportation and the even steeper downward curve of persons arriving in the core by mass transportation. But an unusual facet was brought to light by the statistical information: namely, that in the last three or four years the upward curve denoting those who entered by individualized transportation had flattened out and finally declined. In the case of Milwaukee, we see the vicious cycle completed: The erosion of the core area has proceeded so far that its power of attraction has waned to the point where not only has the number of core activity participants arriving by mass transportation shrunk but even the number of visitors coming by automobile has declined.

Boston, Massachusetts

Boston possesses a core with a proud historical heritage and with the unique urban green area of the Boston Common and Public Garden. In spite of these assets, heart disease has progressed so far that the danger of a coronary attack is being realized now by business and government alike. Revitalization efforts by private enterprise and government are now under way on a scale and in a spirit of cooperation unparalleled in other cities. The Boston *Globe* of September 2, 1962, referring to these efforts, voiced the hope that they would succeed in making Boston "a phoenix rising from the dust of its crumbling brick and mortar."

The symptoms of the disease are similar to those present in the cities mentioned above, but are even more dramatic. Not only has the residential population in the city core been reduced sharply, but the total population within the city's incorporated areas has decreased, between 1920 and 1960, by 7 per cent, whereas the population of the surrounding metropolitan region has increased in the same period of time by 85 per cent. Statistics reveal that the heart of Boston experienced its highest cardiac output, or vitality, in the 1920s and that since that time the number of activity participants has been on the downgrade, being presently about 25 per cent lower than at the time of highest vitality. No wonder, then, that there are vacant offices and stores, that real estate values have crumbled, and that cultural, artistic and social institutions languish. No wonder that retail business has fallen off and that environmental qualities have been on the decline.

These events, in turn, have led to a lowering of the municipal income and a rise in the cost of administration. This, of course, forced the city to raise taxes; high taxes then drove additional enterprises across the city's borders into the outlying region. I will discuss in Part Three the projected measures that are now under consideration to reverse the downward trends.

I could go on describing symptoms of the heart disease of American cities, citing examples at hand of other cities we have studied: Fresno, Santa Monica, and San Bernardino in California; St. Paul, Minnesota; Kalamazoo, Michigan; Green Bay, Wisconsin; Forth Worth, Texas; St. Petersburg, Florida; Rochester, New York; Paterson and Woodbridge, New Jersey; Stamford, Connecticut; Lockport, New York, and those for which core redevelopment projects are being studied or are under way by others: St. Louis and Kansas City, Missouri; Philadelphia; Newark, New Jersey; New Haven, Connecticut, and many more. Suffice it to say that aberrations from the healthy norm are present in all of them and that the symptoms of disease are similar in all cases.

What are the reasons for the drying up of the city hearts? The well-known economist, Sylvia Porter, wrote in 1961 in her daily column, under the title "Abandoned Cities":

> Is business abandoning the big cities, and thus helping to create the vicious circle of downtown degeneration, bigger urban taxes to make up for the abandonment, a resulting further migration of business and a loss of real estate values, more tax hikes and so on and on? The answer is an emphatic "yes." American top executives may work in our big

A daring commuter to downtown is discouraged from repeating such a visit by inconvenience, high costs and time loss.

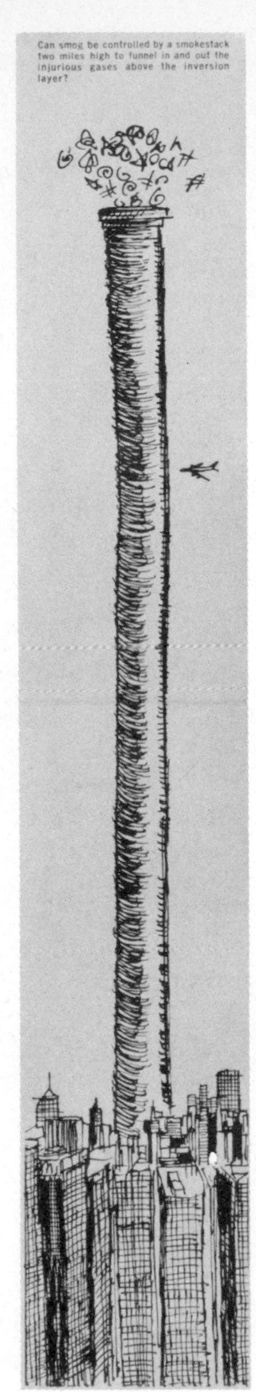

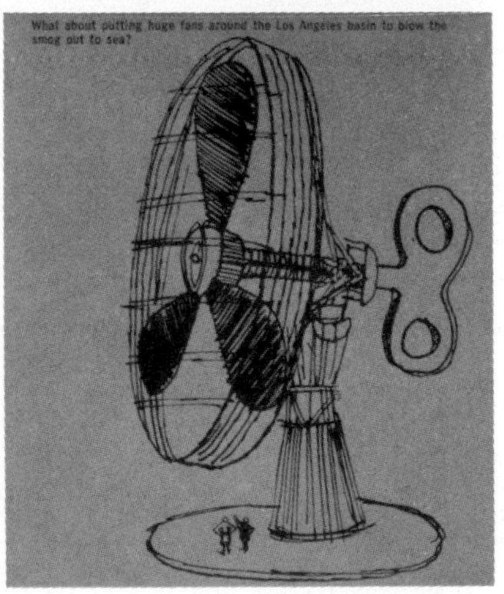

The frantic search for effective means of fighting the smog over the City of the Angels illustrated by this cartoon — towering chimneys for industrial plants, electric automobiles, giant vacuum cleaners and, finally, electric fans are proposed.

> cities, but they do not live in them. A survey of the cross section of U.S. executives reveals that only one third working in cities with populations over 250,000 live in them, and in our ten largest cities, the proportion falls to a scant 27%.
>
> Executives are much better citizens in the communities in which they live than in the cities in which they work. While most businessmen have a distaste for the government of our cities, they do nothing to improve the situation.
>
> One large retail chain reports it expects to lose 10 to 20 downtown stores per year as leases expire. At the same time, of the 348 stores it has opened in the past 5 years, 308 are located in suburban shopping centers. . . . As long as most executives work in one place, live in another, and do nothing but bemoan their city's degeneration, they are acutely defaulting on what they admit is their responsibility.

If one should ask the average citizen why he avoids downtown, why he goes there for one purpose only, namely, to *make* money, but stays away when it comes to *spending* it, he would probably give the following reasons:

1. He can't get into it.
2. He can't get out of it.
3. He can't get around in it.
4. He finds public transportation uncomfortable and distasteful, and he can't use his car because he can't find parking space.
5. The values he receives downtown, as compared with those he can get in suburbia, become less attractive as far as shopping, movies, conveniences, amenities and beauty are concerned.
6. The sacrifices he has to make in time and nervous energy become constantly greater. And finally,
7. The city is a downright dangerous place to live in or to move around in.

Los Angeles, City of the Angels (sometimes known as "Gasopolis"), threatens the health of its inhabitants with that lovely mixture of gases and fog that led to the enrichment of the English language by the addition of the word "smog," which attacks the over-all health of the people, causing them to cry even when they are in a gay mood. (*The National Observer* stated in a recent issue that Los Angeles is now testing its smog, fearing that it may be deadly. Physicians at the University of Southern California have concluded that there is a strong possibility smog may soon be killing some Californians.)

The dangers to life in New York are illustrated in a report of the Accident Records Bureau of the New York Police Department for 1962. According to this report 55,050 people were injured (4,877 more than in the previous year) while riding in automobiles. During that period, 649 were killed in automobile accidents. To walk is slightly less dangerous. Only 435 pedestrians were killed (39 more than the year before) and 14,566 were injured (679 more than in the previous year).

Is it, then, any wonder that those who can afford to avoid the dangers to life, limb and general health, and the inconvenience caused by noise and congestion, and those who are disenchanted by the lack of public safety and the deterioration of public institutions (especially schools) have quit the city as residents, leaving their former homes to those who cannot afford to live anywhere else, but who dream of the day on which they, too, can move out? (Dwight MacDonald, in an article in the January 19, 1963, issue of *The New Yorker,* states that the richest city of all, New York, has been steadily growing poorer; that 49 per cent of its families had incomes in 1959 of less than $6,000, and that a fourth of all New York families were below the poverty line of $4,000.)

Is it any wonder that those who visit the city do so only when it is unavoidable in order to earn their livelihood, but cannot be persuaded to stay any longer than absolutely necessary—and most certainly do not return during the evening or on Saturdays, Sundays and holidays?

In our "case studies" we have referred chiefly to large cities, but the disease of the heart has affected nearly every city of any size in the nation. Philip W. Moore, president of the First Research Corporation, states in an article in the *Lawyers Title News:*

> There are some 192 U.S. cities of more than 100,000 population, which are the victims of their own inflexibility. . . . By and large, it can be safely said that in almost all cities of more than 100,000 population, the share of the downtown business area as such, and the share in the local retail dollar, has been probably cut by at least 40% in the past 12 years, and in many cases more than this. . . . The Plight of Downtown is somewhat more evident in cities or metropolitan areas of between 150,000 and 600,000 population than in cities below that size or above that size.

During the nineteenth century, and in the early years of the twentieth, we believed, perhaps naïvely, that growth of a city and improvement of those qualities which we call urbane went hand in hand. As a new gold-mining town grew in population, it also grew in urbane amenities. It got sidewalks, sewers and an opera house. Nowadays, the contrary is rather the case. As urban population grows, amenities shrink. Sidewalks are narrowed or done away with in order to make space for vehicular traffic, and opera houses close down because traffic congestion makes them inaccessible.

In the beginning of this chapter, I tried to give an inventory of the activities, institutions and buildings that a healthy city heart should contain. If we were to use this inventory as a checklist, we would find that 90 per cent of our cities with over 100,000 population cannot muster within their heart areas more than 10 per cent of the essential features and that, moreover, of the 10 per cent left, only two or three will come close to the target. I know of at least one American city, Miami, Florida, in which serious consideration is being given to moving City Hall, the heart valve of the urban core, into suburbia.

If the deterioration of the hearts of American cities were planfully undertaken by diabolic fiends, they could not devise more effective means of destruction than those presently utilized. Yet most of these measures are not the work of fiends, but of basically well-meaning people, about whom I want to talk in the next chapter, "The False Friends of the City."

8 The False Friends of the City

Defend me from my friends; I can defend myself from my enemies.

—Maréchal Villars, upon taking leave of Louis XIV

History is full of stories of cities that have managed not only to survive attacks and disaster—man-made or elemental—but to preserve their spirit and their culture as well. What enemy attack and destruction by the elements have been unable to accomplish, however, may be managed soon and effectively by nonviolent but persistent efforts of the anti-urban fifth column, the self-proclaimed friends of the city. We find them in all professions and in all walks of life. They may be architects or planners, politicians, economists, administrators, real estate operators, builders, traffic engineers, industrialists, merchants, critics, bureaucrats, lawmakers or experts of any kind. How are we to recognize these false friends of the city? We shall know them by one characteristic they have in common: They are the dehumanizers of the city. Their interests, their love, their industry and their actions are employed first and foremost to serve not human beings but rather the well-being of machines (real or political), for political or economic advantages; their gods are the motorcar, power and money.

The devious methods employed in destroying the city from within are so manifold that one could write a book about them. Inasmuch as I have only a chapter at my disposal, I shall have to restrict myself to mentioning only the main types of the species, and to giving just a digest of their activities.

For brevity's sake, then, I shall direct the spotlight on five major types of false friends of the city:

The traffickist
The bulldozerite
The segregator
The projectite
The economizer

The TRAFFICKIST's habitat is the traffic department of every city and town, although he can often be found, too, in planning commissions, in police departments and in Federal agencies. He lives and dies for the "facilitation" of automobile traffic, and for that purpose he is engaged in an unholy crusade, willing to bring to his goddess, The Automotive Vehicle, as supreme sacrifice, the city and all its inhabitants. Given a choice between removing automobiles and removing buildings and people, he will not hesitate for a moment to choose the latter. The traffickist has hypnotized the nation into believing a) that the term "traffic" means solely the movement of automobiles and trucks, and b) that he is the only one on whom some Higher Being has bestowed the know-how and wisdom to deal with this problem. He has persuaded us that we live in the "automobile age" and that therefore our cities will have to be "automobile cities." An important characteristic of these cities, he has made us believe, is their "deference to the role of the automobile" (this is a quote from the foreword to the New York Zoning Resolution adopted by the Board of Estimate on December 15, 1960) or their ability to adjust themselves to traffic by continuous shrinkage of the areas devoted to structures and human activities and by wiping out that outdated species, the pedestrian, whom the traffickist regards as an outright nuisance slowing down the traffic he wants to facilitate. He firmly believes that cities and people were created to serve traffic, rather than the other way around. He has succeeded in mesmerizing us into forgetting the real meaning of the term traffic, which is movement—specifically the moving of people and goods—and that the earmark of good traffic is that it moves people and goods in the fastest, most convenient, and least disturbing manner possible. Thus, strangely enough, the traffickist is an anti-transportationist. Whenever he hears phrases like "public transportation," "rapid transit," or "pedestrian movement," he sees red, and refers to those who mention those phrases as "ivory tower planners."

This is not astonishing, if one considers that the traffickist is an expert and specialist who wishes to perpetuate the problem from which he is making a living. Toward this end of keeping his beloved specialty a continuous, lucrative enterprise, he very carefully plans his efforts in such a manner that they create new and even more fascinating problems. Thus he not only succeeds in making the city unlivable and unworkable, unreachable and inescapable, but he has even managed to rob that tool of his craft, the automobile, of its usability and practical meaning. Out of that wonderful invention, the automobile, designed to move at a speed of up to a hundred miles an hour, out of this tool of *individual mobility* he has made an instrument of *collective immobility*. He has swept the narrowed sidewalks clear of people, and where once the boys stood, in the words of a popular song, "watching all the girls go by," we now find the traffickist with a stopwatch "watching all the cars go by." As a result of his counting operation, he then decrees the installation of a new forest of traffic signals and signs, the introduction of one-way streets, the wholesale demolition of buildings to make way for more asphalt, the posting of "humorous" signs in which animals such as owls and cats admonish (in bad English) those inferior and childish beings, the pedestrians, to pay deference to traffic at every step. Each time the traffickists do so, traffic problems get more serious, and thus their position becomes more important. Today these inventors of the traffic jam enjoy high standing in society. From the obscurity of subordinate positions they have grown into a powerful and authoritative clique. Mayors, city admin-

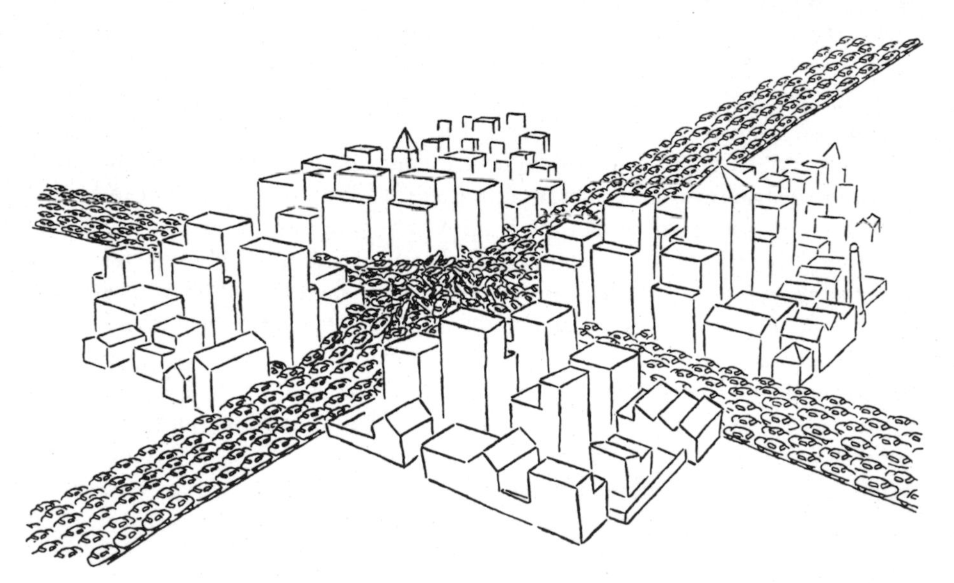

This cartoon demonstrates convincingly what must happen if one moves automobiles from millions of outlying points to one central point.

istrators and city planners bow to their judgment and their demands. In the city budget, more money is allocated to traffic studies, electronic signaling, road building and traffic policing than to any phase of genuine civic improvement. The traffickists have jockeyed themselves into a position where they usurp over-all planning functions while others, scared and puzzled by the seemingly insoluble traffic problems, sit frustrated on the sidelines, finally joining in the game of "watching all the cars go by."

The traffickists have hypnotized us into believing that traffic is an elemental act of God or nature, like an earthquake, a flood, or a hurricane; something which only the expert, with his God-given power and insight, can dare to tangle with.

The BULLDOZERITE is the bosom friend of the traffickist, and they work hand in glove. He owns and operates diabolical machines which can tear down in minutes what it has taken ages to build. The machine is monstrous; it has a big mouth, and an even bigger stomach. It is not interested in small bites, but likes to gobble up large chunks at a time. It is an ideal tool for mass destruction. The owners, operators and lovers of the machine occupy important positions in planning departments, redevelopment agencies, and the construction industries; some of them call themselves architects and planners. The bulldozerite is hell-bent on demolition, and starts to think about the replacement of buildings, communities and urban values only

The original caption under this cartoon reads "Oh, well, it was bound to happen one day."

No longer do we take advantage of existing topography, of hills and slopes and valleys. The bulldozer evens everything out. Thus more sameness, more boredom, is created.

---

after the damage has been done. The bulldozerite's activity is danger-fraught for the heart of the city. Making deep cuts in the living tissue of the urban heart is just as critical an operation as surgery around the human heart, which should be performed only by the most skillful medical expert with the finest scalpel. Yet, in the heart of the city, the bulldozerite does not hesitate to cut with his infernal machine broad swaths for new freeways and expressways, or to demolish entire blocks of structures, even entire communities marked for "redevelopment." More often than not, the living tissue does not grow back and the patient dies. The bulldozerite knows no respect for historic or cultural values, for heritage and continuity. He can prove to you that it is "cheaper by the dozen" to murder wholesale, to destroy in large quantities. He believes firmly in starting from scratch, and scratches his head when the problem arises of how to start. The bull-dozerite also loves to work in the countryside. Here he levels mountains and fills in valleys, and tears down in one swoop what nature has caused to grow over the ages. Trees and bushes, meadows and flowers, brooks and rivers are torn out or leveled, and the operation is admired as a triumph of technology.

Russell Baker, the "Observer," in *The New York Times* (Western Edition, February 7, 1963) has discovered a special species of false friends who take the position between the traffickist and the bulldozerite. The Observer remarks:

> There is a small clique little known outside insiders' circles that will be extremely pained if the Boston experiment [getting commuters off the highways and onto the railroads] should work. The director of this tiny but immensely powerful group, whose tentacles reach even into the Mafia, is known only as The Great Paver.
>
> His dream . . . is to pave the entire United States with concrete and asphalt. He envisions a nation buried under six-lane, limited access turnpikes. When the last blade of American grass is buried, he plans to go on to pave Europe. Then Asia. And on and on until the whole planet is coated in cement. Today America—tomorrow the world. . . .
>
> His philosophy is summed up in the sentence with which he refutes every attempt to stop him: "The world must move cars."

Next let's consider the SEGREGATOR (and I do not use this expression as applying just to racial segregation but in a much wider sense), who is basically a simple, methodical soul. City planning departments, zoning commissions, and planning practitioners, too, are often members of the segregation club. Their goddess is Methodology, and because the segregator believes devoutly, his methodology becomes deadly. Method, of course, is an essential tool in planning. But if the tool becomes more important than the goal of creating a truly human environment, the effects are sterility and inhumanness. Let us illustrate the methods of the segregator by a practical example. We will assume he is confronted with the planning of a new community. Methodical as he is, he starts out with the filling in of an inventory form for the needs and requirements of a community of the given size. He utilizes the best research material available and arrives at a chart listing the various types of structures and facilities needed. He then interpolates the square footage typically found in the average existing community, the number of floors typically utilized, the private open spaces typically occurring, and he arrives at acreage figures for each use category. He then adds, with the aid of endless research material, the needed acreages for streets, roads, highways, parking lots, recreational land, sewerage plants and schools. Thus his final listing may look something like this:

ANALYSIS FOR A NEW COMMUNITY ON A 1,000-ACRE SITE

USE	% OF TOTAL DEVELOPED AREA*	ACRE-AGE	POPULATION DENSITY*	POPULATION	BUILDING COVERAGE	PARKING AREA
Single Family Dwellings	40	400	15 persons per acre	6,000 persons	133	30
Multi-Family Dwellings	3	30	40 persons per acre	1,200 persons	12	10
Commercial	3	30			8	20
Industrial	7	70			28	35
Parks and Playgrounds	6	60			2	3
Public and Semi-Public	5	50			15	20
Utilities and Railroad	11	110			4	
Streets	25	250				
	100%	1,000 acres		7,200 persons	82 acres	118 acres

* *Percentage Figures and Population Densities are arrived at from Analysis of Average Existing Communities.*

The typical methodic planner builds a new community by applying statistics lifted from various textbooks that reflect the organizational pattern of the poorly working "anti-urban" older development. Thus the mistakes of the past are endlessly and thoughtlessly repeated.

Up to this point, the procedure is legitimate. The only disturbing fact is that all the statistical figures utilized reflect, of course, the experience of existing communities and, therefore, all their faults and shortcomings. But the real trouble sets in when our methodological planner, with his instinctive longing for discipline, transfers his figures onto a land map. He takes each of his land-use categories and places it, according to the acreage indicated in his calculation, on a piece of land, thus creating an area reserved for shopping, one for offices, one for a civic center, another for a cultural center, and yet another for a sports or recreational center. He lays out a network of highways and roads, connecting the parking areas reserved for each of the aforementioned uses; and within the various sectors and segments created by those roads, he then places residential areas of varying density to coincide with the economic groups to be expected in each section. Thus, the segregated community is created. On paper it is completely balanced. But it is also a community in which everybody has to drive long distances in order to reach the shopping area, or the civic area, the cultural area, sports area, or place of work. Because it is so beautifully and carefully segregated, each one of the single-use areas is sterile and inhuman, and in each one of the residential areas live people of astounding sameness: those who make one hundred dollars a week in one enclave, those who make two hundred in another, and so on. Thus our segregator-methodologist proves himself also to be an equalizer and a scatterizer.

The work of the segregator could probably have been accomplished just as well—and, I am sure, will be so accomplished in the near future—by an electronic brain. It is void of concern for human relations, and of relations between landscape and topography and community.

Real estate developers, helped by local prejudices, sometimes succeed in shaping our suburbs along segregative lines. One of their successes was described in a creditably frank article that appeared in *Time* magazine on April 25, 1960 that dealt with Detroit's oldest and richest suburban area, called Grosse Pointe (population 50,000). *Time* pointed out that Grosse Pointe is representative of dozens of wealthy residential areas in the United States. The reason for the article—the news angle, so to speak—was the public revelation, which burst into the open during a court squabble between one property owner and the Grosse Pointe Property Owners Association, of the existence of a rigid system for screening families who wanted to buy or build houses in Grosse Pointe. The screening system, the writer of the article pointed out, employed a three-page questionnaire on the basis of which "points" (Grosse Pointes, I guess) were given, which depended on such qualities as descent, way of life (American?), occupation (typical of his race?), swarthiness (very? medium? slightly? not at all?), accent (pronounced, medium, slight, none?), name (typically American?), repute, education, dress (neat or slovenly? conservative or flashy?), status of occupation (sufficient importance might offset poor grades in other respects). Religion was not scored, but weighed in the balance by a three-man Grosse Pointe Screening Committee. All prospects were handicapped on an ethnical and racial basis: Jews, for example, must score a minimum of 85 points, Italians 75, Greeks 65, Poles 55: Negroes and Orientals did not count. *Time* magazine wrote: "What makes neighboring Detroiters smile about the carefully protected Grosse Pointe exclusivity is that the area's permanent well-established residents

The original caption of this cartoon: "The Masked Builder Strikes Again."

somehow include such noted Detroit gangsters as Matthew Rubino (20 arrests), Peter Licavoli (24) and John Priziola (17)."

The segregators are not only busy in the suburbs, or in the planning of new communities, but also in the hearts of our cities. Here they plan and build civic centers that are concentration camps for bureaucrats, who are thus prevented from mingling with common folks; this may explain why they lose their touch with and understanding of the problems of the latter. By concentrating all civic activities in one compound, civic-mindedness is subtracted from the rest of the city. They build cultural centers like, for example, the much-hailed new Lincoln Center in New York, where theaters, concert halls and other institutions for the performing arts are confined to one particular spot, which necessarily will be dead and empty all day long, but upset by monumental traffic jams when the performances begin or end. Obviously the success of suburban shopping centers has influenced the concept of the cultural center, although it can hardly be expected that shoppers will move around from the opera to the concert hall to the ballet and the repertory theater for one cultural super-shopping trip. This concentration of culture in one segregated spot is in part a psychoanalytically interesting confession of the feeling that our cities are so void of culture and so hostile to it that only by putting culture behind figurative barbed wire can it be protected from the vulgarity of urban life. This concentration of cultural activity in one spot, of course, robs the rest of the city of any enrichment through cultural activities, and gives it the stamp of pure commercialism.

A clear expression of our segregator's tendencies are the zoning laws and their administration. Zoning was originally conceived as one of the earliest planning measures, in order to protect residential quarters from the disturbances which industry, then in its baby shoes, brought about through smoke-belching chimneys and earsplitting noises. Zoning has never acknowledged that most industrial activities have lost those obnoxious qualities; it has, on the contrary, steadily deepened and refined its separatist tendencies. There are areas in which one can build only office buildings, others in which only institutional buildings are permitted, yet others in which only residences, and neither stores nor offices, are allowed; and even within each one of these categories, there are further fine distinctions, guaranteeing that each zoning district becomes in itself a boring experience of sameness. The side effect of this type of zoning practice is, of course, that everyone's journey for purposes of shopping or working or engaging in any other activities is significantly lengthened—so much so that it can be negotiated only by use of the automobile.

The segregator succeeds in robbing the hearts of our cities of one of their most essential qualities: variety and small-grained differentiation. He makes impossible the accentuation of cityscape by landmarks. He creates a lack of public spirit in those districts which are solely residential; and, just as he brings into existence city areas that are alive only at night—namely, the reservations set aside for theatrical life and the amusement industry—he succeeds in creating other reservations that are ghost towns from the close of office hours until the offices open again. The segregators are destroyers of urbane qualities and of urban activities; by making human communication as difficult as possible, they are keeping people away from people.

Another false friend of the city is the PROJECTITE. He is helped and abetted by the bulldozerite and the segregator. He has dreams of large complexes of architectural sameness, all constructed at one time and inhabited by people of economic and racial sameness. Unfortunately he translates these nightmares into reality. They then become huge public housing projects, in which one can reside only if one possesses too little money to live decently, or elegant suburban subdivisions, in which one can afford to live only if one possesses too much. The projectite creates urban residential redevelopment projects comprised of herds of identical skyscrapers; these are inhabited by people who can prove middle-class status, which is further divided neatly into lower-, medium- and upper-middle class. Because income in the United States is, to a large degree, scaled along racial lines, these developments become both economic and racial ghettos.

Projectitis is promoted by certain regulations in our Federal, state and city housing laws, which, for example, determine that architects' fees, set up as a percentage of the total building cost, are radically diminished as the number of housing units goes up. The professional fee for a project with 100 housing units, thus, might be 4 per cent of the total building cost. However, if a project contains 1,000 housing units, it may go down to 2.5 per cent of the total construction cost. There is, of course, only one way in which the architect retained for the planning and design can stay out of bankruptcy in the case of larger projects: he has to repeat the same building over and over again.

Projectitis is also caused by building economics. In case of repetition of the same building, construction costs are reduced, and the more often you repeat, the sweeter is the picture for the entrepreneur and the builder. Projectitis, of course, could not flourish if we could get rid of our superstition that bigness can replace quality, and if we could stop the efforts of the bulldozerite and the segregator.

Now, let us take a look at another false friend of the city, the ECONOMIZER. We find him in the role of economic consultant in budget bureaus, in the Federal General Accounting Office, and in the presidential offices of real estate development and building concerns. Gustave G. Amsterdam, chairman and president of Bankers Securities Corporation, a man who, in his professional standing, certainly cannot be suspected of anti-economic tendencies, stated in an address in Boston on April 14, 1960, "If Columbus had had an economist on board the *Santa Maria*, figuring the continent's development needs, the Admiral would have turned right back to Cadiz and no one would have attempted the settlement of America to this day. The point is that we must not let the future scare us." If Columbus had listened to most of the economic consultants who today advise city governments and private enterprises on what they may dare to invest, we undoubtedly would not be discovered yet.

There are, of course, in the economics profession notable and laudable exceptions, some of whom I have the privilege of working with. But, generally speaking, the economy-minded expert—who is often called upon before a plan is even conceived but is called upon most often to judge a completed concept from the point of view of financial return—feels professionally honor-bound to be pessimistic. He feels that it is his duty to be conservative, and he will eye every new concept with the greatest mistrust. This is partly so because the economizer, like his friend the methodological planner, relies solely on the voluminous research material he has collected; and this material, because it reflects only the past, cannot possibly give him a tool by which to weigh properly something that has not been done before. It could be demonstrated that wherever new thoughts and new concepts in building, in technological improvements, and in the creation of environmental units have been actually implemented, this has happened because a particular agency or entrepreneur disregarded the findings of the economist. (If, for example, John D. Rockefeller Jr. had consulted with an economist about the chances of finding tenants for Rockefeller Center, New York would probably have been deprived of this notable landmark.)

Some important statements concerning the role of the economizer were made by Representative Clem Miller of California in the House of Representatives in August, 1962. Congressman Miller's remarks were called forth by the strong criticism expressed in the General Accounting Office of the Federal government with reference to a somewhat unusual housing development in Marin City, California. Mr. Miller questioned GAO's methods of evaluation. He pointed out that the agency had over two thousand accountants and one hundred lawyers, but not a single architect or engineer. He submitted that GAO ignored essential considerations: social, esthetic, maintenance. "We are given," he stated, "the two-dimensional world of the adding machine and told to make from it the three-dimensional world of the value judgment." This, he asserted, can lead to only one conclusion: that public housing would be institutionalized, that every breath of imaginative design would be withdrawn. Representative Miller had other things, which I quote at random, to say about the General Accounting Office:

> It reaches architectural conclusions without an architect, engineering conclusions without an engineer, esthetic and historical conclusions without a planner. It arrogates architecture, esthetics, engineering conclusions without competence. There seems to be not a trace of thought in their minds, yet it seems to me they bring to all projects the built-in conviction of a lifetime that accountancy is the primary value. . . . What does this approach mean to sensible planning? It means sterility at best, chaos and an inability to perform at worst. It hamstrings design to place it at the mercy of unpredictable and ignorant criticism. . . . To

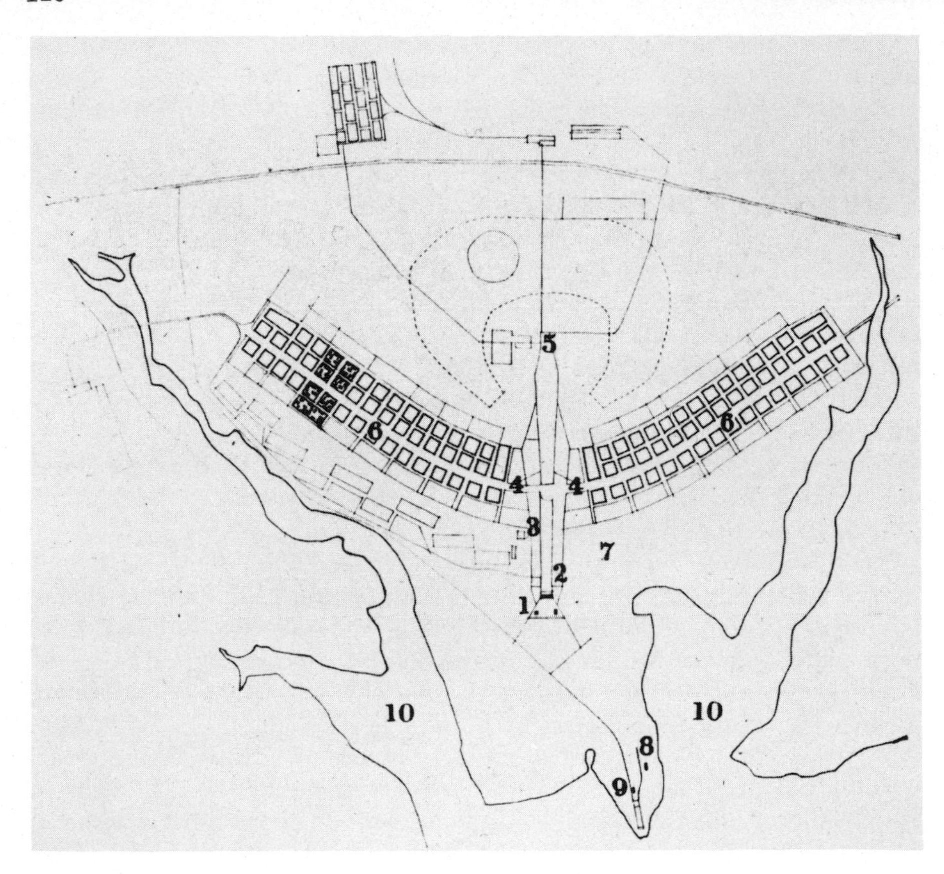

PLAN OF
THE CITY OF BRASILIA

1. Government Buildings
2. Ministries
3. Cathedral
4. Commercial Areas
5. City Square
6. Residential Areas
7. University
8. Hotel
9. President's Palace
10. Lake

Lucio Costa, the planner of the new city of Brasilia in Brazil, is rumored to have won the competition for this undertaking on the basis of a sketch on the back of an envelope. Characteristics of the plan, as illustrated here, make these rumors appear believable. The plan was obviously dictated by a vision of a formalistic pattern, possibly a bird or an airplane, rather than by a deep and intense study of human needs and requirements or by topographic and natural conditions.

some degree, we have become a nation of accountants. The figure sheets have become sacred talismen [*sic*]. Among other things, this leads to the destruction of thought, and let no man say that we can forego beauty for utilitarianism. Utility is beauty, and has been so for all ages. The angry critic who accepts a barbarian architecture at home is crossing to Europe by the planeload to see the outpourings of other cultures and other ages. We need not fear for our country when we are putting up great buildings of imaginative design. We need fear for ourselves when we stop doing so.

The loves and goals of the false friends of the city find expression not only within established urban organisms but in brand-new ones as well. Brasilia, that most gorgeous autocratically planned new city in the Western world, the construction of which has nearly succeeded in bankrupting a nation, pays homage in its planning to the traffickist, the bulldozerite, the segregator and the projectite (but, unfortunately in this case, not to the economizer). Tourists who have been to Brasilia have told me that in order to escape its sterility, people visit the more populous shantytown—originally built as temporary headquarters for construction workers—where, in spite of the disorder, at least some life can be found.

The planner of Brasilia, Lucio Costa, is also chief planning consultant for a newly projected city in Texas, to be called Horizon City. A news release sent out in December, 1959, announced that the city will have 1,500,000 inhabitants, that it will cost $1,000,000,000 in its initial stages, and that it will cover 167 square miles, with the core alone occupying 1,100 acres. (In comparison to this, the core of the city of Boston, which contains nearly 3,000,000 inhabitants in its metropolitan region, covers only a little better than 200 acres.) According to the fact sheet, 30 per cent of the city core will be occupied by a football-shaped park with a man-made lake, and there will of course be a segregated cultural center and a segregated governmental complex. The remainder of the core will be devoted to business and commercial uses. In the description of the traffic pattern, impressive figures about six-lane highways and large thoroughfares are mentioned, but not a word is said about mass transportation.

I brought this plan to the attention of Sibyl Moholy-Nagy, a well-known architectural critic and professor of architectural history, and I quote from a letter which she wrote me in response:

The plan for Horizon City is a document to see and behold. It is a somewhat sad confirmation of the basic formalism of a planner who is so hard to dislike because he is such a nice person. Here he switches from

> a town "conceived in the sign of the cross" to a town "conceived in the sign of the football." It is really amusing because only the shape differs; otherwise he has sold the same set of Brasilian clichés. The "Plaza of the Three Powers" of Brasilia here becomes the "Plaza for the Legislative, Judicial and Executive Branches of City Government." The sliced up plan with its total disregard for contained groupings is so familiar from Brasilia. Imagine the pleasures of a community park with two heliports right smack in the midst of it! And of course there is the by now so well known separation of functions—the Financial Plaza dozens of miles from the City Center and the Recreational Center neatly isolated by multilaned speedways on all sides. The 30 percent solid park area located in the midst of an 1100-acre core benefits nobody because the surrounding business and commercial zones cannot possibly make use of it, and the inhabitants of the residential areas would have to make a multimiled journey in order to get there.

I have heard nothing about building progress in Horizon City since 1959. Maybe it is not possible to arrive at the realization of an autocratic scheme within a democratic society. Yet the danger is always present that something of this order could happen if the false friends of the city do not wake up to the facts of true city life: its values, needs and requirements.

BIRD'S-EYE VIEW OF PROJECTED HORIZON CITY

The planner of Brasilia, Mr. Lucio Costa, was also influential in the shaping of a planning proposal for a projected settlement in Texas (near El Paso), on which he worked with others and which the promoters named "Horizon City." Though a formalistic approach does justice to the first part of its name, since the settlement reaches toward the horizon on all sides, it is so stretched out that it is unlikely ever to result in anything that would justify the second half of the name ("City").

9 Full Speed Ahead on a Dead-End Road

There is more to life than increasing its speed.

—Mahatma Gandhi

An expert is one who knows more and more about less and less.

—Nicholas Murray Butler

While we consider when to begin it becomes too late.

Latin Proverb

In the fall of 1957, a symposium concerning the problems of cities in the motor age was held in Hartford under the sponsorship of the Connecticut General Life Insurance Company. From the report of this meeting, in which I participated, I quote the following: "Our attempt to be urbanized and motorized at the same time has been less than a complete success."

By 1975, we are told, more than 100,000,000 vehicles will be jockeying for position on the highways. If this trend is superimposed on today's metropolitan hodgepodge, America will be faced with an absurd paradox. In spite of achieving the world's highest per-capita income, the majority of our people may have to endure not only poorer standards of transportation but lower standards of living as well. If we continue full speed ahead on the dead-end road of overmotorization, as we are advised to do by the heedless experts, we will lose our cities after killing their hearts.

There is a murder plot afoot against our highly urbanized areas. The method the killers have chosen is that of slowly poisoning the urban body by the injection of foreign particles into its bloodstream in ever-increasing doses. These particles, in the form of automobiles and trucks, cannot be absorbed by the urban body, and therefore cause circulatory diseases. The plotters are assisted by fifth columnists within the city who—by "facilitating" automobile traffic through the widening of streets, narrowing of sidewalks, construction of gigantic garages within the heart area, and the whole electronic hocus-pocus of signaling systems—do everything in their power to attract more and more of the foreign particles into the very heart, until the tissues and cells of this most vital organism are effectively attacked and destroyed. The injection of these foreign particles brings with it not only the clogging of arteries and veins, but those side effects which further hasten the demise of the victim: noise, danger to life and limb, and pollution of the air, to name a few.

Noise, the forgotten nuisance, is more dangerous than we realize. The Armour Research Foundation of the Illinois Institute of Technology published in 1951 a document based on four years of study, from which I quote:

> Traffic noises affect far more people than industrial noises. In Chicago, for example, there are 1500 route-miles of vehicle traffic thoroughfares. Many people live on or very close to these routes. Traffic noise not only is more prevalent, but it is louder than industrial noise. Noise conditions ascribed to an industrial plant often are caused by vehicles associated with industry. Traffic noises are the greatest offenders against human hearing (industrial area noises rank second).

Medical authorities and psychologists assure us that noise is not just a nuisance. It interferes with our hearing ability, it deranges our nervous systems and minds, it causes serious diseases and in rare cases even death.

The poisoning of the air we breathe in our cities is, to a surprisingly high degree, ascribable to the exhaust gases of motorized vehicles. Arthur C. Stern, of Taft Sanitary Engineering Center, predicted that it will soon be necessary for the U.S. Weather Bureau to issue daily air pollution reports and that more and more cities will have to prohibit auto traffic on days when pollution is critical. In Los Angeles such daily air pollution reports are being announced. The air pollution level is determined by the ozone ratio, and the first-stage alert occurs at .50 parts ozone per one million parts air. A second-stage alert occurs at one part ozone to one million parts air, at which time compulsive requirements are supposed to be made on industry and motorists. This stage hasn't been reached yet, though it was nearly attained in September, 1955, when there were .90 parts ozone. The practical value of these first-stage and second-stage alert announcements is doubtful, as the condition might last only for a short time and any action to counter the condition may come too late. A recent newspaper report stated, under the title "Dangers of Air Pollution":

> Does air pollution kill people? Many researchers think it does, and they point to some startling examples. In New York City a research team

> has revealed results of a study of a 10-day period of unusually heavy air pollution in that city in November 1953, showing a marked increase in death. The researchers are convinced that air pollution affects health even when the degree of pollution is not so intense, and the amount of illness caused by it not so dramatic.

Los Angeles, which suffers badly from air pollution and especially from smoke (which is the result of high concentration of unburned hydrocarbons), has for a long time attempted to please the automobile industry and overlook the main causes of the trouble. But when neither the outlawing of private incinerators nor the installation of smoke reduction devices for industrial plants made a significant difference to the ever-growing pollution, action with regard to the real troublemakers started, although hesitatingly. The California Motor Vehicles Pollution Control Board formally approved an antipollution device known as a "blow-by," designed to eliminate certain kinds of automobile crankcase fumes. It is promised that the installation of these and other devices will become mandatory for all California.

Even the Federal government had to take notice. Former Secretary of Health, Education and Welfare Abraham A. Ribicoff said in August, 1961, "Air pollution resulting from unburned gasoline exhaust fumes is not just a problem in smog-ridden Los Angeles. It is a problem all over the United States, not just in the cities but in the suburbs, and even the farm areas." He continued: "If our automobile industry does not come up with a voluntary pledge by January to make antipollution devices standard equipment, I will ask Congress for a law requiring such installation." Since then, at least to my knowledge, no more has been heard of the matter.

Noise and fumes are slow agents of death. There are of course much faster ones available. As Ernest Marples, British Minister of Transport, said in 1960:

> When a ton of steel moving at 30 miles an hour and eleven stone [154 pounds] of flesh and bones moving at three miles an hour share the same surface, accidents must happen. And the flesh and bones can never win.

About this most direct danger to life and limb: the killing and maiming of drivers and passengers of cars, and of pedestrians who get in their way, we have already spoken. Anybody who opens the daily newspapers can get the impact of this mass killing and mass maiming. More people have lost their lives in auto accidents in this country since the invention of the automobile than have been killed in all the wars fought by this country to date.

None of these ghastly facts seems to touch in the least those experts who, although they are all solid and well-meaning citizens, and friends (though false friends, as we have shown) of the city, are unwittingly the executors of the murder plot against the city. As the freeways which they design become more multitracked, the minds of these experts, the traffickists or traffic engineers, seem to become increasingly more single-tracked. This one-track-mindedness has led to the point where they can no longer think of any mode of transportation other than private automobile and truck.

Fred H. Blair, Jr., of the American Institute of Planners, wrote recently, "One of these same gents [the traffic engineers] wrote an article recently in which he protests against the small foreign car because it does not burn enough gas to pay enough gasoline tax to build enough roads." This argument highlights the utter confusion that reigns in the one-track mind of the expert. It appears that we are no longer building roads in order to move automobiles, but that we have to build automobiles that use a lot of gas in order to make it possible to build more roads. Following the same logic: the experts oppose any type of new public transportation because if more people were to use it, fewer people would use cars; thus there would be less income from gasoline taxes, and this would lessen the possibility of building new freeways.

This one-track-mindedness was highlighted by an editorial in the Washington *Post* of May 12, 1962, which declared, "It is now to be considered faintly un-American, apparently, to suggest that the ultimate definition of the public welfare may not lie, after all, in the Federal Highway Act." Autosis has become a religious cult in which, instead of the golden calf, the goddess symbol is the golden Cadillac. The believers whom, for the sake of brevity, I will call auto-crats, have raised their goddess on a high pedestal, and preach complete subjugation to the "higher mechanical being." They accept all manifestations of the goddess in the same manner in which heathen religions have accepted elemental phenomena, the sun and the rain, thunder and lightning, as supreme divine forces with which man cannot presume to tangle. Members of the new cult are perfectly willing to sacrifice people and cities on the altar of their goddess. The evangelists of the new sect have won millions of blind followers: among them are downtown merchants losing business and yelling for more and more parking space to house the symbols of the new divinity, and city administrators prescribing that every newly erected building must provide altars to autocrazity in the form of car storage. Impressed by the evangelistic fervor of the auto-crats, the urban citizens submissively give up privacy, restfulness, beauty, as well as time and money, to please the deity from Detroit.

How far autocrazity has progressed is illustrated in a recent planning report for the rebuilding of downtown Los Angeles, which contains this remarkable statement: "The pedestrian remains as the largest single obstacle to free traffic movement." How deeply the new dogma of autocrazity is felt is illustrated by remarks made by the former traffic commissioner of New York, T. T. Wiley, when I had the pleasure of engaging him in a debate before a New York civic organization. He tried to establish that traffic congestion was not an evil but a highly desirable phenomenon. To prove his point, he said, "No city has ever died from too much traffic, but many have deteriorated because of too little." I replied that basically I agreed with his statement, but that I had some misgivings about his terminology; traffic, in my opinion, had nothing to do with congestion; traffic meant movement of people and goods; the aim of transportation planning should be to provide movement in the necessary quantity and of the highest attainable quality. Quality relates, of course, to speed and convenience. Inasmuch as congestion obviously implied non-movement, it was a force hostile to the flourishing of cities. If he would rephrase his sentence to read "No city has ever died from too much and too smooth movement of people and goods, but many have deteriorated because of too little of this type of movement," I would then agree wholeheartedly with his statement.

That there is too little and too slow movement in Manhattan is clear to anyone who lives, works, or visits there. A group of business executives was discussing this matter at the Arden House Conference in March, 1961. One participant stated, "It costs more to move an orange from the West Side of Manhattan to its East Side than to move it from Florida to New York." The existence of too little movement is also illustrated by a race arranged not long ago on a crosstown Manhattan street by the New York newspaper, the *Daily News,* involving an automobile, a bus, a taxi and a pedestrian: a race which the pedestrian won hands down. The facts, as we observe them in our urban areas, tend to support the theory that the more automobiles we attempt to move, the less "traffic" will result.

The blind belief of the traffickist and the auto-crat in the dogma of auto-crazity was highlighted when the same T. T. Wiley, with the support of some retail merchants, proposed a $52,500,000 garage program for the midtown area of Manhattan, projecting the construction of 10,000 car spaces in fifteen garages placed in the midst of the most productive and citified area in the world, between 31st and 59th Streets and between Second and Eighth Avenues. I am happy to report that, chiefly because of the reasonable and strong attitude of the City Planning Commission and its chairman at that time, James Felt, this program was killed (at least for the time being) and that the new traffic commissioner of New York, Henry A. Barnes, proposes a much more sensible solution. He basically proposes moving garage facilities to the fringe of the core area.

Because Mr. Wiley's proposal for erecting garages in the midst of the heart area of the city is typical of thousands of others proposed for American and European cities, I feel it worthwhile to repeat here some of the findings and conclusions derived from a study of it.

The purpose, as stated in Mr. Wiley's proposal, was to regain lost retail volume for Manhattan, with the hope of generating retail sales of approximately $100,000,000 a year. This purpose, it was hoped, could be achieved by attracting customers from the metropolitan region who are presently doing their shopping in suburban centers. The reasoning behind the proposal was that suburbanites abstain from shopping in Manhattan for one reason only: they cannot find parking space in reasonably close proximity to stores. The argument of the proposal was that if the city were to provide 10,000 parking spaces in immediate proximity to large stores, and if parking fees were set so as to encourage fast turnover and discourage long-time use, then the stores' sales volume would go up, and an overall economic gain for the city would ensue.

I feel that the presupposition of this proposal was erroneous on the following grounds:

(1) Lack of parking space is by no means the only or even the major reason why suburbanites prefer to do their shopping in suburbs. Others are the difficulty and time loss involved in driving on arterial highways leading toward Manhattan and on streets within Manhattan; the physical inconveniences and dangers which the congested Manhattan environment imposes; and the additional costs which such shopping trips to Manhattan involve through operation of the car and parking fees.

(2) I question whether, considering the existing pattern of transportation to and from Manhattan, the importance of the private automobile for mass transportation was not highly exaggerated. The following figures will prove why:

Persons entering Manhattan daily do so by the following means of transportation:

By railroad	233,000
By rapid transit	1,970,000
By ferry-boat	36,000
By bus	249,000
By truck	92,000
Total by mass transportation and by trucks	2,580,000
Total by individualized transportation and taxicab	736,000

Unfortunately, there exists no breakdown for the total of persons entering by taxi and automobile, but it may be safely assumed that one-third of the figure representing both (736,000) might be allocated to taxicabs. Thus it appears that by public and semipublic (i.e., taxicab) transportation 2,825,-000 people arrive in Manhattan daily, and by private car 491,000.

(3) What, I ask, is the main purpose of these 3,316,000 persons who come daily to the heart of Manhattan, which lies below 61st Street? Their main purpose is obviously work and employment, but it must be assumed that those who come to Manhattan to work are also at some time customers of the stores.

(4) Should we assume that a significant number of inhabitants of the New York metropolitan region come to Manhattan for the sole purpose of shopping? I find this a highly unlikely assumption. Even in powerful regional shopping centers in the suburbs, which are much more easily approached by automobile than Manhattan is, people who live more than fifteen minutes' driving distance away will visit regional shopping centers only when they can combine their shopping activity with other pursuits. This is the reason why the best regional shopping centers have increasingly provided for other functions of typical "downtown character" by including medical offices, auditoria, theaters, exhibits, eating places, office space and cultural events. In this manner they have succeeded in attracting customers from a much wider radius, and in keeping them in the center for six hours and more. It can be safely assumed that the experiences of regional shopping centers in the suburbs are valid to a considerably larger degree for Manhattan. Visits to Manhattan by regionites are, in the overwhelming number of cases, undertaken for multiple purposes: visits to doctors' office, to theaters, museums, exhibits, galleries, restaurants, etc. Because of the manifold character of these visits, the stay in Manhattan is extended over a long time period, anywhere from six hours to a full day, or even overnight.

(5) Would visits by regionites, of the nature described above, be encouraged by the proposed garage system? My answer is that in view of the intended parking fees, which would discourage long usage of the stalls through the device of "steeply rising fees," the garage would prove unsuitable for the regional visitors.

(6) Now let us assume for a moment that all my statements about the unlikelihood that persons coming from the metropolitan region would be willing to come for short stays were proved wrong and that Mr. Wiley's program were to succeed in attracting a sufficient number of shoppers to fulfill the expectation of $100,000,000 in additional retail sales volume. The experience of the most successful shopping center (Northland, near Detroit) has demonstrated that 10,000 parking spaces can indeed generate a retail volume of $100,000,000. For this purpose, however, a four-time turnover with garages filled to capacity during the shopping hours would be necessary. Assuming

that the garages would function in this manner—namely, with a four-time turnover and an average two-hour stay for each car during an eight-hour period, then 40,000 private automobiles would be newly attracted into the Manhattan midtown area during a business day. In the area for which the garages are projected, there are available for automobile traffic eight avenues, each with four traffic lanes, or altogether thirty-two lanes. Simple mathematics demonstrates that for the twenty-seven blocks between 31st and 58th Streets a total of 172,000 feet of traffic lanes on avenues are available. Adding to this the twenty-eight cross streets, which have two traffic lanes each and which on the average cross blocks 600 feet long, there are an additional 235,200 feet of traffic lanes available. This, then, results in a theoretical total length of 408,000 feet of traffic lanes. For practical purposes, however, this has to be considerably reduced in order to take into consideration prevailing interfering conditions like construction work on buildings, construction of sewers and underground utilities, and unavoidable breakdowns in traffic. If we conservatively deduct one-third for these conditions, 272,000 feet of available traffic lanes remain.

(7) How much traffic space would be covered by automobiles driving to the projected garages and exiting from them?

If 40,000 cars were to use the garages, and if this usage were spread evenly over the day (which is an unreasonably optimistic assumption), then 5,000 automobiles would enter and 5,000 automobiles would exit from the garages within each hour. Within any given hour, therefore, 10,000 automobiles would be on their way in and out of garages.

A car moving at a slow speed requires 35 feet of one traffic lane; thus, 10,000 cars would require 350,000 feet. Assuming that each car driving through the midtown area would be able to reach a garage in twenty minutes, and would also be able to leave in the same amount of time, the additional automobiles at any given moment would occupy 175,000 feet of driving lanes, or roughly 64 per cent of the entire available space. Unfortunately, the spread would not be even. On certain streets and avenues adjoining the garages, where cars would have to line up in order to enter or where they would accumulate as they left the garages, there would probably be an occupancy by newly attracted automobiles three times the number stated above. Also, during certain peak hours when stores are closing, traffic levels would be much heavier than in other periods, while during the same peak hours heaviest existing traffic would also occur.

(8) What, then, would be the effect on traffic conditions generally, in the midtown area, of the additional occupancy by cars attracted to the projected garages?

The available traffic surfaces during business hours are already filled nearly to capacity, and, during inclement weather, traffic at certain times practically comes to a standstill. The additional load of cars attracted by the garages would lead to a complete loss of mobility during business hours. This would have the effect that buses and taxicabs would find it impossible to operate in midtown. Thus patronage of buses and taxis would diminish, the crossing of streets by pedestrians would become even more time-consuming, dangerous and unpleasant than it is now, Manhattan would become an even less desirable place to live in than presently, and the flight of residents to the suburbs would be accelerated. Those who now come by public transportation for all-day or half-day visits to Manhattan would be discouraged from doing so. Therefore the likelihood exists that the number of shopping patrons who might be gained through the existence of the projected garages would be far outweighed by those who would stay away from Manhattan stores because of the unbearable conditions of congestion the garages would create. There would be, besides, adverse effects on the efficiency of store operations, which are strongly influenced by the punctuality and morale of their employees and by the efficient functioning of delivery and shipping services. As congestion grew, store operation would suffer.

(9) What influence would the garage program have on mass transportation carriers?

Nearly all our mass transportation carriers suffer presently from great financial difficulties. If surface traffic congestion in midtown Manhattan were to be further increased, and if people who up to now have used commuter trains, subways or buses were to become discouraged by the congestion and cease to visit the overcrowded city, then operating revenues of commuter lines, bus companies and subways would further decline, especially during the non-rush hours. Thus mass transportation carriers would be forced either to cease operation or to demand even more heavy subsidization by taxes than they have at this time.

(10) What would be the direct economic effect of the garage building program?

Ten thousand cars need about 3,500,000 square feet of building space. Assuming that the garages would, on the average, be built on six levels, 580,000 square feet of ground in the most expensive real estate area of the world would have to be devoted to this purpose. Not only would this make construction of the garages unreasonably expensive but, because the garages would be publicly owned, the real estate on which they would be erected would be removed from the tax roll. (If the same land area were utilized for the construction of twenty-story office buildings, 11,600,000 square feet of high-tax-paying office space could be created.)

(11) Would the midtown garage program thus make a contribution to an over-all solution of New York's problem?

No. On the contrary, it would increase the difficulties under which the city administration now labors. It would require public expenditures, which have to be contributed directly or indirectly by New York taxpayers. It would necessitate the expenditure of public funds for the acquisition of extremely expensive land for the construction of municipal garages.

It would make increased subsidy to public transportation carriers necessary.

Simultaneously, it would adversely affect tax income by taking off the tax roll the land used by the municipal garages and, in addition, by diminishing the real estate value of existing structures because of the deteriorating effects of increased congestion.

The points made under (1) to (11) I stated originally in a more detailed fashion in a document called "Appraisal and Proposal," which, at the time of the publication of Mr. Wiley's plan, was distributed to all parties who should be interested. At that time I also described an alternate proposal, which I will discuss in greater detail in Part Three of this book.

I said earlier that I felt justified in delving into the Manhattan garage project at some length because similar projects either have been built or are under consideration all over the United States and in Europe as well. Each one can be shown to have violently deteriorative effects on the economic structure and civic life of its city. Statistics that list, year by year, the total number of visitors to the heart area of any given city, when related to statistics that list transportation methods utilized by these visitors, strongly suggest the existence of a mathematical ratio. The formula that results from this comparative method, if simplified and generalized, can be stated as follows: *For each additional automobile penetrating the heart area of a city, one visitor or inhabitant of the same heart area is lost.* Thus, if a city attracts, during a given year, 10,000 more automobiles daily, it can be reasonably assumed that the number of core activity participants (the inhabitants plus those who arrive in the city core for the purpose of working, or for shopping, or for visits to hotels, theaters, restaurants, museums, meetings, etc.), will drop by 10,000 persons.

This is the inescapable arithmetic of heart failure. The process is automatically self-accelerating; after it has reached a certain point, as it has in downtown Milwaukee, even the automobiles will stay away. That point is reached when there is little or nothing left that would cause people to visit the heart of their city. It is the end of the dead-end road.

And yet our traffickist speeds happily along with his eyes glued to the automobile in front of him, watching the rearview mirror for the car behind,

ABOVE A typical filing cabinet for the automobiles that are poured by the hundreds of thousands into the core areas of our cities, replacing structures serving human activities (office buildings, churches, civic buildings, stores) which once contributed to truly urban life.

ABOVE LEFT The Delaware River Bridge in Philadelphia, one of the many facilities (bridges, tunnels, freeways, toll roads) constructed by the traffickist in order to bring hundreds of thousands of automobiles from the surrounding region into the heart of the city, where they can be neither moved nor stored satisfactorily.

---

and looking to neither left nor right. Driven by his one-track mind and by his devout belief in the infallibility of his goddess (the motorcar), he proceeds with his work of destruction along several avenues or on a multilane approach. With a certain genius he kills several birds (not to speak of a few pedestrians) with a few well-aimed stones. First of all, he attempts to drag to the city center as many automobiles as he can find lurking in the metropolitan region. For this purpose he constructs bridges, tunnels, toll roads, which converge from every direction like arrows to the heart. In doing so, he bankrupts public transportation, which, though painfully overcrowded during rush hours, loses customers during the rest of the day. Deprived by this action of a large part of its revenue, public transportation is forced to cut down on the quality and quantity of its services, to stop improvements and new investments. This makes public transportation unpopular, and as a result an additional army of automobiles streams into the core. This kind of aggravated traffic congestion is highly welcome to the traffickist, as it makes the need for his services apparent to everyone. Businessmen and the general populace, cowed into submission by the monumental traffic jams, offer no

Aerial photograph of the downtown area of the city of Rochester, New York, illustrates the erosion of the urban fabric brought about by the widening of streets and introduction of parking areas. This is typical of nearly every American city core.

further resistance, and the traffickist can now proceed to destroy one of the most essential qualities of the city core, namely, its compactness. He proposes (and usually gets permission for) street widenings, crosstown highways, freeway-like main arteries through the heart of the city; and once they are constructed, he can point justifiably to the fact that the many cars he brought in must also somehow be stored. He then proceeds to build garages and parking lots on sites where people used to live or work, or watch theatrical performances, or otherwise engage in urban activities. He thus loosens the fabric of the city, destroying the experience of continuity, of shopping or window-shopping, and endangering the lives and limbs of those who had felt safe at least on the sidewalks, which now become entrances and exits for the garages. The end result is that the very heart areas of American cities, when seen from the air, resemble the bombed-out cities of Europe after the Second World War, with only isolated buildings remaining forlornly in a vast sea of tin automobile roofs. At this point, the day of glory of the traffickist has arrived. He can proudly point out that traffic downtown is moving. He forgets to mention it is about the only thing that is moving: merchandise is not moving, and all movement in the fields of culture, sociability and civic endeavor has stopped.

Few in our highly efficient industrial life could hope to get away with the kind of bungling the traffickists engage in. Imagine, for example, what would happen to the most backward student in a plumbers' kindergarten, voted by his colleagues the most unlikely to succeed, if he were to build an irrigation system in such a manner that water in gigantic pipes would be carried at high velocity from all directions toward one little central spot, within which he would place rusty, narrow pipes, crisscrossing each other; and if, furthermore, he were to propose that this inadequate internal pipe system should take care not only of irrigation, but also of drinking water, sewage and drainage. Obviously, he would be immediately expelled from the plumbers' kindergarten, and take up some other profession, possibly traffic engineering. In that career, he would then design what we are now blessed with in all our metropolitan areas, gigantic pipes in the form of highways and freeways, all converging on one little spot called downtown, there emptying into a crisscross pattern of the pipelines of streets and roads, which he would then assign to the combined use of private cars, stop-and-go buses, stop-and-go taxis, trucks, pushcarts and people. To make things more interesting, he would call on the help of other people like double parkers and "dig we must" construction crews; and would also arrange for some assorted holes in the pavement, and occasional but heavy rain and snowfall. But no amount of bungling can discourage the traffickists.

On a recent television show concerning the traffic situation in Manhattan, the following statement was made by a defender of the man-made mess: "All efforts to separate machines from man are doomed to failure, because deep in human nature there is the irresistible desire of everybody to drive a car, and to drive it right to the door of the building for which he aims."

Now, if everybody were allowed to do as he wishes, nobody could do what he wants. If, for example, everybody wanted to reach, by car, the door of one of Manhattan's great department stores, Macy's, that store would have to have an estimated 40,000 doors along a frontage of 40 miles. Should this prove impossible, then one could, of course, construct instead a parking lot—which, however, would have to cover thirty-three blocks, let us say from Third to Eighth Avenue, and from 30th to 38th Street. Though this might possibly satisfy Macy's—one can't help wondering: what would Gimbel's say?

There comes, of course, a time when the bungling becomes so obvious that the citizenry starts to rebel. This is how the long-planned Broome Street Expressway which would have cut through a community in lower Manhattan was defeated. *The National Observer* of December 24, 1962, wrote under the headline LITTLE ITALY WINS STUNNING VICTORY OVER BIG HIGHWAY: "They mobilized their energies and helped defeat what one candid city official calls 'the most intractable bureaucracy known to modern man.'" The writer of the article said, "Their victory over 'City Hall' . . . would have little interest outside New York were it not for the fact that it represents the kind of struggle occurring elsewhere today in the United States—in Boston, Pittsburgh, West Palm Beach, San Francisco, Los Angeles."

Because an awareness of the tremendous havoc caused by the insatiable appetite of the private motorcar for space in urbanized areas is slowly being recognized, proposals for the contruction of new mass transportation are, for the first time since the beginning of the century, making some headway. In San Francisco the construction of a new system costing in excess of $700,000,000 has recently been approved by the voters.

Washington, D.C., has held hearings concerning a new transportation system. At these hearings, witness after witness has spoken out against the construction of further urban highways and freeways and in favor of public mass transportation. A report on Bill S 3193 concerning Washington transport, printed in June 1960, states:

> It is becoming increasingly evident that any attempt to meet the area's transport needs by highways and private automobiles alone will wreck the city—it will demolish residential neighborhoods, violate parks and playgrounds, desecrate the monumental parts of the nation's capital, and remove much valuable property from the tax rolls. In any case, an all-highway solution to the area's traffic problem is a physical impossibility. Reliance on the private automobile to carry all commuters to work each day would require close to thirty freeway lanes in the north-central corridor lane alone, and would turn downtown Washington into a concrete sea of highways and parking lots. For this reason, the Washington area, like several other metropolitan areas, is showing renewed interest in public transportation. It is generally recognized that a healthy mass transportation system is essential to every metropolis.

Well, it may be generally recognized. But this does not perturb our friends the traffickists, who have forgotten that such a thing as public mass transit even exists. They opposed, and are still opposing, all proposals made for public transit in Washington, and should they be forced by public pressure to take steps they will probably do so hesitatingly, creating some inadequate form of transportation, in the hope it will work unsuccessfully and thus prove their point. This attitude moved Hillard H. Goodman, executive vice-president of the Citizen's Transit Improvement Association of

Washington, to write, "The deterioration of the nation's capital will proceed at an accelerating pace if Congress and the executive branch follow the advice of highway and traffic engineers whose mission seems to be to perpetuate and increase the jobs of such engineers, who think in terms of motor vehicles instead of human beings, and who promote an endless series of projects that, instead of solving our transportation problems, greatly complicate, delay and increase the cost of electric railroad rapid transit construction and operation.

"In Washington as elsewhere, highway and traffic planners are dominating urban and regional planning with the result that mass transit, instead of being used to help guide the direction of public movement, patterns and growth, and the character of economic development, is expected to serve mainly as an overflow transportation facility, with rapid transit to be built only as a last resort."

Henry A. Barnes, New York's enlightened traffic commissioner, quite logically pointed out that the introduction of express buses on New York's parkways could take thousands of automobiles off the road, and prevent them from infiltrating Manhattan. But the traffickists told him that this was an impossible and fantastic idea. They masked themselves, this time, as friends not only of people but also of trees, plants and flowers, and declared that parkways, as the name implied, were really parks, and were legally restricted to pleasure driving. It may be true that when the parkways were first designed and constructed, their originator, Robert Moses, had a vision of families driving slowly along, stopping from time to time to have a picnic along the sometimes handsomely landscaped boundaries. Mr. Moses, who now protests against the use of parkways by buses, has overslept the last thirty or forty years. The only place where pleasure driving can still be noticed is in the colorful ads of automobile companies, in which there is regularly pictured a single gorgeous car, alone on the road, surrounded by trees and meadows, or along a seacoast or lakefront. Driving an automobile may once have been a pleasure, even in urban areas. But those who use New York's parkways today are either commuters going to or from work, or people rushing to the airports, which are accessible through parkways. If a law permitting only pleasure driving on parkways were to be enforced, there would not be a single car left on Mr. Moses' parkways.

The traffickists' arguments against public transportation are manifold:

a) It is un-American. A true, red-blooded American is an individualist, and has a sacred right to drive his own automobile wherever he wants to go. It does not disturb the traffickist that he himself interferes with this "American freedom" by telling automobilists in which direction they may move, when they have to stop and when they may go, and that movement at those times when one most desires it consists of crawling and stopping.

b) Public transportation has been proved uneconomical, unsound, and has to be subsidized by taxes, which is abhorrent to the concept of free enterprise.

c) Public transportation is unpopular, and no one will ever succeed in persuading Americans to use it as long as they find it possible to steer their own cars.

These arguments, supported effectively by automobile manufacturers and highway builders, do not fail to make an impression on the public.

Interesting clues concerning the mentality of traffickists can be found in reports about the National Highway Users Conference, which took place in early March, 1962, in Washington, D.C. (One cannot get rid of the suspicion that this is a front organization for highway builders and the automobile industry.) In this conference "Freedom of Automobility" was declared. One of the speakers, William S. Canning, engineering director of the Keystone Auto Club, said that "it has become socially acceptable to oppose good roads and to damn the auto. One wonders how a movement could have arisen so suddenly in America where the automobile has been so long a symbol of our high standard of living." Mr. Canning concluded that two persons were primarily responsible for the growth of this movement: "Messrs. Lewis Mumford and Victor Gruen." The conference then expressed special displeasure with the fact that there are people who now suggest there might be an alternative means of transportation for urban areas—such as rapid transit and other kinds of mass transportation.

The nervousness that hovered over the entire Highway Users Conference probably has some justification. In spite of the fact that mass transportation was declared dead quite some time ago by traffickists and their friends, it is still quite alive. Americans do use public transportation if it is convenient, speedy and competitively priced. For example, they use to an ever-increasing degree the airplane; they are using to a surprisingly high degree, and in spite of combined attacks, commuter trains and rapid-transit systems in our most urbanized cities (and they are using, within their office and apartment buildings, public transportation in the form of elevators).

As far as the question of subsidy for public transportation is concerned, it may be worthwhile to take a hard look at the public cost of private transport. Private automobile transport is subsidized to a higher degree than we ever have subsidized railways, subways, buses or airlines. It is subsidized out of tax moneys through the construction of roads, highways, freeways and overpasses (after the land is first acquired for them). It is subsidized by the tremendous police force needed to keep private transportation going, by the construction and operation of signaling systems, and by the construction of public garages or, where those do not exist in sufficient number, by providing—mostly free of charge—public streets and highways as stable yards for automobiles.

I am not in principle opposed to subsidy for private automobile transportation, but I feel strongly that subsidy for mass transportation—to a far greater extent than has been forthcoming anywhere up to now—is in order. Mass transportation is a public service needed for urban health, just as is a sewerage system, street cleaning system, or a police force. Public subsidy should be used to obtain the best possible urban transportation system for people and goods; one that will not interfere with economic and human values of the city. As far as the hearts of our cities and surrounding urbanized areas are concerned, it can be proved that an optimal system would have to be based to the largest degree on mass transportation instruments and media, with individualized transportation playing a very minor role.

Unfortunately, the rebellion against destruction of the city through assault by surface mechanized traffic is still weak, and word of it has not reached the ears of those who are in charge of the fate of our cities. The 26th World Congress on Housing and Planning, which assembled in Paris in September, 1962, was under the spell of traffickist sentiment. Robert Bradbury, director of housing in Liverpool, England, remarked (I hope with tongue in cheek), "Traffic is the life stream of the twentieth century. It is a sign of success and prosperity. After all, what is a pedestrian? He is a man who has two cars, one being driven by his wife, the other by one of his children."

These men concluded that maximum city populations in future should be held to 700,000, as in cities of this size it would be possible to arrive at reasonable automobile traffic arrangements. Thus we have—alack and alas—come to the point where the automobile will dictate the size of our cities. We will have to demolish Paris, London, Berlin and Vienna; Chicago, Philadelphia and Boston. We will have to divide Metropolitan New York into approximately twenty-two cities, and proceed in similar fashion with all the other large cities in the world. What this Congress has decided about the fate of the inhabitants of these cities—whether they should be killed outright or deported—I wasn't able to learn. But I do know that cutting down the size of cities to 700,000 would not solve the problems that automobiles create in these cities. As long as we follow the traffickist's high-speed ride on a dead-end road, we will not arrive at anything that would deserve to call itself a city.

10 The Land Wasters

In the nineteenth century and the early years of the twentieth, mankind was disturbed by problems that had been created by the Industrial Revolution. The smoke, the noises and the stench created by primitive industrial plants, the soot and smoke-laden fogs covering whole cities like London and Pittsburgh seemed then to the thoughtful to spell the end of urbia. The grimness and monotony of industrial towns, their shabbiness and dirt, formed the background of the socially conscious novels of writers like Émile Zola, Romain Rolland, Upton Sinclair, Arnold Bennett, and others.

Somehow these problems have been pushed into the background. Technological and sociological improvements have taken the sting and the stink out of the industrial plant. Modern factories, powered by electricity and with electronic equipment, operate quietly and form respectable neighbors. They are no longer very different from the modern office, which, in the meantime, has acquired its own industrial park of machinery, from typewriters and adding machines to duplicators and computers. We have learned how to control effectively smoke and poisonous fumes, and though we do not always take full advantage of our knowledge (serious problems concerning air and water pollution and disposal of industrial waste are still acute because of negligence), we know that one day we will be able to live in peace with the industrial establishment.

Obnoxiousness has shifted from the production plant to transportation. The noises and fumes, the dangers that beset us today, no longer emanate mainly from factories and other places of work but from propeller planes, jets, automobiles, trucks, buses, helicopters, and machines for road building and road repair. Beyond that, twentieth-century transportation endangers the urban environment through one other significant and outstanding characteristic. It wastes one of our most essential natural resources: land—either directly or indirectly.

Architectural Forum, a widely read architectural publication, in September, 1956, devoted its entire issue to the problem of the future of our cities. In the introduction to this issue, the editor stated:

> The U.S. is heading into a growth crisis the like of which was never seen before. It is an unprecedented crisis simply because we are an unprecedented nation of centaurs.
>
> Our automobile population is rising about as fast as our human population and promises to continue for another generation. Since 1946 we have added 24 million humans, 26 million car registrations. In 20 years we shall have 56 million more people and, conservatively figured, 50 million more passenger cars in use.
>
> Right now every human in the U.S. commands an average of 12 acres. Seven raise food for him, giving an average of 5 for all other purposes. Optimistically assuming the same farm acreage supporting 162 million people now [N. B. That was in 1956.] will support 218 million in 20 years, the average acreage per person for all purposes will drop about 20%, and because asphalt will not grow potatoes, the pavement that will be demanded by two cars for every one we have today will have to come out of that other purpose acreage. There's the rub. For the car is not only a monstrous land eater itself: it abets that other insatiable land eater—endless strung out suburbanization.
>
> Our old way of figuring density by so many persons per square mile has now become irrelevant. The crucial figure for U.S. planning is now density of cars. For some time this has been true, though little recognized, for cities. Traffic and all it means is the key factor in urban renewal. Now we must recognize that this renewal is only part of an over-all pattern of urbanization, taking in spaces far beyond and between the old cities. Cities used to be an incident in countryside; now countryside is become an incident in city.

As a nation we cannot in the long run afford or permit the waste, despoilment and pollution of land. We are fast running out of this commodity in those areas where urban concentration exists or can exist. Land is irreplaceable. It cannot be imported from other places, and we had better learn fast how to use it economically and in a manner in which it can serve us best.

The problems that threatened us during the early years of the Industrial Revolution, or until—let us say—thirty years ago, have been to a large degree resolved, or at least we have learned how to approach their solution.

I submit that it should also be possible to solve the problems brought about by the "Transportation Revolution." It appears to me reasonable to hope, and indeed to expect, that we will attack successfully those problems which threaten to make our cities, our nation, and indeed our globe unlivable.

Let me illustrate the direction of possible progress by just one example: The areas needed for the terminal facilities of air transportation have grown steadily since the beginnings of aviation. As traffic density grew and as new and faster planes were invented, landing and takeoff strips continued to stretch out until today airports have become prime and significant land wasters. Yet there seems to be hope that technology may in the near future develop vertical takeoff and vertical landing, in which case land required for airport facilities will be cut to a small portion of what is needed today.

Similar technological improvement will be necessary in order to cope with the insatiable appetite for land of automobiles and other transportation carriers; but, most important, if we wish to maintain a varied pattern of urban culture, agricultural land, recreational area, landscape and natural beauty, we will have to develop planning schemes and planning methods that aim to be land-conserving instead of land-wasting. In order to approach this task, it will be helpful to take a good look at the land wasters of today and analyze their performance.

There are two interlocking and interacting forces that carry the main responsibility for conspicuous waste of land:

(1) *Mass transportation by rubber-wheeled vehicles* (the automobile, the truck, and to a minor degree the bus), which because of their conspicuous land consumption are tearing the urban pattern to shreds and creating in their wake the molestations and dangers of congestion, poisonous fumes and obnoxious gases; and

(2) *The desire to flee from the transportation-created havoc,* a desire that can be fulfilled, at least up to a certain breaking point (the point of no return), through the even more extensive usage of individual transportation carriers.

The more land is gobbled up by the refugees from congestion, the greater is the need for even more *transportationscape* with all its auxiliary facilities; and wherever or whenever new transportation and the nuisances that attend it reach the saturation point, new flight patterns spread and new refugees start on the outbound track.

The tendency toward spread and scatterization is further heightened by the sociological revolution paralleling the transportation revolution, which has put at the disposal of the many the financial means to acquire one, two, three or even more automobiles and the means for acquisition of more private space. Because as a nation we have become wealthier, and because this wealth has been spread from the thousands to the millions, we have, as a nation, attained many of the characteristics of the *nouveau riche*. One of these characteristics is an egocentric concentration on the raising of private living standards and, as a side effect, the neglect of public living standards. The result of neglect of the public environment drives us even further into efforts to improve our own immediate personal surroundings. In escapist fashion we are running away from the upsetting dangers and ugliness of the public environment; our love for the detached house, the private swimming pool, and fenced-in garden are some of the expressions of this trend. We have taken over from our British friends the dictum: "A man's house is his castle." We have even gone a step further and made it a "fortified castle," armed with curtains to keep out the ugly vistas of the public environment, with air filters to keep out spoiled public air, with front yards to move us farther away from the ugliness of the public streets. We tend to reduce all intimate and personal relations with the outside world, relying more and more on the telephone, the radio and television for communication. In doing so, however, we soon run afoul of some basic, deeply human needs: the need for sociability, deeply imbedded in man who is a gregarious beast, and the need to earn one's living, a necessity at least for most of us. We are forced to make sorties and forays from our fortified castles, and whenever we do so we encounter the hostility and dangers, the ugliness and chaos of the over-all public environment.

We are also finding out, to our dismay, that our fortifications cannot be built strong enough to resist, in the long run, the troubles that exist around us in the public domain. *The house beautiful in the city terrible proves to be impossible*. Smog robs us of the enjoyment of our gardens; public neglect brings about catastrophes like fires, floods, landslides; and the din and stench of chaotic Anti-city seem able to penetrate with increasing success the walls of our private castles.

This desire of a prosperous nation for more and more space for the individual is historically as well as sociologically understandable. Yet two questions arise: first, can we afford to indulge forever in this luxury, and second, are not the disadvantages which possession or control of large private space involves outweighing the advantages? Let us try to strike a balance.

We still admire the palaces and castles set down in lavish gardens and parks which the rich and the rulers of former centuries created. No doubt life in these palaces and castles was agreeable. But if we conclude from this fact that what was desirable and attainable in former times for the few can now be adopted or adapted by the millions in the form of 1,000-square-foot castles and palaces on one-eighth acre lots, we are engaging in a dangerous miscalculation. The feudal lords of the past could afford to cut themselves off from society because the services of society were at their command whenever they desired them. Troubadours came to them, bringing their lyric art; theatrical groups performed in their parks or private theaters; writers and poets were attracted to their households, and jesters took care of their amusement. An army of servants was constantly available within the confines of the great house, or in the villages clustered outside its walls. Merchants brought their wares from all corners of the world into the lordly mansion; craftsmen rushed into the palace at the call of the mighty.

But what was feasible for a small number of feudal lords is no longer obtainable in an economically democratized society in which neither serfs nor absolute lords exist.

For the luxury of overly large private space we pay a heavy price. We pay for it directly in time, the time we have to invest in order to get to and return from our work and to reach friends and relatives and places of social, cultural and recreational enjoyment. We pay a high price in nervous energy and in health whenever we wish to, or have to, leave our private fortresses. Finally, we pay for it in cash for the help we need in order to build, maintain and operate our private establishments, and for taxes needed to make our private castles accessible through streets and highways, and to have them served by utilities, transportation and schools.

But there is a hidden price we are paying, which may be even more significant. Because we are not the only ones who surround ourselves with excessive private space, because our friends and relatives and indeed nearly everybody else do so simultaneously, we are robbing ourselves of the values of social intercourse and human relationships, especially of those all-important human relations which come about impromptu and by chance.

Life in suburban Los Angeles, the city in which the most people have the most private space—the prime example of scatterization—illustrates the case. Because men are gregarious, even in Los Angeles there is a social life of sorts. But because everybody is far from everybody else, this social life is based solely on the carefully planned, prepared, arranged and organized party. People meet other people in their detached houses at dinners, barbecues, garden parties and swimming parties. The results are many beautifully organized but generally dull gatherings, very rarely offering human experiences of interest, or the opportunity to get outside the charmed circle and encounter new faces and ideas.

Visits to theaters, concerts, exhibits also must be planned well in advance because they involve long and tortuous drives. Wife and husband often arrive in separate cars—she from home and he from the office. At concerts in the open-air Hollywood Bowl, smart people come two hours early and have picnics before the concert in order to avoid traffic jams at starting time, and very smart ones leave before the last program number. Thus, social and cultural life, though it exists in Los Angeles, is artifically inseminated and exceedingly sterile.

There is a saying that the best things in life are free. Those best things are hard to come by in the sprawling environment of the modern American metropolis. One of the best things in life that comes free is a chance meeting with another human being, which in more concentrated and urbane cities occurs in everyday life on the streets, in the parks, in stores and on buses, streetcars or other public conveyances. These chance meetings, not predesigned by efficient hostesses, more often than not are the most rewarding ones. In Anti-city they cannot come about because the places that create the occasions do not exist. There are no sidewalks, there are no public squares, and there are very few, if any, public conveyances. Even if in spite of the lack of sidewalks one should set out on a simple stroll in suburban Los Angeles, it is hard to accomplish, as I know from my own experience. You will be stopped either by a policeman, as I said before, or by kind motorists who will offer you a ride in the belief that your car has broken down. The right to walk is in jeopardy all over suburban America, as a newspaper item from Salina, Kansas, proves. A Mr. Hans Sutter was repeatedly stopped by police when walking. Serious problems evolved because Mr. Sutter couldn't speak English, but everything was cleared up when he hung a poster around his neck whenever he went out on foot. The inscription on the poster was: "I am from Lungern, Switzerland. I cannot speak English. I walk two hours every day for my health. If any information is needed, please call my son-in-law." Chance meetings at stores, which might include a chat with the merchant or with other shoppers, have been severely cut because the existence of the refrigerator and especially the deepfreeze reduces the number of shopping trips to a minimum.

I still count among my friends many whom I originally met as a boy in the "poor" city of Vienna, in the public parks where I had approached them or they had approached me as strangers, with the simple question "Do you want to play with me?" The child of a high-living-standard friend of mine living in modern suburbia, being driven to school and back home again with no street, park or common playground to frequent, may become acquainted with other high-living-standard children in school; but if he wants to continue the friendship and deepen it, his friends have to be invited to his own garden by his parents or he has to be invited into other people's gardens by the parents of friends. I have often in my life made new friendships or new acquaintances by joining somebody else's table at a sidewalk cafe in Vienna or in a *bistro* in Paris, or by getting into conversation with someone on the streetcar, the bus or the subway. I have often renewed acquaintance by running into someone on the street whom I had known earlier but lost sight of. This was possible because I went on foot. Had I run into somebody in an automobile, it would have resulted only in a lawsuit.

By detaching our houses from each other, by isolating them from their neighbors, we have detached ourselves also from human experiences; we have isolated ourselves from our fellow men.

The balance sheet of private space might very well be negative. Compact urbia is a melting pot; spread-out Anti-city is a segregator. It creates segregation of income groups, of races, and, as a result, a monotonous, boring and tiresome society.

Inasmuch as we are living in a middle-class society, we acquire only middling-size space and build on it middling houses with middling gardens.

In spite of this, we insist on sealing ourselves off hermetically, and in doing so we are losing some elementary advantages. Let me relate a fairy tale showing how we could "live happily ever after."

Once upon a time there were three brothers who, in spite of what the psychologists tell us about sibling rivalry, were deeply attached to each other. When all three of them had married, they got together and decided to flee the ugly, sinful city and move out to the lovely, untouched countryside. Jointly they bought a nice piece of land comprising about 25,000 square feet (that is, between one-half and two-thirds of an acre), not too far from the city yet located in a peaceful, quiet spot.

Their dreamland was situated at the intersection of a major highway leading into the city and a quiet side street. They decided to divide the land into three parts, each measuring 70 feet in width and 120 feet in depth, and since they had been advised by their good real estate fairy that the corner piece was the most desirable, 100-per-cent-perfect location, they all agreed that the eldest brother should have it. Each of the brothers retained his own architect and they started out happily planning their dream homes.

These three loving brothers were very similar in most respects: in income —even in their choice of wives. Thus it was no surprise that the instructions they gave to their architects were nearly identical. Each one wanted a 3,000-square-foot house on one level in ranch-house style because he had read in a fairy decorator's magazine that this was the thing to do these days. Each one desired a representative front yard with an elegant driveway, a nice lawn on which he hoped to be able to display some fairy-tale figures such as dwarfs, or possibly some bright pink flamingos, and each of them wanted a two-car garage.

One happy, cheerful morning, the three brothers and their wives met to reveal to each other their individual plans. It was quite a shock to them to find that the plans were nearly identical. But they accepted this graciously as further proof of their brotherly affection. What they could not accept with the same grace, however, was a bit of bad news related by the eldest brother. He had discovered that a wicked developer had started to build houses on the land backing up to their own fairyland, and it seemed that the developer's sinister plans included the construction of houses all around them.

Their mood became even more somber when they inspected their own plans more closely. "I don't like the idea of having your kitchen window and back door and your garbage can and laundry yard right smack in front of my dining room picture window," complained Mrs. C. to Mrs. B. Mrs. A. sadly remarked that her bedroom would get hardly any light because Brother B.'s house was only ten feet away. Brother B., on the other hand, was pondering aloud how much privacy he would have in his living room with only forty feet separating it from the garden fence of those backyard neighbors who would be moving in when the wicked fairy developer finished construction. To which Mrs. B. added, "And what's more, there probably won't be more than eighty feet between my beautiful full-glass-wall indoor-outdoor living room and the windows of the back-yard neighbors." "I only hope," said Mrs. C., "that they won't have too many children and that they won't turn their television up too loud. It looks as if we'll have to put up high walls at the back line of our fairyland."

All were silent and thoughtful for a moment. Finally Mrs. A. said, "By the way, we have news. We are expecting a blessed event." "So are we!" said Mrs. B. and Mrs. C. in chorus. When the mutual congratulations were over, there was another moment of silence. "I wonder where our kids are going to play," said Brother A. "That back yard of mine is about the size of a postage stamp. About all we can hope to put in it are three bushes and a tree." "And I had dreams of a swimming pool, a barbecue pit, a children's playground—but I guess that was expecting too much," sighed Brother C., who was the eldest brother with the corner lot. "Besides," he added with a touch of asperity, "I think you two played a dirty trick on me when you gave me the 'choice' land on the corner. I was out there last Saturday and I'm beginning to wonder how we're ever going to sleep with the rumbling of trucks and the swishing of automobiles on the main highway all night long."

A deep dark cloud of unhappiness floated in through the window and

A

Three brothers bought a nice piece of land comprising about 25,000 square feet.

B

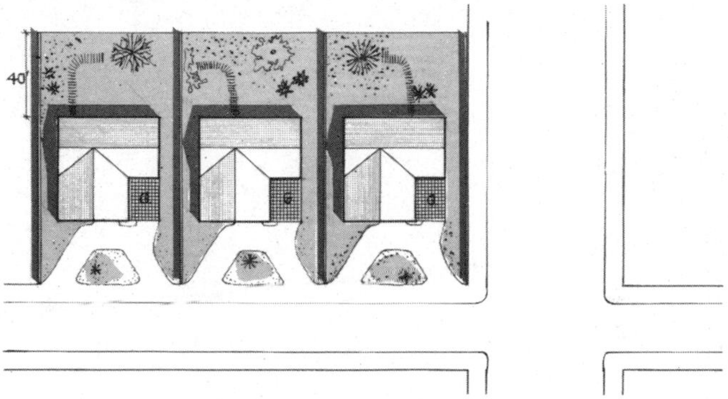

They divided it into three building sites. Their architects planned for them three nearly identical dream houses.

C

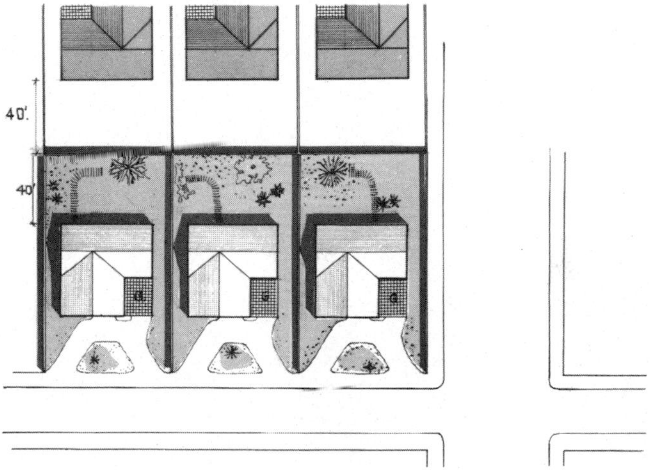

A wicked developer started to build houses on the land adjoining their own fairyland.

D

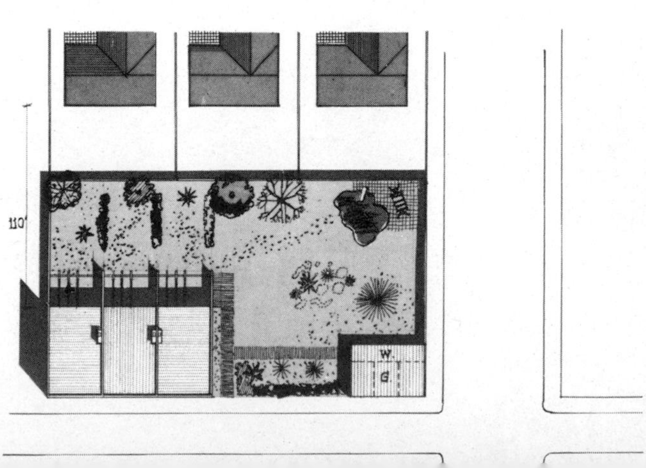

A "magician architect" came up with a brand-new plan.

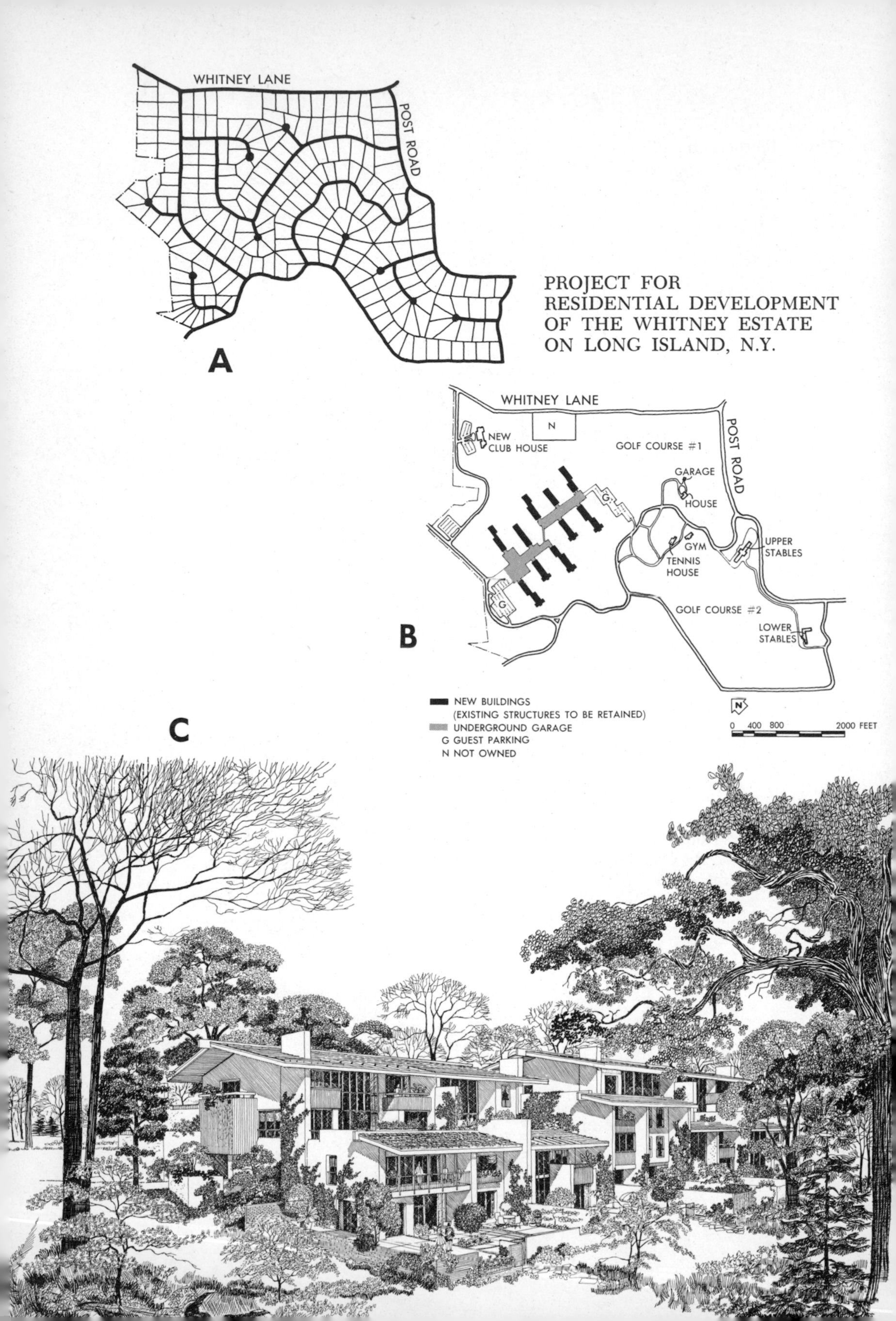

PROJECT FOR RESIDENTIAL DEVELOPMENT OF THE WHITNEY ESTATE ON LONG ISLAND, N.Y.

settled over the three couples. There was a long, depressing silence. Finally the eldest brother said, "Is this really all we're going to get as a reward for moving into fairyland? I think we have more quiet and privacy in our city apartments right now. There must be a better solution."

Together they decided to visit an architect who was rumored to be a magician, and to lay their problems before him. He came up with a brand-new plan. He convinced the brothers that they just didn't have enough space for one-story bungalows and that they should instead build two-story houses adjoining each other on the quietest part of the land as far from the highway as possible. "Behind the houses," he said, "you can each have a secluded living patio, and then, behind that, a private garden. The distance between your back windows and those of your back-yard neighbors will now be increased from eighty feet to a hundred and ten feet." On the corner nearest the highway, he proposed building a common garage with a workshop behind it for the three brothers, who all enjoyed tinkering. "Now," he said, "we have still nearly half the land left over. Here you can have lots of trees—maybe even some fruit trees—a good-sized swimming pool, a

---

OPPOSITE These illustrations are related to a project which illustrates, on a larger scale, the "moral" of the fairy tale of the three brothers. The beautiful Whitney estate on Long Island, New York, could no longer be kept up by the owners and was sold to a real estate developer, Mr. Norman E. Blankman. The developer, deeply desirous of preserving the parklike landscape and existing structure, entrusted to our organization the challenging task of creating a plan that would take these aims into fullest consideration. Illustration A shows schematically what would have to happen in order to comply with existing zoning ordinances, which provide that detached houses should be built on lots of an average size of one-half acre. This solution would necessitate the demolition of all existing buildings, the destruction of forests and meadows, and the construction of a large number of roads in order to make all the lots accessible. Illustration B shows the proposed arrangement by which the same number of residences would be clustered along the spine of an underground parking facility on a small portion of the total area. And C illustrates the appearance of these townlike residential facilities. The proposed solution provided that all of the remainder of the parklike area would be kept in its present natural state, uninterrupted by roads but utilized for recreational areas, golf courses, footpaths, wooded areas, bridle paths, etc. The existing buildings would remain and be utilized as clubhouses, restaurants, riding stables, etc.

This story did not have a happy ending. The administration of the town decided that the existing zoning regulations had to prevail. The project therefore had to be abandoned.

playground for the children and a flower garden. You may have noticed," the architect added, "that I have eliminated the front yards. Think of all the lawn mowing that will save you. You won't have any windows or doors along narrow side yards because you won't have any side yards. All your windows will be directed toward the quiet side street and toward your own garden, so that you will have complete privacy. And to top it all, you will save yourselves a lot of money because your houses, by adjoining each other, will have considerably fewer exterior walls than the detached ones would have had."

He waved his wand (which really was a T square) and said, "I shall fulfill all your wishes. You will have the same amount of living space that you had before. You will have three times the useful garden area, and you will even have money left, because of the savings I will bring about, to pay for some of the furniture you will have to buy."

Gratefully the three couples decided to go ahead with the architect's plans. But they fell into a state of complete despair when the wicked Zoning Commission turned down the architect-magician's plan because the land the brothers had bought happened to be located in an area zoned for detached houses with setbacks for front yards regulated by the Zoning Ordinance.

But inasmuch as this is a fairy tale, we must have a happy ending. A Good City Planning Spirit came along and said, "Life can be made happier and richer through cooperation and understanding. Useful and enjoyable open space can be gained if we are willing to move closer together. If we share the land with our brothers (and all regionites and all men are our brothers), we can get more out of life." So saying, he threw the Zoning Ordinance out the window, the brothers went ahead with their plans, and they all lived happily ever after.

In most cities and communities such a "Good City Planning Spirit" never appears. Zoning regulations, which in their provisions concerning lot sizes and their insistence on detached houses are land wasting, are kept in operation because they are controlled by those who already live in the area (the "ins") in order to keep out those who want to move there (the "outs"). In so-called better communities they are designed to attract only people of the higher income groups who can afford a larger piece of land, in which case, then, a larger and more expensive type of residence would be prescribed.

Bulletin No. 100 of the Regional Plan Association, which I have earlier recommended for study, takes note of the fact that in the New York region there is a definite tendency toward zoning of larger and larger lot sizes, and a chart of the zoning of vacant land in 1960 shows that 16 per cent of all residential land is zoned for two acres and over; 28 per cent for one acre; 18 per cent for one-half acre; and 20 per cent for one-quarter acre. Only

10 per cent is used for under one-eighth of an acre or multifamily buildings. Thus, urban spread over unnegotiably long distances is artificially promoted.

The land wasters in suburbia, as well as in urbia and the heart of the city, are to a large degree influenced in pursuing their activities by something that, in the planning lingo, is called "density." One speaks of high, low or medium density in order to indicate how many families live, or how many buildings of any type are constructed, on a land area of a specific size. Thus density is measured in terms like 200 families per acre, which is regarded as medium density; or 600 families per acre, which is regarded as high density; or 3 families per acre, which is regarded as low density. In the case of office buildings or other structures, density is often prescribed by rules and regulations which dictate that the building areas on all floors may not exceed a multiple of the land size; for example, it might be ruled that the building area cannot be more than three times the land area. Planners also set up rules concerning land coverage. In many redevelopment projects, for example, it is ruled that only 20 or 30 per cent of the entire land may be covered with buildings; the rest of the area must be devoted to open space of some type.

Certain rules, of course, are necessary in order to exercise some control over speculative builders; but unfortunately there exists in the souls of most planners a superstitious belief that low density and low land coverage are basically angelic and that high density and high land coverage are necessarily inventions of the devil. The basis of this superstition is quite rational. Slumlike quarters with airless streets into which sunshine never infiltrates, suffering from complete lack of privacy and making life miserable for everyone but the slum landlords, are of course a shameful monument to *laissez-faire* planning. But it is a mistake to believe that high density and high building coverage are the only or even the most important creators of slum conditions. Brand-new public housing projects with extremely low building coverage and medium density have in many cases become—sociologically speaking, at least—slums also.

The confusion reigning in the minds of planners and laymen alike concerning the virtues and disadvantages of high density or low density is so great that it may be worth while to relate these terms to an environmental unit with which any female reader at least will be thoroughly familiar: the kitchen. Let us see how the following terms can be applied to the kitchen:

HIGH DENSITY, or compactness.
OVERCROWDING, or disorderliness.
LOW DENSITY, or sprawl.

Let us first assume that we have a kitchen of a given size, originally designed for the use of one small family. Due to a family crisis, the kitchen suddenly has to be used also by the mother-in-law and the grandmother. The new condition might be termed OVERCROWDING and will lead in all likelihood to frayed nerves, inefficiency and, if tempers should really flare, possibly to attempted murder. In other words, it will create all the conditions that make a city slum: an area in which the living units are overcrowded.

Now let's assume that this kitchen is so badly planned and constructed that it also forms the main passage between the only entrance of the house and all other rooms, including the bathroom; that all pipes are laid on the outside, some of them forming obstacles on the floor; that smoke and poisonous gases are not taken out by chimneys but can only escape by the window, which, however, cannot be opened when it is cold. The housewife in this kitchen would be faced with conditions of extreme *disorderliness* resulting from the fact that utilitarian functions are not separated from human ones. Just like the inhabitants of a poorly planned or unplanned city, she would be beset by traffic problems occurring whenever a member of the family passes through the kitchen; by dangers, because she might trip over the pipes; by inconvenience, and by health-endangering pollution of the air.

Up to now we have talked about a kitchen of a specific size. Now let us enlarge it to ballroom size, make it light and airy, have it utilized by only one family and have all plumbing and equipment in first-rate, up-to-date order. The kitchen stove would be placed in one corner of this large room, the sink 20 feet away in another, the icebox in the third one, and storage for pots and pans and other utensils in the fourth corner. Somewhere between would be the various storage cabinets for cooking ingredients. This kitchen expresses the pattern of LOW DENSITY, or urban sprawl, and the housewife working in it would have to cover wide distances for every single task; in spite of the wide-open spaces she would be unhappy and would probably end up on the psychoanalyst's couch.

And finally, let's consider the compact kitchen—one in which all utilitarian, backstage functions are removed from sight and hearing, one where all through traffic is strictly excluded but where, on the other hand, the "urban" activities of the kitchen are closely and logically related to each other, bringing food preparation, food storage, equipment storage, sources of warming and sources of cooling into closest proximity to each other, requiring of the housewife a minimum of bending down or stretching up. The kitchen is comparatively small, yet it is not overcrowded. It expresses the idea of optimal HIGH DENSITY achieved by thorough study and imaginative design.

It is the kitchen that most of my female readers will recognize as the "dream" kitchen.

Thus the devilish inventions ruining the city are not high density or high coverage but overcrowding and disorderliness. High density or low density, high coverage or low coverage, can be good or evil, depending on how and where they are applied. Low density and low land coverage within the heart of a city are land-wasting and destroy urban compactness, thus interfering with the ease of human communication. In the heart area we therefore should strive for *optimal density and land coverage*. By these terms I mean to imply a pattern created through the employment of the greatest ingenuity in the process of planning and architectural design, with the aim of utilizing the heartland of the city most intensively without sacrificing humanly desirable qualities with regard to health, convenience and delight.

Those who attempt to introduce low densities and low land coverage patterns into the hearts of our cities, who try to transplant suburban concepts into urbia, sin against the spirit of the city. Some of the new urban housing projects, whether public or built by private interests within the framework of redevelopment programs, are examples of the attempted suburbanization of the city. Because of prescribed low land coverage, buildings are set far apart. The space between them is utilized either for surface parking or for meaningless, poorly landscaped and even more poorly kept-up lawn areas, which become, at best, purposeless holes in the urban fabric and, at their worst, stages for criminal activities.

There are finally those who waste the heartlands of our cities by using them for nonurban activities, for warehousing or for storage (and that includes the warehousing and storage of automobiles and trucks) and for all types of secondary or utilitarian functions placed on the surface of the land. They are not only land wasters but the creators of disorderliness and urban anarchy and thus the instigators of the flight of urbanites into outlying areas. They are not only directly wasting the land they mistreat, but, by killing the vitality and usability of the city core and surrounding areas, they are causing further land wastage on the outskirts, and so become land wasters by remote control.

The manner in which existing planning tools (zoning for various land usages, restrictions concerning density and land coverage) are utilized represents an attempt to find an easy way out of the urban crisis. Unfortunately, there is no easy way out and the application of these zoning tools has exactly the opposite effect: that of creating a vicious circle leading to ever-increasing land wastage and scatterization. As long as we engage in land waste, our cities must waste away.

11 The Sins of Omission and Commission

THE TRAGIC CONDITIONS in most of the heart areas of American cities can be laid at the door of two specific types of sin: the sins of omission and the sins of commission. The two are inescapably interconnected. As long as we commit the sins of omission, we are forced by an iron logic to pursue the sins of commission.

The sins of omission could also be termed FAILURE TO TAKE EFFECTIVE ACTION. The sins of commission could be characterized as FUTILE AND DAMAGING ACTION.

Our failure to take effective action is inherent in our neglect to separate from each other urban activities and urban elements which by their characteristics are bound to interfere with each other in a most violent manner. These functions and elements are so hostile to each other that they inflict mortal wounds on each other and finally kill each other off.

The futile and damaging action is what we are forced to take in an attempt to quiet the furor of the adversaries, to persuade them to wound each other as lightly as possible and thus to postpone the *coup de grâce* as long as we can. By our failure to take effective action we create chaos.

Through our futile activity we sacrifice essential virtues of urban life—intimacy, diversity and variety.

Both types of foolish behavior can be observed not only within the hearts of our cities but throughout the urban organism. This sad condition is due to the fact that we hold no true convictions about urban and human values. If we were to act decisively in those areas where we now fail to act, we could avoid the otherwise inevitable futility of those measures on which we are now concentrating. Before we can accomplish this, however, we must recognize a few simple principles.

The city, a creation of man, should serve man and should be molded to do so.

Out of this consideration would come a hierarchy of values in which primary human activities would have first priority for the best and most desirable space, whereas all serving and utilitarian activities would have second priority, being placed in locations where they would least interfere with the comfortable enjoyment of human urban experiences.

Acting on this premise first priority, then, would be given to living and working quarters, places for the exchange of goods, places for learning and enriching the mind and the soul, areas serving social, cultural and recreational functions.

Second priority, as far as location is concerned, would be reserved for those activities basically serving the primary needs: warehousing and storage; communications of all types such as telephone cables, wires, public and private transportation media; utilities like water lines, heating plants, air conditioning plants and their distributory systems; pipes carrying gas and oil or sewage and drainage. Special provisions concerning space allocation and location would have to be made for those functions which create obnoxious disturbances, like certain industrial activities, mining activities, etc., and those which use a disproportionate amount of land in relation to their urban usefulness and for which, therefore, peripheral locations would have to be found, such as cemeteries, dumping areas, agriculture, and so on. Wherever we take effective action in the direction of separating primary and secondary functions from each other, giving primary functions prime space, we are no longer forced to engage in the futile reactions I have called the sins of commission. We no longer have to separate—at least not in a radical manner—residences from shops and stores, offices and non-obnoxious plants from either of these two categories, or cultural and civic functions from all of them.

The relationship between primary and secondary functions, between human experiences and backstage serving functions, can be readily observed and understood if we consider for a moment the operations of a large theater or an opera house. The planning and construction of such a building for the performing arts is an extremely complex, technical task. Ventilation, air conditioning, lighting, aisle space and seating arrangements, entrances and exits, all have to be carefully arranged in order to make the audience comfortable and enable it to follow, without distraction, the action on the stage. Even more complex is the design of the stage structure, of which only a small part ever becomes apparent to the theatergoer. Behind the scenes are arrangements for moving scenery and actors forward, backward and sideways—even upward and downward; intricate lighting arrangements, dressing rooms, tailoring shops, workshops, storage space, thousands of mechanical and electronic devices, amplifier systems, and so on. The greatest care is taken to keep these backstage functions visually and aurally away from the consciousness of the audience. If any one of them ever, through some slip, interferes with the emotional impact of the play itself—the primary human function of the theater—and becomes visible or audible to the audience, it is regarded as scandalous and has been known to cause the suicide of the director. The impact and the enjoyment of the human experience depend on the noninterference of the serving utilitarian backstage functions; in fact, on the certainty that their existence cannot be detected by any of the senses, since otherwise the spell of communication would be broken. This noninterference must be accomplished in spite of the need for an ever-increasing complexity and quantity of such serving mechanical apparatus.

If we now translate the meaning of the conditions that must prevail in a theater into those that are essential on the vaster stage of the city, we may draw some significant conclusions. The performance of the city today is unimpressive and unenjoyable precisely because the backstage functions have taken over the scene and the auditorium, creating such confusion, such noises and such an overall racket that the voices of the actors—the citizens—are drowned out; human communication has become impossible; every human emotion, every human expression, is dwarfed, stultified and subjugated.

In earlier times, when utilitarian and mechanical features were less complex than they are today, we recognized their subservient and secondary nature and managed to remove them, as civilization progressed, from those places where they would interfere with our senses and our sensibilities. It has always been an earmark of the civilized city that it removed its sewage from the gutter and put it underground. We have retained some sensitivity concerning such functions as electric cables, telephone wires, water lines, gas mains; and, at least in city cores, we attempt to remove them from obvious positions. Even when we were so fascinated by the invention of the

Utilitarian and mechanical features intermingled with human activities are a serious threat to urban society. A drawing from *Harper's Weekly* of May 14, 1881, depicts convincingly the disturbing visual effects as well as the hazards and dangers created by dangling wires strung along poles within a central city.

---

railroad that we termed a whole epoch the "Railroad Age," it did not take us long to learn that railroad tracks on Main Street were a nuisance, and we proceeded to remove them, placing them underground, away from the eyes, ears and nose of the urbanite. Even in the case of that other great technological novelty, air transportation, we adjusted ourselves with comparative speed by moving airports to the outskirts.

But one technological event has swamped us with such overwhelming vehemence that we have surrendered urban life and urban values to it—not only without a struggle but even with a certain enthusiasm. I am referring to the advent of the gasoline-driven vehicle, the private car and the truck, as a means of mass transportation. This unconditional surrender is difficult to understand when one considers that the dangers to life and limb caused by this particular utilitarian function are, as demonstrated by the yearly figures of the killed and maimed, at least as great as those once caused by open sewers. The disrupting and deteriorative influence on the

urban pattern of mass transportation by private vehicles is infinitely greater than that of all other utilitarian serving functions together; much greater, for example, than that of the railroad trains on Main Street that ran not continuously but in accordance with an established schedule.

The suddenness of this propulsion into an age of machines that grow at a faster birth rate than the human population and cover, individually, many times the space required by the single member of the human race, may explain in part our failure to act with the same logic that we employed with regard to other utilitarian functions. But while the suddenness and vehemence with which the invasion took place may explain our sins of omission—namely, the neglect to separate what is usually referred to as traffic from the human domain—it does not excuse us. We can no longer continue on our errant path without destroying the city and civilization itself.

The danger of the situation is illustrated by the kinds of palliative measures we find ourselves forced to resort to as a result of our failure to keep at bay our mechanical slaves generally—and our transportation hordes specifically. Because we refuse to separate the drama of living from the backstage functions, we are, so to speak, forced to separate the actors from each other. Instead of separating those functions which by their nature clash with each other, we separate those which depend on each other for their very existence. We are trapped into futile and abortive sins of commission, which lead to a silly compartmentalization of our lives.

We now separate stores and shops from residential areas, although obviously it is the residents who are desirous of buying things. We are consigning structures of cultural and artistic purpose to compounds separated from both residential and retail areas, though obviously it is the people in their role of residents and shoppers who would like to visit these institutions. We are enclosing in special enclaves our places of work, our office buildings, government structures, industrial plants, keeping them apart from all the aforementioned categories, thus forcing the breadwinner to take long and tedious trips every day in an effort to reach them. We have not yet grasped the fact that, having grown out of the baby shoes of industrial development, the degree of separation that might once have been necessary, in the days of smoke-belching factory chimneys, in most cases is no longer needed. We are separating government workers from the public at large, confining them in ghettos called "civic centers," removing them from normal life, and thus promoting the development of the "bureaucrat." We are further separating by careful compartmentalization the living quarters of the rich from those of the middle classes, the upper-middle class from the "middle-middle" and lower-middle classes, and all of them from the economically least successful whom we put into concentration camps called slums or public housing projects. In doing so, we are not only creating a highly prejudiced society but making it extremely difficult, if not impossible, for those with higher incomes to obtain the services of those with lower incomes and for those who render domestic service to reach their places of employment. We are striving to separate theaters, concert halls, museums and galleries from all the other categories, and by doing so we are not only isolating them until they become "hothouses" in which the arts are then influenced by snobbish cliques, but we are also impoverishing the rest of urbia by extracting from it the amenities which give it the zest of life.

We are forced into taking these irrational measures of separation as a direct result of our original disregard of intelligent planning (our sins of omission). It is a vicious cycle: Working places, stores, theaters and concert halls attract large quantities of traffic, automobiles and trucks, which not only create dangers and offend our senses but also need a lot of space for their movement and storage. In order, therefore, to protect the health and sleep of the city's residents, however slightly, we are compelled to legislate against the existence, in those places where people reside, of stores, shops, working places, theaters, social gathering places, or anything else that attracts traffic. By virtue of this compartmentalization and separation we, of course, create ever-greater quantities of that evil from which we desire to protect ourselves: traffic. By making it impossible to reach the various human activity areas by means of one's own two feet, we are promoting with astounding success the manufacture and operation of more and more automobiles and trucks. We are, as stated before, speeding ahead on a dead-end road, and as long as we carelessly, and with blind enthusiasm, continue to sin in this direction, our cities will go to hell, and utter chaos will take over. All efforts to stop this inevitable and ultimate disaster are doomed, as long as we proceed at an accelerating pace on our present headlong course.

Those cities which flourish and have remained dynamic centers of urban life and culture—those cities in which millions of American tourists each year engage joyfully in the art of walking—are also those which show the least tendency toward segregation and compartmentalization.

Look, for example, at Paris. Its famous opera house sits in the midst of stores, shops and residences. Before entering or after leaving the opera house, you may enjoy window-shopping, you have a choice of hundreds of nearby restaurants and cafés, and a few steps away you will find large department stores and hundreds of specialty shops, ranging from the luxury type to the French version of the dime store. Above the shops and stores are living quarters of all types: luxurious apartments, hotel rooms, and moderately priced space for people who have low incomes but feel happy in the midst of urban life. Dozens of other theaters and office buildings are sprinkled all over the urban scene.

The President's Palace fronts one of the busiest shopping and residential streets, and from the doorway of a little millinery shop I have casually watched M. de Gaulle coming and going, accompanied by the colorful spectacle of picturesquely uniformed guards.

The Academy of Fine Arts is surrounded by structures that contain living quarters on the upper floors and *bistros,* cafés, art galleries and antique shops on the ground floor. Whenever and wherever I visited the offices of friends or clients, architects or planners in Paris, I found right around the corner a wide selection of places where one could enjoy anything from a cup of coffee to an elaborate meal. Around the Church of the Madeleine there is an array of stalls and structures devoted to a wide variety of activities, a flower market, apartment buildings, restaurants and stores of every description, including the mouth-watering show windows of delicatessen stores. Neighboring buildings may contain elegant apartments or cheap ones. And although in recent years the streets and boulevards have also been swamped with automobiles, just as in the United States, they have never quite succeeded in uprooting deep-seated urban traditions. Street vendors, flower stands, newspaper sellers, souvenir peddlers (including the ones who sell the famous "filthy" pictures, which usually turn out to be reproductions of paintings in the Louvre), seem to resist successfully the dictatorship of utilitarian gadgets.

In contrast to the hearts of American cities, the core areas or inner cities of European towns, as a direct result of their resistance to compartmentalization, are still filled, morning and evening, day and night, weekdays and Sundays, with urban dynamism.

Although unfortunately such sins of omission as the permitting of utilitarian functions like surface traffic to invade the city have begun to be committed lately in Europe too, at least the sins of commission are not as energetically pursued. Certain beginnings are detectable, but so far they express themselves more strongly in the outlying metropolitan regions. The central areas resist, maybe because of their long urban history, which has bred living traditions too deeply rooted to be torn out by segregators and traffickists.

Consider, as another example, my home town of Vienna, where I spend a few weeks in the fall of every year. From my residence there I can reach, within a few minutes' walk, places of the most diversified character: the opera; the famous concert hall of the Musikverein; the Konzerthaus and two theaters; shops and stores of every type and description; elegant restaurants; *Beiseln* (the counterpart of the French *bistro*); both elegant and modest cafés; the central market for fruit, meat and vegetables (the so-called Naschmarkt); the Modern Museum; the Belvedere; and the art galleries at the Künstlerhaus and Sezession. My windows open onto a spacious square with a park and the largest fountain in Europe. Around the corner is one of the most important baroque churches, the Karlskirche, masterwork of Fischer von Erlach. Along the great square are the headquarters of organizations that are the counterparts of our National Association of Manufacturers and Chamber of Commerce. But also located there are the French Embassy and an Austrian Ministry. The other buildings contain apartments and offices. If I want to relax, I can choose between the little park around the fountain and two larger ones a few steps farther away. In the neighboring buildings there are "hole in the wall" stores, a tobacco shop, a tiny *espresso* and a *Greisler,* the Viennese equivalent of the old-fashioned general store; and a few steps from these modest shops is the headquarters building of one of the largest electrical industries. The residents of the area represent a potpourri of all economic and cultural groups, from modest workmen to millionaires; but because the mixture is so small-grained, because no single economic or national stratum overpowers another by sheer numbers, to live in the city is still a highly desirable goal, just as it is in Paris and London, in Rome and many other European cities.

In European cities, in fact, it is still the fringe that is regarded as the least desirable area for residence. The core still attracts people who want to live there, and even more so people who want to shop or enjoy themselves. On evenings and holidays the streets of the heart area are full of window-shoppers who may connect their *Spaziergang* (aimless walk) with a visit to the theater or a gallery, a concert hall or a museum.

By refraining from futile action in the direction of compartmentalization, segregation and separation, even smaller European cities, towns and villages manage to conserve their heart areas as pulsating, urbane and interesting centers. In contrast to this, the hearts of our cities in the United States, even those with millions of inhabitants, have lost their liveliness.

Not only are we failing to separate backstage functions of utilitarian character from human ones; we are even starting to glorify them, thus manifesting our opinion that machines are more important than people. An excellent example is a new municipal garage in the core area of New Haven, which the gifted architect, Paul Rudolph, was commissioned to design. The February, 1963, issue of *Architectural Forum* devotes six pages to illustrating and describing the architectural features of this storage building for automobiles. It calls it "a perforated cliff of concrete," an expression of Mr. Rudolph's "personal architectural ambition . . . almost imperial. Roman." *Forum* writes that the garage "cost $5,000,000 (almost twice the usual

Municipal garage in New Haven, Connecticut. In an article in the magazine *Show* of December 1963, Wolf Von Eckardt refers to it as "the most imposing shrine yet built to the automobile," and in discussing the shopping center to be built next to it, states, "Its only virtue is that it will largely hide Mr. Rudolph's monstrous prehistoric garage."

---

austerity model), is two full blocks long and sits so strongly in the middle of New Haven that, at first glance, the other city buildings around it appear astonished. . . . [The garage] is an enormous, unabashed piece of sculpture."

Having visited New Haven repeatedly in the course of consulting activities for the city, I can state that the other New Haven buildings look not only astonished but sadly dwarfed. Human activity centers, the nearby city hall, the three lovely churches on the green, and the various civic and commercial structures are reduced to complete insignificance by comparison with the glory, bulk and impressiveness of the new storage building for cars. The facts stressed by the *Forum*—that this garage became the expression of the personal ambition and talent of an architect and that instead of a strictly utilitarian storage facility, New Haven has gotten a monument to the automobile—are only a minor part of the over-all problem. The root of the trouble is of course that because of a lack of efficient mass transportation the heart of New Haven cannot be approached by any means other than the private car and that therefore a large storage facility had to be constructed. Even then, however, proper respect for the superiority of man over machines would have prevented the use of surface land for utilitarian purposes. The same number of automobiles now stored in the two-block-long garage could have been stored on two underground levels of the three large blocks that comprise the redevelopment project of which the garage is a part. The costs would have been, if anything, smaller, and the entire surface of the land would have been available for human and productive functions. The talents of the architects could have been employed then in shaping man-used instead of machine-used buildings, and a monument to men instead of a monument to the motorcar could have been erected.

We will be freed from the compulsive desire to take futile action in the direction of compartmentalization, segregation and scatterization, once we have a clear understanding of urban and human values. This understanding will direct our action toward efforts to separate backstage functions of a serving nature from primary human functions—and in doing so, we will clearly recognize that priority for the most desirable space belongs to those activities which are primarily human.

12 The Chaotic State of Architecture

Even our biggest and richest cities today fall short of the ideal possibilities that our age has opened up. We have not had the imagination nor the forethought to use the immense energies modern man now commands; our architects have frittered them away on constructive trivialities and superfluities that have often defaced the environment without improving the human condition or the architectural form.

—Lewis Mumford, "The Future of Our Cities," *Architectural Record*, February, 1963

Finding myself completely in agreement with Mr. Mumford's statement, which introduces this chapter, I have often asked myself the question, "Why have architects failed so dismally in a task that should be their immediate and deep concern?"

Many of course will claim—and some very well-known architects take this point of view—that architecture should be solely concerned with the design of the individual structure and that the responsibility for the shaping of the man-made and man-influenced environment belongs to others. This view, in my opinion, lies at the root of the trouble and is the reason for the presently prevailing confusion in our profession, which has been referred to by *Progressive Architecture* as "the period of chaoticism."*

The original Greek term, *architekton,* implied a much wider activity than the practice of the modern profession encompasses. The *architekton* was the master mason or master builder, the creator, and the leader and coordinator of a vast team of artisans.

* March, 1961, first article in symposium on "The State of Architecture."

In our time, specialization has not only whittled down the architect's sphere of influence, but has even created divisions within the architectural profession. The architect no longer designs the structure of a building. This is done by specialists—structural, mechanical, electrical and civil engineers. He is no longer a builder; construction is executed by a general contractor and an endless number of subcontractors. He no longer decides about the placement of major buildings on the site; this is done by planners, planning administrators and lawgivers. No longer does the architect act as sculptor or painter, and most important of all, no longer does he function as leader and coordinator of the building team.

Even in his narrowed field of endeavor, he is fenced in by the inflexibility of building codes and zoning ordinances, by the real or imagined harshness of economic facts, which are analyzed not only by him but also by the client or his economic adviser; by the frequent narrow-mindedness of major lending institutions; and, in the case of large public or private clients, by the fact that they predesign their buildings before the architect is ever called in. Richard Roth, an architect who probably has to his credit the design of more office buildings in New York than anyone else, stated in a discussion held at the Museum of Modern Art in New York that with regard to most office buildings he had no other function than to translate into blueprints the dictates imposed on him by others. Zoning ordinances, he said, prescribe not only the use of the building but also its height, shape and form. Building codes and economic considerations ultimately create the interior layout, and the wishes of moneylenders dictate materials and building methods. Whatever free choice there appears to be as to the selection of colors and textures is greatly influenced by the tastes or prejudices of the client.

Similarly, Mrs. Jane Jacobs had earlier declared that non-architects were making significant planning and design decisions. Public housing agencies and urban renewal offices are preordaining many important matters, so that "it becomes a big deal for the architect if he is permitted the leeway of using colored glazed brick or deciding whether to use balconies."

There is no doubt that the architect's creativity and imagination suffer from imprisonment within tiny cells behind iron bars of legal, administrative and economic restrictions. It is no wonder therefore that the profession as a whole experiences a sense of disenchantment and frustration.

Even the shrunken world of the architect has been subdivided like a piece of suburban acreage by a society that trusts only the specialist who devotes his practice exclusively to one or two particular types of building. We are now blessed with interior architects who work independently of those who design the exterior. We have architects specializing in private residences, tract housing, or apartment houses. Others have as their specialties hospitals, movie theaters, stores, shopping centers, garages, office buildings, and so on. The specialist is sought after by the client because his exclusive activity in one particular area allows him to use over and over not only past experiences but even the blueprints of buildings previously executed, permitting him to operate at a lower fee. The other side of the medal is characterized in the aphorism: "A specialist is somebody who repeats a mistake he once made over and over again." Specialization thus becomes another step in strangling creative ability.

Some people somberly predict that mass production, prefabrication, specialization, together with the waning of the influence area of the architect, will lead to the death of architecture as a creative profession. They point to the fate of painting as an art, which they feel for similar reasons is facing disappearance.

The painter's function has dwindled with the arrival of photography, the motion picture, television and modern printing techniques. Where he once was the only one able to record visually the faces and figures of people, the features and sites of foreign lands, historic events and the contemporary scene, he has been far surpassed in speed and accuracy and nearly supplanted by the means which modern technology has put at our disposal. Thus it is said that some painters, frustrated by the loss of their effectiveness on society, have become completely absorbed in their own egos and in self-expression, giving up every effort to communicate with the rest of humanity. Painting therefore no longer forms part of the over-all pattern of human life but exists only as easel painting exhibited in the artificial climate of hothouses, or art galleries, for viewing by groups of connoisseurs. And though the products of these painters are being sold quite successfully, sales are made for reasons that have little to do with art appreciation. The purchase of paintings has become a speculative enterprise, similar in character to speculating in stocks; in other cases, it is motivated by the desire to achieve tax advantages.

Whether or not this analysis of the status of contemporary painting is correct, I for one do not believe that it is analogous to the status of architecture. Painting is an art but architecture is a profession, which, when it is truly creative, may contain elements of art but must also contain elements of technology and sociology. Architecture, in the still-accepted terminology, must meet, according to Vitruvius, "three conditions: Commodity, Firmness, and Delight." Architecture does not have to die. It is needed more than ever, but must rid itself of its shackles and expand its area of activity to the larger scale demanded by the sociological, technological and political developments of the twentieth century.

Architecture, like the city, needs "transfiguration," deep-seated changes and over-all adjustments to changed times and changed conditions. All the feverish activities now under way to draw architecture out of its quagmire by the invention of new styles and new isms may help some individual practitioners but will not solve "the crisis of architecture." Architecture is still riding on the momentum of the great architectural revolution which, originating in Europe (notably in Holland, Austria, France and Germany) some sixty years ago, started, like all revolutions, with the destruction of the old order: in that case the classic orders. It marched under banners bearing slogans like "Form follows function," "Down with ornament," and "Long live the machine for living," and was actually nothing more than a necessary and belated acknowledgment of the Industrial Revolution that had preceded it. Nothing of consequence has happened since; yet, in our fast-moving times, in which every year brings new technological and sociological developments, standing still means retrogression.

The confused state of architecture is excellently illustrated in an article that appeared in *Vogue* in September, 1961, under the title "Are You Illiterate About Modern Architecture?" In this article a well-known architect, Peter Blake, attempts to explain to the the layman what modern architecture in the United States is all about and succeeds in the task beautifully by making it absolutely clear that it is impossible to find the answer. Mr. Blake explains that "many modern buildings are not architecture" and then helpfully states that "modern architects may build with almost anything from prehistoric rock to irradiated plastics, and their forms and spaces may recall anything from the piazza at Vigevano to twenty-first century science fiction." He is most constructive when he explains what modern architecture is *not*. It "is not particularly cheap" and it is not based on the belief that "ugliness is necessarily synonymous with goodness." He then confesses that "it is much harder to say what American architects do believe."

"A good many architects," he writes, "now seem to have a fixation about 'expressing structure.'" And he goes on to say that this fixation has produced some very odd results. He mentions architect Victor Lundy's "fabulous acrobatics with laminated wood arches" and calls attention to the fact that many famous architects "have begun to decorate their buildings with symbols that are meant to 'express structure' but in truth have little to do with it." He calls noted architect Philip Johnson's Fort Worth Museum (page 160) a "lovely piece of outdoor decoration," with sculptured arches that appear to the unsuspecting eye to be formed concrete but actually consist of travertine stone fitted around steel pipes. The famous architect, Mies van der Rohe, he assures us, has been doing this for quite some time, and this cult of "expressing structure" through seemingly functional means,

LEFT The Seagram office building on Park Avenue, New York. Architect, Mies van der Rohe; Associate Architect, Philip Johnson. The enlivenment of this bronze-and-glass cage by geometric patterns created by shades drawn or half-drawn was probably not foreseen by the architects.

RIGHT Amon Carter Museum of Western Art, Fort Worth, Texas. Architect, Philip Johnson Associates.

which actually consist of applied pilasters and porticos, is about to receive quite a workout in New York's Lincoln Center. Mr. Blake remarks that architect Philip Johnson "takes an almost sadistic delight in parading his eclecticism before his more purist (and utterly infuriated) colleagues."

The article then speculates that some of the pioneers of the revolutionary architectural movement must be rotating in their graves. He refers especially to Auguste Perret, the famous French architect and teacher of Le Corbusier, who said, "Decoration always hides an error in construction." "On occasion," Mr. Blake says, "the cult of 'expressing' or 'symbolizing' structure may take on an almost surrealist aspect by creating structures that look like gracefully thin concrete shells but in reality violate every known principle of engineering."

He then introduces us to a new approach that attempts to express, visually, utilitarian services instead of structural forms. One of the representatives of this cult is the well-known Philadelphia architect, Louis Kahn, who adorns his buildings with towers that dramatically symbolize utilitarian services like air conditioning and ventilating shafts in a manner which, according to Mr. Blake, "no cost accountant could possibly justify." This leads the author to speculate "that we may soon see buildings with mail chutes, telephone wires, pneumatic tubes and soft drink dispensers all applied to, or expressed on the outside."

The article then switches to Edward Stone, architect of the Pavilion of the United States at the World's Fair in Brussels, referring to him as "a beauty seeker" and quoting some modernists who describe Mr. Stone's work as "pretty" rather than beautiful. The Edward Stone school of architecture, it is explained, is referred to as the "ballet school of architecture" or as "exterior decoration." In contrast to this, it is stated that Louis Kahn feels buildings should have "character" rather than beauty, an argument which Mr. Blake feels has been "brazenly stolen from the sisterhood of spinsters."

The layman is then enlightened about the existence of another architectural cult, "Brutalism" or "New Brutalism," which sails under the motto "Beauty is Ugliness." Mr. Blake remarks, with smiling satisfaction, that the "New Brutalists in Japan have spoiled everybody's fun because it is absolutely impossible for Japanese craftsmen to build *im*perfectly—hence, the 'New Brutalist' architecture around Tokyo and Kyoto turns out to be rather pretty."

Mr. Blake concludes his article with these sentences, with which I am wholeheartedly in agreement: "But the central problem of American architecture is no longer the individual building but the entire city and its environs. Recently, one American critic started to talk about 'Chaoticism' as a movement—it is a non-movement. It is the by-product of an apparent absence of civilization. . . . More and more architects of the younger generation in this country are trying to do something to halt this blight, to create a civilized, even beautiful American townscape. The first step, to them, is simply to create a sense of order, without which neither civilization nor beauty seems attainable." In spite of great difficulties, he adds, "the new

The Richards Medical Research Building of the University of Pennsylvania, designed by Architect Louis I. Kahn, F.A.I.A.

American architects continue, with the zeal of missionaries. It has been said that it took this country close to 200 years to create a workable political system, and that the next step is to create a civilization. These new architects have that sense of historic mission, and men with that sense are dangerous and hard to stop."

Mr. Blake has in this last paragraph paid an enlightened and important tribute to those men who believe in the transfiguration of architecture and work with missionary zeal but, unfortunately, are rarely accorded recognition for the creation of a better environment. All the orchids in the national press, and even in architectural publications, go to the "innovators," "form-givers" and creators of new styles, simply because their products, so often original for originality's sake, are news-making. In our time, in which communications media can make or break the reputation and livelihood of a professional man, it is no wonder that many a professional will prefer to design a building which shockingly explodes its surroundings—and which, being newsworthy, will therefore bring fame to its creator—than one which would, with a certain amount of humility, try to integrate itself into its surroundings and attempt to serve the purpose for which it was designed.

Edward Stone wrote in a recent article, "Everybody in this country is too insistent on his own identity—on building a billboard." The correctness of this remark can be appreciated by objective observation of some of those buildings which have been hailed publicly as outstanding examples of modern architecture but only too often are expressions of the quest for originality, the products of vanity and, even more often, of the commercial desire of the client for publicity. The commercial client, in some cases, encourages architectural vanity, urging originality at any price, disregarding cost or the basic functions of the building. This happens in the case of those buildings which are more important for publicity and advertising purposes or for the establishment of what the public relations profession calls the "corporate image" than for the purpose which they supposedly are serving.

An illustration of how this desire for publicity can influence the architect's work can be found in comparing two air terminal buildings designed by the same architect, the late, extremely gifted Eero Saarinen. One of these buildings, the TWA terminal at Idlewild, New York (now John F. Kennedy International Airport), obviously was based on the client's desire to outdo all its competitors' displays of originality and glamour as they are lined up in that "World's Fair" of air terminal buildings at the International Airport. The result is a *tour de force* that offers some excitement but little comfort or convenience to the air traveler. The second air terminal building designed by Eero Saarinen is at the Dulles Airport in Washington, D.C., and inasmuch as it is one central structure serving all competitive airlines, the desire for advertising was not present. The result is an excellent, handsome structure offering innovations in the transport of the passengers to the plane which will probably pioneer similar arrangements all over the world and which, as far as the human users are concerned, will provide quietude, convenience, comfort and "delight." Yet I will not be surprised if that superior terminal in Washington will create less furor and excitement in our mass communications media and in the architectural press than did the first one.

Just as in the world of modern painting, there are in architecture a number of highly voluble critics whose business and livelihood consist in the discovering of new styles and reading into an architect's creation intentions and ideas that never occurred to him. Albert Bush-Brown, president of the Rhode Island School of Design, does not belong to this group. In an article that appeared in *Horizon* in September, 1962, he writes thoughtfully about Louis Kahn's work under the title "Architect's Hero: Louis Kahn," considering the work of this imaginative and creative man from various angles. In discussing the Richards Medical Research Building at the University of Pennsylvania, he states:

> By conventional standards the Richards Medical Building is not a beautiful one. You are likely not to like it when you see it. Its brick towers, massive and stark, bristle on the skyline; the concrete structure below seems brutish; ugly pipes, ducts, and wires gnarl its ceilings. . . . If you seek a quiet, serene, or pretty architecture, you will not find it here. . . .
>
> As we move about the structure we are offered powerful vistas from one tower across a small court and into the adjacent tower—spaces we can visualize as inside, then outside, then inside again. No previous architecture, in my opinion, is so powerfully three-dimensional in its ability to impress on you continuously, as you move through it, its functional, structural, and mechanical origins. . . .
>
> The Richards Building won Kahn the Brunner Prize for 1960, annually awarded by the National Institute of Arts and Letters to the architect who contributes most to "architecture as art." . . . It was greeted enthusiastically in the architectural magazines of Japan, England, Italy, France, Germany, Scandinavia, South America, and Canada. Indeed, few recent buildings anywhere have been so well-celebrated.

After this tribute to Kahn's Richards Medical Research Building, Albert Bush-Brown continues:

> Kahn has become a hero too quickly, and too few of his fellow architects have listened to the scientists who have to work in his building. The latter complain that Kahn's rigorous integration of space, structure, and services has been purchased at too great an expense. The generalized studio spaces do not divide easily. Essential equipment—like refrigerators, public telephones, centrifuges, and cabinets—protrudes into the maze of corridors because no place was specially fitted to receive it. Secretaries have to sit in hallways. To correct glare, especially at the corners, the occupants have stretched aluminum foil across the windows, an unsightly improvisation that could have been avoided by protecting the windows and eliminating the transom. . . . One hopes Kahn's pursuit of the bold silhouette will not lead him astray.

One hopes indeed. I do not believe that the pursuit of bold silhouettes or the searching for new forms and new styles will lead us out of the chaotic state of architecture. I doubt seriously that we are creating new styles. I rather believe that we manufacture short-lived fads and fashions, similar to those we find in millinery and ladies' wear generally.

The Swiss art historian, Sigfried Giedion, states that American architecture has become "a playboy architecture . . . an architecture treated as playboys treat life, jumping from one sensation to another and quickly bored with everything."

Wolf von Eckardt, in an article about the city in *Show* Magazine of December, 1963, says: "The trouble with our architecture is not its exuberance but its prima donna complex. It is narcissistic and neurotically antisocial. It refuses to restrain itself in the company of older architecture."

Styles throughout history have not been intentionally created but have been recognized subsequently for what they were from the viewing tower of the art historian. Some of the elements of style formation are missing anyway in our times. I refer to the restrictions that existed in various epochs of history and were of technological or regional origin. New technological inventions, like the arch or the cupola or the dome, resulted in new styles. The regional availability of materials like stone, brick or lumber was a decisive factor in style evolution. The wealth of materials and building methods which modern communications and modern technology have put at our disposal make it possible for an architect designing a building to choose among a number of materials and methods, and the decision very often is based far less on style than on building economics. Regional differences seem to be disappearing, and the glass box built on Park Avenue today may be seen copied tomorrow in places as far removed as Tokyo, Hong Kong, London and Honolulu. I would not be surprised indeed if historians of future ages should recognize as "twentieth-century style" structures with which the architects had nothing to do, like freeways, cloverleaves, hydroelectric plants, and the subdivisions of suburbia.

Mr. Blake stated in his article that those new dangerous American architects who, with missionary zeal, work on the improvement of the over-all environment feel that the first step is simply to create a sense of order. This is indeed the most urgent task. It is the establishing of the foundation from which architecture as individual, free expression can rise again. As long as we permit the chaotic condition of the man-made environment to prevail, architectural self-expression is forced to be originality-seeking, as it otherwise could not even make itself noticed in the over-all disorder. And even though such "original" buildings may be noticed, they will not succeed in truly serving human needs. Of what use are glamorous glass walls when the view out of them opens up on blight, disorder and smog? How can we hope to reintegrate art with architecture as long as the contemplation of such integrated work is made impossible because of the compelling need to observe the traffic instead? As matters stand today, it might be stated that any architectural creation so outstanding that it would force observation and appreciation would have to be forbidden by law because of the traffic risks it would engender.

Thus we architects, wishing to create structures that can offer delight within and without have but one choice: to use our energies, our knowledge, our imagination, creativity and perseverence toward the aim of creating, first of all, *order,* and then environmental qualities in our cities that will permit the contemplation of future buildings and their undisturbed functioning for the purposes for which they are designed—structures that will enhance the enjoyment of those who observe them, live in them or otherwise use them.

13 Appearance or Disappearance: That Is the Question

Make no little plans, they have no magic to stir men's blood.

—DANIEL BURNHAM, architect, 1907

THIS STATEMENT BY Daniel Burnham, creator of the Chicago plan, is probably one of the best-known quotations of its kind; also one of the most misunderstood and misused. All too often, Mr. Burnham's demand for "no little plans" is interpreted to mean that *large* plans are the answer. Thus, the quotation is used as a justification for plans that are large as far as the amount of money to be spent is concerned, large in building area or cubage, large with respect to the amount of required demolition involved, large in regard to sacrifices necessary in order to make their implementation possible. However, according to Webster "large" and "big" are not the only opposites of the word "little." There is also "great." The plans that "stir men's blood" are the great plans, based on great ideas, on philosophical thought, on deep conviction.

A great plan may or may not involve demolition or destruction; it may or may not be costly; it may not even involve the construction of a single new building. But a great plan will always be one which distinctively improves the human environment, which changes existing patterns, and which manifests itself in something that, for lack of a better word, I shall call "appearance." This is a term used in regular discussions that take place yearly in the city of Washington, D.C., concerning "The Appearance of the National Capital." These discussions are sponsored by the Metropolitan Washington Board of Trade and the Chamber of Commerce of the District of Columbia. I have attended one of these discussions and studied the records of another. It is clear that all participants agreed that "appearance" signified much more than just the visual impression. The well-known Washington architect, Cloethiel Smith, upon looking up the word in a dictionary, found a synonym in the word "aspect," denoting implications related to the object itself *or* felt by the beholder. For purposes of this discussion, I would like to include in the term "appearance" the inherent quality of an object itself plus its impact on those who experience the object through their senses.

In that sense, then, appearance takes in the sum total of the physical and psychological influence of an environment on human beings. Appearance, therefore, can never be decisively affected by the surface treatment of cosmeticians, or by any skin-deep actions alone.

Appearance is to be measured by the physical and psychological reactions of man: how well he feels, how comfortable he is, how much inspiration he gets, to what degree he is enabled to live undisturbed, unmolested and free of interference.

Good appearance, in this context, widens the scope of individual freedom, and of free choice of expression and experience.

Good appearance in a city can only be built upon certain prerequisites which must be present as the floor from which to strive upward toward the summit: a foundation without which everything higher up would crumble. Chief among these prerequisites is the protection of human life and health from dangers, disturbing noises and obnoxious smells. Another prerequisite is the over-all legal framework, within which the greatest and most reasonable amount of personal latitude is assured while care is taken that no individual's whim or expression will interfere unreasonably with, or injure, another, or the community at large.

The tragedy of man's city in our day is that the prerequisites for good appearance, those fundamental features upon which we can build, are partially or even totally lacking and that therefore all our efforts to improve by superficial means, even through "large" projects, are doomed to fail.

That is the reason why a few handsome buildings here and there have no true impact, why all the efforts of well-meaning beauticians, with their slogan "Beautify Your City," are pathetic and sometimes ridiculous. Millions have been spent, for example, to introduce terrazzo sidewalks with the names of movie stars embedded in the pavement on Hollywood Boulevard in Los Angeles. The street has remained as shabby and dreary as before, its shabbiness is merely underlined by "glamorous" and vulgar high-intensity lighting fixtures.

That is why the appearance of State Street in Chicago has not been elevated in spite of the great sums spent for new fluorescent lighting on standards that carry artificial flowers.

When, in the City of New York, concrete plant containers with bushes and flowers were arranged along the sidewalks on some avenues, the bushes soon looked tired and dirty, the containers became filled with trash, and it did not help matters when, in some places, signs were affixed with the polite request: "Don't steal the flowers."

The placards one sees posted in many cities appealing to the public to "keep your city clean" have only added to the confusing forest of signs, warnings and advertisements which spread all over the cityscape. Nor are the efforts undertaken by some institutions to add cultural flair, to introduce sporadic expressions of art into the chaotic urban environment, of any help. Sculptures and murals, unobserved by anybody, just gather dust.

That individual efforts alone cannot cope with the problem of improving the appearance of the city is not surprising; neither do many of the larger projects sponsored by Federal agencies, city administrations or public-spirited groups of citizens, unless, as is only too rarely the case, they deal with fundamental aspects. Usually they aim only for an exchange of merchandise, which might be likened to that with which department stores are plagued right after Christmas: They exchange old structures for new ones, old fads for modern ones, and in doing so more often than not spoil the very appearance they are trying to improve.

Ada Louise Huxtable, critic and historian in the field of art and architecture, recently wrote an article in *The New York Times* about conditions prevailing in Washington, D.C., in which she bemoans the sad state of architecture, as expressed in the individual newer buildings. Yet she concludes that there is something admirable in Washington. "If Washington has kept its beauty, it is because of the spaciousness of its avenues, the pleasure of its parks, the vision of its plan." In her judgment, with which I agree, it is the over-all *appearance*, the great plan which, at least in those parts of Washington that we as tourists know as the official center of government, is so strong that it can maintain its impact in spite of the mediocrity of individual structures.

Two important plans have come to fruition in Pittsburgh. One was a great plan, yet it did not involve the demolition of one single structure or the creation of a single new one. It has not even created anything visible to the human eye but, quite the contrary, has removed something that bothered human sensibilities. I am referring to the plan that has been successfully implemented to free Pittsburgh of the smoke and soot that had covered it for a long time. The second plan has involved a lot of demolition and many millions of dollars' worth of new buildings. It is the Golden Triangle project, which replaced a downgraded neighborhood with new office and hotel buildings. Now, although the effects of this project can be seen by everybody, it is a *little* plan that has not decisively changed the appearance of the city in the sense in which I have defined this term. Because it was not concerned with the creation of a superior pattern, with the establishment of the prerequisites, it has resulted in a sea of moving and parked automobiles, out of which rise disconnected islands of tall utilitarian buildings.

The new Pan American building in Manhattan, with its 2,000,000 square feet of building area, is the largest office building ever constructed. It has not improved the appearance of Manhattan: rather, it has diminished it, and this in spite of the fact that untold millions of dollars were involved, that two of the most famous American architects (Walter Gropius and Pietro Belluschi) were retained as design consultants, that its builder, the late Erwin S. Wolfson, was motivated, at least to some degree, by praiseworthy aims. The fact is that by virtue of its location this building contributes to a deterioration of those prerequisites which are vital to a city.

In order to create and implement truly great plans, one must be prepared to use a radical approach. The word "radical" has fallen into bad repute, unjustly and unfortunately. Its true meaning, derived from the Latin *radicalis,* "having roots," implies that a radical solution is one that goes right down to the root of the problem. The problem then is: What makes the appearance of a city superior?

We may get a clue to the answer by observing the few spots still left in some of our cities to which tourists and visitors flock. Most visitors to New York will go to Greenwich Village, in spite of the fact that there is hardly an outstanding structure there. What the tourists seek and admire is what they call "atmosphere," which, when one digs deeper, is found to be the result of small-grained variety and diversity. The admixture of buildings old and new, small and large; the potpourri of nationalities, races and economic groups; the intermingling of shops, stores, restaurants, bars, institutions of learning and theaters with residences of all types—all this diversity attracted artists and others who do not admire conformity. However, because so few areas of this type exist, the very popularity of this particular one begins to threaten its attractive qualities. It is becoming a self-conscious tourist trap. It is also being flooded with luxury apartment buildings ever since people with money found out that it is a desirable place to live. There is now a danger that another "high income reservation" may be in the making.

Tourists in Manhattan are also shown Rockefeller Center. If you should ask any of them what the architecture of this remarkable urban element is like, they would not have the faintest idea. But what they do remember with great enjoyment is the pedestrian mall with its flower exhibits and fountains; the ice-skating rink which in summer becomes an outdoor eating place; and what they instinctively feel as an agreeable feature is a strongly expressed unity in the character and placement of the original building (this is, unfortunately, not true of the new ones) and the variety of open spaces between the buildings, which acts as a relief from the standard gridiron pattern of Manhattan. They will also remember with pleasure the view from the top of the highest building, opening up vistas over Central Park, the Hudson and East Rivers, and down the Battery to the tip end of the Island of Manhattan. Rockefeller Center is one of the very few examples of a great plan in this country. It is amazing and disturbing that, in spite of its economic success, it has found no true imitators.

The tourists in Manhattan will also be impressed with that part of Fifth Avenue which is clearly terminated at both ends by two important urban elements: the Public Library on 42nd Street, and Central Park (the product of one of the *really* Great Plans) on 59th Street. Why is this stretch of avenue, which is no different in width or in length from other New York avenues, singled out as an attraction to New Yorkers and tourists alike? It is because, together with its immediate surroundings, it offers true urban variety. Rockefeller Center, the Public Library, St. Patrick's Cathedral, and a number of other churches and public buildings are to be found along its borders. Nearby are such institutions as the Modern Museum and the Whitney Museum, as well as apartments of all types. The first and second floors of the structures bordering that part of Fifth Avenue are occupied by stores and shops of all types and sizes, competing with each other in the glamour of their show-window displays. Lately, a few too many banks have invaded this milieu, interrupting the continuous interest of the window-shopper, and maybe that is one of the reasons why the area has lost some of its magnetism. Yet this stretch of Fifth Avenue is the only dynamic area in the United States which, in its attractiveness, can compete with similar streets in London, Paris, Rome or Vienna.

San Francisco is another American city to which tourists flock. Strangely, one of the most popular features is a former service alley called Maiden Lane. It is bordered by the rather grim rear façades of buildings that turn their main fronts to parallel neighboring streets. But the fact that it is free of automobile traffic, that it is an area in which the pedestrian has been made king and it therefore draws people, has encouraged the merchants to move their main entrances to the lane; in fact, a number of them have entrances only along the former alley, including the famous V. C. Morris store, designed by America's most eminent architect, Frank Lloyd Wright.

The local Chamber of Commerce of Los Angeles will prove by statistics that that city is a major tourist center. But were one to ask where those tourists go, or what they come for, one would discover that only rarely do they show up in the heart of the city, the downtown area. If they do so, they are attracted by the one little building group with atmosphere, Olvera Street, a leftover from Spanish colonial times, which, with its pedestrian area and its rather phony stores and restaurants, represents an urban element kept alive by artificial respiration. Otherwise one will find the tourists spreading out into the sprawling suburban area. They come to Los Angeles in order to see Disneyland (27 miles from the city center) or Marineland (30 miles from the city center). They stay at hotels in Beverly Hills or Bel Air or Santa Monica. They try to enjoy the climate, if that happens not to be ruined by smog, and the beaches, if they happen not to be polluted. They go to Palm Springs (100 miles from the city center) or to Santa Barbara (95 miles from the city center). In other words, it is not Los Angeles as a city that attracts them, but some of the features, natural or man-made, that can be enjoyed in Southern California.

Arriving in dozens of cities in the United States, in my role as an architect and planner, I am often treated, by kind clients or civic officials, as a visiting tourist. I am shown the sights, and in most cases I find they are not located in the city. I am dined and wined at the Country Club. I am entertained in plush suburbs. I am taken to a neighboring lake, or state or national park. In the great majority of American cities, appearance is of such low quality there is nothing left of interest to the residents, or of possible interest to visitors.

I have discussed earlier the prerequisites of appearance, and I have submitted that their creation or resuscitation is a dire and fundamental necessity. But prerequisites alone do not create good appearance. Much more is needed to reach this aim, and one of the most essential ingredients is variety. Any experience in life becomes dull if it is constant and repetitive. We need versatility, change of pace, the dramatic and monumental interspersed with the quiet and intimate. The art of music should be an inspiration to the creators of man-made environment. A musical composition plays on human emotions not only through the differentiation of notes and the tone color of the instruments, but also by changes in rhythm, in emphasis and in tempo. There are intervals filled with sound, and intervals filled with silence. There is ever-changing rhythm, indicated by the musical vocabulary that contains such instructions for variations: largo, adagio, andante, allegro, allegretto, presto, prestissimo.

Just as a symphony could not be enjoyed without basic prerequisites like quietude in the concert hall, together with comfort, weather protection, good acoustics and appropriate architecture, and without the multitude of sounds and tone colors, of changes in emphasis, so will the urban symphony be unable to reach heights of appearance if it is not given soul and content in a similar manner.

The appearance of the heart of a city that has neither taken care of the prerequisites nor managed the full register of expressions of human thought and activities has to be abominable. The city area that has become only a working place for public and private administration; the city core that is only a shopping place; the city core that wishes to devote itself exclusively to any other specific type of urban activities—every one will unavoidably dry up and wither away because the only alternative to good *appearance* is *disappearance.* No compromise is possible with regard either to the fulfillment of the prerequisites or to versatility.

We have neglected the appearance of our cities for at least a half century. The damage caused by long neglect can no longer be cured by superficial means: neither by large plans, which are not great plans, nor by so-called beautification. The trends that have infected the hearts of our cities with a fatal malady are firmly entrenched. If we want to reverse them, we must radically change the conditions that have brought them about and are keeping them alive. If we do not want the city to be destroyed, if we do not want Anti-city to bury us, we have to prepare for an all-out counterattack.

This is the subject of Part Three of this book.

PART THREE

THE COUNTERATTACK

When a city begins to grow and spread outward from the edges, the center which was once its glory . . . goes into a period of desolation inhabited at night by the vague ruins of men, the lotus eaters who struggle daily toward unconsciousness by way of raw alcohol. Nearly every city I know has such a dying mother of violence and despair where at night the brightness of the street lamps is sucked away and policemen walk in pairs. And then one day perhaps the city returns and rips out the sore and builds a monument to its past.

—JOHN STEINBECK,
Travels With Charley

14 The Search

A disease known is a half cure.

—LATIN PROVERB

IN PART ONE, "THE CITY," I have discussed the criteria by which we come to recognize a city: its anatomy, its values. I have devoted Part Two to a discussion of the forces that threaten and destroy the city, and which, if left unchecked, finally pave the way for anti-city. It is my hope that once the wish to be cured has been created or strengthened by directing a searchlight on the diseases, "half a cure" has already been effected.

The most difficult part still remains: How does a city regain its health and vigor?

A cure for modern man's ailing city has been sought for a long time and at various levels. There is the search for ideas, which, though more often than not conceived outside the realm of practicalities, has extended great influence. This is the search conducted by thinkers who rarely have a chance to implement even a fraction of their concepts but who only too often have to witness the disappointing misapplication of their ideas by "doers."

Then there is the pragmatic search of those who, being basically enemies of planning, oppose every effort as futile, pointing to the existing economic distress, which in the first place was caused, not by *over-all,* but by *laissez-faire* planning.

And between these two goes on a search by architects and planners like myself who, fully respecting the value of ideas and ideals, are attempting to give direction and implementation to curative measures by engaging in practical action toward the improvement of the urban environment.

As to the many and varied ideas for new patterns of urban organization that have been put forth, I have become acquainted with most of them at various stages of my professional activity through reading and research, during conferences and discussions and, with some of them, during my research for this book. I confess that, not being a scholarly man, I have never methodically studied the history of planning ideas and concepts but have rather arrived upon many of them through the search needed to solve problems posed in my professional work. Often I find myself in the happy position of recognizing that somebody else has had a thought on which I hit much later, and sometimes I find myself violently disagreeing with ideas I read about, feeling that they are conceived in violation of the urban spirit.

During my student years I read with great enthusiasm Le Corbusier's books about city planning. I owe deep gratitude to the master because his writings awakened in me the profound interest I have felt ever since in the architecture of environment. When I recently reread *La Ville Radieuse* I was impressed with the prophetic gifts of Le Corbusier, who, at a time when only a few thousand automobiles cruised through the streets of Paris, foresaw that the motorcar would become a means of mass transportation and based his concepts of the new city, as best reflected and visualized in the "Voisin Plan for Paris," on a welding of nature and buildings, placing individual tall structures of uniform design into a parklike area, with broad boulevards forming a grid for automobile transportation. In my youth I could not help but be impressed by the idea of people living and working in tall towers, able to look out from their windows over wide vistas of greenery, with other tall towers in the background. But as I became confronted with actually executed building groups—which, though poorly translating Le Corbusier's concepts into reality, were nevertheless based on his thoughts—I began to realize that the idea was not only unworkable but also pregnant with the danger of bringing forth Anti-city. The unworkability has to do with the very understandable fact that Le Corbusier, though he foresaw a great flood of automobiles, underestimated the proportions of the deluge. The amount of traffic necessary to establish any kind of connection between the widely separated towers is indeed of such a scale that it automatically destroys part of the dream. Where Le Corbusier visualized nature and parks, traffic and parking lots are bound to take over. The Golden Triangle project

Three views illustrating city planning concepts of the architect Le Corbusier. Towerlike structures of uniform design are set far apart from each other. In the center picture they are arranged in relation to stetched-out lower apartment buildings. In viewing these drawings one realizes to what a high degree they have influenced planning and architecture all over the world.

The Golden Triangle Development in Pittsburgh, Pennsylvania. The triangular land area in the foreground is mostly used for automobile roads, and though landscaped areas in the segments remaining between roads are quite generous in size, they are also inaccessible. The new buildings adjoining this open area are spaced far apart, but the open spaces between them are with minor exceptions devoted to the automobile—its movements and its storing.

Model of Frank Lloyd Wright's project for Broadacre City. The concept was based on a Jeffersonian contempt for life in the city. In Broadacre City every family would live on a large rectangular plot, presumably finding escape from boredom in long automobile trips.

in Pittsburgh is a direct, though possibly subconscious, imitation of Le Corbusier's concept. High structures of similar design are spaced far apart from each other in splendid isolation, but what occurs between them is an ugly morass of moving, stored and stalled automobiles, an asphalt desert that can be negotiated only with the greatest danger and inconvenience by those who seek direct communication with the workers or residents of other buildings. Le Corbusier's ideas are undoubtedly at the base of the attitude of "the false friends of the city" toward low land coverage and the destruction of intimacy, variety and compactness.

Much later, during my life in the United States, I was exposed to Frank Lloyd Wright's plan for Broadacre City, according to which every family would live on at least an acre of land. Though I appreciated the orderliness and discipline of the master plan and the love for the values of the rural life, I reacted strongly against a scheme that would spread population even farther apart than in the most land-wasting sub-suburban pattern and would therefore multiply the problems already bestowed on us by sprawl and scatterization.

In an exhibit called "The Road," at the Museum of Modern Art in New York in the summer of 1961, I became acquainted with plans that would make the city an appendage to the highway, using its buildings as a base for the roads above. Some ideas actually provided for cities many, many miles long with all their buildings arranged underneath highways. Others arranged endless strips of buildings on both sides of highways. These ideas appeared to me to be the final word on the subjugation of human beings to their traveling machines. The scheme of "Motopia" by G. A. Jellicoe, arranged in a grid pattern, with the roofs of all structures representing auto roads, belongs to this species. In spite of the fact that many of these schemes are regarded even by their authors as utopian, we find them very often proposed and actually executed by practicing planners. Los Angeles' Wilshire Boulevard, which exists in smaller editions in nearly every metropolis, is nothing but "Roadtown" executed. "Corridor towns," as proposed in the master plan for Washington, D.C., and the ideas of the Greek planner, Dr. C. A. Doxiadis, which sail under the catchy name of "Dynapolis," represent practically implementable variations on the utopian concepts. Dr. Doxiadis bases his Dynapolis concept on his belief that growth per se is good and that lineal growth is best. He proposes to start the building of a new city with a short stretch of high-rise buildings for office and merchandising purposes on both sides of a traffic way backed up on either side by residential and other buildings, and then to let the city grow in preplanned fashion by adding, every few years, a similarly patterned increment,

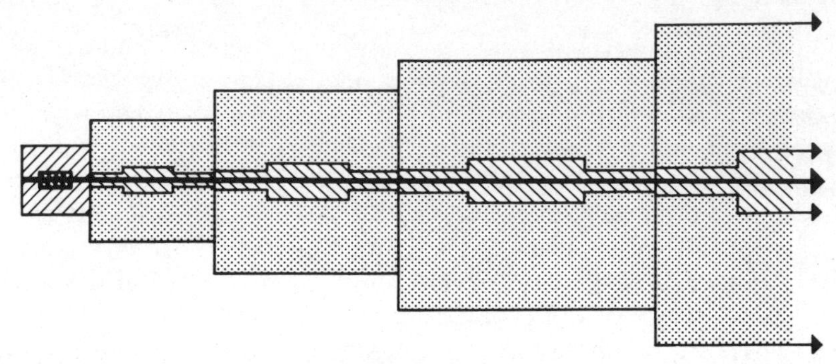

Schematic drawing illustrating city planning concepts of Dr. C. A. Doxiadis. Being preoccupied by the problem of dynamic growth, Dr. Doxiadis proposes that the city would start to grow (on the extreme left edge of the illustration) as a commercial core surrounded by residential areas, and that in future years it would continue to grow (toward the right edge of the picture), adding increments of the core area along a central artery and new residential areas at the same time.

---

giving Dynapolis, at least theoretically, the possibility of stretching out the full length of a continent.

I also have difficulty sympathizing with those who, as Jean Gottmann does in his book *Megalopolis,* are willing to accept the disorderly, cancerous growth that occurs along the East Coast of the United States as the present and future form of urbanization.

What I feel is wrong with all these ideas, concepts or utopias is that, in their search to discover new ways for untrammeled dynamism, they are destroying the physical confines of the urban organism and thereby all chances for organized community life and for differentiation between cityscape, landscape, agricultural land and nature. Much more significant, I feel, are the writings and planning efforts—and the actual developments resulting from them—that seek to arrive at comprehensively conceived communities and groupings of communities that are defined as to size and shape. The most successful of these searchers seem to me to be those who have aimed at achieving reasonable compactness with regard to the areas devoted to habitation and other urban activities, utilizing the land thus saved as nature reserves of one type or another, with the idea that these nature reserves should also act as separators between urbanized elements.

The planning of many communities in our time has been influenced by the ideas of Ebenezer Howard in whose book *Garden Cities of To-Morrow,* published in 1898, the schematic pattern was set for such contemporary model towns as Vällingby and Farsta, near Stockholm, and the New Towns in England, the older green-belt towns in the United States, and many others. I shall discuss these principles of cluster development in the chapter "The Emerging New Urban Pattern."

I spoke earlier of the search that is going on at two other levels: the search by those forces of the American economy which, because of inefficiency resulting from the *laissez-faire* pattern, are now turning to planning experiments; and the search (in which I myself, as a planner, am deeply involved) for means of channeling the uncertain and uncrystallized desires for improvement into meaningful patterns which can be actually implemented within our democratic free-enterprise system.

These efforts might be termed the development of a strategy of counterattack against the forces of Anti-city. In order to be as constructive as possible, I will to a large degree illustrate the strategy by referring to actual examples either in the project stage or already executed. I am aware of the built-in disadvantage this procedure holds because each of these actual examples is diluted to some degree by necessities that stem from existing conditions, or by need for compromises; yet these examples are important because they reflect clearly the degree to which progress is attainable in our time, under prevailing conditions. In a later chapter I shall discuss the manner and means by which prevailing legal and administrative tools could be modified in order to make possible the raising of our goals and in order to speed up planning and implementation processes.

In discussing the elements of the counterattack I shall, as I explained in the first chapter, choose as examples chiefly projects undertaken by our own office, not because I believe they are the only significant ones but because I am most intimately acquainted with their nature and background and thus am best able to describe and illustrate them.

The search for elements of the counterattack on Anti-city, interestingly enough, started within Anti-city in the thinly populated fringe area of the metropolitan region. This happened partly because chaotic conditions arose there with such speed that some action had to be taken and partly because inexpensive land was amply available. Thus we have witnessed in Suburbia, U.S.A., during the last twenty years a tendency toward recentralization, an effort to create, within the vast deserts of spread city, nuclei that would establish meaningful urban oases. These new nuclei for the most part suffer from deficiencies. Often devoted to only one type of activity, usually too small to be meaningful, and very often victims of land-wasting arrangements, they have nevertheless shown themselves to be useful experimental proving grounds. By the dynamism with which they develop they furnish undeniable proof that the desire for the creation of meaningful centers has not quite died in the era of sprawl.

Such nuclear elements—activity clusters for various purposes—have grown up by the dozen in practically every metropolitan region of the nation. There are educational nuclei like the Air Force Academy in Colorado Springs (Skidmore, Owings and Merrill, architects and engineers); the Foothill Junior College, Los Altos Hills, California (Ernest J. Kump and Masten & Hurd, associated architects); the University of California at Irvine, Orange County, California (Master plan by William L. Pereira & Associates). There are new, self-contained, or at least partially self-contained, communities like Park Forest, Chicago (Loebl, Schlossman & Bennett, architects); Babbitt, Minnesota; White Pine, Upper Michigan; and Silver Bay, Minnesota (Pace Associates, Chicago, architects); Don Mills near Toronto, Canada (Don Mills Development, Ltd.). There are industrial nuclei and there are office activity centers like that of the Connecticut General Life Insurance Company near Hartford (Skidmore, Owings and Merrill, architects), and many others. There are new residential nuclei, most of them unfortunately only bedroom towns, and there are regional shopping centers.

Because the regional shopping center is in many ways most closely related

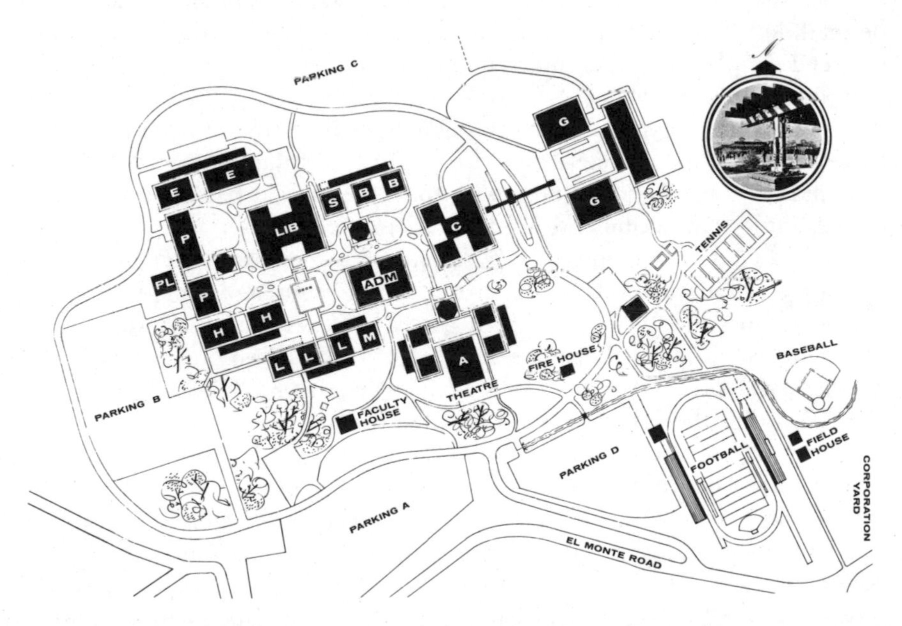

A plan of Foothill College, Los Altos Hills, California. Here, structures serving administration, education, and student residences are grouped into one cluster surrounded by parking areas and circulatory roads. In the central cluster, only pedestrian traffic is permitted.

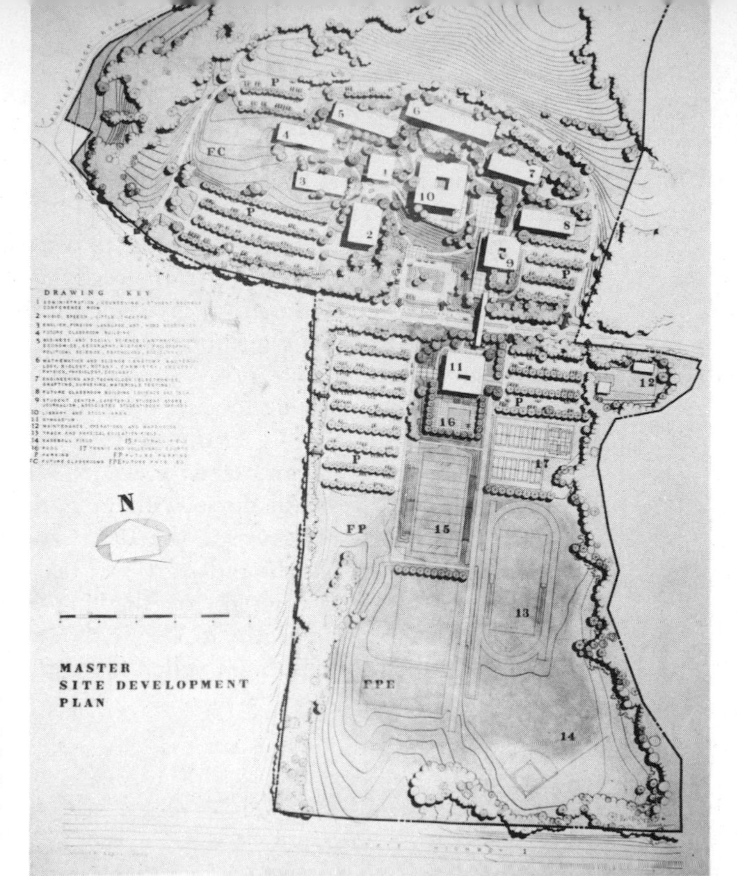

Site plan of Cabrillo College, Santa Cruz County, California. A clusterlike arrangement similar to the one discussed in the Foothill College plan is apparent.

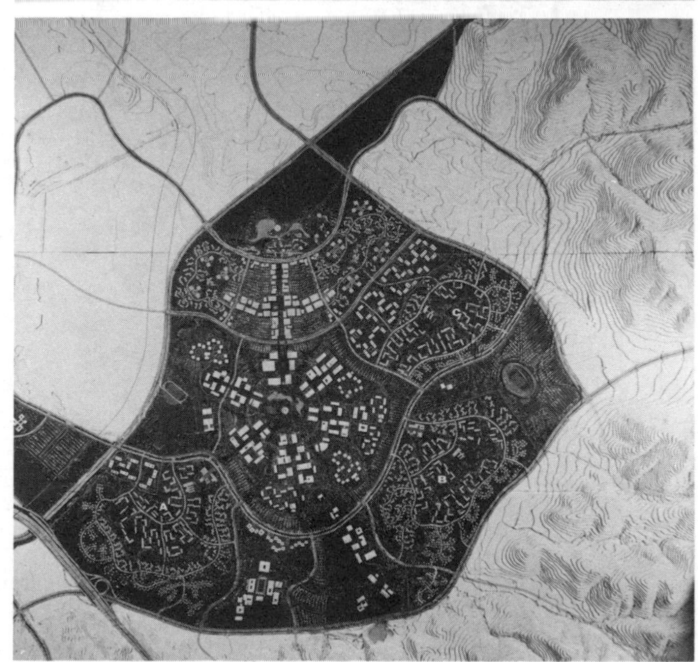

A plan of the University of California campus at Irvine, Orange County. In this case of a much larger university, six clusters are arranged around a large circular common area.

to the problems at the heart of our cities and because in its development some potent weapons have been forged (applicable with some modifications to the core areas of cities), I would like to discuss it at greater length.

The reason for the emergence of the regional shopping center is identical to that which has created many a great city in the past: commercialism. Let us follow the path of its development through the experiences of one individual merchandising enterprise, John Doe's Fashion Emporium. It had been founded by John Doe toward the end of the nineteenth century and was established successfully in the heart of the core area of Middle City, U.S.A. Business was fine and when John, Jr., who preferred to lead a life of leisure, took over, he could do so without hurting the success of the store. John III inherited the business in the 1920s, and he was quite an ambitious young man. He felt that the old store had become run-down and needed a face-lifting as well as a complete overhauling of the interior, but just about the time when he was ready to begin the work of renovation, business started to drop off. Attempting to elicit the reasons for bad business from his

On miles and miles of suburban highway, developments of commercial facilities occur, all hoping to cash in on the traffic moving by.

Once it became apparent that sufficient parking space could not be provided to maintain business in stores along the highway, rear parking areas were arranged. The illustration shows a typical shopping center in Los Angeles, California.

manager, he discovered that his best customers had left the area and fled to the suburbs. Mrs. Fox had moved to Lake Valley, Mrs. Wolf to Beauty Acres, Mrs. Badger to Sunnyside, and so on. True enough, new people had moved into their apartments, but they were not the type of customers whom the Fashion Emporium was seeking. John III postponed the alterations and business went downhill fast. Being an able and energetic young man, John III decided that action was needed, so he rented stores along some of the main highways in Lake Valley, Beauty Acres and Sunnyside, giving up the downtown lease. John III's enterprise and daring paid off, and he used to stand smiling in front of one or the other of his three stores, counting the ever-increasing number of automobiles on the highways along which they were located with unconcealed satisfaction.

The story of John III's success spread like wildfire; on both sides of the highway, stores and all kinds of other retail enterprises were opened by fugitives from the center of the city—until there was a mile-long stretch, fully developed, lining the highway. In true cooperative spirit, the merchants got together in order to promote their common welfare. At both ends of the strip they erected large signs with the words MIRACLE MILE—which, however, they found they had to move out a little farther every few months. In a second session of the Miracle Mile Association, business conditions were discussed and the various members confessed to each other that in spite of the fact that more automobiles than ever could be counted going by their stores, they now moved rather slowly and sometimes not at all. The other trouble was that because of the growing traffic congestion, the municipality had forbidden curb parking so that suddenly no customers were able to park their cars in front of any of the stores. The decision was made to acquire land areas behind the stores and to build parking lots there (see illustration page 187). The result was not quite what was hoped for. John III found that the ladies who would be likely customers for the Fashion Emporium did not appreciate the fact that they had to walk in through the narrow rear door, through which deliveries also moved in and trash moved out. And thus, in spite of the great expenditure for the acquisition of land and the construction of parking lots, business diminished markedly.

John III, never slow to act, said to himself that the area in which he had been located for five years had obviously gone to hell and that he had better move still farther out, to highways in the new suburban developments to which Mrs. Fox, Mrs. Wolf and Mrs. Badger in the meantime had moved. (They had become disgusted with traffic congestion and cheap commercialism.) But like his first move, the second was also copied by many, and after another five years John III was faced with the identical difficulties, in spite of the fact that in the new location he had made one significant improvement: placing his parking areas in front of the store instead of behind it.

One of the reasons for the new trouble was that public authorities, reacting to the popular complaints about unbearable traffic congestion between the rows of suburban stores, had constructed a six-lane freeway bypassing the traffic-ridden area. On the morning when the freeway opened, merchants along the highway strip noticed that traffic congestion had indeed disappeared—but so had all their customers. A sign which they persuaded the authorities to erect along the freeway reading EXIT FOR ROADSIDE BUSINESS was of little help.

Now John III heard about three regional shopping centers, then in the planning stage, strategically located near the freeway ramps and within easy reach of his most desirable customers in the northern, eastern and southern areas of the metropolitan region. He negotiated leases and in spite of the somewhat surprising conditions imposed in these leases, John III, being a pioneering character, established his stores. At first he was quite upset about the manner in which he, a desirable tenant, was treated by the shopping center management. He was told not only where he should locate his store within the shopping center but also how much space would be allotted to him. He was told to arrange his main entrance doors along interior courts, malls or lanes in which no automobiles would be permitted; and only after it was convincingly put to him that his customers were actually people and not cars could he reconcile himself to that idea. He was told that he could receive and load merchandise only in specified areas in the basement, and that the loading areas would have to be approached by his trucks over an underground road especially reserved for this purpose. His greatest shock came when he was informed that his storefronts and signs would be subject to approval by the shopping center management and that the letters used to advertise his firm could not be higher than three feet and could be affixed only to a certain portion of the storefront. When he was reassured, however, that the same regulations would be imposed on everybody else he shrugged his shoulders and said, "Well, in that case I can save myself a lot of money. As long as nobody else can yell louder than I, I certainly don't mind."

Thus John III opened his three new stores in three well-planned regional shopping centers, and for the first time in his business life he was able to relax and abandon the continuous search for suitable locations.

Planned regional shopping centers, like those into which John III moved, are one of the few new building types created in our time and in the United States. Their history goes back to the village type of shopping environment, which made its appearance in the 1920s. An outstanding example of this, the Country Club Plaza, built in 1925 in Kansas City, Missouri, is still flourishing. This was a pioneering act in the sense that it moved the shopping environment away from arterial highways, that it formed an integral part of a large new residential district consisting of apartment buildings and single houses, and that it established a high degree of architectural unity through exterior treatment and the preplanned location of major stores. The Country Club Plaza found many imitators all over the country, most of them (for example, Westwood Village in Los Angeles) not living up to the quality of the original. Though some of these shopping districts of the village type are still doing reasonably well, they are suffering from automobile congestion and parking problems generated by the local shopping traffic because the idea of separating pedestrians from automobiles had then not been part of this shopping area concept.

Decisive progress, however, was made after World War II. In the 1950s the first of the large regional shopping centers attempting to bring into being a new orderly pattern opened their doors. Northgate, near Seattle, designed by John Graham & Co.; Shopper's World in Framingham, near Boston, designed by Ketchum, Giná and Sharp; Northland, near Detroit, designed by our office, were put into operation. Since then, dozens of regional shopping centers have made their appearance in every metropolitan area. The ones illustrated on these pages exemplify some of them and illustrate various development stages. Let us first analyze the features which these regional shopping centers have in common.

They are usually constructed on large tracts of land, anywhere from 60 to 120 acres, frequently former cow pastures or farmland. The land is selected with an eye on good surrounding highways, favorable physical characteristics, and a location within reach of a sufficient number of people (anywhere between 200,000 and 500,000) in a driving-time distance of about twenty minutes.

What is novel and revolutionary is the manner in which the store buildings are placed. Instead of being arranged conventionally, directly bordering the surrounding highways, they are located in the space theoretically least visible from the public roads and least directly accessible to automobiles: in the center of the site. There the buildings form a cluster of great compactness, with spaces between them reserved for pedestrian use only and equipped with such amenities and improvements as landscaping, rest benches, fountains and even, in some cases, works of the creative arts. The ring-shaped area around the building cluster is then utilized as a storage area for automobiles, offering between 3,000 and 10,000 car spaces. The car storage area is ringed by an internal distribution road, which, at various points, is connected with the public road network. In order to eliminate interference by delivery and service vehicles with the customers' cars or foot traffic (created by those who, after leaving their cars, enter the shopping center or, after leaving the stores, return to their cars), special roads for service traffic are arranged. These, in the larger shopping centers, dip underground and enter the basements of the stores, where loading docks and utility lines are located. In some of the shopping centers special roads are also constructed for public transportation, with bus terminals and taxi stands provided.

Thus the regional shopping center has actually implemented the concept of separation of utilitarian and human activities, and through the general popularity and economic success of this arrangement has proved that the concept is feasible and practical. Separation is achieved in a horizontal sense as far as automobile storage and automobile movement are concerned, by relegating these functions to the fringe of the core development; and it is achieved in a vertical sense with regard to the transportation of goods and the provision of services and utilities, by relegating them to an underground level.

All the regional shopping centers have created superior environmental qualities within the building core. In many of them we find weather protection achieved through the introduction of colonnades and crosswalks, and some of them are esthetically as pleasing and as busy as the long-lost town square of our urban past.

Thus they represent a great step forward. They are clearly defined urban organisms, either constructed from the beginning in their ultimate size or preplanned for inner growth. Their developers, architects and planners have decided from the beginning on their optimal shape, form and size, with full knowledge that any planless future sprawl would destroy their usefulness. The attitude of enlightened shopping center developers is that if population in the area should markedly increase, this event would necessitate the *con*struction of a new nucleus and not the *de*struction, through sprawl, of the old one.

None of these shopping centers, however, has treated successfully the appearance of the area immediately surrounding the building core, which appears like an asphalt desert occupied fully or partially by thousands of automobiles. And even where some attempts at beautification through the introduction of trees in the parking area have been made, the walk from the parked car to the building core, which might be as long as 600 feet, is not an enjoyable one. Because one of the attractions of the regional shopping center is the provision of ample and free parking, car storage is, for cost reasons, arranged only on the ground level, and thus an extremely land-wasting concept is created. In the average regional shopping center, four to five times as much land is devoted to parking and interior roads as to buildings and pedestrian areas. The wide ring of parking and transportation area surrounding the building core makes it undesirable to approach the shopping center on foot from the outside—even for those who might be living or working nearby. This is very much in contrast to the Swedish shopping centers in Vällingby and Farsta, where surface parking areas are comparatively small because many of the shoppers arrive by public transportation and where, at least on two sides of the shopping center's site, intimate contact between the building core and surrounding high-rise apartment houses is achieved; footpaths and bicycle paths lead directly from the residential area to the central building group.

Yet the regional shopping center represents an important and significant step in the right direction. It has proved that it is able to play the role not merely of a commercial center but of a social, cultural and recreational crystallization point for the up-to-then amorphous, sprawling suburban region. Shopping center planners and developers, recognizing the importance of this function, have year by year increased the number and types of facilities that would enable the regional shopping center to play more fully its role as a new heart area. Medical office buildings, general office buildings, hotels, theaters, auditoria, meeting rooms, children's play areas, restaurants, exhibit halls have been added to an environment that originally served only retail activities.

Each of the shopping centers illustrated on these pages represents some

ABOVE View of Northgate Center near Seattle, Washington. Example of the striplike arrangement typical of early regional shopping centers.

LEFT One of the landscaped pedestrian areas of Northland Center near Detroit.

BELOW Aerial view of Northland Center near Detroit. A tight cluster of buildings with a large department store in the center is ringed by a transportation area and parking area, which in turn are surrounded by a green belt and the circulatory highway network. In the center of the picture is the down ramp which brings service vehicles into the basement of the store cluster.

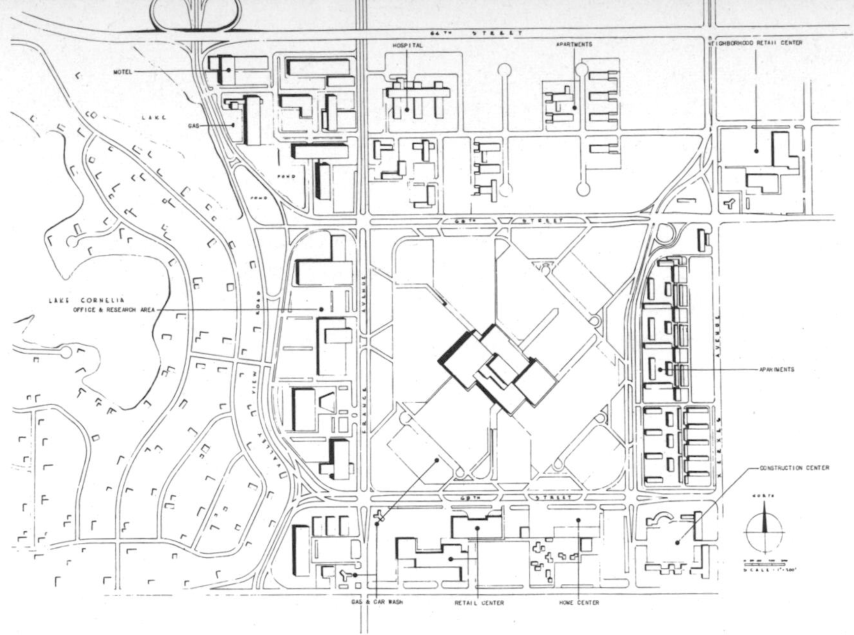

ABOVE Master plan for Southdale Shopping Center in Edina, near Minneapolis, Minnesota, showing the regional shopping center in the middle of the site with its surrounding parking and buffer areas. Future development of the surrounding area, controlled by the same owners, with apartment buildings, office buildings, hospitals, medical buildings, etc., is indicated. (This development has already been implemented to a large degree.)

RIGHT An interior view of the main enclosed air-conditioned pedestrian area (the Garden Court) of Southdale Center in Edina near Minneapolis, Minnesota.

RIGHT BELOW A partial interior view of the same garden court area during a symphony concert.

BELOW A view of the largest landscaped pedestrian area of Eastland Center, near Detroit. Its spaciousness permits the holding of large public events of all types.

milestone in the development of this building type. Northland Center, near Detroit, represents the first example of the cluster type of center (in contrast to the striplike arrangement executed in Northgate, near Seattle, and in Shopper's World in Framingham, which opened slightly earlier). *Architectural Forum* characterized Northland as "a new yardstick for shopping center planning." It has also been, from its beginning and up to the present time, commercially the most successful of all shopping centers. The Northland plan is also significant because from the beginning it envisaged the development of the surrounding area of about 250 acres in a manner that would be in harmony with the shopping center itself, and during the last ten years office buildings, apartment buildings, a hospital, a hotel, research laboratories, etc., have been constructed.

Eastland Center, also in the Detroit area, is in many ways similar to Northland, but at least one of the pedestrian courts is much larger than those created in Northland Center; when Eastland was constructed, the demand for public gathering space had become more apparent. The arrangement for the bus terminal is also more elaborate.

Southdale Center, near Minneapolis, confronted the planner with a new challenge. The climate in this Middle Western area is especially rigorous, with extremely cold winters and very hot summers. Climatic conditions made it appear that outdoor public pedestrian spaces would be attractive to shoppers during only a few days of the year. The answer to that challenge was inspired by the covered pedestrian areas of the *gallerias* in Milan and Naples. In Southdale, for the first time in the United States, pedestrian areas were not only covered but also air-conditioned, heated in winter and cooled in summer, thus achieving springlike temperatures all year round. Because the roofing-over and air-conditioning of pedestrian areas created additional expense, an attempt was made to reduce the size of these pedestrian spaces, without, however, losing spaciousness and airiness. Buildings were moved closer together and were developed vertically, with two main shopping levels and a partial shopping level in the basement. In order to achieve equally strong foot traffic on the two main levels, the surrounding car storage area was graded in such fashion that some of the parking lots, by sloping upward, could give direct access to the upper level while others, by sloping downward, could lead directly onto the lower level. Within the main pedestrian court, a centrally located public escalator facilitates exchange between the two levels. The *Architectural Forum* in March, 1953, referred to Southdale as a market square "reflecting a teamwork of a store-owning family whose third generation is already planning for the fifth; an economic consultant equally determined to put the center beyond the reach of competition; and an architect eager to go far beyond what any previous center has attempted and really tackle the problem of preventing community blight. . . . [It] is a beautiful example of how to plan a lot of fun into a serious, functional circulation scheme. . . . For tangible climate and intangible atmosphere, the like . . . has never before been seen in a northern city."

In this connection, I found it interesting recently, while reading Ebenezer Howard's *Garden Cities of To-morrow,* to see that he proposed and foresaw not only the regional shopping center but its latest version, the shopping center with completely enclosed pedestrian areas. As one of the features of the new garden city he planned a ring-shaped "Crystal Palace" to serve as a "shopping center" (he uses this very term). He writes, "Here manufactured goods are exposed for sale, and here most of that class of shopping which requires the joy of deliberation and selection is done. The space enclosed by the Crystal Palace is, however, a good deal larger than is required for these purposes, and a considerable part of it is used as a Winter Garden—the whole forming a permanent exhibition of a most attractive character." In describing the operation of the center (the Crystal Palace, to which he also refers sometimes as a grand arcade), he introduces suggestions concerning leasing of the space, which contain such well-known present-day terms as exclusivity for certain tenants; he also warns against selling monopolies.

Winrock Center, near Albuquerque, New Mexico, opened in 1961. Its pedestrian areas are neither open to the sky (as in Northland and Eastland) nor completely enclosed and air-conditioned (as in Southdale). Climatic conditions in Albuquerque, though generally favorable, called for protection from direct rays of the sun. The main pedestrian shopping area is covered at a two-story height. The space between the one-story store buildings and the roof of the pedestrian area contains an open grillwork, permitting free air circulation but preventing the infiltration of sunrays. A second new feature of Winrock Center is the integration of a hotel into the building cluster. The hotel restaurant and lobby are directly accessible from the pedestrian shopping area, and the outlying parking lots are utilized by both the stores and the hotel.

Randhurst Center, in Mount Prospect, near Chicago, "the largest shopping center under one roof," was opened in 1962. It contains three department stores, which jointly own and operate the shopping center. Its building group is arranged with extreme compactness, and though the square footage of rentable area is equal to that of Northland, the central cluster, consisting of buildings and pedestrian areas, covers only approximately half of the land area required in Northland. Randhurst exemplifies the "introvert" type of shopping center. It has abandoned those last vestiges of the former highway store: entrances and show windows of individual stores directed toward the parking area. (The department stores form the only exceptions in this re-

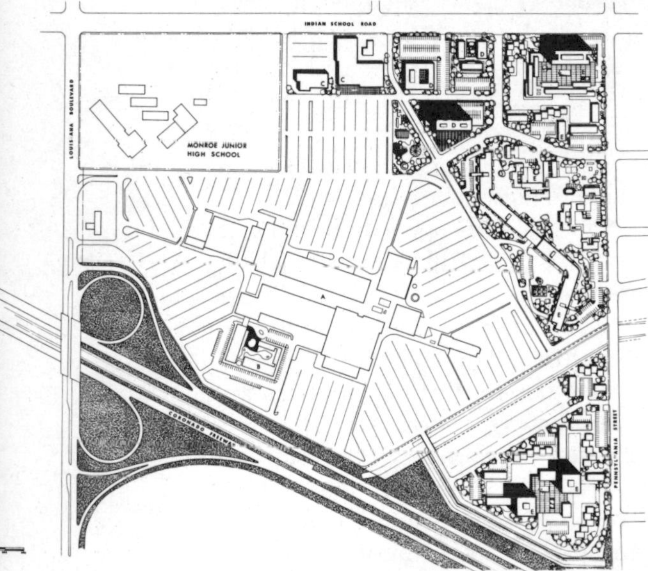

ABOVE A view of the gardens of the hotel in Winrock Center. The hotel, in this case, is an integral part of the shopping center.

LEFT Master plan for Winrock Center, near Albuquerque, New Mexico, and its surrounding area. The central area: the shopping center plus hotel, surrounded by parking areas and circulatory roads. The fringes: development by hotels, apartment buildings, office buildings, etc. Left upper corner: an existing school.

BELOW A view of the main pedestrian area of Winrock Center.

ABOVE The central pedestrian court, covered by a large dome, of Randhurst Shopping Center near Chicago, Illinois.

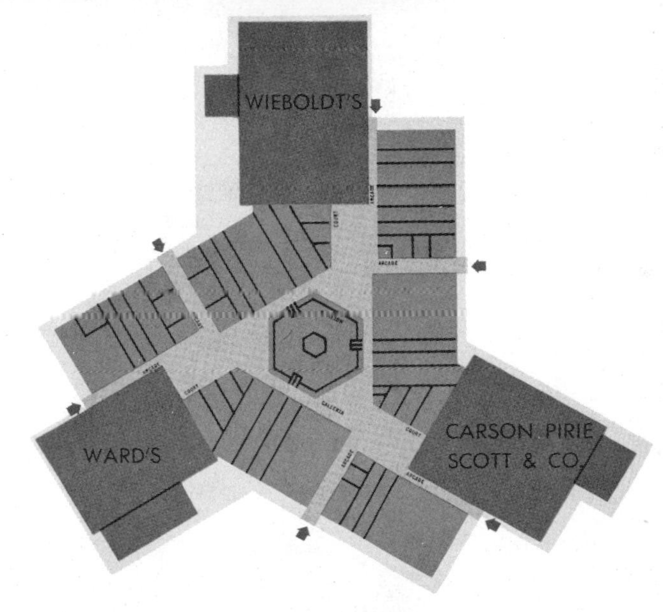

RIGHT Plan of Randhurst Shopping Center near Chicago, Illinois.

BELOW Interior view of the main pedestrian area (Cherry Court) of the Cherry Hill Shopping Center in Camden, New Jersey, near Philadalphia.

spect.) Otherwise Randhurst represents one large ring of buildings surrounding a hexagonal, domed court, which is entered through three pedestrian arcades from the parking area.

These five centers with which I am personally familiar exemplify the characteristics of the hundreds of other regional centers either existing or in construction. Among those, I should like to mention Old Orchard, near Chicago (Loebl, Schlossman & Bennett, architects) for its especially beautiful treatment of landscaping and particularly for its tree-shaded parking area; Exchange Park in Dallas, Texas (Lane Gamble & Associates, J. N. MacCammon & Associates, associated architects) because it combines large office buildings and hotels with the shopping complex; Cherry Hill in Camden, New Jersey (Victor Gruen Associates, architects) for the tropical park atmosphere of its main court; Fashion Square, near Santa Ana, California (Pereira & Luckman, architects) for its elegance; and a small center, The Boardwalk, in Tiburon, California (John Lord King, architect) for the excellence of its architecture. There are other excellent examples, too numerous to mention here, which I have gone into in some detail in an earlier book devoted specifically to the shopping center.*

The search for weapons for the counterattack against urban sprawl and anti-city chaos is continuing on a growing scale and with increasing sophistication—a search, one may hope, that will have two significant results:

A coalescing effect on the thinned-out, scatterized metropolitan regions through the establishment of powerful and versatile regional centers, which may ultimately form the cores of clearly defined satellite towns or cities.

Important gains, as far as experience and know-how are concerned, in the forging of new planning and architectural tools, which, if properly applied, could be effective in the revitalization of the heart of our cities.

* Victor Gruen and Larry Smith, *Shopping Towns USA,* Reinhold Publishing Corporation, New York, 1960.

15 Separate and Meld*

* *Meld* . . . [*Blend of* melt *and* weld]: MERGE

—*Webster's Third New International Dictionary,* 1961

I HAVE ATTEMPTED earlier to demonstrate that the sins of omission (our failure to separate mechanical, utilitarian functions from human functions) have forced us automatically to take defensive measures that I call the sins of commission: that in the long run these are ineffective as remedies, consisting as they do of misguided attempts to separate human functions from each other and thus compartmentalize them. I have stated my belief that the ultimate effect of the twin sins of omission and of commission is the destruction of urban civilization in general, and especially of the heart of our cities. I will now set out to show that in those cases where the sins of omission are *avoided*—where effective, constructive efforts are made to separate utilitarian, mechanical functions from purely human ones—new opportunities for the melding of human functions of all types are created, and that by making use of those opportunities a new and better urban order, a better environment and a richer human experience can be gained.

I would like to make my case on the basis of experiences in regional shopping centers, because they do represent significant steps in the attempt to avoid the sins of omission and also because they reflect in many ways, on a small scale, the problems and potentialities inherent in the hearts of our cities.

It is significant, for example, that the arguments raised in the early days of shopping center development by developers, prospective tenants and the population in surrounding areas were very similar to those that today only too often stymie all efforts to improve patterns in the core areas of cities. When we designed our first large regional shopping center, Northland, we were extremely fortunate in having as clients people of vision and foresight —quite especially Oscar Webber, who then was president of the J. L. Hudson Company. Due to this fortunate circumstance, the architects and developers were able to overcome the opposition that was strongly voiced by lending institutions, prospective tenants, the maintenance people and surrounding property owners against the principal planning features as well as against some of the planning and architectural concepts that concerned environmental quality.

A number of tenants seriously doubted that any business could be conducted if cars were not permitted to drive to their front doors and park right there or nearby. Nearly all the tenants were quite dubious about the idea of including in the shopping center concept any features or functions which were not directly related to the selling of merchandise. They were unhappy with the idea of creating spacious pedestrian areas, as they felt that shoppers would not be exposed directly enough to their show windows. They were appalled by the concept of introducing beauty and enjoyment into the environment, fearing that trees and sculpture would block the view of their signs and show windows, and that flower beds, trees and rest benches would distract their customers from the one activity they were supposed to engage in: namely, buying as much merchandise as possible. There was, for example, the prospective tenant for a luncheon pavilion, located in the midst of a large landscaped pedestrian area, who felt absolutely certain he would go bankrupt after two weeks of operation because his enterprise would be some distance away from the car-parking area. We were only partly successful in persuading tenants to concentrate their display efforts along the pedestrian area frontage and to bear in mind, when organizing their merchandise, that since most people would enter not from the parking-lot side but from the pedestrian area, the so-called pickup items, usually located near the main entrance, should be arranged to take advantage of that fact. There were bitter fights about the advisability of having all service facilities, including loading and unloading, underground, and the fear was expressed that this would cause additional operating costs. There was great opposition to sign controls, which had the aim of avoiding blatant commercialism and preventing garish signs and storefronts from exploding the unifying architectural framework. There was a tough battle against the experts in the maintenance and cleaning profession. They wanted the shopping center designed exclusively with an eye toward achieving the lowest cleaning and operating costs. These proponents of "janitorial architecture" vehemently opposed flower beds because they were convinced that all flowers would be stolen on the first day. They were against fountains, assuring us that children would fall into them daily. They opposed spacious pedestrian areas, sidewalk cafés, and outdoor eating places because of the trash problem that would be created. They fought valiantly against every piece of sculpture, pointing out the difficulty of keeping it clean. Bright, clear colors on buildings were opposed because they would show dirt, and the recommendation was made to paint everything a grayish green, the most practical color because it looked dirty from the beginning and would not need much care. There were bitter arguments against the introduction of trees and planting wells in the parking areas because they would complicate snow removal and also because tree roots might break the pavement.

Financing institutions were extremely wary because of the novelty of the concept, arguing that they could not risk capital entrusted to them for untried experiments. At a public hearing, adjoining property owners opposed the construction of the center, claiming, with some justification, that inasmuch as all commerce in suburbia brought with it a lowering of property values, this very big commercial development might do so on a larger scale.

Within a few weeks after the opening of Northland, its dramatic business success quieted the critics. The insurance companies, which had up to then refused adequate financing, became greatly interested. The tenant of the lunch pavilion beamingly observed the lines that formed all day long in front of his doors and never again mentioned the distance of his enterprise from the parking lot. Merchants who had organized their stores in the sure expectation that most people would enter from the parking lot rearranged their interior schemes and their show-window layouts when they found that 70 per cent of all shoppers entered from the pedestrian area. Those who had been unhappy with the sign restrictions contentedly observed the fact that since nobody was permitted to have bigger or louder signs than theirs, the need for high expenditures for this purpose was eliminated. Loading and unloading over the especially reserved truck route worked without a flaw and saved time and money. Since it was soon demonstrated that sculpture, fountains, flower beds and rest benches attracted people, management actually began to get complaints from those merchants in front of whose stores such features had been omitted. The merchants' association, after observing the crowds which public events drew into the shopping center, got busy arranging more and more elaborate ones. The maintenance people discovered to their great surprise that flowers were not stolen, that trash was not thrown around, but that, on the contrary, the 70,000 persons who visited the center on an average day took possessive pride in the beauty offered to them. No need was found to erect signs similar to those found in neglected downtown environments, such as KEEP YOUR CITY CLEAN or THROW YOUR BALLOT IN THE TRASH CAN or DON'T STEAL THE FLOWERS.

When the surrounding property owners, who had evinced hostility to the project from the beginning, saw that the value of their properties was enhanced by the existence of a shopping center that protected its own surroundings, through the introduction of a vast landscaped buffer strip and through carefully worked-out traffic arrangements that prevented the use of residential streets by visitors to the center, their hostility gave way to friendly approval.

How quickly opposition had melted away was demonstrated a few years later when plans for Eastland Center, also for the J. L. Hudson Company, were developed. When, at the public zoning hearing, one property owner got up to protest against the development, he was yelled down by thousands of irate women who accused him of attempting to rob them of something that would give more pleasure and content to their lives. The client who had been, to say the least, lukewarm to the introduction of sculpture in Northland reminded us most forcefully that the sculpture program must be considered as one of the most important features of Eastland Center. Thus all opposition to a new type of urban environment was swept away in the case of the suburban regional center. What was revolutionary dreaming ten years ago has now become, at least in the majority of cases, accepted planning procedure.

Unfortunately some opposition still can be found when plans based on the same principle are proposed for the revitalization of a city core: from merchants who are afraid of losing direct contact with automobile traffic, garage owners who tremble for fear their business might suffer if car storage areas are moved to the fringe of the core, and all the "practical" people who claim that such improvements are newfangled and can't be financed.

I set out to prove that in separating mechanical, utilitarian functions from the human ones, new opportunities for an intimate melding of human functions of different types were created. As planning and development concepts of regional shopping centers matured, they began to include an ever-growing number of varying activities, and to date they have fallen short in only one respect. That is the failure to include residences. Otherwise, they have furnished proof that the separation and compartmentalization of various *human* activities is unnecessary if utilitarian functions are separated; moreover, they are proof that the melding results in significant economic and human advantages. It has been demonstrated that professional and general offices, civic facilities like post offices, public libraries, police stations, educational institutions, legitimate theaters and movie houses, hotels, bars, restaurants and of course stores of all types can peacefully coexist once the prerequisites of urban order have been created.

But—more important, and beyond all this—an unexpected phenomenon has been observed. The participation of the inhabitants of the region in the newly created environment has proved to be of an intensity and expressed itself in forms which even the most optimistic of us did not quite foresee. I remember the surprised faces of my clients when we drove out to a shopping center on a Sunday and found the parking area full. The courts and malls, the lanes and promenades were filled with milling crowds dressed in their Sunday best, engaging in an activity that was believed to be long forgotten: family groups strolling leisurely, their youngsters in go-carts and dogs on the leash; relaxed and admiring the flowers and trees, sculptures and murals, fountains and ponds, and, incidentally, using the opportunity for window-shopping. To the joy of the merchants, this last resulted in strong business activity on the following weekdays.

The public auditorium and the meeting rooms, the promotion of which had cost management a lot of headaches, were within weeks booked up for a whole year by civic clubs, church meetings, lectures, chamber music concerts, amateur theatrical performances, folk dancing groups, and so on. Garden clubs asked for permission to hold their flower shows within the landscaped areas. Camera clubs arranged photo competitions and exhibits. Groups of artists arranged for art exhibits. National minority groups arranged for special musical and folk dancing evenings. The United States Army displayed its newest planes; home builders erected model houses for display on the huge terrace in front of the department store.

The quiet, protected pedestrian areas proved to be the fulfillment of pent-up demands and desires for which no opportunity had previously existed in the suburban environment. The shopping center became the place where friends met, where new friendships were started, where gatherings of all sorts were held, where ladies met for luncheons and families met for dinner. Inactive civic, cultural and art organizations became active, and many new ones were started because they finally had a place in which to meet. The theater in Northland, at least during the summer months, is the only one in all of Detroit which shows legitimate plays, and the vast public areas are the ideal setting for popular concerts, Fourth of July celebrations, and political gatherings around election time.

Thus it can be safely stated that in those regional shopping centers where the separation of utilitarian functions from human activities has been forthrightly carried out, where the sins of omission have been avoided, integration of manifold human activities has been made possible; and wherever the provision of these prerequisites of order was accompanied by the achievement of high environmental quality, decisive successes, economic and human, have resulted.

The success has been much less marked where compromises precluding the complete separation of utilitarian from human functions have crept in. This holds true for those centers in which unloading facilities were not completely separated (where loading and unloading are allowed over the sidewalk from the parking areas), or where insufficient care was taken to remove from sight, sound or smell utilitarian facilities like television antennas, air-conditioning or heating equipment, ventilation ducts, piping, cables, etc. All such compromises have a detrimental effect on the number of visitors and a blighting effect on the surroundings. Another type of compromise that has disadvantageous effects is interference with compactness. Even now there are certain tenant groups who wish to be located as close as possible to the surrounding highways, and outside the building core. They are the proponents of scatterization, the enemies of compactness, and therefore potentially destructive elements for the successful regional shopping center. The desire of banks with drive-in facilities, or of drive-in restaurants, office building promoters and others, to settle in locations along the highway results in a double threat to the health of the central core area. The customers and other visitors to these facilities do not become core participants. The person driving to the bank counter or to the drive-in restaurant will not leave the car and therefore never will get into direct contact with the activities of the center. The second part of the threat is just as serious. Not only do these detached facilities occupy space that would be better used for a landscaped buffer area, but each one needs separate circulation and car-storage areas, and this separate traffic interferes with the over-all main circulation pattern. This type of scatterization within a regional shopping center is anti-urban in character and leads as a final result to flight and blight.

The tendencies described above, which not all regional shopping centers have been successful in fighting off, lead to a conclusion, and a very important one, with regard to the hearts of our cities. There can be no compromise with regard to the completeness of the separation between utilitarian and human functions, and there can be no compromise with the principles of compactness, variety and diversity, if a successful urban environmental element is to be created. A schizophrenic attitude in this respect can be observed with great regularity, not only in new environmental elements in the suburbs but in redevelopment planning and in revitalization plans for core areas of cities. I felt forced to point this out when I was invited to discuss the master plan for Washington, D.C., which was drawn up in 1962. I said then:

> The [Washington] planning report stresses in words the need for great concentration and for open land. But instead of forthrightly concluding that this aim can only be secured on the basis of complete separation of all utilitarian from all human actions, it sidesteps the issue. It speaks of the creation of "*relatively*" compact suburban communities. It advocates "great reliance on mass transportation," but a few pages later, it states that "more and more" people rely on individual forms of transportation, and that there will be a "continuous tendency" toward dispersal. A paragraph further on, it reverses itself, stating that people will be living at close quarters. It propounds the idea of creating new compact towns, but it carefully specifies that their density should only be "somewhat higher" than is typical of today's suburban development. In the design of the new towns, it relies on the old recipe of compartmentalization by dividing each community into hermetically closed-off office centers, shopping centers, community centers and residential areas with varying particular densities and, therefore, varying economic status. It supports a doctrine of defined urban clusters, separated from each other by open countryside, but it ranges these clusters along super new highways, with only a "token" public transportation in the central strip, in such manner that one town flows into the other.
>
> The report professes that only public transportation can fully serve the "metrocenter," but proposes that an elaborate network of new superhighways leading from the corridor towns into the heart of the city should be constructed. The report goes so far as to state that "although the transit system will be built to the highest possible standards, most automobile users will be converted to the public system only after congestion on the highways reaches intolerable levels." From this statement it would then follow that if a new highway network were not built at all, then the rapid transit system would have a chance to exist economically much earlier!
>
> By projection of new radial highways which are laid out in such a manner as to bring a good portion of the projected three million new inhabitants to the heart of the city in their automobiles, it automatically creates the necessity for more roads, more garages, more gas stations within the core. Thus, it is killing from the outset any chance of reshaping "metrocenter" into a truly urban, compact organism.

> Now, I was told that the document for Washington was only to be regarded as the general master plan. Knowing as a practical planner that during the execution of a plan some compromises will have to be made at least temporarily, it seems to be doubly important that such an over-all master plan reflect forthright uncompromising thinking, if it is to yield any worthwhile results. It will serve as a basis for more detailed planning only when it represents an underpinning of truly urban thought.

I have mentioned before that the creation of trouble-free, safe, and well-designed public spaces opens up a chance to reintroduce visual delight into the urban environment in the form of flowers, trees, fountains, ponds, sculpture, murals and mosaics. It has also offered the same opportunities to music and the performing arts. The reason is simply that these well-protected, safe and well-designed spaces, free of traffic and its noises and smells, uncluttered by any expressions of mechanical service, re-establish in the individual the ability and desire to contemplate, to view, to listen and observe. Having been put back on his own two feet, without interference and feedback from the technological apparatus, man is enabled to amble along, observing as he passes, stopping if something catches his attention, and taking in

Safe and well-designed public spaces open up the opportunity to reintroduce the arts into the urban environment. This picture shows a symphony concert being held in the pedestrian court of the Mondawmin shopping center near Baltimore, Maryland.

impressions fully. We are not yet completely equipped, especially in the fields of sculpture and painting, to take full advantage of the phenomenon which a broad public interest in the viewing of art presents. Our artists have been cut off so long from participating creatively in the shaping of the urban environment that they will slowly have to get used to this new opportunity. But I believe it can be safely stated that a renaissance of artistic expression could be achieved if new environments, conducive to contemplation in sufficient number and of high quality, set the stage for it.

We have also observed that the new environmental scenery offers an opportunity to battle successfully one of the worst scourges of both suburban and urban visual experience: garishness in advertising and billboards. In the hearts of our cities and along highways, the misbegotten products of commercialism overpower nearly every other visual impression—the forest of signs (for the most part poorly conceived) that sprout from every lamppost and power mast; the billboards that mar or completely hide landscape (where it still exists) along highways; the screaming store signs, announcements of sales, movies, sports events which cover like a rash the façades and roofs of buildings, fences, subway stations, railroad terminals, etc., outyell and outweigh whatever architects may have dreamed up or nature has created.

Sign regulations and certain basic rules about the treatment of storefronts, together with a framework strongly expressed architecturally, have created in many regional shopping centers a sense of visual order and discipline.

A sharp line, however, has to be drawn between the desire to create visual order and authoritarian discipline resulting in sameness. Those few regional shopping centers in which an attempt was made to prescribe a uniform treatment of all store exteriors have, in my opinion, acted misguidedly. In these cases it was not fully understood that the planner of the man-made environment should provide only the framework within which individual expression can flourish. Otherwise the effect can be either deadly sameness and dullness or a revolt against the rules, which usually takes place sooner or later.

A word must also be said about the planning and design of landscaping for the pedestrian areas of the regional center which are basically urban squares and streets. The treatment must obviously be very different from that of either a private garden or a public park. The slogan "Grass on Main Street," which has been so widely broadcast, betrays a defeatist attitude suggesting the injection of suburban values into an essentially urban environment. There should be more pavement than planting, and the pavement, moreover, should vary in character in a way that can be sensed by the eye and by the foot. The right elements for this kind of urban landscaping, it appears to me, are tree wells, small islands of flower beds, and plants in movable containers that can be put aside in case more space is needed for large public events.

I have dwelt at some length on the theme of the search for new environmental forms in suburbia and the effects this search has brought about, because I firmly believe that these new suburban clusterizations represent experimental workshops where we can learn more about how to achieve the transfiguration of the hearts of our cities. But before we can attempt to successfully translate these suburban experiments into the urban vernacular, we will have to discuss the complex problem of transportation required to give accessibility to the urban core and to enable us to get around within it.

16 The Taming of the Motorcar

People will use automobiles as long as nothing better is available.

—Stanley Berge, *Atlantic*, May, 1960

Though I have often been accused of being an enemy of the automobile, and have even been violently attacked on that score, I should like to take this occasion to state categorically that I have nothing but admiration for the automobile itself as an ingeniously conceived means of individualized transportation. I am convinced, however, that our present attitude toward it is fundamentally wrong. In fact, I believe that if we were to change this attitude we would create better living conditions for people and for automobiles, too. We must adopt a sensible pattern of behavior toward the automotive population.

The urbanized areas of the United States are now inhabited by about 125,000,000 members of the human race, and an automotive population about 82,000,000 hoods strong. Thus, the automotive population is still a minority group, although steadily growing in relative strength. But the automobiles have certain race characteristics that actually put them in the driver's seat. Hood per head they are physically stronger, bigger, and enjoy the advantage of being free of psychological and nervous problems. The automobile population has a higher birth rate than the human one. *The New York Times* of July 29, 1963, states:

> There will be about 4,167,000 human births this year. In car production the 1963 model year that is just about ending will set a record of more than 7,340,000 cars. The motor vehicle population 20 years from now is forecast at 115,000,000 hoods and the human population at 267,000,000 heads. Road building has a hard time catching up with automobile population growth. In 1941 there were 11.4 cars for every mile of road and street. Today the figure is 22 cars for every mile.

We have already arrived at a point where the human majority has been cowed into submission; not only is it in steady retreat but—as we have demonstrated before—in routlike flight from the city. It appears that the internal combustion engines, in their mass assault, have led to the external combustion of the city.

The degree of submission varies as far as individual members of the human race are concerned. There is a lunatic fringe, the members of which are completely unsettled. These autorotics feel deep affection, bordering on love, for their cars, spoiling their beloved ones in every way possible, spending their free hours in washing and polishing them, giving them "workouts" by taking needless drives, buying them trinkets in the form of useless so-called accessories, and taking them to beauty parlors, cosmeticians and doctors. They will happily go into debt for them, willing to ruin their own careers. Autorotics feel about their cars the way other men feel about their mistresses or highly decorative wives; to parade them builds up their egos and their masculine pride.

Less affected than this lunatic fringe are those to whom an automobile represents a status symbol, a highly visible financial statement supporting its owner's credit rating.

But even apart from these special cases, the majority of the human population group seem to be utterly confused concerning the relationship between the human race and the automotive race, willingly acknowledging the supremacy of the automotive being, and agreeable to adjusting themselves, their cities and their lives to its demands.

Through the ages, man has been faced with problems caused by roaming members of other than human hordes. He had to deal, for example, with the problem of tremendous herds of wild beasts, which threatened, in various parts of the world and in various epochs of history, not only the comfort and safety but the very lives of human beings.

Certain techniques were employed in such cases. Ages ago, man built his communities on high stilts, making them inaccessible to ferocious beasts, which were, so to speak, kept on a lower operating level (an application of the principle of vertical separation). Even today, in some of the so-called primitive areas of the world, communities can be found in which this kind of separation still exists. In other parts of the globe, and at other times, stockades, walls and enclosures of all types have been erected to deflect dangerous interferences. Thus was introduced the method of horizontal separation.

In the early days of his development, man realized that certain members of the animal kingdom could be made useful to him. The horse, the cow, the dog and many birds were domesticated, and out of a dangerous, disturbing animal population were created some of the most useful helpers of human development, serving as transportation for people and goods and as suppliers of food.

Because automotive beings are man-made creations and not supplied by nature, it seems we have felt hesitant to apply similar methods. And yet if two types of creature which constantly interfere with each other are to find a pattern of coexistence, something obviously has to give. In respect to this, there are today two schools of thought. The more powerful and prevailing one is that the problem of coexistence should be solved by taming and domesticating man. It is felt that by training the members of the human population, by teaching people certain tricks, like walking at "green" and stopping at "red," by putting them behind fences or chains along curbs, their spirit of individuality and independence can be broken so that they will be willing to submit to the regime of the automotive beings.

I have recently read the report of an International Conference of Traffic Engineers held in Salzburg, Austria, in August and September, 1962; in this convention of human animal trainers, a number of highly interesting methods for the taming and training of people were discussed and recommended. It was suggested, for example, that people who want to cross the roaming grounds of automobiles should wait behind turnstiles and queue up, and should then be allowed, only in small groups, to trickle across. Others went further, and favored complete elimination of sidewalks—which, they presumably hoped, would lead to the elimination of people.

There was quite general agreement that structures utilized by members of the human race would have to be cut down to a minimum in order to create sufficient lebensraum for members of the automotive race. Wherever and whenever traffic experts meet, they take it upon themselves to devise plans for the redesigning of the human environment. They have, in fact, to an astounding degree, become the dictators in all questions concerned with city planning.

To realize the abnormality of this situation, one need only try to visualize for a moment a convention of plumbers dictating to architects and the entire construction industry how buildings should be designed, inside and out, in order to a) increase the employment opportunities in the plumbing fixtures industry, and b) facilitate their installations.

They would then dictate that every room in every building must have a bathtub, water closet and three washstands—otherwise unemployment in the appliance industry might result—and that plumbing pipes of all types must no longer be forced into positions where they are hidden in walls and ceilings, but should be permitted to run any odd way, diagonally, vertically or horizontally, through living rooms or offices. This demand would be rationalized as the facilitation of water and sewage traffic, as demanded by our era of technology. Every protest against these measures would then be ridiculed as reactionary—or, worse, as "idealistic"—and an attempt to turn the wheels of history backward.

It is not hard to recognize, from this fictitious plumbing-convention story, that the traffic planners really do not behave too differently. They, too, demand that we accept as gospel the proposition that more and more automobiles should be manufactured, as otherwise the automotive appliance industry might be underemployed, and they most definitely insist that their plumbing pipes crisscross the public living rooms and working rooms of our cities. Anybody who opposes their views is characterized as either "an ivory tower planner," "a reactionary out of step with the miracles of technology," or an outright imbecile.

I am perfectly willing to risk the attacks of the traffic planners when I insist that the solution to coexistence of the human and automotive populations *does not lie in the taming and training of people, but in the taming of the motorcar*. I am not in favor of the destruction of automobiles, not even necessarily of the diminution of the automotive population; but I am most definitely in favor of domesticating it, and making it useful to the human race, just as we did with the horse and the cow and with various types of poultry. I further submit that in doing so we will enable these machines to develop to the fullest their excellent inherent characteristics of mobility. Thus even the autorotics should agree with me, because if the automotive beings, as they seem to believe, have emotions, they will most certainly be happier if they do not have to crawl along at a slow pace, or stand around for hours in a traffic jam, but can employ their abilities to the highest degree. (In this connection it is significant that the magazine *Motor Sport*, commenting editorially on my ideas concerning the taming of the automobile, wrote that they agreed with them because, as lovers of the automobile, they felt that the measures I proposed would make driving a car more pleasurable.)

I believe that the automobile industry does an injustice to its own product by underestimating its importance. The industry should be reminded of the fact that along with growth in size and growth in importance comes growth in responsibility. The childhood years of the motorcar are most certainly over. It is no longer a mechanical toy or the subject of an exercise in gentlemanly sport or even a pleasure vehicle (though some people, influenced by the advertising of the car industry, still believe so). The fact is that the automobile has become a means of utilitarian mass transportation. Having grown into this role, it must be approached with the same seriousness and concern that are devoted to all other important and significant utilitarian, mechanical functions. It is no longer less important than the railroads or the sewerage and utility systems. And if we want to keep the automobile operating as an efficient and useful instrument of mass transportation, then in the interest of the automobile industry itself, ways must be found to accomplish this without bringing about the destruction of our cities and their inhabitants.

I have been personally attacked as the enemy of the automobile and the automobile industry. What utter nonsense! Could one say that somebody is an enemy of sanitation because he is in favor of installing an efficient underground sewerage system to replace one that lets the waste products flood the streets? Could one say that somebody who is against the construction of a jet landing strip on Main Street is an enemy of aviation? The contrary is obviously the case. The future of the automobile industry depends on the development of patterns and methods by which its product, ingeniously invented as a tool for individual mobility, will be prevented from becoming a tool of collective immobility and a destroyer of urban and human values.

How, then, can the taming of the motorcar, the domestication of the automotive population, be accomplished? The lessons learned from the historic pattern dealing with protection from wild animals and the final domestication of some of them will be highly valuable. Also significant might be a consideration of the steps taken by cities for effective defense against threats posed by human enemies.

Our forefathers have presented us with a number of approaches to the solution of our problems. We have already talked about the human communities whose dwellings were built on stilts in terms of vertical separation, and of those other human communities, which protected themselves from wild beasts by building stockades, fences and walls around human activity areas, as examples of horizontal separation. We also know that people who domesticated animals reserved for them special grazing grounds, and that only in the most primitive peasant huts was livestock allowed in man's living room.

In the defense against hordes of human enemies, cities built complex defense systems consisting of series of concentric rings of fortified walls, of which the outermost were supposed to slow down the mobility of the enemy troops, with closer-in lines of defense rings acting as a further brake, or even halting the enemy if possible, while the innermost ring was supposed to be strong enough to definitely stop it.

The city of Vienna, which successfully withstood two sieges of the Turks who had swept over all of Eastern Europe, was able to do so because of a defense system consisting of such concentric defense rings. The strongest and best armed of these immediately surrounded the city proper; outside this wall, as I mentioned in Chapter II, was a deep, water-filled ditch, and beyond that an open area, the so-called Glacis, kept free of all buildings so that one could shoot comfortably from the wall at the enemy troops. The second system, the so-called Linienwall, surrounded outer communities in a wider ring. It was constructed in accordance with similar principles. And then there was a ring of outlying fortifications, which had the function of a holding operation, and of slowing down the enemy.

How a similar system of concentric defense lines could be employed to repel the invasion of mechanical hordes into those areas where they create havoc was first indicated by a plan which our office developed for the revitalization of the city center of Fort Worth, Texas. The defense system here also consists of concentric rings—an outer loop, an intermediate loop, and an inner loop. Each of the loops is a major limited-access highway, along which are arranged storage facilities for automobiles. The outermost of these defense rings would hold some of the onrushing motorcars, which would be stored in fringe parking lots or garages, while their drivers and passengers would then continue the trip into the center by rapid public transportation. Other motorists coming from the metropolitan region would follow this procedure along the intermediate defense lines, and only the most determined ones would infiltrate to the strongest fortification, the inner loop. This inner loop would be so designed that its fortifications would be impenetrable. In the case of Fort Worth, it was designed as one multilaned, in some places multilevel, freeway-like road, directly and intimately connected with large, multistory parking garages with a total of 60,000 parking spaces. The fortification system would be strengthened by physical and legal arrangements which would make any further penetration by privately owned motorcars impossible.

In order to improve traffic—that is, the movement of people and goods—three measures were recommended as part of the plan:

In an era when defense of the city against common enemies was essential, Vincenzo Scamozzi designed an ideal city. His design was carried out in slightly changed fashion in Palma Nova, Italy. For a modern version, see page 216 top photograph.

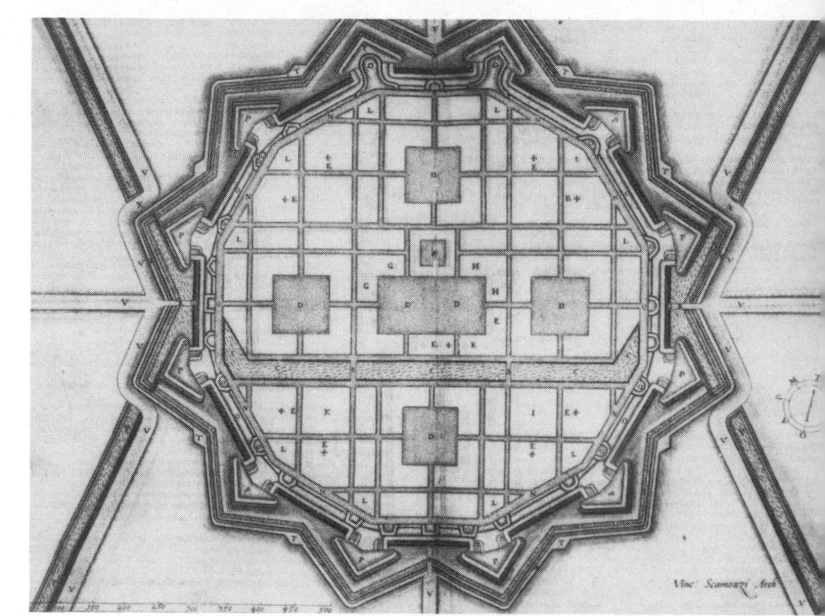

Am Tabor
Bahnhof
Wirthshäuser
Wurstelprater
Kaisergarten
Prater
Stern
Panorama
Circus
Chaussee
Prater Allee
Rondo
Wienerwasser
Erdberger Linie
Währinger Linie
Währing
Auf der Sichenals
Brändl Bad
Herrnalser Linie
Exercier Platz
Herrnals
Lerchenfeld
Lerchenfelder Kirchhof
Mariahilfer Kirchhof
Mariahilfer Linie
Fünfhaus
Neustädter Canal
Belvedere Linie
Eisenbahn
Bahnhöfe
Favoriten Linie
Wasserstation
Kirchhof
A
B
C
D
E
F
G
H
N

1. A marked increase in the quality, quantity, speed, and convenience of public transportation, and low fare structure.
2. A system of underground roads for the handling of service traffic within the heart area of the city. These underground roads would connect with loading and unloading facilities, storage facilities, etc., in the basements of all buildings.
3. An accessory pedestrian transportation system within the human activity area of the core, consisting of moving sidewalks within the garages, and of small slow-moving, electrically driven vehicles which would circulate in the pedestrian area, transporting people during inclement weather, and available for use at all times by those who are unable or not inclined to negotiate the short walking distances (about 2½ minutes from garages and public transportation terminals) within the pedestrian area.

Thus, in the case of the plan for the revitalization of the city of Fort Worth, the method of horizontal separation was employed with regard to automotive traffic, and that of vertical separation with regard to service traffic within the core areas and storage of automobiles in multilevel structures. Even the concept of a building-free green zone (which we found in the arrangement of the Glacis) was utilized. Each of the defense lines (the loop roads) was conceived as being located in a landscaped green belt to establish a buffer for protection from noises and smells, to act as a separator, and also to provide opportunity for sports and recreational activities. Similar green-belt arrangements were proposed along the main arterial roads, to shield urban developments, and suburban developments between them, from technological nuisances, as well as to encourage a pattern of defined and organic urban clusterization.

The plan for the heart area (the core) of Fort Worth was an attempt to take full advantage of the "bonus" potential which the elimination of surface

---

LEFT TOP Air photo of the Pentagon in Washington, D. C. Though at first glance highly reminiscent of the ideal city designed by architect Vincenzo Scamozzi, it is essentially different. It is not a city but an office building for 25,000 employees. It is not surrounded by countryside but by huge parking lots and freeways.

LEFT BOTTOM Plan of Vienna showing the inner defense ring around the inner city (dark gray); the so-called *glacis,* a permanent open area between the city and its satellite cities; second defense ring (zigzag line) around the satellite cities. Around the outside of the outer defense ring are some of the green areas which were protected and still exist.

REVITALIZATION PROJECT FOR CORE OF FORT WORTH, TEXAS

LEFT TOP Aerial view demonstrating how the city core of Fort Worth, Texas, would look if the revitalization plan were carried out.

LEFT BOTTOM An aerial view of one section of the envisioned revitalized downtown core of Fort Worth, Texas. Some of the buildings depicted exist, some are projected. The uniform grid pattern of streets of equal width has been enlivened by the introduction of plazas, the narrowing of some streets, the construction of new buildings, the covering of some streets, and by the introduction of various exhibit and selling facilities in the center of streets and plazas.

RIGHT Visualization of the change in character an existing downtown street in Fort Worth, Texas, would undergo. Bridge in the foreground connects one of the multi-story fringe garages with an existing hotel. Street is made more convenient and interesting through introduction of landscaping, tree wells, flower beds, a variety of pavements—changes in width and character.

---

movement by mechanized vehicles offered. An opportunity for new freedom in the organization and size of public spaces became evident and was utilized. No longer was it mandatory that all public streets and roads be of a minimum width; no longer was it necessary that they be unbroken and straight; no longer was space needed in the heart of the city for garages, automobile salesrooms, parking lots, repair shops, and so on. Thus the original regular gridiron pattern, lacking in landmarks or terminating vistas, could be greatly modified. In some cases, large plazas and squares could be provided where space, until then utilized for automotive accessory facilities, became available. In other cases, streets were narrowed either by adding new structures on one or both sides or by introducing structures within the area formerly used for vehicular purposes. It was proposed that some streets be roofed over so that they might form protected, air-conditioned business and shopping environments; for others, colonnades and arcades were proposed, to furnish protection from sun and rain. Thus a pattern of great variety and interest was created, providing a continuous change of pace and atmosphere to those who would work in the core or visit there. Some public spaces would be large, even monumental; others would be narrow and intimate. Some would be open to the sky; others would be covered and skylighted, similar in character to the regional shopping centers we discussed in "The Search." Many of the public spaces would have landscaping in the form of tree wells and flower beds, fountains and sculpture; areas for public meetings and events would be introduced.

Jane Jacobs, commenting on the Fort Worth plan in the chapter she wrote for the book *The Exploding Metropolis* characterized it in this way:

> The plan by Victor Gruen Associates for Fort Worth . . . has been publicized chiefly for its arrangements to provide enormous perimeter parking garages and convert the downtown into a pedestrian island, but its main purpose is to enliven the streets with variety and detail. . . . To these ends, the excellent Gruen plan includes in its street treatment sidewalk arcades, poster columns, flags, vending kiosks, display stands, outdoor cafés, bandstands, flower beds, and special lighting effects. Street concerts, dances, and exhibits are to be fostered. The whole point is to make the streets more surprising, more compact, more variegated, and busier than before—not less so.

Mrs. Jacobs also pointed out that the plan had influenced the thinking of many planners, but that, unfortunately, in many cases only certain surface features had been implemented, without the spirit being understood.

It is, unhappily, true that, although the principle of separation finds many adherents, some basic misunderstandings exist concerning the very nature of separation. It is rarely understood that even proper separation represents only the fulfillment of the *prerequisites* for the improvement of the appearance of the city, but does not in itself create better appearance.

Let us deal first with those who misunderstand the nature of separation. The main reason for this misunderstanding is the lack of an establishment of hierarchic values. Only if we fully comprehend that the mission of separation is to subordinate serving functions of a utilitarian or mechanical nature to human ones can we proceed properly. Too often this comprehension is lacking. There are those who would put human beings underground, converting them into moles who would hardly ever see daylight, and would generously give the machines the place in the sun. There are others who would reserve the easily accessible ground level for vehicles, demanding that people should climb stairs or ride upward on escalators to a secondary level, where they would move on balconies and breathe the exhaust fumes of cars. There are projects which, in order to create easily separated movement for vehicles, propose to demolish entire city cores and thus make it feasible to build many layers of streets and parking spaces for the use of the automotive population. There are quite a number of utopian projects which, in trying to achieve full separation, sacrifice cohesion and compactness, like those I mentioned in the chapter "The Search." To this category belong also all the well-meaning proposals by traffic engineers, which are directed mostly toward the aim of getting rid of that nuisance, the pedestrian, and which propose separation only in order to make it easier for the herds of motorcars to roam.

One of the greatest shortcomings of most plans that pay lip service to separation is that their designers wear blinders and approach the problem on the basis of automobile traffic only, closing their minds to all other methods of moving people and goods. For example, members of the faculty and student body of the School of Architecture at Columbia University in

Core revitalization project, Dallas, Texas. Longitudinal section through building complex. Buildings of various heights rise from pedestrian platforms. Storage of automobiles is projected in deep wells (the depth equals about 50 stories of an office building). Within these wells there is visualized a continuously moving elevatorlike arrangement. Arriving automobiles would be driven onto a platform and would then move first down and then up again. Owners who wish to pick up their cars might have to wait up to 30 minutes before their automobile appeared on the surface. See also illustrations on pages 232, 233 and 234.

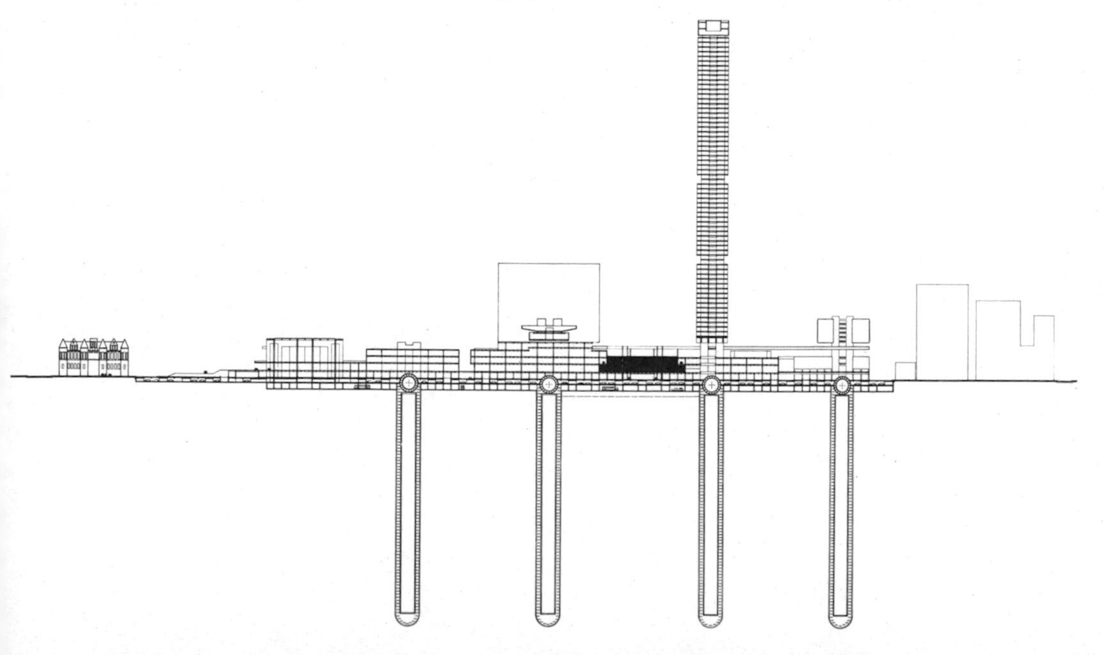

New York, in developing a plan for downtown Dallas, showed themselves unwilling to recognize that public mass transportation might be an important factor in reaching the center of a large metropolis; instead they engaged in mental acrobatics in an effort to achieve the impossible; namely, the storing of large numbers of cars without occupying land for this purpose. They dreamed up deep vertical wells into which automobiles would be sunk by continuously operating platforms attached to endless moving belts. This, of course, gets the automobiles nicely out of the way, but the arrangement makes it necessary for those who would like to re-enter their "instruments of individual mobility" to wait about thirty minutes until their cars, after a vertical ride, appear again on the surface. It would seem that a short waiting time for a subway train would be preferable.

To anybody who observes the performance of functioning, relatively healthy city cores in Europe or America, it must become quite obvious that only in those cities where a major part of the entire transportation load is taken care of by mass transportation can compactness and cohesiveness, those mainstays of urban health, be preserved. I will have more to say about this problem in the next chapter.

And now to those who believe that separation per se, without other efforts, leads to the re-establishment of urban values. One of the most popular issues discussed in cities small and large is the idea of the "pedestrian mall." This matter concerns me deeply because I have been repeatedly referred to in various publications as "the father of the mall." I want to take this opportunity to disclaim paternity once and for all, because I believe that as a halfhearted and partial attempt it cannot solve our problems.

In the minds of most people who advocate the introduction of downtown malls, sometimes only on an experimental basis, the recipe is extremely simple: take the main shopping street of any town or city, place a sign at each end CLOSED TO AUTOMOBILES, and presto, the mall is completed, and the city is saved. The advantages of this quick-change act are:

a) It is cheap (the two signs are a negligible expense).
b) It causes publicity.
c) If it does not work, one can always remove the two signs again, with no damage done.

Nevertheless, considerable damage is done. Initial publicity causes, for a few days, a flocking in of crowds and improved sales for merchants. When the recipe does not work out, as—for reasons to be discussed later—is inevitable, then the resultant disappointment causes criticism, which is not directed toward the stupidity of the idea but toward all attempts to improve the appearance of the city; and progress is set back for years. The pedestrian mall, even if it consists of a little more than the two signs—even if a few plants, a portable merry-go-round for children, and a number of garden dwarfs are added—must necessarily fail because it is "an easy way out," a surface promotional measure lacking any comprehensive planning concept.

The improvement of the appearance of our cities cannot be accomplished merely by subtraction (that is, the subtraction of automobiles from one busy street) but rather by addition (the addition of positive measures to facilitate the moving of people and goods, and to utilize the potential which the existence of these prerequisites offers). By subtracting automobile traffic from one street without adding anything to its environmental qualities, a deadly atmosphere is created similar to what one can observe in any city street around three o'clock in the morning. Traffic eliminated from one street is, perforce, transferred to neighboring streets, and unbearable conditions of congestion are thereby created. Introducing *one* pedestrian mall into a city core area without taking the necessary steps to improve circulation and provide automobile storage space, only serves to multiply the troubles instead of eliminating them. If a point of attraction is created for the sake of the crowds who for a few days will flock there, and improved accessibility to this new attraction area is not offered simultaneously, those who have been attracted by the mere novelty will be thoroughly disenchanted and will probably never return. Thus in the wake of an abandoned mall experiment comes an avoidance of the downtown area as a whole, usually greater than before the experiment started.

An interesting case of misunderstood separation is one proposed by the highly imaginative architect Louis Kahn. In schematic fashion, he has thought out ideas for new city cores, which, interestingly enough, lean heavily on the example of the fortified medieval city that I have already referred to. But Mr. Kahn gets swept off his feet by romanticism, and proposes the construction of circular, towerlike garages which, like medieval watchtowers, would surround the city core and become a dramatic architectural expression of modern technology. The sketches look impressive indeed and the towers threatening and forbidding. This, in my opinion, is exactly where the trouble lies. Mr. Kahn believes, generally, that utilitarian functions should be clearly and openly expressed, in order to reflect the spirit of our times. He is in favor of leaving the apparatus of technology—the plumbing lines, ventilating ducts, air-conditioning machinery and water towers—in the most visible positions on every structure, letting them determine the appearance of the structure. He believes that he can thus create a style for the century of technology. Mr. Kahn's schemes, beguiling as they may appear to some of the architectural critics, actually express a lack of appreciation for the hierarchy of values. His aim to push the backstage machinery into the limelight necessarily renders the stage unusable for truly human expres-

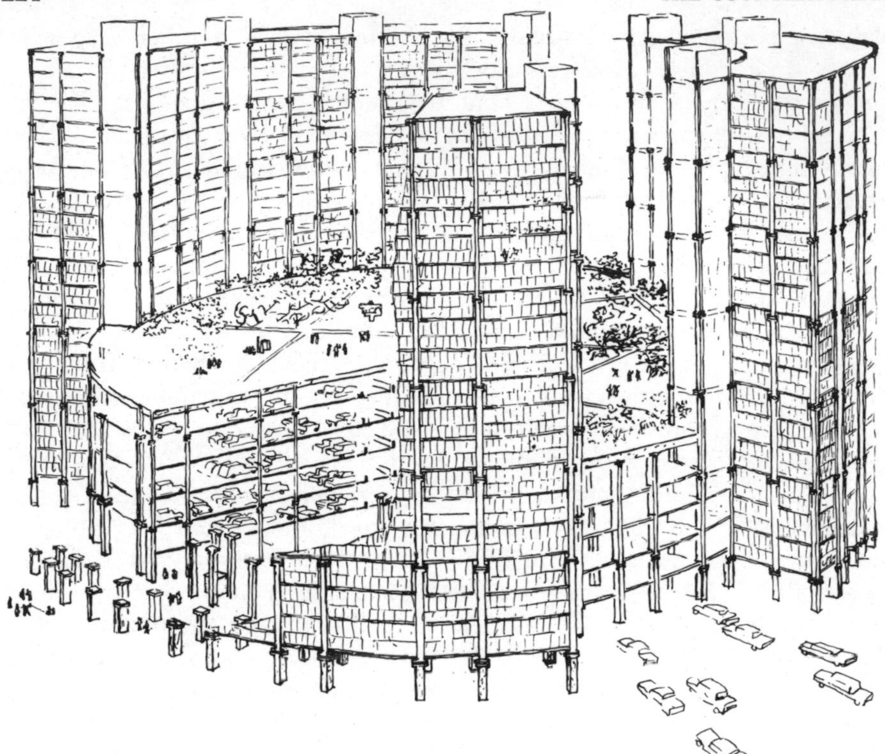

Circular garages resembling medieval fortification towers, projected by architect Louis I. Kahn.

---

sions. I have nothing against romanticism, but I would rather romanticize human thought, human emotions, man's soul and man's heart than garages or air-conditioning equipment.

Illustrations on pages 226, 227, 230 and 231 represent schemes which, following the basic principles established in the plan for Fort Worth and directed toward the revitalization of core areas through taming of the motorcar, have been developed during the last few years. These plans have been so devised that they can be implemented within the framework of existing legislation and particularly of the urban redevelopment laws. All of them therefore had to take into consideration certain limitations and shortcomings inherent in the present legislation. (We will discuss these shortcomings in the chapter "Are We Equipped?") The most glaring of these shortcomings is that—to date, at least—no legal tools have been provided to significantly improve public mass transportation. Thus, in designing these schemes, we had to accept the fact that improvements would first have to be accomplished chiefly by regulating automobile, truck and bus transportation.

In presenting a master plan for the heart of the city of Cincinnati (pages 232, 233 and 234), we went beyond the established limitations of the redevelopment law, hoping that because we dealt here with a large city, we would find some flexibility with state and Federal authorities. (I have discussed the condition of the core area of Cincinnati in Part Two, Chapter 7, "The Tired Hearts of Our Cities.")

At the time when we (in association with Larry Smith & Company, economic consultants) were entrusted by a citizens' committee with the development of a master plan, an ambitious freeway network was in part completed, partly in construction and partly in an advanced planning stage. In order to be realistic, therefore, we had to consider the new freeway network as an accomplished fact. But we had to point out that it would not, in its present form, fulfill the role of an effective inner defense line. In this respect, it was faulty for these reasons: It framed the core on three sides, but left the northern side, from where most regionites would enter the city by automobile, undefended. We set out to prove that unless the freeway network were adjusted, it would lead to traffic confusion, additional congestion within the core, and finally to ultimate traffic chaos. We therefore provided an additional northern link to the defense line, connecting it with the already projected freeways. We then proposed the addition of two further fortification systems: an outer one-way loop road between the core fringe (the area with the least dynamic urban activity) and the core frame (a medium-high activity area), and an inner loop road surrounding the most active portion of the core, a fifteen-block area containing the most significant structures and public spaces.

Basically we proposed that the heart of the city, the inner core, should be kept free of all mechanized surface traffic, with only limited surface traffic permitted in the core frame and core fringe areas. In order to achieve this aim, we proposed a system of "use classifications" of public street surfaces. We pointed out that up to now such use classifications within the framework of zoning legislation had been applied only to land allocated to buildings, and not to public areas. We explained that use classifications for public land were justified because it was in these areas that the greatest conflict in usage arose, thus affecting the usefulness of adjacent buildings. With proper use classification in public areas, we could be considerably more lenient in use classifications of building areas, and the aim—bringing about a greater intermingling of varied uses, greater variety and greater

REVITALIZATION PROJECT

FOR THE CORE OF FRESNO, CALIFORNIA

This plan reflects measures for redirection and taming of automobile traffic in relation to the actual heart of the city (indicated in black in the small sketch in the left corner), the core frame and the core fringe. The freeway network surrounding the central area visualized as "an outer defense line." There is a second such defense line around the core fringe; finally, a loop road system around the heart of the city itself. Along the third one, all automobile traffic is stopped. The core of Fresno is reserved for pedestrian traffic only.

Fulton Way, one of the major pedestrian thoroughfares which is to be created on the basis of the revitalization plan. At the time of writing, plans for the conversion of the core into a pedestrian area are moving toward implementation.

Fulton Street before conversion into Fulton Way.

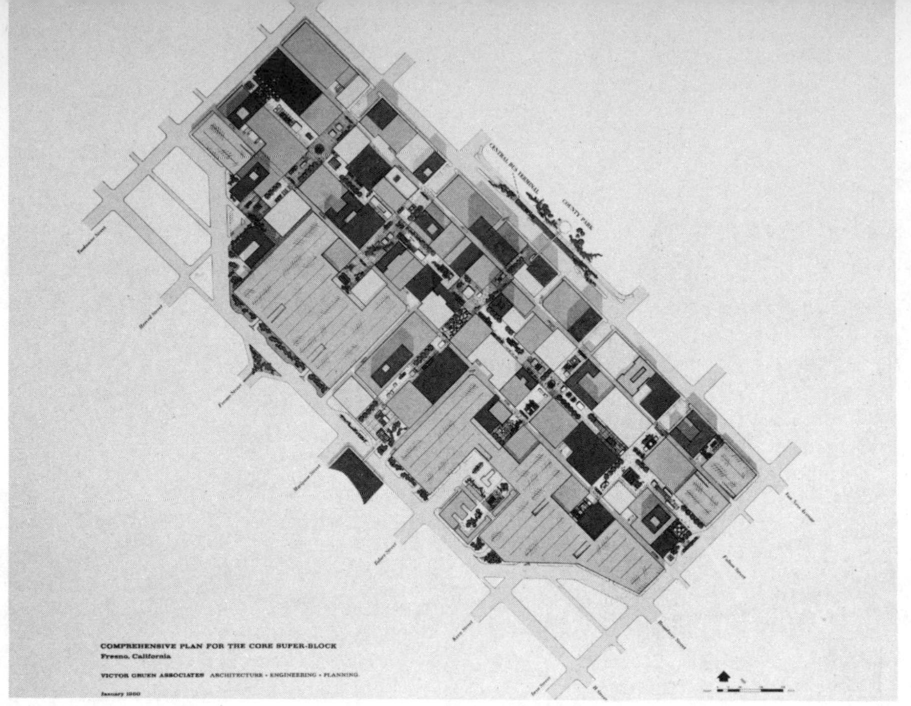

Detail of the central area plan for Fresno, California. On this map is shown solely the core area of Fresno, located within the innermost traffic loop. Multi-level parking decks on the southwest, underground garage to the northeast directly accessible from the loop road system. Remaining area remains free of all surface traffic.

Construction in the pedestrian areas of the heart of the city of Fresno, California, is in progress at this writing. The illustration shows plans and elevations of the treatment of one section of the pedestrian area and its enlivenment by patterned pavement, fountains and ponds, shade-providing shelters, groups of rest benches, planting beds and trees. Designed by Victor Gruen Associates in association with Garrett Eckbo, landscape architect.

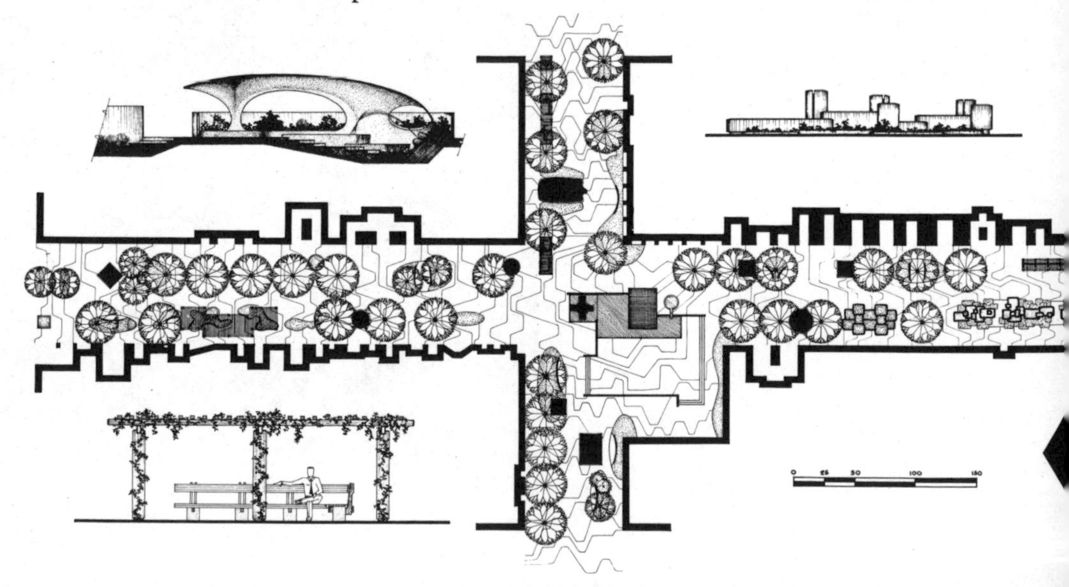

diversity—could be accomplished. (This describes the relationship of the sins of omission and of commission in another form.)

We proposed seven use classifications, assigning No. 1 to that with the highest usage quality. In all the various use classifications, emergency vehicles like fire trucks, ambulances, etc., would of course be permitted.

Our aim for this particular proposal, which had to be as realistic as possible, was to apply these usage classifications initially over only the central core and the core frame, with the recommendation that as it proved successful it should be expanded.

At the time we started our planning efforts, there was in existence an official redevelopment plan for the city core. It directed itself solely to the demolition of existing deteriorated or underused structures and their replacement by new buildings serving as offices, hotels, stores and residences. The city had invited proposals from developers who would undertake the demolition of the old buildings and the construction of the new ones, in the hope that interested parties would be found—a hope that was probably justified since, thanks to the possibilities the redevelopment legislation establishes, land could be sold at considerably reduced prices.

We analyzed the situation that would exist if these new buildings should actually be constructed. We had to conclude that their completion would in all likelihood have the undesirable effect of emptying out older structures, whose tenants would leave to move into the newer ones (equipped with air conditioning and otherwise offering more conveniences and prestige). Such an occurrence, of course, would only move blight from one location to the other—leading to further redevelopment programs, which once again would empty out the slightly older buildings—and in sum total would not contribute anything to the greater strength and vitality of the core. The reason for these disquieting prospects was to be found in the simple fact that the official redevelopment project did not provide any measures capable of reversing the long-established downward trend of the downtown core.

We posed the following question: "Assuming that all the new buildings were to be filled with tenants and their employees, that all the new stores were to become economically sound, that the new hotels would fill with visitors, that all the additional activities for which the new buildings provided space were to flourish, and that all this could be done without diminishing the already languishing economic status of existing facilities, how many more people per day would then have to be drawn into the core area?" The figure we arrived at was a needed additional daytime population of 28,000 persons. We then asked, "Would the continuation of a situation in which the existing facilities operate at their present, unsatisfactory level, which expresses itself in empty stores, low occupancy rate of hotels, unsatisfactory

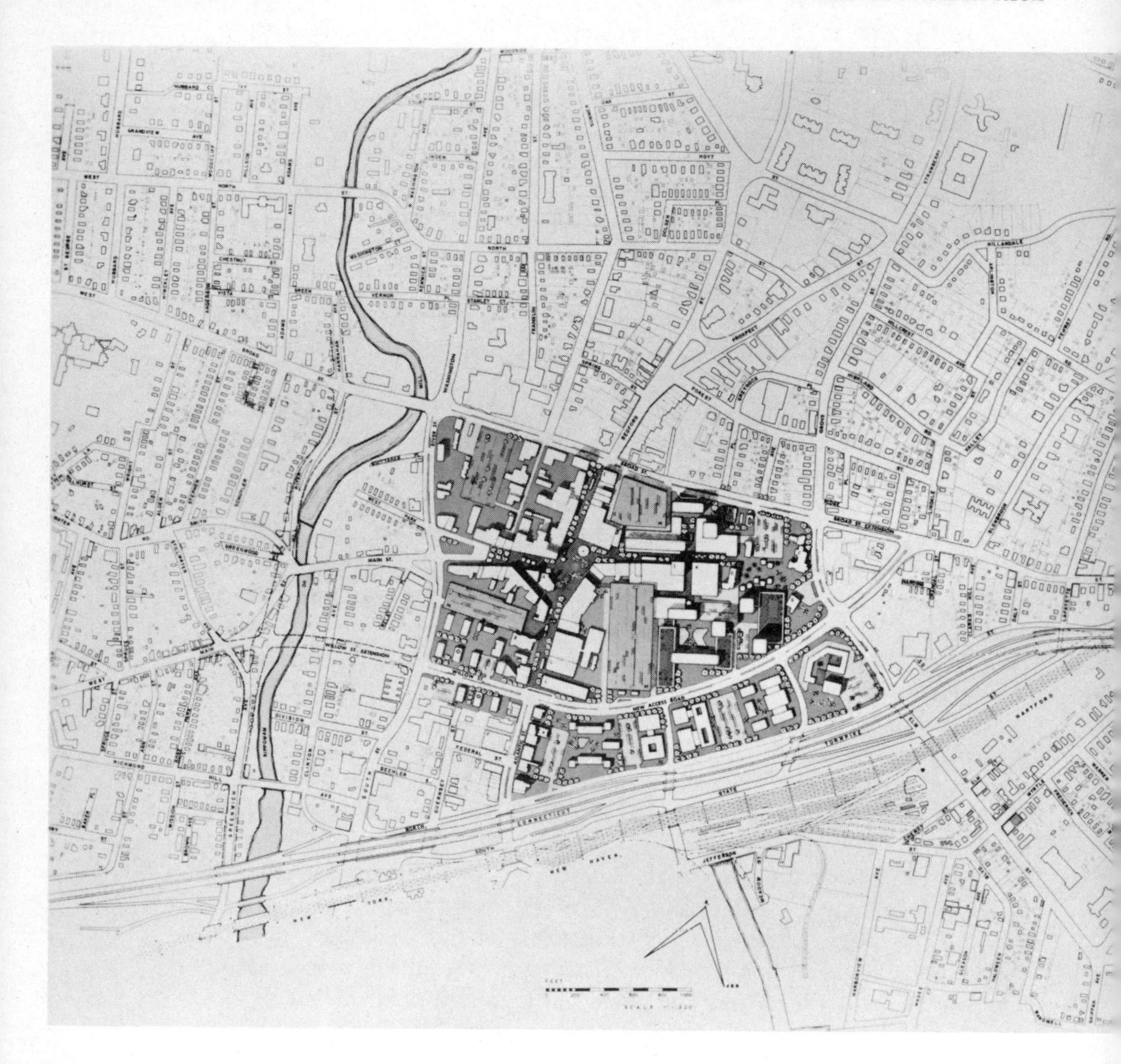

Central area plan of Stamford, Connecticut. Here, too, the heart area of the city is freed of all mechanized traffic. Parking facilities and bus terminals are reachable from innermost loop. A minimum of demolition is planned for this project, which is to proceed within the framework of redevelopment legislation, but the functioning pattern is radically changed. A comparatively large number of urban residences is included within the core area. (At the time of this writing, the plan is moving toward implementation.)

Central area plan of Paterson, New Jersey. Principles underlying revitalization planning for cities of relatively recent vintage, like Fort Worth and Fresno, are here applied to one of the oldest cities in the U.S.A. The core area ringed by innermost loop, by which access to terminals for automobiles and buses can be gained, is kept free of all mechanized surface traffic. Streets, squares and plazas are converted into attractive pedestrian areas. A regional park is projected on both sides of the river and facing it, directly adjacent to the core, are new urban residential facilities. (At the time of writing this plan is moving toward implementation.)

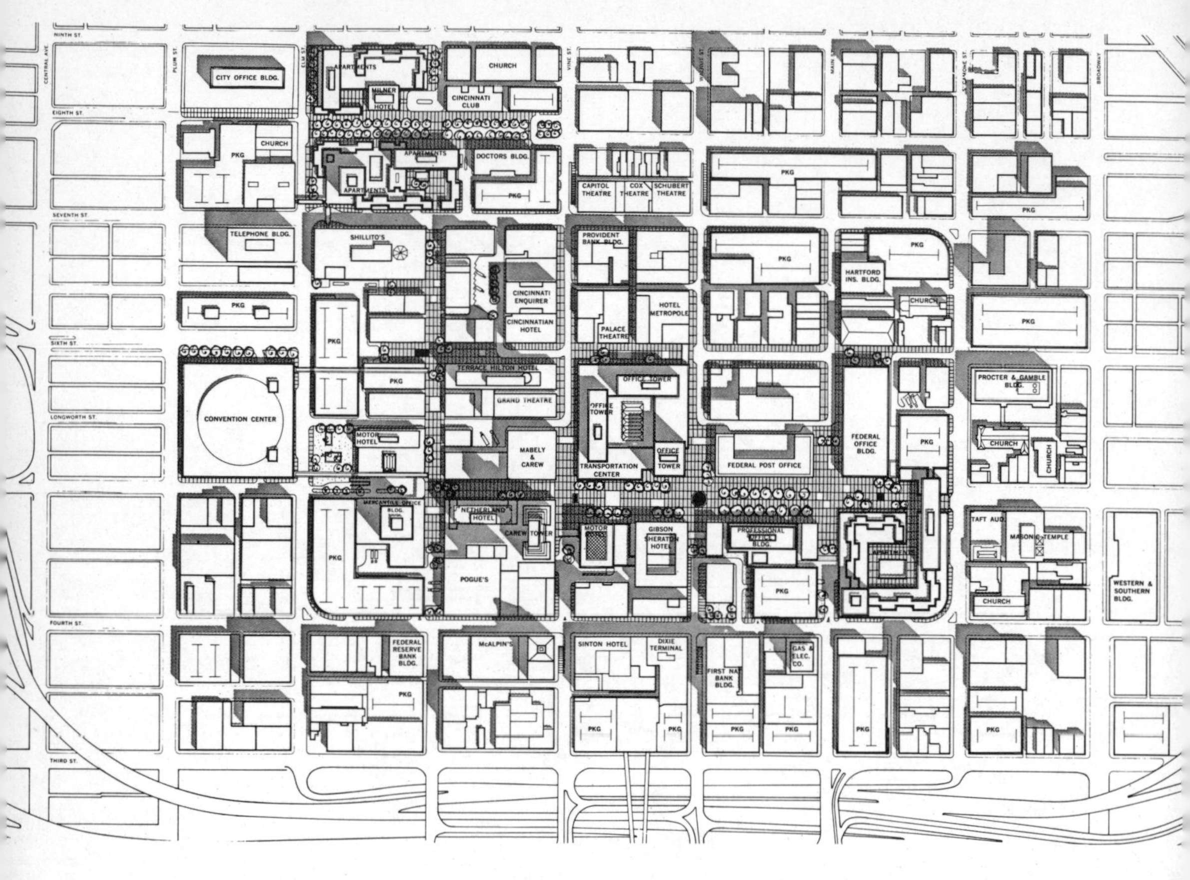

CENTRAL AREA PLAN FOR CINCINNATI, OHIO

The 15-block core area is ringed by a double one-way loop road. One leg of this loop road encloses the core itself; a second leg, the core frame. Within these two legs of the loop road, parking facilities are to be arranged. In the geometric center of the core one large block is to be converted into a public transportation terminal, underground facilities of which are reachable by roads routed underground within the core area. Surfaces of streets are to remain free of mechanized traffic of any kind.

---

business for the stores, disintegration of cultural, recreational and amusement facilities, really constitute the desired revitalization?"

The answer was: If one were to attain this satisfactory condition, an additional 40,000 visitors daily would have to be attracted to the core (this would interestingly re-establish the number of core visitors that existed in 1945). As these figures were generally accepted, our next question was: "How would these people reach the downtown core?" And we demonstrated

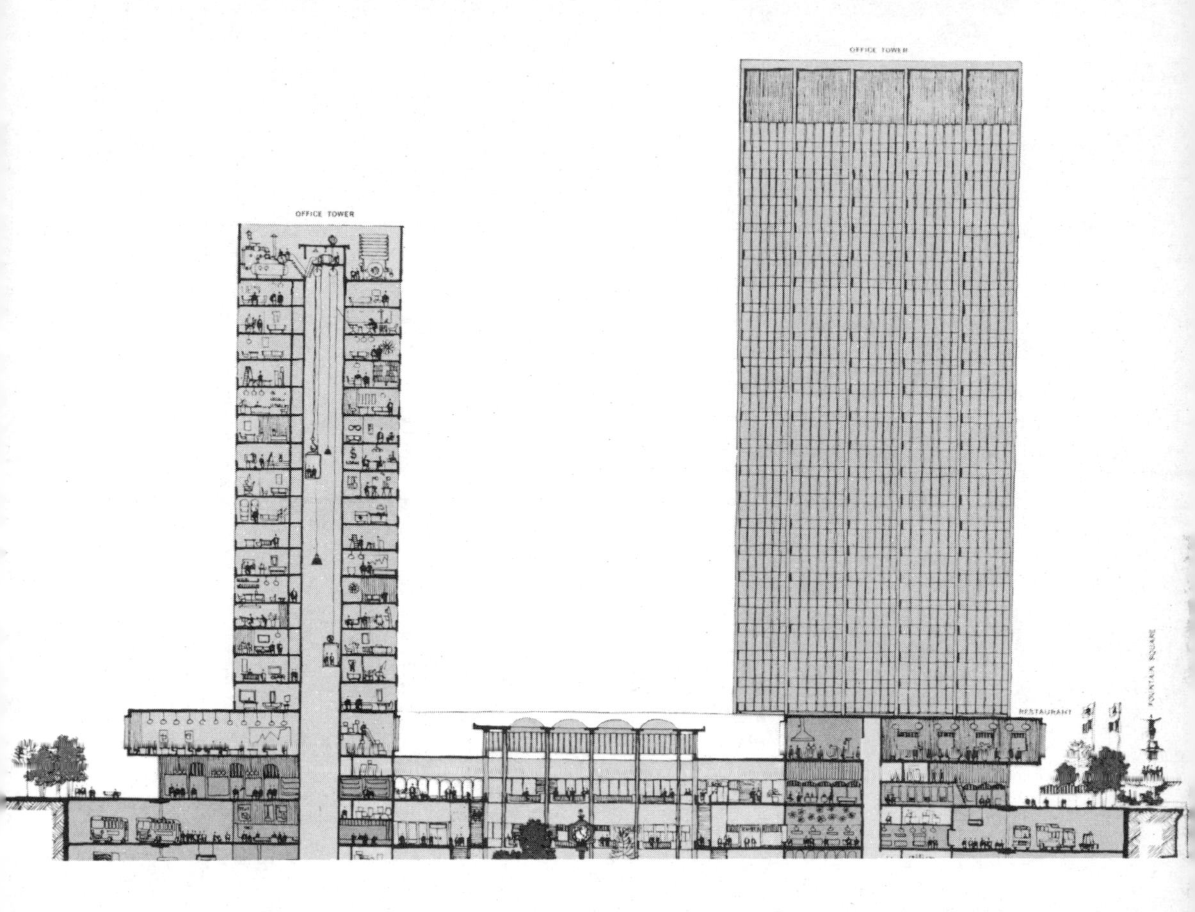

Section through transportation center projected for the central block in the heart area of Cincinnati, Ohio. Basement level reaching under adjoining street surfaces utilized as transportation terminal. Buses, airline limousines and taxicabs reach the terminal by underground streets. The ground floor is a covered air-conditioned pedestrian area surrounded by shops, stores and eating places. Above the ground rise office buildings, hotels, apartment buildings, etc.

---

that even if the present ratio between users of mass transportation and users of individualized transportation were to be maintained (which, in the light of existing trends, seemed unlikely), then it was very probable that the capacity of the access-street network, including the new freeways, would be insufficient and that the necessary car storage capacity within locations reasonably close to the core area (because of physical limitations and because of enormous cost) could not be created.

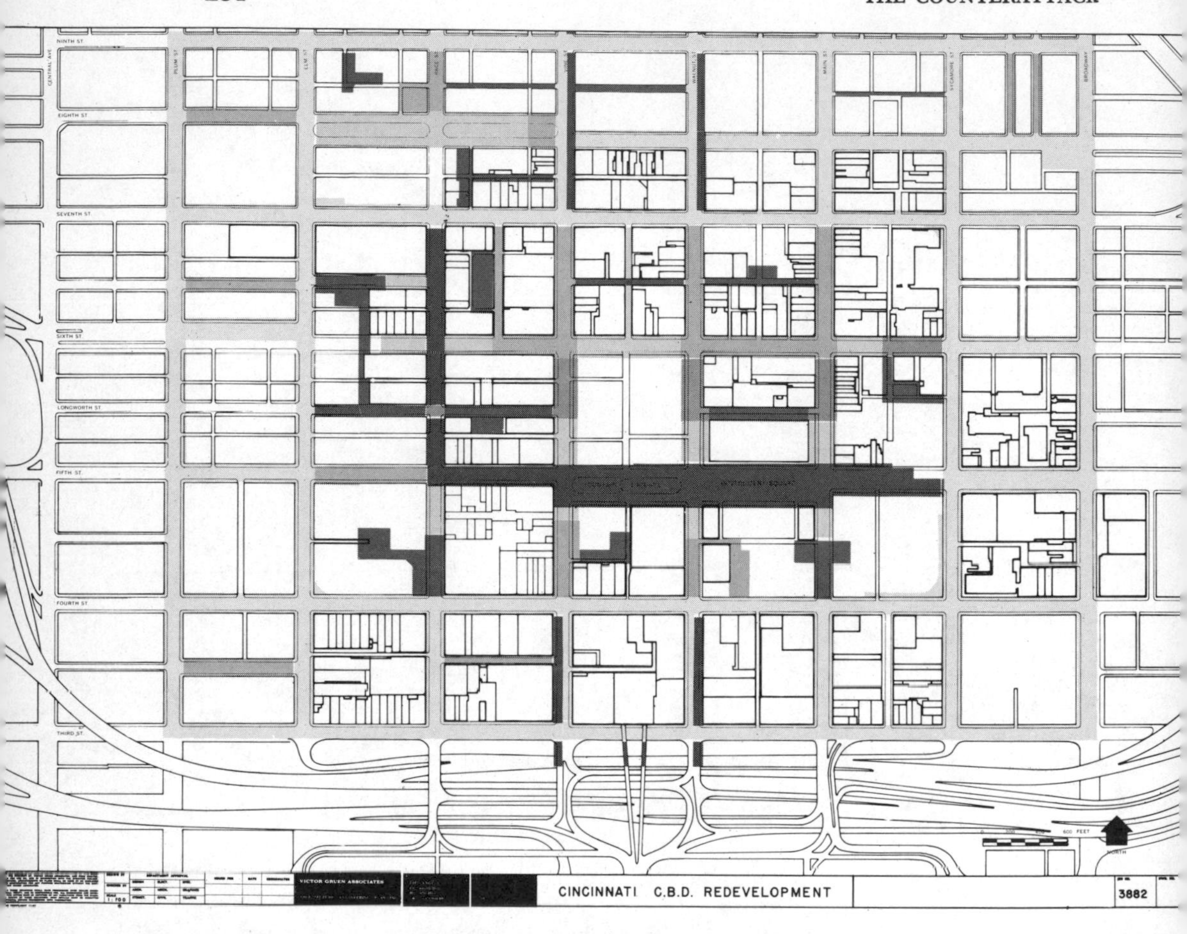

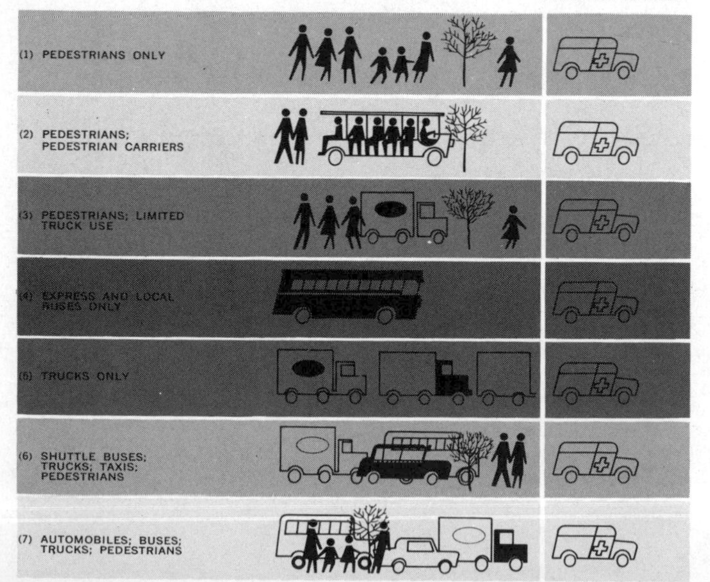

Central area of Cincinnati, Ohio, illustrating the proposed use classification for public areas.

We concluded therefore that only if arrangements could be made that would reverse the existing trends and result in an increased use of mass transportation could a solution be found.

In order for mass transportation to regain popularity, it would be necessary to equip it with certain advantages to the consumer, providing convincing proof that riding public transportation would be a good buy. We stated that a final solution for a metropolitan area of the size of Cincinnati could be found only through the introduction of a modern, convenient rapid-transit network. Inasmuch, however, as no such network existed, and inasmuch as, up to then at least, funds for the construction of such a system were not available through Federal help, we recommended the enlarging and improving of the existing bus service.

Obviously public transportation, if imposed on the sprawling pattern now existing in most of our urban regions, has one disadvantage that cannot be fully overcome. It is impossible to establish a sufficient number of public transportation lines to bring them within easy walking distance of each suburban home. Therefore, it appears likely that a large percentage of regionites would still have to use their cars for short rides to approach the nearest stop of a public transportation system, and changing from one vehicle to the other would be mandatory. In order to make public transportation workable, this inherent difficulty has to be countered by bestowing on public transportation certain marked advantages over private transportation, and by giving it a low, subsidized rate structure.

What are these measures that can bring significant advantages to the use of mass transit over individualized transportation? We proposed the following:

1. Free parking lots immediately adjoining outlying express bus stops
2. Reserved lanes for bus transportation on all express roads leading to the core, enabling buses to proceed at a speed greater than that which private vehicles could attain during heavy traffic periods
3. Special roads for buses and other public transportation vehicles, reserved exclusively for their use and routed underground within the fifteen-block heart area of the city
4. Location of a main public transportation terminal in the geographic center of the fifteen-block core area; construction of this terminal in a manner that would offer greatest convenience and comfort—yes, even beauty and glamour; arrangement of convenient facilities within the public transportation terminal for the transfer of persons from one bus line to the other, and from express buses to local buses and pedestrian vehicles like minibuses, airline limousines, taxicabs, etc.

We pointed out that in the case of Cincinnati there was, by lucky coincidence, in the geographic center of the city core, an underused land parcel measuring 400 feet square already programed for complete redevelopment. Utilizing two basement levels as a public transportation terminal combined with shopping facilities and services, it would still be possible to erect aboveground a group of high-rise office buildings, stores, and so on. (The economic consultant stated that the existence of the underground public transportation terminal would offer such economic advantages to tenants and owners that a developer would be justified in constructing all necessary public improvements for the public transportation terminal without any cost to the city government.)

Inasmuch as terminal facilities for private cars—namely, garages—would in accordance with our plan be constructed only in the area between the two loop roads or outside that area, walking distances to most buildings in the core would be considerably shorter for those arriving by public transportation. Thus the combination of advantages held out to the user of public transportation is:

A. Lower cost
B. Avoidance of the wear and tear on the nervous system, necessarily involved in driving into a city center, looking for a parking space, etc.
C. Higher speed resulting in shorter travel time
D. More strategic location of arrival points in the heart area
E. Ease of transfer to other types of transportation

These advantages would undoubtedly persuade increasing numbers of people to leave their cars at home or at the outlying free parking lots. If the number of private car users could thus be significantly reduced, it would be possible to construct the necessary number of parking stalls for them in locations logically suited to this purpose, and driving on the access roads would lose at least some of its disadvantages.

The fact that in this plan for the revitalization of Cincinnati we were proposing to give certain advantages to public transportation of course resulted in outraged cries of "foul" from the auto-crats and traffickists, who claimed that by giving certain advantages to mass transportation, we were interfering with the "constitutional" right of free choice of transportation.

As of this date, it appears that in Cincinnati, for the time being at least, the traffickists will win out, that redevelopment of the core will proceed only in the form of "commercial slum clearance" through Federal subsidy. No change of the functioning pattern, no separation of utilitarian from human functions, appears to be contemplated. Any expectation that the basic downward trend will change seems, under these circumstances, overly optimistic.

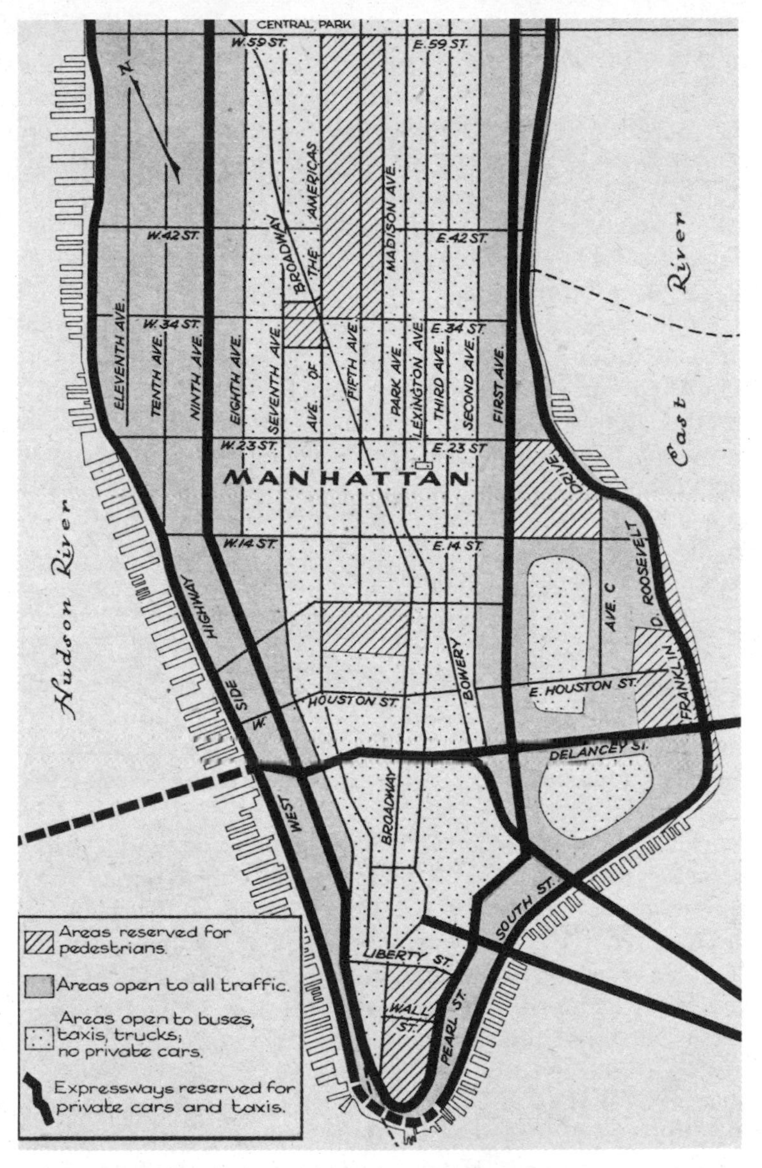

Schematic plan of the island of Manhattan from the Battery to 59th Street. This sketch plan was drawn to explain the proposal of land usage classifications for public areas within Manhattan, as suggested by the author. Only the gray areas along the fringe of the island would permit use of all types of vehicles. The central portion and certain areas now containing or projected to contain major residential developments would be restricted to public and semi-public transportation only. Some areas, as indicated, are to be reserved solely for pedestrian movement. (This sketch plan was published first in the Sunday magazine section of *The New York Times* on January 10, 1960.)

In Chapter 9 in Part Two, I discussed at some length the now defeated Midtown Garage Project for Manhattan, and indicated that I would describe, later on, a possible alternate proposal. It now appears that a proposal I submitted in a memorandum to the City Planning Commission and other authorities is being considered, at least in part. It applied the grand strategy of outer defense lines by proposing that a larger number of outlying garages than those already in existence near the terminals of subway and commuter lines should be constructed so as to drain off, at outlying points, some of the automobiles now inundating Manhattan and thus encourage the use of public transportation. As far as the inner, impenetrable defense ring of Manhattan is concerned, we are unfortunately forced to establish it on the island of Manhattan itself, because the numerous tunnels, bridges, toll roads, etc., constructed in the past, have opened floodgates which, at least for the time being, cannot be closed. Realizing the unavoidability of taking care of the automobiles that have been cordially invited to Manhattan, I proposed a pattern of usage classifications for Manhattan similar to that discussed for Cincinnati. The outer ring of Manhattan, which already contains the West Side Highway and the Franklin D. Roosevelt Drive, would be zoned for private transportation usage, and within the land devoted to this classification would then have to be located fringe garages of sufficient capacity to permit the storage of those automobiles which, in spite of improvements to public transportation, would still be driven into Manhattan.

The core of Manhattan, roughly between Eighth Avenue and Third Avenue and between Battery Park and 63rd Street, should be devoted, as far as its public land is concerned, to various use categories. There might be some areas—possibly Fifth Avenue between 42nd and 59th Streets—and some residential areas in Greenwich Village and other localities—that would be reserved for pedestrians only. Other public land would then be zoned for mass transport and semipublic vehicles (buses and taxicabs), and for service traffic at specific, limited times. Yet others might be zoned exclusively for service traffic. Emergency vehicles, of course, would be permitted in all usage classifications.

The number of parking stalls located in the fringe garages would probably have to be considerably higher than the 10,000 spaces proposed by the former traffic commissioner. However, since land in the fringe area is considerably cheaper than in midtown locations, the larger program probably could be built for the same capital investment. (Since the fringe garages could be larger, allowing for construction methods like prefabrication, lower construction costs would result.) In order to bring people who leave their cars in the fringe garages into central Manhattan, it would be necessary to establish additional means of public transit (crosstown buses, or completely new types of mechanized transportation). And inasmuch as traffic surfaces would be freed not only of moving private cars but of parked cars as well, the speed with which existing and new bus lines, taxicabs, service vehicles and emergency vehicles could operate would be markedly increased.

This concept was published in *The New York Times Magazine* on January 10, 1960, and popular reaction to it, as I was able to convince myself in talking with merchants, housewives, taxi drivers, and other city dwellers, was enthusiastic. Most of the experts, on the other hand, feel that it is utopian and impracticable. What, then, I ask, is their alternative? The present policy in New York is that of bringing more and more automobiles into Manhattan every year and of trying, with greater or lesser degrees of success, to take care of them once they have arrived. In the process, public transportation is being robbed of its fare-paying passengers, and in spite of penny-pinching policies with regard to upkeep, maintenance and improvement, it is being driven into bankruptcy. The long-range aim of the present policy, then, seems to be to stop public transportation altogether, and put everyone who wishes to approach Manhattan from the surrounding region with its 14,000,000 inhabitants behind the wheel of his own car. This kind of action is reminiscent of the efforts of the good citizens of Schilda, who, when they discovered that they had forgotten to equip their city hall with windows, tried to carry sunlight into the dark rooms in baskets.

A few figures will prove that to continue along the present path is utter madness.

At this point, some comprehension of relative space requirements might be useful: A very thin man riding in a subway train during rush hours occupies 2 square feet of floor space. A fat man standing comfortably needs 5 square feet, while a man who is walking requires 8 square feet. A man in a hurry, who is running, needs 15 square feet. The same man, sitting in an automobile that is standing still, requires 200 square feet, but when he drives this automobile at a reasonable speed, he needs 600 square feet. Going at 60 miles per hour, he requires 1,200 square feet.

I have, just for the fun of it, calculated what the space requirements would be if everybody coming into Manhattan today, whether by commuter train, subway or other means of public transportation, were forced to use a car. (I don't want to bore my readers with the calculation, but anybody with any skill at all in mathematics can figure it out for himself.) The results would be as follows: If 1,000,000 transit passengers were to drive in to work or to shop, they would occupy approximately 750,000 automobiles. If, having reached Manhattan, they were satisfied merely to stand still, bumper to bumper, they would cover 150,000,000 square feet of road surface. To make space for them within the main business area of

Manhattan, we not only would have to eliminate all sidewalks, but would have to demolish every last structure, and then double-deck a part of Manhattan Island now covered by office buildings, hotels, theaters, stores, etc. Inasmuch as standing still, bumper to bumper, would be a highly undesirable and fruitless activity, and as people obviously will want to move around, we will have to provide three times that space; that means we will have to build six layers of transportation area covering the entire business core. If we also desire space for taxicabs, trucks, service vehicles; if we consider that there might be occasional accidents and stalled cars; and that it will be necessary to build some ramps, stairs, elevators and escalators, nine levels will be required. On top of the ninth level, we could then start from scratch and construct new buildings to house those facilities which we had to demolish in order to make space for motorization.

Now let me inquire: Who is "utopian and impractical"? The traffickists, who oppose all measures for true transportation improvement and are dead set against all efforts to "tame the automobile," who, if allowed to proceed freely, would make the demolition of all of Manhattan's structures mandatory . . . or those planners who believe in a balanced transportation system which, as it relates to core areas, would necessarily give main attention to the improvement of mass transportation, and who propose by the taming of the automobile to save the city from destruction?

The last argument against any proposal concerned with the taming of the motorcar is usually that it cannot be carried out because it has never been done. My answer to this is that it *has* been done. It has been done in the United States in those new suburban environmental clusters which I described in the chapter called "The Search." It has been done in portions of certain city cores, which I will discuss in the chapter on "The Revitalization of the Heart." It has been done long ago in a number of European cities: in the *gallerias* in Milan and the arcades in a number of West German cities like Bremen; more recently in Coventry, England, and in some of the New Towns around London. It was done in Copenhagen in the fall of 1962, when the long main shopping street, the Strøget, was closed to all mechanized traffic. A newspaper report stated, "Recently there was a singular type of popular festival to be observed in Copenhagen. 40,000 people triumphantly followed a brass band through the decorated Strøget. The joy expressed itself in uproarious manner. Merchants and shoppers showered the mayor and his staff with flowers and presents, including, of all things, a grandfather clock."

It has been done in the center of Stockholm, where pedestrian streets many blocks long were opened and where the flood of automobiles was vastly reduced by the new, efficient and handsome subway. It has been done even more effectively in Vällingby and Farsta, the satellite towns of Stockholm, where pedestrian areas in new town centers are directly accessible by escalator from subway lines. It has been done in the center of Rotterdam, where the new business district, the Lijnbaan, represents an outstanding pedestrian reserve.

Strangely (or perhaps not so strangely), such examples of the taming of the motorcar are kept secret by the fraternity of auto-crats. How short a distance news travels in this respect I learned recently in Vienna, where local traffic experts assured me that taming of the automobile was not possible. By chance, I arrived while on an excursion, at the local county seat of St. Pölten, only 24 miles from the metropolis, where I found that the main business street, the Kremserstrasse, had been freed of all automobile traffic and zoned "for pedestrians only." I also learned from a local policeman, who explained the situation with a great show of knowledge and enthusiasm, that the local merchants had been deadly opposed to the idea but, in view of their subsequent success, had changed their opinion. Practically every storefront on that street had been remodeled, and on Sunday evenings, although the rest of the town was as dead as a doornail, I found Kremserstrasse crowded with promenading window-shoppers.

The taming of the motorcar can be achieved if we keep a few basic rules in mind:

A. The automobile represents one form of transportation, but it is by no means the only one. There is a wide range of transportation media suitable for various purposes and within various types of environment. (I will discuss the gradation of transportation in the next chapter.)

B. A clear distinction has to be made between core-bound and distributary transportation. Core-bound transportation—namely, that which converges from the regional area along radial lines toward the heart of the city—should ideally be handled by mass transportation media only. Circulatory transportation lines, which basically form concentric rings within the metropolitan area at varying distances from the core, can be formed partly by loop roads serving individualized transportation and partly by distributing, mass transportation lines. Transportation within a thinly populated area will, until such time as a coalescing of the suburban pattern can be achieved, have to be taken care of by feeder roads, freeways and general roads serving automobiles, and by mass transportation in the form of buses, over special reserved rights of way.

C. Transportation within the city core can be handled partly by pedestrianism and partly by special inner-core mass-transportation media which, because of the short distances, may provide slow speeds but should offer comfort and continuity of service.

D. The automobile has obviously become an important transportation medium. In those areas where it represents the most logical carrier, it should be provided with a suitable environment in which it can perform in accordance with its full technological potential. It should, above all, be given all those advantages which result from a strict separation of utilitarian from human functions.

At a meeting of prominent executives of the automobile industry, which I was privileged to attend, the over-all problems of the urban crisis with relation to automobile traffic were discussed. One of the executives commented sadly that the automobile was beginning to have a bad "public image," that it had become the butt of endless jokes and the target of popular ill will.

I stated then: Nobody really hates the automobile. It has served a useful purpose in our lives and will continue to do so. But in order to restore the "public image" of the automobile to its former glory, we will have to channel its force. Not only is the taming of the motorcar essential to the amelioration of our urban problems, but it is vital to the continued prosperity of the automobile industry itself.

17 Pedestrianism and Other Future Modes of Transportation

THE SAME DEADLY SPIRIT that is responsible for the uniformity, sterility and boredom in the man-made environment generally, because it is opposed to variety and diversity, also prevails with regard to transportation methods. Mass production has given us vehicles like motorcars and buses in tremendous quantity, but even though they are produced by a number of manufacturers, and even though each company dreams up new, catchy names each year to denote mutations of its product, basically they are all the same. In an epoch in which the genius of mankind is employed in inventing vehicles of enormous complexity to conquer space, there is a remarkable dearth of new ideas for transportation here on earth. Even the automobile, an invention born more than half a century ago, has not changed basically from its early prototype; and we are still riding on the same subway, railroad and commuter train systems that our fathers used. Even the one so-called "new" invention, the monorail train, was actually first installed in Wuppertal, Germany, some sixty years ago.

That there is a public desire for new types of public ground transportation is demonstrated by the hundreds of thousands who flock to Disneyland or

For some odd reason the catchy name "monorail" created the impression that we are faced with a brand-new invention, a major contribution to the solution of the transportation crisis. Here is a drawing of a monorail train driven by a steam engine, projected in the 1890s. A number of years later a monorail system was actually installed in Wuppertal, Germany.

Monorail installation for Seattle, Washington, World's Fair.

to Seattle in order to have a ride, at considerable cost, on this highly overrated "new" transportation carrier.

There are a number of new inventions, most of them under study or in the experimental stage, but none of them has so far been actually utilized for mass transportation.

If we are to succeed in the creation of a new, diversified urban pattern, we will require new and diversified means of public transportation. As we create public areas with different characteristics and new types and arrangements of urban elements, we will need transportation types scaled and engineered to the specific uses for which they are destined.

Right now there is a complete disregard for gradation in urban movement, with the result that, since we do not have at our disposal a sufficient variety in types of public transportation, we are forced to use existing media in the wrong places and in the wrong manner. A new urban pattern will create a challenge to inventors, technicians and manufacturers to supply us with new kinds of transportation carriers, and improve existing ones.

Let me try to develop schematically a *scale of gradation of movement,* as it may exist in the nation once a new urban planning philosophy starts to be implemented:

MOVEMENT AREA No. 1: For distances of 1 mile and below

The most suitable means of locomotion for this movement area is pedestrianism, supplemented by various types of slow-moving carriers.

MOVEMENT AREA No. 2: 1–2 miles

The small bus, the taxicab, and various transportation media of modest speed but continuous availability (the latter based on the moving-belt principle, with or without seats) and, for the transportation of goods, moving belt systems.

MOVEMENT AREA No. 3: 2–5 miles

The larger urban bus; new types of underground rapid transit; and for the transportation of goods, rail and trucks on special roads, etc.

MOVEMENT AREA No. 4: 5–30 miles

Rapid transit, commuter trains, the regional bus, the private automobile; and for goods, rail transportation, water transportation, trucks.

MOVEMENT AREA No. 5: 30–60 miles

Track-bound transportation, either railroad or vehicles (already invented but still to be developed) riding on air cushions; the long-distance bus, the private automobile.

MOVEMENT AREA No. 6: 60–400 miles

Small jet planes, new types of track-bound transportation, the private automobile; and for the transportation of goods—trucks, airplanes and waterways.

MOVEMENT AREA No. 7: Continental travel

The large jet plane, new speedy track-bound transportation; and for goods—rail transportation, planes and waterways.

MOVEMENT AREA No. 8: Intercontinental travel

The supersonic plane, new types of ocean liners; and for goods—jet planes and shipping.

There are two types of existing transportation that I have not mentioned: the helicopter and the private plane. I believe that neither of them will be able to make a significant contribution to mass transportation, because of the noise caused by the helicopter and because both these modes of transportation will, in the long run, be able to function only where the airways are not too crowded.

In comparing the means of transportation within various movement areas, I have mentioned a few that are not in use at all, others that are in use but not for the suitable gradation categories. For example, we use the airplane for distances where track-bound transportation could do a better job. The popularity of flights between New York and Boston, or New York and Washington, can be explained only by the fact that track-bound transportation is not offering sufficient speed and comfort, nor is it running on sufficiently frequent schedules. A plane ride over these medium distances involves an expenditure of considerably more secondary, unproductive travel time than primary travel time. For a flight that lasts only 50 minutes, we have to invest anywhere from 40 minutes to an hour in order to get from the airport to the city and vice versa, and inasmuch as we have to be at the airport at least 15 minutes ahead of time and, if we carry baggage, have to wait at least 15 minutes before we receive it, the ratio of primary travel time to secondary time is extremely unfavorable, about 1:2. If we had express trains similar to those which the European railroad systems run between large cities (furnishing a nonstop trip, for example, between Paris and Brussels), equipped with extremely comfortable seats and serving drinks and meals on the way, the over-all time expenditure would be less, the trip itself much more comfortable and the strain on the nerves almost nonexistent. Air travel—which, between nearby cities, is already completely saturating air space and airport facilities—could then be reduced.

We are using basically one type of bus for transportation within city cores, where the big vehicles move clumsily through narrow streets and heavy traffic, and where their capacity for operating at 60 miles per hour is never utilized. These buses have the additional disadvantage of developing obnoxious exhaust gases, and in view of their extremely slow speeds and the continuous need of stopping, they are noisy and uneconomical to operate. Quite especially with regard to the bus, we need a pattern of

Motor-driven Minibus as now used on an experimental basis with a 5¢ fare in downtown Washington, D. C. This picture shows just one of the dozens of types (some of them electrically driven) that are presently being tried out on an experimental basis in various cities in the United States.

---

gradation. For the heart areas of our cities we will need slow-moving and extremely quiet electrically driven vehicles ("minibuses") in which the seating is so arranged that boarding and leaving can be accomplished in seconds; vehicles that will develop neither smells nor noises, and will be easily maneuverable.

We will need for the inner loop-road system slightly larger vehicles, also extremely maneuverable, which will not have to develop a speed faster than 25 miles an hour, and which should produce a minimum of noise and fumes.

We will need for the remaining urbanized areas a medium-sized bus; and only for longer trips within the region will a bus similar to that which we are now utilizing everywhere be necessary.

And finally, we will need a long-distance bus, which should be considerably more comfortable than the types now in operation.

Our present city bus system suffers from another problem: the one-man operation, which is almost universally used in American cities. This is in great contrast to European cities, where the bus driver is carefully shielded from all contact with the passengers so that he may concentrate on the business of driving. A special conductor—or more often a conductress—takes care of collecting fares. Usually he or she is seated at a little counter near the rear entrance. Because this individual is not overworked, he is happy to give information and direction to the passengers. We frequently criticize our bus drivers for being impolite but if one considers that theirs is probably the only nonspecialized profession left in the United States, comprising the duties of a chauffeur, a money collector, an information bureau and a policeman, the ragged state of their nerves should be no surprise. This system of one-man operation of buses within urban areas is driving people away in droves from public transportation. The understandable impatience of the driver, plus the serious time loss that occurs at every stop, where—at least in New York—the driver often misses the change to green lights twice, plus the sudden stopping and starting, are sufficient reason to make bus transportation unpopular. I believe it could be shown that one-man operation is also bad business for the bus company. Operation techniques with driver and conductor, as used in Europe (and as formerly used here), would speed up traffic considerably, would make riding more enjoyable, and therefore increase the number of customers; moreover, it would also result in considerable savings for the bus company, in fuel and oil, and in wear and tear on the vehicles. The end result, I firmly believe, would be that in spite of the additional expenditure for one more employee on every bus, revenue would go up considerably, other operating expenses would go down, more trips could be accomplished within the same over-all operating time, and currently existing deficits could be converted into profits.

Another means of transportation hardly utilized at all is pedestrianism. There exists a widespread rumor that Americans of all ages and of both sexes are not only unwilling to walk, but actually unable to do so. This rumor of course is highly exaggerated. I have, on the gradation chart, indicated that pedestrianism would be the most suitable mode of transportation for distances of under one mile. Actually, people walk—and enjoy walking—much longer distances. The desire to walk does not depend only on distance. It is influenced to a much higher degree by the qualities of the surrounding environment. Walking in the desert heat for five minutes might be highly undesirable, but walking the same length of time in a beautiful landscape would be regarded as highly pleasurable. Careful research concerning regional shopping centers has demonstrated that persons leaving their automobiles parked in the car storage area will absolutely refuse to walk more than 600 feet and that a distance of about 300 feet between parked car and building core is the one most acceptable to shoppers. Yet the same shopper will walk for many hours, negotiating many miles, within the attractive pedestrian area of the shopping core, along the show windows or through the aisles of the stores. In a supermarket, for example, the aggregate of aisles between merchandising displays may easily amount to as much as half a mile. A woman living in the New York region will refuse to walk five minutes to the nearest subway or bus station, and would rather take her car, but she will happily walk up and down Fifth Avenue between 42nd and 59th Streets, a distance of over a mile if she takes in both sides, with her eyes glued to the appetizing displays.

Walkability also depends on comfort and the absence of disturbance. Where colonnades, arcades, roofed overhangs for rain and sun protection are provided, where rest benches for brief relaxation are available, walkability is extended over considerable distances. On the other hand, where continuity of vista enjoyment is interrupted by buildings without life or interest or of outright ugliness, or where the pleasure of continuous physical movement is interfered with by automobiles turning into or leaving garages or parking lots, or by the need to stop at red traffic lights every few hundred feet, or where the danger and smell of traffic disturb the senses, walkability is considerably reduced in radius. One has merely to observe the impressive pedestrian achievement of American tourists once they come to Europe. There a pent-up need for an activity no longer possible in urban areas of the United States finds its expression.

The following tabulation attempts, in a highly simplified and schematic fashion, to list the distances, and the time involved in covering these distances, which the average healthy human being is willing to walk, under varying environmental conditions. It takes under consideration desirable walking distances as they may exist in urban areas, making the point that there are significant variations within the definition of "desirable walking distances" in this respect. One could add to the tabulation—in order to prove that such differences of desirability of walking exist—the case of the man who might conceivably be required to walk in the Sahara Desert on a hot day in a sandstorm. The desirable walking time in that case would be zero and the desirable walking distance would also be zero.

	MINUTES	FEET
In a highly attractive, completely weather-protected and artificially climatized environment	20	5,000
In a highly attractive environment in which sidewalks are protected from sunshine and rain	10	2,500
In an attractive but not weather-protected area during periods of inclement weather	5	1,250
In an unattractive environment (parking lot, garage, traffic-congested streets)	2	600

This tabulation refers to the lazy walker and to the one-purpose trip without interruption. If there are interruptions like resting on benches, in sidewalk cafés, shopping or taking meals, additional walking time will be acceptable.

Pedestrianism will be the transportation mode of the future, not only within the repatterned hearts of our cities, where experiences similar to those in today's outlying regional shopping centers will be available, but also in other core elements of urbia, wherever new environmental clusterizations are created. The rise of pedestrianism as a mode of transportation will have an excellent, beneficial influence on national health.

As a vital factor in the contemporary scene, pedestrianism has begun to receive recognition even by various legislative bodies. Of particular interest in this respect is the California Pedestrian Mall Law of 1960, Section 11100, from which I quote this statement:

> The Legislature hereby finds and declares that in certain areas in cities and particularly in retail shopping areas thereof, there is need to separate pedestrian travel from vehicular travel and that such separation is necessary to protect the public safety or otherwise to serve the public interest and convenience. The Legislature further finds and declares that such objective can, in part, be accomplished by the establishment of pedestrian malls pursuant to this part.

Wherever large areas with pedestrianism as the main mode of transportation are created, we have suggested the introduction of accessory means of transportation with the idea that these would serve during inclement weather, and would also be used by those who have overestimated their walking capacity, are laden with packages, or, because of age or sickness, are incapacitated. Such assistance to pedestrian transportation has been utilized in the past at World's Fairs and similar events, and has always enjoyed great popularity. Accessory transport media must be small and easily maneuverable, and must move at a slow speed, to enable them to mingle with the walking majority. Seats must be so arranged that boarding and getting off take only seconds. Either this transportation must be available free of charge or a fare collection system must be arranged that will not slow down movement and prolong stops.

The potentials of transportation systems based on the moving-belt principle have hardly been touched yet as far as their utilization for urban transportation is concerned, though their use in industrial plants is widespread. I regard them as highly adaptable for the movement of people over

Moving sidewalk and continuously moving train with benches, utilized in the World's Columbian Exposition in 1893. These are predecessors of the Speedwalk and Carveyor Systems described in the text.

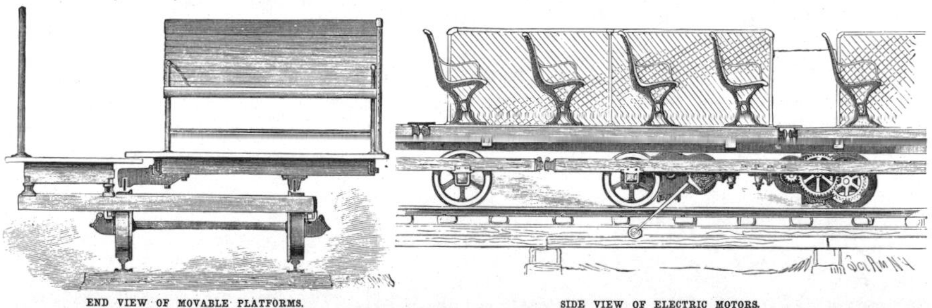

A ramped speedwalk installation in a shopping center. The safety of the system is illustrated by the baby carriage.

medium distances and quite especially for the movement of goods within city core areas.

Two transportation methods based on this principle have been developed and are, in some cases, being used; in others, they are at least in the experimental stage. One is the moving sidewalk. Some of these have been installed in airports like the one in Dallas, where the operation, because of certain small technical deficiencies, has not been altogether satisfactory. The improved version of the sidewalk appears to be the so-called Speedwalk (manufactured by Goodyear and Stevens-Adamson), which allows for entering from the side at any designated spot; though without moving handrails, it appears completely safe. Moving sidewalks, including the Speedwalk, move approximately at pedestrian pace. If one continues to walk while on it, one approximately doubles the usual walking speed. The installation of such moving sidewalks or speedwalks appears to be especially desirable within large parking areas or within large garages, and from such parking areas

Full-size model of a Carveyor train. The picture shows how passengers are boarding a continuous row of cars over a speedwalk which moves at the identical speed which the Carveyor itself maintains at the station stops, where its speed has been decelerated from the one which it maintains between station stops.

---

and garages to the nearby core area of the city. Inasmuch as a moving sidewalk installation interrupts the cross movement, it would be necessary to have it grade-separated and thus operate either below or above the pedestrian level. In our project for the revitalization of the Boston core area, we are proposing a moving sidewalk installation in an underground tunnel leading directly from a 3,000-car garage to a central point in the core area.

A speedier method of transportation based on the moving-belt principle is represented in the so-called Carveyor (also developed by Goodyear and Stevens-Adamson). This system provides for a moving belt that operates at about a 15-mile-per-hour speed. Riding on this moving belt are platforms, and on these platforms seats are mounted. Depending on the width of the belt, the individual platform can carry from four to sixteen seats. On open stretches between station stops, the platforms, which may be visualized as little cars with their seats, ride some distance from each other on the moving belt. As stations are approached, individual platforms are transferred over rollers from the 15-mile-an-hour moving belt onto a second belt which moves only at walking speed, achieving in this way a gradual deceleration. As soon as walking speed is achieved, embarking or disembarking from the individual cars is then accomplished by means of a parallel loading belt, which also moves at pedestrian speed, so that to the passenger the individual cars appear to stand still. When the individual cars leave the station, they are transported over a series of accelerating rollers until they again reach the 15-mile-per-hour moving belt. This Carveyor system was originally envisaged for the shuttle line between Times Square and Grand Central Station in New York. Because this system operates with a minimum of personnel, it was opposed by the transportation union and thus never installed. However, in those cities where its installation would not result in a cut in employment but, on the contrary, in some additional employment, there seems to be no reason why it should not be possible to implement this idea; it has been worked out in the greatest detail, and a full-size mock-up section has actually been constructed and operated.

The Carveyor system or some similar principle seems to me highly suitable for connecting large terminal facilities at the fringe of the city—whether these facilities serve mostly mass transportation (i.e., commuter lines), rapid transit lines, or private transportation (in this case, large garages)—with the central sections of the city core. The Carveyor system, of course, would also have to be installed on a grade-separated level either above or below pedestrian areas. In our planning for the revitalization of the Boston city core, we have proposed such a Carveyor line installation on a balcony within an enclosed pedestrian environment, leaving from a combined terminal facility projected at the present South Station in Boston to the heart of the downtown core at the crossing of Washington and Summer-Winter Street.

Another Carveyor installation was proposed by us for a project that envisages the conversion of Welfare Island in New York to a model residential community completely free of automobile traffic. Its purpose would be to transport people on a balcony located within a two-story-high enclosed pedestrian promenade stretching along the full length of the island, making possible the interconnection of all apartment house lobbies with subway line terminals and other transportation stops. The Carveyor line envisaged for the Welfare Island project would be about 10,000 feet long, would have station stops every 500 feet, and, besides facilitating connection with transportation terminals, would also be utilized by the projected 40,000 inhabitants of the island for reaching shopping facilities located on the island, schools, and so on. Total travel time for the 10,000-foot distance was estimated roughly to be fifteen minutes. Preliminary economic projections showed that the system could be operated and amortized at the 5-cent fare.

The use of the moving-belt system for the transportation of goods within core areas seems to have great potential. Electronic devices have been developed which would make it possible to distribute goods from warehouses located on the fringe of the core area to any chosen location. Such belt systems would be located either underground or on a second-story level, possibly on top of overhangs protecting the sidewalk from sunshine and rain. All truck traffic could be eliminated from the core areas of our cities.

And now, let us consider various means and methods of rapid transit, all of which have been abysmally neglected in the United States during the past thirty years; not only have no new techniques been employed, but the

Visualization sketch of a pedestrian concourse which is to form the spine of a residential community to be called East Island (the present Welfare Island, located in the East River alongside Manhattan, New York). The concourse, approximately 10,000 feet long, is visualized as a pedestrian area connecting all building lobbies with subway stations and other public transportation terminals. Stores and shops, schools, theaters, and entrances to the buildings are directly accessible from the concourse. Because of the great length of this concourse, it was suggested that a continuous means of public transportation in the form of a Carveyor train be introduced as an additional movement facility on a balcony level. (At the time of writing, this project is still in the discussion stage.)

old installations have not even been kept up to date. Instead, governmental agencies have engaged, to an ever-increasing degree, in a one-sided and unbalanced system of subsidy available to private transportation only, and it is a miracle that in following this policy we have not destroyed, by now, all urban mass transportation. The fight against public transportation systems, about which I have spoken more fully in the chapter called "Full Speed Ahead on a Dead-End Road," has a double thrust. Not only does it rob public transportation of the funds it needs for improvements and operations, but it simultaneously drains the public transportation system of passengers. Yet, surprisingly, there is still some life in the beaten and neglected carcass. In the fall of 1962 the New York Transit Authority reported that both passengers and revenue had increased. This rise is a continuation of one that started in 1958, at which time it was announced with joy, but with a certain amount of surprise as well, by city officials. The surprise stems from the fact that the Transit Authority can state in good conscience that it has done nothing significant to make riding in New York's subway system, which was already one of the most unattractive in the world when it was built, more pleasurable or convenient. The only explanation for the phenomenon must be found in the fact that traffic congestion on access roads and within Manhattan has become so unbearable that even the horrors of a subway ride are preferable.

The problem of urban transportation has always inspired discussion, and how lively this discussion has been is reflected in the endless flow of ideas brought forth by inventors, writers and laymen. Like everything else that engages the public interest to a large degree, public transportation problems have always been reflected in cartoons, jokes and humorous drawings and, in America, on the pages of comic strips. That there was already a serious urban transportation problem in 1895 is witnessed by a drawing in *Fliegende Blätter,* the German *Witzblatt* (difficult to translate, because it scarcely exists any longer in our day: A magazine devoted chiefly to humorous and satirical stories, still represented in some respects in England's *Punch*) published that year in Munich. The drawing quite clearly proves that at that time serious thought was already being given to the separation of technological equipment from purely human activities which take place on the street level. There is visible on the street a single automobile with the trademark "Benz"; otherwise the street contains only bicycles and pedestrians. On the upper level, we can discern a means of continuous transportation bridging the road surface, which obviously had already been invented then, nearly seventy years ago, but which still has not been utilized. On the next level, we find on the right side a big suspended pipe with the lettering PNEUM, obviously referring to a pneumatic mail delivery system, in which letters and packages are shot by

the high pressure of compressed air through tubes, a type of mail service which for a time played an important role in European cities. (I understand that in Vienna the pneumatic mail service was still available until a few years ago, at which time some traffickist found that motorcyclists could do the job just as fast. This was at a time when automobile traffic was still light in Vienna. By now I am sure that the speed of the motorcycle delivery has slowed down considerably. The concept of pneumatic transportation, which can still be found in some of our stores and office buildings, may be one to be considered again.)

Above that, the cartoon shows something resembling a monorail train, guided right through the centers of buildings, which, it is interesting to note, is also old hat. There is an elevated railroad train to the left and right, and above that a cable car train; still higher up, in the air, flies the granddaddy of the helicopter.

Of special interest in the United States is the development of the science-fiction cartoon. The artists who draw these cartoons always seem to be predicting things, with great accuracy, which scientists later invent, and which usually are developed many years afterward. As early as forty years ago, missiles and rockets flew into outer space, at least in our Buck Rogers comic strips. If one looks at these old illustrations, one finds a disturbing similarity to the actual product. These artists seem to have a knack of being able to read the inborn desires of mankind, and of foretelling the future.

In this context, then, it may be encouraging to observe, now that rockets actually fly into outer space, that the prophecies of the artists are currently directed toward public transportation, and many cartoons showing speedy trains being shot through underground tubes, stopping in airy, glass-domed stations, are beginning to make their appearance. Inasmuch as these cartoons have always been a few years ahead of reality, and inasmuch as they have always expressed what people desired, we may be quite optimistic about the development of public transportation.

Although European cities also commit their share of sins in facilitating and thereby increasing automobile traffic within urban areas, they seem at least to engage simultaneously in a parallel effort to improve public transportation media. There is right now, in fact, a rash of new subway network construction in European cities, and the ones I have seen are of an astoundingly high quality as far as speed, coverage, attractiveness and convenience are concerned. Even in the United States it has been demonstrated that subway cars do not have to look drab and dirty. The new subway trains in Philadelphia with their colorful, cheerful interiors are a revelation to any New Yorker. I have, personally, not seen the famous subway system of Moscow, but friends who have had the opportunity to ride it tell me that it is an object of civic pride. Large clocks in every station, with hands that indicate the seconds, invite all passengers to check the punctuality of the service. If it is announced that trains are running every 120 seconds, people are amazed if they are one or two seconds late. The pride is so great that in spite of the fact that smoking is permitted, nobody in fact would do so, as this might interfere with the cleanliness of the equipment. The old stations are ridiculously ornate, the newer ones less so; all of them are said to possess great spaciousness and good ventilation.

When we think about rapid transit to serve the new urban pattern of the United States, we should be daring enough to envisage something better than what was provided at the beginning of the twentieth century. New technological methods by which vibration and noise can be eliminated are now available. Speeds can be increased, and the jolts that accompany stops and starts can be done away with. (The Paris Métro recently announced its

Station of the Philadelphia subway system. Though extremely simple, it has an orderly and clean appearance. The trains themselves are modern and colorful, with cheerful interiors.

A station of the New York City subway system: a disorderly and drab appearance caused by exposed construction features and drab color schemes.

ABOVE The desire to effectively separate utilitarian traffic from pedestrian traffic is nothing new, even in our country. (A proposal for elevated sidewalks and pedestrian bridges connecting docking facilities. *Scientific American,* 1890.)
BELOW A freeway in Chicago, Illinois, with rapid transportation in center strip. Most freeway construction in Chicago provides for the introduction of rapid transit facilities either simultaneously with freeway construction or later.

introduction of noiseless trains on rubber-covered wheels.) Furthermore, stations need not look drab and dingy, as do those of the New York subway, which follow the dictates of the "janitorial style" at present. There can be beauty and dignity in public transportation.

For greater distances, superior public transportation—taking advantage of the well-advanced experimental work on vehicles that glide smoothly and noiselessly at speeds of 200 miles per hour—could be introduced. Our railroad managers—who, it seems, have been preoccupied in recent years solely with problems and opportunities presented by real estate holdings—would be well advised to take a few trips to Europe and ride, for example, on the fabulous express trains of Italy, and on the trains of the European Rapid Train System. They would find that with such equipment the competition of bus lines, and even air lines, over medium distances would not have to be feared.

There are, however, definite indications in Europe, and in the United States as well, that the day of the one-sided subsidy for private transportation is nearing its end. Even traffic experts seem to have realized that we have reached the end of the dead-end road on which we have been speeding.

At the 35th International Traffic Convention, which took place in May, 1963, in Vienna, findings were made concerning a definite renaissance of rail-borne mass transportation. The convention expressed agreement with the results of a worldwide poll concerning traffic problems of 76 cities in 20 countries:

1. The private automobile cannot solve contemporary problems of transportation. Only public mass transportation will be effective.
2. Public transportation must be given separate routes, for complete separation from private transportation.
3. Governmental assistance is necessary in order to provide good mass transportation.
4. The use of rail transportation in the form of subways, commuter trains and even street cars is now expanding.
5. Even cities of below one million population are now able to build subway lines.

And then the conclusion: "Our cities must be prepared not for more vehicles but for more passengers."

Even in Los Angeles it has come to be realized that the construction of hundreds of miles of city freeways does not solve the traffic problem. After lots of talk about a rapid-transit network, things now seem to be getting serious. An editorial in the Los Angeles *Times* of May 22, 1963, states:

> This could be the year that mass rapid transit finally gets the green light in metropolitan Los Angeles. The State Legislature has at last started to act instead of just talking about urban transit problems.

And the editorial ends with this significant sentence: "We believe that once motorists understand that an adequate mass transit system is essential to drivers as well as commuters, they will support the program."

San Francisco has developed for its metropolitan area an ambitious plan for a rapid transit system, which was submitted to the voters; a bond issue was passed in November, 1962.

Atlanta, Georgia, is seriously considering a subway system.

New York has for the first time in decades decided to construct new subway lines, for which plans are now being drawn up.

In Washington, D.C., a long struggle between those who wanted to construct more and more freeways and those who were in favor of a new rapid-transit system has been going on for a long time. The late President Kennedy may have helped a decision in favor of rapid transit by declaring himself publicly for that solution.

The New York Times of June 3, 1963, under the heading "Victory for the Underground," editorialized:

> The President, accepting the recommendations of the National Capital Transportation Agency, has called for a downtown subway with suburban rail connections. He has deferred construction of proposed automobile freeways through the city and asked for a re-study of those projects. These decisions, if carried out by Congress, will preserve the beauty of Washington and enhance its economy. If there is anything the Capital doesn't need, esthetically speaking, it is a great swath of concrete sweeping across its face and attracting even more automobiles into town. The convenience of rapid transit underground is overdue in Washington.
>
> The President's decision has significance for more cities than Washington. Across the country the battle between rapid transit and the highway builders is being waged. The push for highways at whatever cost has behind it powerful automobile, concrete and other lobbies. In Washington the highway lobbyists were out in full force with the support of the local press. Fortunately they have lost, at least temporarily. Their setback is a victory for all hard-pressed American cities, and for those trying to save them from strangulation by concrete and the internal combustion engine.

There is also a promising change in the attitude of Federal agencies. They now consider requesting that the scope of urban renewal be widened so that assistance for public transportation might be included in Federal grants.

Congress has now under consideration a $5,000,000 allocation proposed by the Administration for a study of, and assistance to, public transportation in American urban areas. In an editorial entitled "Hope for Mass Transit," *The New York Times* of March 11, 1963, remarks:

> After many disappointments, the prospects appear brighter this year that Congress may respond to the needs of the nation's large cities for improving their mass transit systems. . . . Throughout the nation it is possible to discern a greatly increased interest in finding the alternatives to strangulation of cities by automobile traffic. . . . Congress, so extravagantly generous to the farmer, owes some help to the city and suburban resident.

What influence even a poorly conceived and executed public transportation system like the New York subway can have is illustrated by some notes on the history of this system, which appeared in a subway map and guide, 1958 edition. It says:

> Some 90 years ago, the Metropolis of New York ran out of space. Employers were leaving the city. They packed their machinery on drays and barges, and moved to the towns of Westchester, Long Island, New Jersey and Connecticut, followed by their employees, to places where workers could have sunlight in their rooms. New York, they foresaw, was dying. It was strangled by its population of 700,000 which it could never handle.
>
> Then rapid transit began. At first with the construction of an elevated railroad in downtown Manhattan. Employers returned. The population soared. Subway building started in 1900, and the first underground train ran in 1904.

If we would stop insisting that the type of system built in 1900 is still adequate in our day, we would be able to take steps now to stop flight and blight, spread, sprawl and scatterization.

There are straws in the wind now indicating that industry is accepting the new challenges of public transportation and that new ideas and new techniques are in the making. There is, for example, the new type of electronically controlled bus, first displayed at the American Transit Association's annual meeting in Dallas. It is planned that this bus will start out in suburban areas, operated by a regular bus driver. After collecting its passengers, it enters an expressway where it is coupled with other buses into a continuous bus-train, which then moves at high speed toward the heart of the city. As soon as the bus arrives at its reserved lane on the expressway, it operates automatically on electronic guides embedded in the pavement.

The experimental bus that was displayed was viewed very favorably. It is manufactured by The Flxible Company, Loudonville, Ohio, and Barrett Electronics Corporation, Northbrook, Illinois. It was regarded as a new solution for rapid transit; cheaper, as far as capital investment is concerned, than a railbound operation, and also considerably more economical in operation. This bus-train concept would, it appears to me, solve one of the problems which the prevailing low density of our suburban area presents. It provides, in a single vehicle, the necessary medium for collecting passengers in suburbia and moving them electronically at rapid speed, in a train formation, toward the core. Thus the disturbing need for transferring from bus or private car to public transportation, and the time losses which such transfer entails, can be avoided.

A similar concept is represented in Pullman's Commuter Piggyback operation. Designed for commuter train service, it proposes that buses, after collecting passengers in suburbia, be loaded on trains without requiring the passengers to leave their vehicles.

Westinghouse has developed a system operating by means of small, separate, but connectible, rubber-tired cars running by automatic controls on two-minute headways via an elevated concrete loop structure. The electrically driven aluminum cars are planned to operate in trains of from one to ten units each, depending upon the traffic density, and it is claimed they are capable of handling 5,000 to 14,000 riders per hour.

How great public interest in mass transportation has become is shown by the fact that one of the largest of the mass media (*This Week* Magazine) devoted a good part of its issue of February 3, 1963, to an article by Ralph Stein entitled "Tomorrow's Railroads in the Sky." The subtitle reads "Sixty Miles—Home to Downtown—in a Quarter of an Hour! New supertrains, some without rails or wheels, will soon revolutionize city and suburban transit." The author discusses the "Levatrain," which rides on a one-eighth-inch-thick cushion of air and was developed by the Ford Motor Company. It is said to be capable of shuttling between cities 90 miles apart in 38 minutes. He mentions the British "Hovertrain," which rides on a half-inch cushion of compressed air generated within the train. Its track is a concrete trough. According to the inventor, Christopher Cockerell, forward motion of 300 miles per hour would be accomplished by electric power. An interesting sidelight to this article is that its author is otherwise active as the automobile editor of *This Week*.

Thus it appears that after sixty years of hibernation, government, inventors and technicians have awakened and are getting back on the mass transportation track. The opportunities that will be created by transfiguration of our urban pattern and revitalization of the hearts of our cities should prove challenging and rewarding to American ingenuity and industry.

18 The Emerging New Urban Pattern

In approaching the problems of the hearts of our cities it is essential that we recognize the *interdependence* existing between them and the surrounding urbanized areas and metropolitan regions. A healthy heart within a chaotic region is just as unworkable an absurdity as a metropolitan region with a dying heart. In the chapter "The Search" I have talked about some of the more encouraging developments taking place in the metropolitan regions of our country—the regional shopping center, the new types of college campus, the emerging of office and business centers, industrial centers, apartment house groupings and integrated residential communities. What is happening today within the sprawling metropolitan regions, however, is due to the instinctive reaction of some enlightened individuals and enterprises rather than to an over-all conscientious effort. It is a fact that a trend toward recentralization is detectable in nearly all metropolitan areas, expressing itself in a greater demand for living quarters close to places of work and shopping facilities, and that this increasing demand leads to apartment house construction, town house construction, planning of row housing, etc.

In Los Angeles County, for example, where the land-consuming detached single house held a monopoly position in the thirties, a new trend toward multiple residences (apartment houses) is discernible.

NUMBER OF DWELLING UNITS CONTAINED IN PERMITS
FOR NEW RESIDENTIAL CONSTRUCTION IN THE CITY OF LOS ANGELES
1941–1962

YEAR	SINGLE FAMILY DWELLINGS	% OF TOTAL UNITS	APARTMENTS & OTHER MULTIPLE DWELLINGS	% OF TOTAL UNITS	TOTAL UNITS	%
1941 (JAN–NOV)	10,730	63.6	6,146	36.4	16,876	100.0
1942 (JAN–NOV)	4,092	32.6	8,462	67.4	12,554	100.0
1943	1,536	60.6	1,002	39.4	2,538	100.0
1944 (JAN–NOV)	6,148	72.0	2,393	28.0	8,541	100.0
1945	6,192	70.2	2,629	29.8	8,821	100.0
1946	13,819	62.9	8,147	37.1	21,966	100.0
1947	15,724	70.6	6,545	29.4	22,269	100.0
1948	17,017	52.6	15,341	47.4	32,358	100.0
1949	15,926	56.9	12,079	43.1	28,005	100.0
1950	22,285	68.4	10.294	31.6	32,579	100.0
1951	14,195	70.0	6,085	30.0	20,280	100.0
1952	18,075	61.0	11,559	39.0	29,634	100.0
1953	15,309	48.7	16,102	51.3	31,411	100.0
1954	16,422	58.0	11,903	42.0	28,325	100.0
1955	14,730	59.0	10,231	41.0	24,961	100.0
1956	15,028	52.2	13,785	47.8	28,813	100.0
1957	11,045	37.4	18,505	62.6	29,550	100.0
1958	8,269	31.6	17,869	68.4	26,138	100.0
1959	11,600	48.8	12,155	51.2	23,755	100.0
1960	8,975	37.6	14,896	62.4	23,871	100.0
1961	8,295	32.0	17,588	68.0	25,883	100.0
1962	7,434	24.2	23,270	75.8	30,704	100.0

The table shows the number of dwelling units contained in permits for new residential construction in the City of Los Angeles between 1941 and 1962. (The statistics concerning this for the County of Los Angeles are very similar as far as the relation between building permits for single family dwellings and multiple dwellings is concerned.) The startling result one gains from studying this table is that in 1941, 63.6 per cent of all building permits concern single-family dwellings and this percentage, reaching an all-time high of 70.6 per cent right after the war, was reduced from then on pretty regularly until it reached, in 1962, 24 per cent. On the other hand, the building permits for apartments and other multiple dwellings have increased in their percentage from the total of 36.4 per cent in 1941 to 75.8 per cent in 1962.

Thus we are obviously faced with a clear trend toward recentralization. This recentralization, however, proceeds without direction and without planning, and its expressions are, more often than not, found in the wrong places, or in arrangements that are inimical to each other. The new centers, whether they be residential, shopping or working centers, are not large enough to be meaningful, and—most important of all—no provision is made for separation between them by open land, so that the advantages that centralization should bestow are lost.

Regional shopping centers, for example, are often constructed too close to each other, with the result that they suffer from overcompetition. In other cases, such regional centers are built in close proximity to existing older towns or existing city centers, with disastrous results—usually for the older centers but sometimes for both the old and the new. The Lloyd Center in Portland, Oregon (John Graham and Associates, architects), represents, for example, a very large concentration of retail and business activities in a location only a mile and a half distant from the historic core area of Portland. Its economic strength is damaging to the old established stores; on the other hand, it appears that there is enough strength left in the old downtown section to prevent the new shopping center from achieving the fullest use of its potential. It must be concluded that the *unplanned* recentralization movement now taking place constitutes a serious danger to the hearts of our cities, to the core areas of smaller towns and villages, to lasting economic stability with resulting consequences of more flight and more blight. It also results in a waste of land and of economic and human resources.

New center developments not only draw off the economic lifeblood of older established communities but in doing so very often destroy historic, social and cultural values. The new centers have a tendency to replace only the profitable enterprises which the old town center possessed, without attempting to make up for other values which the old community core possessed. Thus, when the old town center folds up, urban culture is dealt another blow.

Laissez-faire planning for our cities and metropolitan regions is a luxury we can no longer afford. In order to institute comprehensive, creative planning, however, we need a clear image of a desirable organizational pattern for our cities and metropolitan regions.

I will attempt in this chapter to arrive at such an image of a new urban pattern. Before doing so, let me recapitulate and describe schematically the main features of our existing pattern and the reasons for the difficulties under which it operates.

The diagram below shows, schematically, metropolitan organization as it has developed throughout the nineteenth century. The main structural element of this pattern is the "string." The organism somewhat resembles a spider web, with the main actor sitting in the center spinning out threads in all directions. Most of the strings represent streets and roads that serve a twofold purpose: first, to act as guidelines along which, like beads of a necklace,

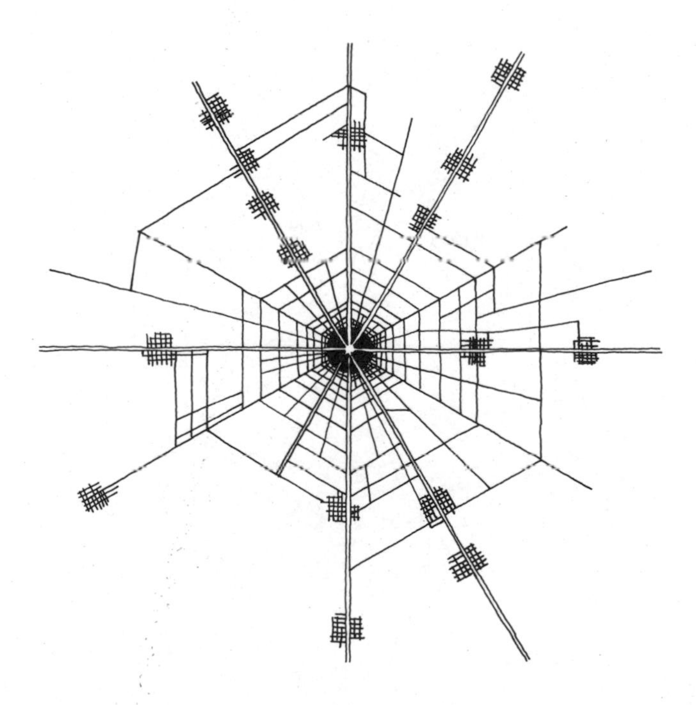

A spider-web type of urban pattern was developed throughout the nineteenth century. Components of this spider web are strings, all converging in the central city. Most of these strings are roads for surface traffic. Some of them, indicated here by a double line, are mass transportation media. On the outskirts of the metropolis we find clusterlike formations of urban activities alongside the station stops of such mass transportation lines.

structures serving multiple types of functions are strung; and secondly, to serve as media for communication and transportation. There are, however, some strings that have an exceptional role. They represent the rights of way for mass transportation (tram lines, subway lines, elevated train lines, commuter train lines, etc.). Along these lines we find, wherever station stops occur, tight web formations in the form of clusters, their size governed by the walking distances from the station.

This pattern functioned, as a structure, comparatively efficiently. The problems of the city during the era in which this pattern was created stemmed rather from the human misery engendered through bad housing conditions, created by a society that lacked social consciousness.

The diagram below illustrates schematically the urban pattern as it exists

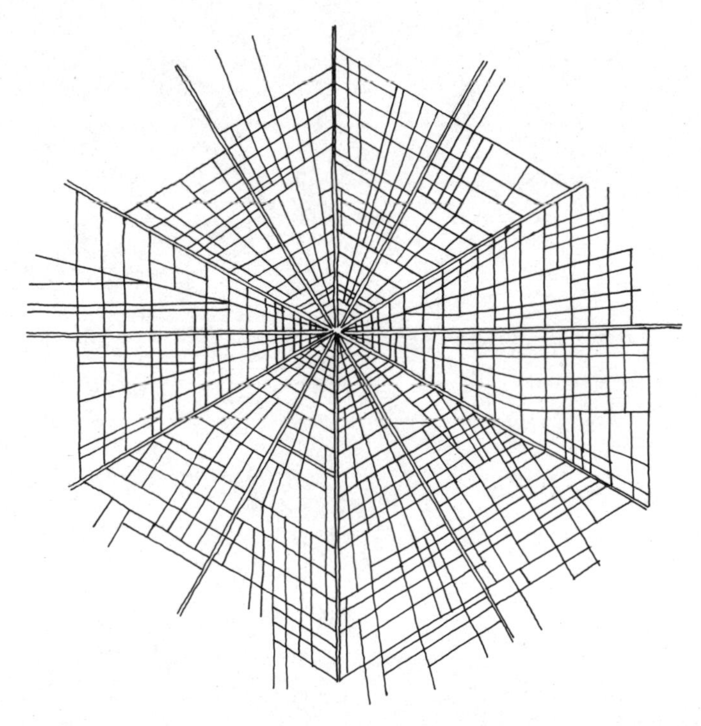

The spider-web type of pattern changed in the twentieth century because of the influence of the automobile as a medium of mass transportation. The pattern spread in all directions, engulfing the former urban clusterizations along stops of mass transportation lines; open areas between these clusterizations have been eliminated and the area flooded by scatterized growth. Public transportation has become less effective and the heart of the city has shrunk.

now, around the halfway mark of the twentieth century. Its base structure is the same spider web that was spun previously, but it has experienced some changes through the influence of the automobile as a means of mass transportation. The pattern has grown significantly, and spreads in all directions. It no longer shows the clusterizations that formerly existed around station stops of the mass transportation carriers, nor does it show the open spaces that existed between those clusters. The strings indicating mass transportation lines have either completely disappeared, or have become thinner and less frequent. The main actor in the center of the web, the old city core, has become weak and small. All differentiation between open areas and citified areas has been wiped out, and uninterrupted sprawl has taken its place.

What we have done, then, is to superimpose on the old nineteenth-century pattern, which depended for its functioning on public transportation, new technological and sociological factors with the result that the livability and workability of the old pattern are hopelessly destroyed.

We need a new pattern in which the new technological apparatus is adjusted to human and urban needs. In searching for such a new pattern, we may profitably observe how nature has shaped its complex organisms. The magazine *Guideposts to Knowledge* discusses the organization and properties of living matter in these terms:

> The basic unit of life, whether plant or animal, is the same. Millions of cells enter into the structure of higher plants and animals but the simplest forms of life are one-celled organisms.
>
> Cells show great variety of shape, being spherical, disk-shaped, elliptical, oblong, etc.
>
> A typical cell consists of a mass of protoplasm, in the center of which is a denser mass called a nucleus. . . . *Most cells are surrounded by cell walls.** . . . In the more highly organized plants and animals the vital processes are carried on by groups of cells that form specialized organs.

This type of organization of living matter seems to repeat itself in the smallest and the largest systems known to man, from one-celled amoebas to the planetary system. I submit that this cellular system is applicable to the urban organism as well.

I can visualize a metropolitan organism in which cells, each one consisting of a nucleus and protoplasm, are combined into clusterizations to form specialized organs like towns which, in turn, are meaningfully grouped

* Italics are mine. V.G.

together to form cities, and finally, in a still more highly developed organism, the "metropolis of tomorrow." Or, to use a different metaphor, I could compare such a metropolitan organism with our planetary system, in which planets, like cities, are surrounded by satellites, or moons, which might be regarded as towns, and in which all the planets are held in the magnetic field of a star of superior magnitude and attractive power, a solar body which we might call the metropolitan core.

To make the visualization of the cellular metropolis of tomorrow possible for the reader, a schematic plan has been included and may be found on the accompanying fold-out.

But before viewing this plan, I would like to have the reader keep in mind that this drawing represents an extreme schematic simplification. It shows simple geometric forms, mostly circles, which indicate the various cells and clusterizations. For reasons of simplicity, the basic cellular forms are all shown to be of equal size. In reality, if such a plan were to be implemented, the patterns of course would be highly irregular. There would not only be different sizes and shapes developing as far as the cellular units are concerned, but also the spaces between them would vary in shape and size. They would all be influenced by topography and characteristics of the landscape, by existing or newly-to-be-created bodies of water, by forests, hills and mountains, and if the pattern were to be applied to an existing metropolitan area (which I strongly feel is possible) then of course the pattern would be influenced by existing man-made structures and economic conditions. Yet there are a few principles which the schematicized drawing clearly expresses. One such principle, recalling the organization of living patterns, "most cells are surrounded by cell walls," is that each one of the cells and nuclei is clearly defined. Their boundaries are pre-established in order to guarantee permanently the open spaces between them.

The diagrammatic scheme is drawn to scale, and thus certain conclusions are possible concerning the relative average size of cellular formations and the distances between them. We will also be able to conclude what the land use demands of the various cluster formations and of the entire metropolitan area would be. And we would, finally, be able to conclude how, generally, the means of communication would work and what time-distances would be involved in transportation among various cells and clusterizations of cells, and from all surrounding clusterizations to the main body of the urban core.

The schematic plan has been arrived at on the basis of certain assumptions concerning population densities and transportation media, which, though they are in some respects different from those to be found in today's sprawling metropolis, have nevertheless been tried and proved in some established communities.

OPEN THIS FOLD-OUT
FOR SCHEMATIC DRAWINGS
OF THE CELLULAR METROPOLIS OF TOMORROW

Now, with the warning that the schematic plan of the metropolis of tomorrow constitutes an oversimplified image of something that, in its implementation, would be translated into a pattern of great variety, let us consider the principles as they are expressed on the drawing.

In order to start somewhere, I assumed that the metropolitan area to be designed would have a population of 3,300,000 people. That is about the median size of an existing American metropolitan area.

We see before us a planetary system with ten planets (each a city of 280,000 population) held in the magnetic field of one solar body, the Metrocore (with a population of 500,000). Taking a closer look at one of the planets, we find that each is a stellar system in itself. In each one, ten satellites (towns with a population of 25,000) revolve around a star (a city center with a population of 30,000). But this type of cellular organization goes still further. Each town represents another stellar system with a center of 3,400 population and with four communities around it (each one with 5,400 population). And finally, each community represents another cellular cluster consisting of a community center (population 900) and five neighborhoods around it (each with a population of 900).

This is the extent to which I was able to show, on a drawing of this size, the cellular system, but actually the cellular character continues. Each of the neighborhoods consists of groups, each of the groups consists of families, and each of the families consists of individuals.

The principle of nature that creates each cell as a nucleus and protoplasm, with cell walls around the protoplasm, is carried on throughout. The nucleus of the family would be the parents; the nucleus of a group of families, a group center; the nucleus of the neighborhood, a neighborhood center; and of the community, a community center. The town has a town center; the city a truly urban city center; and the entire constellation of cells and cellular clusters would then have as its nucleus the metropolitan core.

In illustrating the metropolitan core, I have tried to show that in itself it would represent a clusterization of cellular elements. Around the central core I have shown ten circles representing elements of the core frame. These elements would perform certain serving functions for the heart of the metropolis itself and would also contain residences.

The most central circle, which represents the most densely built-up and most intensively utilized land area, would in itself be, again, a clusterization of a number of cells with their nuclei.

In observing this pattern, the reader will note that each one of the cells is separated from the others by open space. This space varies in size and is relatively smallest around the smallest cells, larger around constellations of cells, and widest between the planets (or cities) which form the entire constellation. There are wide contiguous green belts between city and city, and between all cities and the Metrocenter. There is an even wider permanent green belt around the entire metropolitan organism, separating it effectively from outlying communities, cities and possibly other metropolitan areas.

In order to bring more clarity into this complex organizational scheme, I have included a number of tabulations.

Table No. 1 gives population figures for each of the individual cellular clusters. Table No. 2 represents a summary for the entire metropolis with regard to dwelling units contained in each of the nuclei of the cellular organization. It lists the nuclei of each type and the assumed number of inhabitants per dwelling unit, and on this basis arrives at over-all population figures for each nucleus—and finally for the whole metropolis.

From this it can be noted that a high density of population has been assumed for Metrocenter and Metroframe, in which about 15 per cent of the total metropolitan population resides; a medium high to medium low density for city centers, town centers and community centers where about 30 per cent of the total population reside; and a low density for the neighborhoods where about 55 per cent of the population live.

Table No. 3 lists densities per gross acre but including the open spaces located between the clusters of the cellular formations.

Table No. 4 gives information about densities of nuclei excluding cell-separating open spaces.

The densities here shown, then, point up the fact that the low densities in the neighborhoods (50 persons per gross acre) are considerably higher than those we find in our sprawling suburban areas, and that the highest density, shown in Metrocenter (216 persons per gross acre), is considerably lower than that to be found in parts of existing cities.

Within this framework, it is possible to arrive at a wide variety and choice of living quarters: from single-family houses with gardens arranged in rows or as groups, to multiple residences two to six stories high, and to high-rise apartment buildings. (The space-devouring detached single house was not considered as suitable.)

Table No. 4 also gives information about the land occupied by each of the cellular organs. Adding up these acreages, we find that all cities and the Metrocomplex together occupy, including the open spaces within them, 138,640 acres; that the industrial areas (which we will discuss later) occupy 40,500 acres; and that the large contiguous open spaces between cities and between all cities and Metrocenter occupy 265,345 acres.

Of the total of 444,485 acres which the entire metropolitan organism occupies, more than half is thus devoted to large contiguous open spaces,

TABLE NO. 1 — THE METROPOLIS OF TOMORROW

POPULATION OF INDIVIDUAL CELLULAR CLUSTERS

NAME OF CLUSTER	STANDARDS	TOTAL
Neighborhood	250 Fam. @ 3.6 per Family	900
Community	Center = 250 Fam. @ 3.6 = 900 + 5 × NH. = 900 + 4,500	5,400
Town	Center = 1,000 Fam. @ 3.4 = 3,400 + 4 × Comm. = 3,400 + 21,600	25,000
City	Center = 10,000 Fam. @ 3.0 = 30,000 + 10 × Town = 30,000 + 250,000	280,000
Metroframe	10,000 Fam. @ 2.5 = 25,000 × 10	250,000
Metrocenter	100,000 Fam. @ 2.5	250,000

which would represent parks, orchards, recreational facilities, forests, lakes, and so on.

The total size of the metropolitan area, expressed in square miles, is about 694.5, and the over-all population per square mile is 4,750 persons.

Table No. 5 lists a number of standard "metropolitan statistical areas" in the United States, in order to permit a comparison with the "metropolis of the future." We find, for example, that Los Angeles, with roughly twice the population of the schematic metropolis, occupies seven times its land area. Yet—in contrast to the over 50 per cent of open space easily accessible from every single part of every community in my scheme—there is hardly any such facility existing in the City of the Angels.

We find that the population of the metropolitan area of Boston (2,589,301), representing about 80 per cent of the total population of the schematic metropolis of tomorrow, occupies 969 square miles, or roughly 50 per cent more than our scheme, without providing the easily accessible large open spaces of the metropolis of tomorrow. Boston is one of the more concentrated American metropolises. Contrasts to this theoretical scheme are much sharper in a metropolis like Dallas (population 1,083,601) which, representing about one-third of the population of the schematic metropolis, nevertheless occupies a land area (3,653 square miles) five times as great. By utilizing

TABLE NO. 2 THE METROPOLIS OF TOMORROW

POPULATION SUMMARY

NAME OF NUCLEUS	NO. OF ELEMENTS	DWELLING UNITS PER NUCLEUS	TOTAL DWELLING UNITS	PERSONS PER DWELLING UNIT	POPULATION PER NUCLEUS	TOTAL POPULATION	PERCENT OF TOTAL METROPOLITAN POPULATION	TYPE OF DENSITY
Metro-center	1	100,000	100,000	2.5	250,000	250,000	15%	High
Metro-frame	10	10,000	100,000	2.5	25,000	250,000		High
City Center	10	10,000	100,000	3.0	30,000	300,000	30%	Med-High
Town Center	100	1,000	100,000	3.4	3,400	340,000		Medium
Community Center	400	250	100,000	3.6	900	360,000		Med-Low
Neighborhood	2,000	250	500,000	3.6	900	1,800,000	55%	Low
METROPOLIS —		—	1,000,000		—	3,300,000		

the figures as they appear in Table No. 5, the reader will be able to make comparisons with other metropolitan areas.

The schematic plan also indicates five industrial center areas. In these locations, each one is closely related to three of the cities. There would be space allocated to those industries which, because of their need for large horizontal structures or because of their disturbing production activities (noise, fumes, smells), could not be successfully integrated into the nuclei

TABLE No. 3 THE METROPOLIS OF TOMORROW

POPULATION DENSITY
OF CLUSTERS

NAME OF CLUSTER	ACRES	POPULATION	POPULATION DENSITY PER GROSS ACRE (INCL. OPEN SPACES)
Neighborhood	18	900	50
Community	151.7	5,400	35.6
Town	987.5	25,000	25.6
City	12,645	280,000	22.1
Metropolis	444,485 (694.5 sq. mi.) = 4,750 persons per sq. mi.	3,300,000	7.42

themselves. Also located in these industrial centers would be warehousing facilities, distribution centers for goods, trucking terminals, etc.

As to the network of communications operating within this metropolitan organism, I have shown on the schematic plan only those that would take care of travel over considerable distances. Thus, one of the main transportation media, namely, pedestrianism, is not indicated at all. Pedestrianism will play a main role as a transportation medium within every single one of the nuclei. They are all sized to such scale that walking distances are short, and inasmuch as in all of them mechanized traffic is excluded from the surface, a pleasant walking environment will be created.

Within each of the neighborhoods, within the community centers, the town centers, the city centers and the various nuclei of Metrocenter, there will be a pattern of pedestrian walks and plazas, and this pattern will extend into the green areas surrounding them, in order to connect various nuclei with each other.

Again, I was not able to show, on this small scale, local vehicular roads and highways which, related to each one of the nuclei, will be established as loop roads surrounding each nucleus and connecting up to car storage

TABLE NO. 4 THE METROPOLIS OF TOMORROW

SIZE AND POPULATION OF INDIVIDUAL CELLULAR ELEMENTS

NAME OF NUCLEUS		ACRES	POPULATION	POP. DENSITY PER GROSS ACRE (EXCL. LARGE CONTIGUOUS OPEN SPACES)
Neighborhood		18	900	50.00
Community Center		6.5	900	138.50
Town Center		18	3,400	190.00
City Center		162.3	30,000	185.00
Metro-complex	Metroframe	4,500	250,000	55.6
	Metrocenter	1,154	250,000	216.00
All Cities Plus Metrocomplex = 12,645 × 10 + 12,190		138,640	3,300,000	23.8
Industrial Area		40,500		
Large Contiguous Open Spaces		265,345		
Total Acreage		444,485 = 694.5 sq. mi.		

facilities located on the fringe of each nucleus in the form of underground or multiple-deck garages. In a neighborhood, for example, garages will not be attached to every residence; instead garages for groups of families will be located on the outskirts of the neighborhood, easily reached within a few minutes' walk from each residence. The various centers—community center, town center, city center, Metrocenter, and the nuclei of the Metroframe—will be ringed by smaller loop roads, which, in the larger nuclei, will be continued underground to provide for goods transportation and services for all the structures.

TABLE NO. 5

STANDARD METROPOLITAN STATISTICAL AREAS OF U.S.A.—1960
POPULATIONS OF MORE THAN 1 MILLION

CITY	POPULATION	POP. PER SQ. MILE CENTRAL	POP. PER SQ. MILE TOTAL	TOTAL SQ. MILES
Baltimore	1,727,023	11,886	956	1,807
Boston	2,589,301	14,586	2,672	969
Chicago	6,220,913	15,836	1,675	3,714
Cincinnati	1,071,624	6,501	1,468	730
Cleveland	1,796,595	10,789	2,611	688
Dallas	1,083,601	2,428	297	3,653
Detroit	3,762,360	11,964	1,915	1,965
Kansas City (Mo.)	1,039,493	3,664	633	1,642
Los Angeles-Long Beach	6,742,696	5,638	1,393	4,842
Milwaukee	1,194,290	8,137	1,502	795
Minneapolis-St. Paul	1,482,030	7,326	702	2,111
New York	10,694,633	24,697	4,977	2,149
San Francisco-Oakland	2,783,359	11,013	840	3,313
Washington	2,001,897	12,442	1,348	1,485

The roads necessary to connect the main loop around the community, town or city with the nuclear center will, in order to avoid disturbances, be bedded either in an open depression or, as far as larger nuclei are concerned, underground.

On the schematic drawings, five transportation systems are indicated. They follow the principle of gradation which I discussed in the preceding chapter:

1. Air transportation over long distances, establishing connection with the national and international airways, is taken care of by an air terminal located between the metropolitan boundary and the outer loop freeway.

2. Long-distance rail service, establishing connections with the national rail system, connects with all industrial centers and interconnects with the Metro transit system.
3. The metropolitan high-speed transit system connects all city centers with the Metrocore and further connects all cities with the industrial centers and all cities with each other.
4. Intercity transit connects all town centers with all city centers.
5. Automotive transportation moves over a freeway system surrounding the cities, interconnecting with each other and with the ring road around Metrocenter, and connects further at five points with the national highway system. Roads and highways are linked to the freeway system and surround, in the form of loop roads as mentioned above, each one of the nuclear elements. This system for automotive traffic will be used for the following vehicles:
   a. Express buses on reserved lanes and highways and on special mass transit highways.
   b. Local buses between communities, and connecting communities to town centers, as well as between town centers and city centers
   c. Minibuses between neighborhoods and town centers, and as supporting transportation within pedestrian areas
   d. Private cars for transportation into the areas of nature reserves; for out-of-town travel; for communication between neighborhoods, between neighborhoods and community centers, and between communities.

Since it may be assumed that public mass transportation will offer greater convenience, higher speed and lower cost for those who wish to travel between town centers and city centers, and between city centers and Metrocore, it may also be assumed that private automobile traffic will not be utilized for such trips but for those within the peripheral area. The freeway network shown on the drawing, therefore, does not have to thicken as it approaches Metrocore. It is not designed as a radial system in which, as in the spokes of a wheel, all traffic is guided toward one point (which unavoidably would cause traffic congestion) but rather as a system of loops evenly spread and interconnected with each other.

Table No. 6 lists the types of transportation media envisaged for the metropolitan transit system, the speeds that could be projected on the basis of existing technology, and the travel time that would be involved. It may be noted from this table that a trip to Metrocenter from a city center located in an outer ring of cities, on an express train with a speed of 60 miles per hour, would involve a travel time of 12.5 minutes; one from a city center located in the inner ring, about 7.3 minutes. The longest trip indicated is one from the Metrocenter of the metropolitan air terminal, with 16.5 minutes elapsed travel time. If speeds higher than 60 miles per hour were to be introduced—which, with the aid of some of the already invented but not yet developed travel methods should be easily possible—these travel times could be cut.

As for the activities and land uses in each of the cellular units, I visualize that there would be a variety of them in each one of the nuclei but that as far as their importance and size are concerned, they would be scaled to the needs and requirements of the individual cellular organization. There would

TABLE No. 6 THE METROPOLIS OF TOMORROW

MASS TRANSPORTATION BETWEEN NUCLEI

		TYPE OF TRANSPORTATION	SPEED	TIME IN MINUTES
1. Outer Ring City Center to Metrocenter	= 12.5 miles	Express Rapid Transit	60 mph	12.5
2. Inner Ring City Center to Metrocenter	= 7.3 miles	"	60 mph	7.3
3. Outer Ring Town Center to City Center	= 2.4 miles	City Transit	30 mph	4.8
4. Inner Ring Town Center to City Center	= 1.25 miles	"	30 mph	2.5
5. Community Center to Town Center	= 0.44 mile	Local Bus	20 mph	1.3
6. Inner City Center to Industrial	= 5.7 miles	Express Rapid Transit	60 mph	5.7
7. Outer City Center to Industrial	= 6.7 miles	"	60 mph	6.7
8. Metrocenter to Industrial	= 13.0 miles	"	60 mph	13.0
9. Metrocenter to Air Terminal	= 16.5 miles	"	60 mph	16.5

be, for example, places of work, shopping facilities, cultural and recreational facilities, churches, social meeting rooms, in each one of the centers (neighborhood, community, town or city center; Metroframe and Metrocenter), but they would be graded in size and character in accordance with the size of the nucleus. One might illustrate this best by considering school distribution. The community centers, for example, would have two elementary schools each; the town centers one elementary school, two junior high schools and one senior high school each; the city centers, six elementary schools, three junior and two senior high schools and one junior college each; the Metroframe units, six elementary schools, three junior and two senior high schools each; and Metrocenter, 60 elementary schools, 30 junior high schools, 15 senior high schools, two state colleges and two universities.

The fact that the institutions of higher education are placed within Metrocenter might appear strange in light of our tradition of removing such institutions to rural areas or small towns. I have indicated them as located in Metrocenter because I believe that the urban campus will expose the students most effectively to urban life and will at the same time enrich the vitality of the city core through the influence of the scholastic and scientific life.

What I have just visualized here is a metropolitan system which, on the one hand, would establish close connection—thanks to short travel distances—between each neighborhood, community, town and satellite city and the metropolitan core; but which, on the other hand, would give to each of these communities, down to the very smallest of them (the neighborhood), its own individual life and its own sphere of governmental influence; a pattern in which urban features are not reserved for the metropolitan core alone but, in the form of community, town and city centers, are immediately accessible to every metropolite. It is a pattern that would succeed, also because of the definition of the boundaries of all its elements, in bringing nature and landscaping, and recreational areas, within reach of all inhabitants, wherever they may live. It is a pattern that does not force all to engage in *one* mode of living since it represents a wide choice in types of residential accommodation—from the single house close to nature to the skyscraper apartment close to dynamic urban life.

One of the questions that undoubtedly will be raised is: How would such a metropolitan area grow? There are a number of possibilities in this respect:

1. It could grow by adding an additional ring of cities, again separated by stretches of permanent open land. Inasmuch as the circle grows larger with the distance from the core, it could double its population in this manner. Such an enlargement would become practical if higher-speed

transportation between cities and between the outlying cities and the core can be implemented.

2. It could grow through inner growth, i.e., by increasing the density of the building and population pattern within each of the cellular forms. (The population densities assumed are low enough to open up such a possibility without creating uncomfortable living or working conditions.)
3. Obviously there is a limit, somewhere, to the workable size of a metropolitan area, on the basis of communication systems, existing or to be developed. When that size is reached, then it would be wiser to limit further growth and to start with a new metropolitan region in another location.

The scheme of the metropolis of tomorrow which I have tried to develop here will undoubtedly be called utopian by some. In the following pages I hope to prove, by pointing out existing implementations which at least go in a similar direction, that it is not utopian and that I have learned, to my sorrow, that it isn't even new.

I had arrived at the idea of the cellular organization after a period of many years, and I wrote about it for the first time in an article published by *Architectural Forum* in September, 1956.

When, quite recently, in the process of doing research for this book, I read Ebenezer Howard's *Garden Cities of To-Morrow,* I experienced that double-edged feeling which comes from learning that somebody else had your idea before you did; on the one hand, a certain sense of disappointment that I had not been as original as I thought and, on the other hand, satisfaction that there must be some logic to my thoughts if they had been enunciated sixty years earlier by a man who undoubtedly was a profound thinker. Ebenezer Howard's little book in favor of the construction of semirural garden towns actually culminates in a description of large metropolitan organisms. His diagram No. 5 illustrates this system, which he describes as follows:

> Garden City is built up. Its population has reached 32,000. How will it grow? It will grow by establishing . . . another city some little distance beyond its own zone of "country," so that the new town may have a zone of country of its own. I have said "by establishing another city" and, for administrative purposes there would be *two* cities; but the inhabitants of the one could reach the other in a very few minutes; for rapid transit would be especially provided for, and thus the people of the two towns would in reality represent one community.
>
> And this principle of growth—this principle of always preserving a

belt of country round our cities would be ever kept in mind till, in course of time, we should have a cluster of cities, not of course arranged in the precise geometrical form of my diagram, but so grouped around a Central City that each inhabitant of the whole group, though in one sense living in a town of small size, would be in reality living in, and would enjoy all the advantages of, a great and most beautiful city; . . .

I have said that rapid railway transit would be realised by those who dwell in this beautiful city or group of cities. . . . There is, first, an inter-municipal railway connecting all the towns of the outer ring . . . so that to get from any town to its most distant neighbour requires one to cover a distance of only 10 miles, which could be accomplished in, say, 12 minutes. These trains would not stop between the towns—means of communication for this purpose being afforded by electric tramways. . . .

There is also a system of railways by which each town is placed in

---

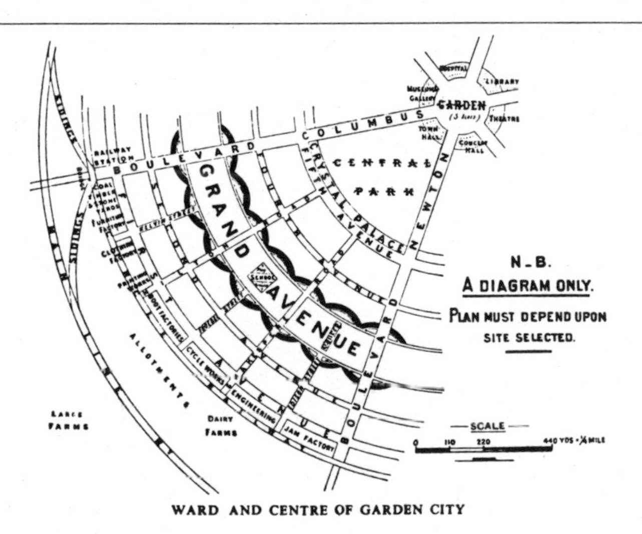

WARD AND CENTRE OF GARDEN CITY

Illustration from Ebenezer Howard's book, *Garden Cities of To-Morrow*. The original caption is "Ward and center of Garden City." We would call it today "Core and Core Frame." Ebenezer Howard describes this picture thus: "Six magnificent boulevards—each 120 feet wide—traverse the city from center to circumference, dividing it into six equal parts or wards. In the center is a circular space containing about five and a half acres, laid out as a beautiful and well-watered garden; and, surrounding this garden, each standing in its own ample grounds, are the large public buildings—town hall, principal concert and lecture hall, theater, library, museum, picture gallery and hospital. The rest of the large space encircled by the 'Crystal Palace' is a public park containing 145 acres, which includes ample recreation grounds within very easy access of all the people."

direct communication with Central City. The distance from any town to the heart of Central City is only 3¼ miles, and this could be readily covered in 5 minutes.

The reader who observes the schematic drawings illustrating the urban cellular pattern as I see it will, of course, be struck by its similarity to Mr. Howard's scheme. It was quite a relief to me, therefore, upon reading further, to discover that he had had an experience similar to mine, in relation to his own book. He writes in a footnote:

I may, perhaps, state as showing how in the search for truth men's minds run in the same channels, and as, possibly, some additional argument for the soundness of the proposals thus combined, that, till I had got far on with my project, I had not seen either the proposals of Professor Marshall or of Wakefield . . . nor had I seen the work of Buckingham,

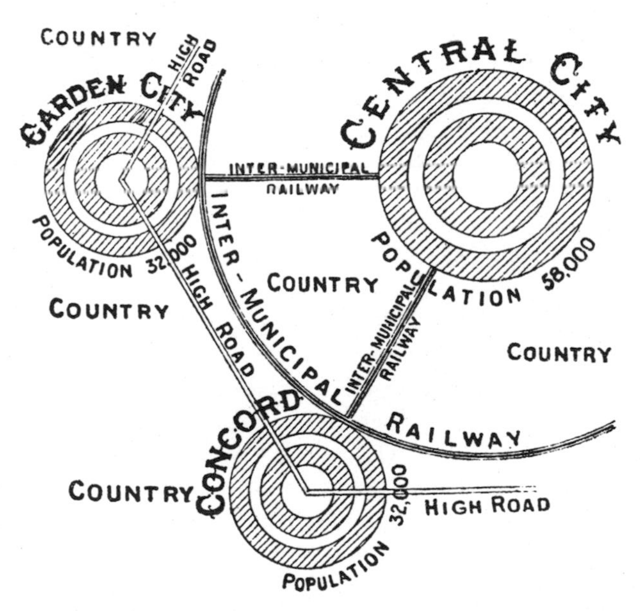

Illustration from Ebenezer Howard's book *Garden Cities of To-Morrow*. The original caption for this illustration is "Correct principle of a city's growth." The subtitle reads "Diagram illustrating correct principle of a city's growth—open country ever near at hand and rapid communication between offshoots." In modern planning language we may stick to the term "central city," but we may be calling the offshoots "satellite cities." What Mr. Howard designates as "the correct principle of a city's growth" seems to this author still applicable today.

> which, published nearly fifty years ago [N. B. That would be around 1850], seems to have attracted but little attention.

The differences between Ebenezer Howard's diagram and my schematic drawing are due to the stormy development of technology and sociology in the intervening sixty years, which have affected our lives more radically than anything for hundreds of years previously. Thus the principles expounded by Mr. Howard seem to me still valid. But where the concepts concerned the size of cellular elements, transportation, density of population and location of places of work, they had to be brought up to date.

Ebenezer Howard's philosophy has influenced many American urbanists, such as Lewis Mumford, Clarence Stein, Catherine Bauer-Wurster, Carl Feiss, who have planned or spoken out in favor of garden cities or new towns. Some such garden cities were actually built in the 1930s (Greenhills, Ohio; Greendale, Wisconsin; and Greenbelt, Maryland). In 1929 the town of Radburn, New Jersey, was constructed on the basis of plans by Clarence Stein.

The satellite towns of Stockholm, especially Vällingby and Farsta, are excellent examples, too. Vällingby itself is a clusterization of six defined communities separated from each other and from the rest of the city by wide permanently protected green areas. (The communities are Hässelby Strand, Hässelby Gård, Grimsta, Råcksta, Blackeberg and Vällingby.) Each of the communities is connected to an industrial center; each of them with the exception of Vällingby has a small shopping and cultural area; Vällingby itself represents the main town center containing shopping facilities, cultural facilities, office buildings and churches of much larger size. The town center in Vällingby is connected by high-speed rapid transit with the central core of Stockholm through an underground terminal directly accessible to the pedestrian area on the main level. Supplementary stations of the rapid transit system are situated in three of the other communities.

The satellite town of Farsta, also connected by high-speed rapid transit with the core of Stockholm, is organized in accordance with similar cellular planning principles, as are a number of other satellite towns, already constructed or in the project stage.

To anyone who would like to experience the visual effects of the cellular organism, I recommend a trip from Stockholm's handsome new airport to the city center, and I would suggest he then compare it with a similar trip in any American metropolis. Like most others, I made use of the very efficient system of express buses. While traveling over excellent roads, one may observe through the windows, on either side of the bus, vistas of peaceful, beautiful countryside. There are no commercial string develop-

Vallingby near Stockholm, Sweden: a satellite town cluster. Ebenezer Howard's "correct principle of a city's growth" has found practical application here. A rapid transit underground railroad connects the six defined communities with each other and with the town center of Stockholm. The urban nuclei are separated by green areas.

Town center of Vällingby, Sweden. In the center of the picture the shopping and office facilities are served by underground rapid transit; around this center and within easy walking distance of it are high-rise apartment buildings.

The New Town of Cumbernauld near Glasgow, Scotland. Photograph of model.

ments, no automobile cemeteries, no hot-dog stands; instead there are forests, lakes and meadows. As one approaches the city, a number of clusters of white towers become visible in the distance, increasing in frequency as the trip goes on. I was still waiting for the typical signs of urban blight when the bus stopped in front of a handsome terminal building. As I stepped out of the bus and looked in the direction from which we had come, I saw forests. When I turned around I saw, rising steeply like walls, the multi-storied structures of Stockholm's city core. From the air terminal one travels either by small city bus or taxicab. Within minutes of departing the rural scene prevailing around the terminal, one finds oneself in the hustle and bustle of a dynamic city core.

The New Towns around London, the completed ones as well as the projected town of Hook, as satellite towns express the cellular approach. In contrast to our suburban areas, they are self-sufficient to a large degree by virtue of the fact that they provide working places and urban centers for their inhabitants.

A small but extremely handsome new community, both as to design and execution, is Tapiola Garden City, a new town approximately six miles from the center of Helsinki, Finland, created by a private, non-profitmaking organization known as "Asuntosaatio" and designed by a team of Finnish architects. The town center was the subject of a competition which was won by the architect Aarne Ervi. The town consists of three independent neighborhoods, each with 5,000 to 6,000 inhabitants, all grouped around and served by the town center.

One of the outstanding examples, which has come to my attention through the kindness of the Cumbernauld Development Corporation, is to be found

The New Town of Cumbernauld near Glasgow, Scotland. Pedestrian ways between residences.

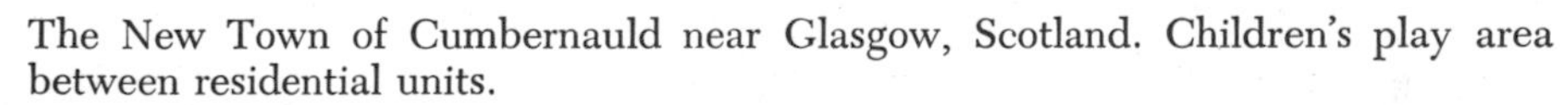

The New Town of Cumbernauld near Glasgow, Scotland. Children's play area between residential units.

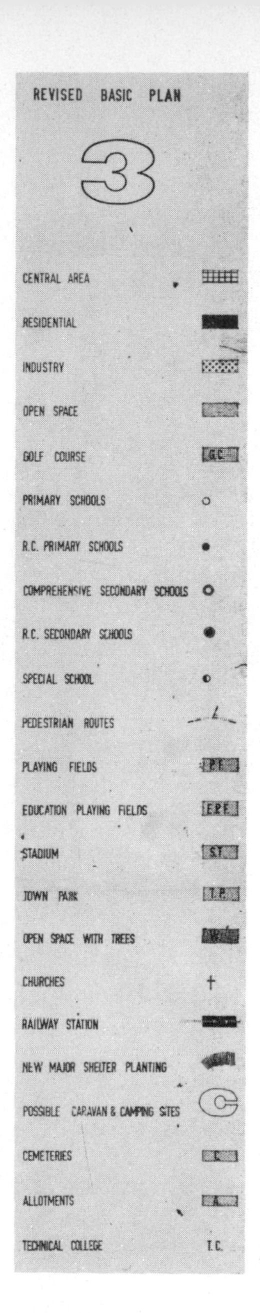

The New Town of Cumbernauld near Glasgow, Scotland. Overall plan.

76
77
78
79
Cumbernauld
Mainhead Plantation
P.E.
T.P.
E.P.E.S.
G.C.
S.T.
C.
A
73
74

in the plan for the New Town of Cumbernauld near Glasgow, Scotland. This plan represents an approach which, though similar to that of the New Towns around London, has profited much from their experience and is more principled and more sophisticated. The New Town of Cumbernauld, projected for 70,000 inhabitants, is already in construction, with some parts completed. The town is of cellular pattern and is organized into five nuclei, each one a separate village. The planning proposal (second revision, published in 1962) parallels so surprisingly the principles of the schematic plan for the metropolis of tomorrow that I would like to quote from it some pertinent portions:

> The town is to provide accommodations and facilities for a total population of 70,000. In addition to the main hilltop site developments are proposed at four villages, each complete with local shops and other minor facilities but depending on the main town centre for the principal shopping, entertainment and cultural activities. . . .
>
> Special sites have been reserved for industry and great emphasis is given in the employment pattern on offices and services. . . .
>
> A town footpath system embraces the whole of the designated area and has been extended to provide links to the surrounding countryside. . . .
>
> The central town center is developed for complete separation of utilitarian and human functions with all traffic movement and parking space at the lowest levels and a series of pedestrian decks above. . . .
>
> A comprehensive open space system has been worked out to surround the built-up areas of the town. . . .
>
> The overall pattern is to be regarded as that of a cluster city in which one major urban center is surrounded by, but separated from, a number of smaller compact urban units of varying size, the whole being linked by an efficient road and footpath system. . . .
>
> Considerable attention has been given to the idea of obtaining the maximum separation of pedestrians and vehicles throughout the town. . . .
>
> The concept of streets lined with houses on both sides has been dropped in favor of designs in which the movement of vehicles and pedestrians and the planning of the individual dwellings to achieve the best possible living conditions are highly integrated.

Among the large number of our own projects in which we have attempted to express the principles of cellular urban organization, there are just two I would like to touch on. One is a project we developed for the Board of

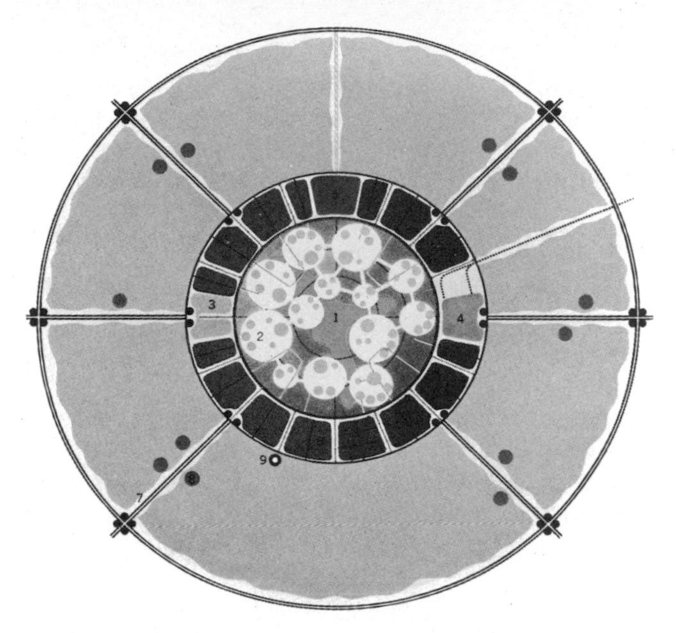

Schematic plan for the projected World's Fair 1964 (see page 294). This plan was developed for the Washington Metropolitan Board of Trade in a bid to place the 1964 World's Fair on a large available site in Maryland, between Washington and Baltimore. The concept was to plan the World's Fair from the beginning in such manner that it could be converted subsequently into a satellite town of about 100,000 inhabitants. This illustration demonstrates the use of the site during the fair.

This illustration demonstrates how the land would be used after the fair was closed and conversion into a satellite town had taken place.

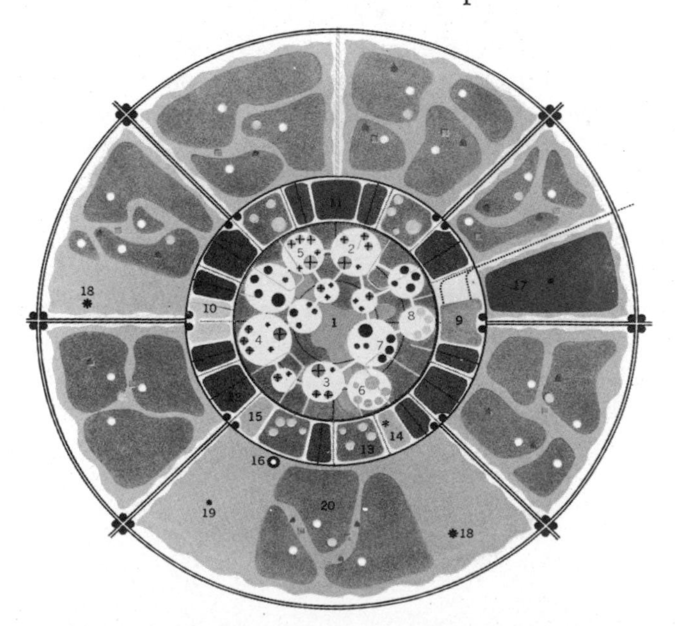

Trade of Washington, D.C., when the likelihood existed that that city might be the site of the World's Fair in 1964. Inasmuch as the application of the city of Washington was turned down in favor of New York, the project was not executed. The plan has, however, attracted great public attention, partly because it seemed to demonstrate that all the economic and human sacrifices which the planning and construction of a Fair entails do not have to be wasted as soon as the Fair closes its gates, and partly because it seemed to develop new ideas for the economics of a World's Fair enterprise. Both of these achievements are brought about through the concept of permanency that underlies the plan.

The idea was to construct all basic improvements in such a manner that at the closing of the Fair operation the site could be converted, with the greatest ease and economy, into one for a satellite town with 100,000 inhabitants. The two illustrations on page 293 show respectively the plan of the site during the Fair operation and after its conversion into a satellite town.

One glance at the illustrations will reveal the cellular organization. But before discussing these illustrations, I would like to caution the reader as I did with regard to the schematic plan for the metropolis of tomorrow: Inasmuch as we were asked only to provide a concept for the Fair, we restricted ourselves to schematized drawings expressed in geometric figures. The central circle represents the main exhibit area during the Fair, and the city core of the future satellite town. It is in itself a clusterization of nuclei which, visualized as platforms raised about 20 feet above the ground level, would carry, during the World's Fair, exhibition buildings of various types within a pedestrian environment. These exhibition buildings would later be replaced by office buildings, apartment buildings, hotels, government structures, etc., located in the same pedestrian environment, for the satellite city. The space underneath the platforms would contain all utilitarian functions: heating plants, air-conditioning plants, facilities for storage, loading and unloading, and terminals for internal transportation, and would remain unchanged in function for both the World's Fair and the satellite city. The various platforms are connected by pedestrian bridges. The space between them is a park with lagoons and lakes constructed during the Fair but utilized later in the core area of the city.

Around the central circle there is an inner ring area which, during the Fair, is utilized exclusively as a terminal facility for regional transportation. Here are transit terminals for lines to Washington and Baltimore, freight terminals, railroad terminals, bus terminals; also, parking lots for private cars. Most of these installations would remain when the satellite city operates. However, since the transportation load of the satellite city would be smaller than that of the World's Fair during peak hours, parts of this transportation ring would be converted into industrial centers, core frame elements, and so on.

The outer ring would be used during the World's Fair as a many-purpose area for the following: circulatory road systems, approach roads, temporary housing, trailer camps, flying fields for private planes, etc. After the Fair, there would grow in this wide ring a clusterization of towns, communities and neighborhoods, all separated from each other by green areas, in a manner similar to the concept developed for the metropolis of tomorrow.

Another project is that of a new city near Cape Kennedy (formerly Cape Canaveral), which is to serve the needs of 60,000 workers and their families who will be employed shortly in connection with the Federal lunar probe program.

The illustration of the plan of this city again reveals a strongly expressed cellular formation. We were, however, in the case of this project, not able to achieve the density patterns we felt would be desirable. The attitude of clients and consultants, based on the belief that the American public was unwilling to accept anything but detached single housing schemes, led to a compromise in this matter.

An interesting example of how a project that starts out with a cellular conceptual idea can go wrong because of *laissez-faire* planning is Disneyland near Anaheim, California. The nucleus of this cellular constellation is organized in a forthright manner as a compactly arranged grouping of buildings, exhibits and surrounding pedestrian areas. In these pedestrian areas we find some supporting transportation in the form of old horse-drawn streetcars, antique buses, etc. Though Disneyland was originally conceived only as an amusement park for children and, to some extent, for their parents, it has also become a shopping center, a social center, and a center of national and international tourism, opening its doors to everyone in the world but Mr. Khrushchev, who, justifiably, was upset about this. Disneyland possesses two public transportation systems, one in the form of an old railroad train, and the other in the form of a modernistic monorail train, which serves not only as a sightseeing vehicle but also as a means of transportation between the core and a large hostelry nearby. The building nucleus is properly surrounded by a transportation ring containing parking areas for buses and automobiles. Intermediary transportation carriers (small electric trains) carry visitors from the various parking lots and bus lots to the entrance to the car area.

Like any dynamic central core, Disneyland has generated, in an astonish-

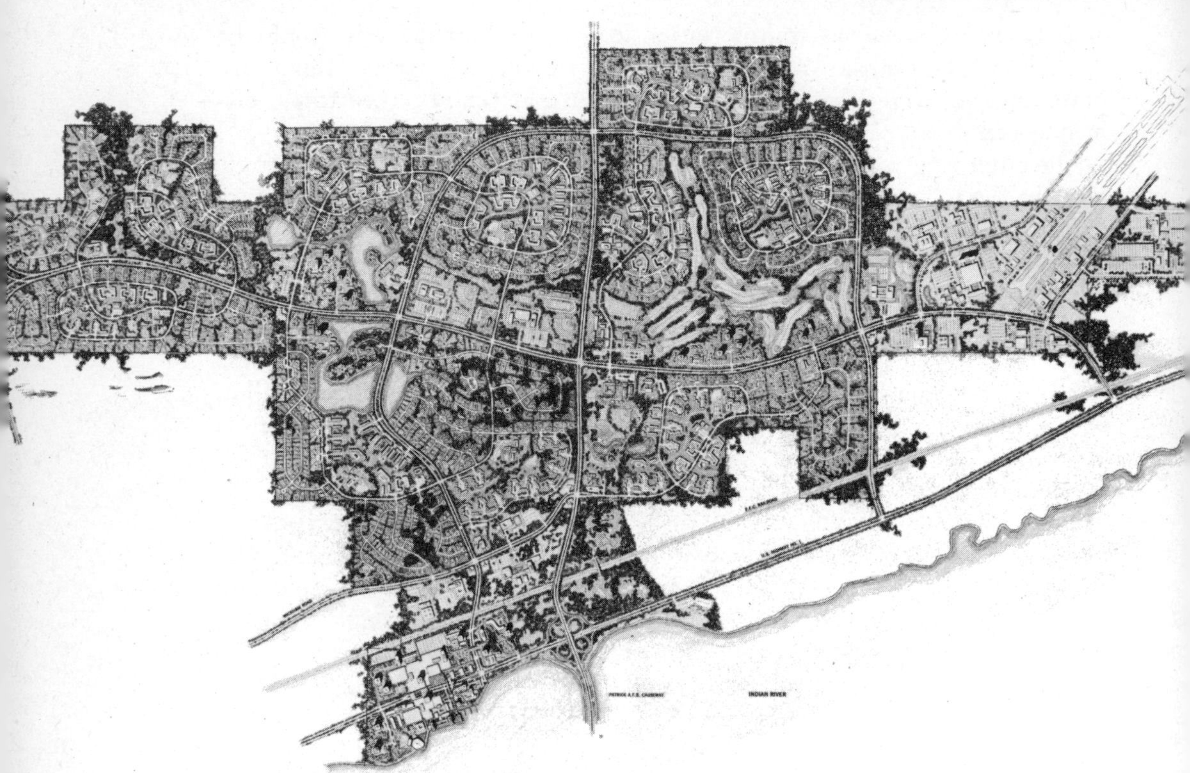

Plan of a projected new city to provide living quarters and urban facilities for the workers of the Federal moon shot program near Cape Kennedy. The cellular organizational pattern is strongly expressed.

---

ingly short time, satellite developments. Here, however, is the rub. The satellite developments proceeded without benefit of any planning, and suburban pandemonium took over. Dozens of hotels, stores, office buildings, restaurants, bars, banks, nightclubs, gas stations, lunch counters, hot-dog stands and billboards clutter it up, creating traffic congestion, disorder and blight.

The emerging new urban pattern will be created only if there emerges a strong will for forthright planning. The cellular planning concept, I believe, points the way in the right direction. It is a concept applicable not only to new communities, cities and metropolitan areas, but also, if we are given the proper legislative tools, to existing metropolitan areas.

19 The Rebirth of the Heart

A NATIONAL MOVEMENT toward the revitalization of the heart areas of our cities is under way. Redevelopment projects in dozens of American cities, dealing partially or totally with core areas, are now in process. I, personally, know of about forty major ones, but I am sure the number is much greater because many of these projects have not yet come to public attention.

In an even greater number of cities, citizens' groups formed specifically for the purpose of redevelopment of the core areas are discussing this goal.

If one were to accept the quantity of efforts as a measuring stick, one would conclude that the outlook for a rosy future of the city is excellent. In any case, the impressive quantity proves that there is a popular desire for urban improvement.

What is questionable is whether the quality of all these undertakings is such as to give hope that the deep desire will be fulfilled. In this respect, revitalization efforts vary widely. Though all of them deal with the problem of the core, few of them go to the core of the problem.

At the core of the problem lie purely human considerations. The hearts of our cities will function in a healthy way only if they fulfill the desires in the hearts of people, if they effectively serve human hopes, aspirations and needs.

There is in most people an inborn desire to be with others when experiencing life expressions, whether these expressions are to be found in parades or baseball games, in concerts, gatherings, in work or in leisure.

This desire is potent enough to create a willingness to accept a certain amount of difficulty arising from such obstacles as travel, crowding, time loss, etc. The relation between the desire for participation in urban life and the amount of difficulty which the average human being is willing to accept in order to fulfill this desire could be expressed as a mathematical equation:

$$A = D - O$$

A represents Attractive Power. *D* represents Desire. *O* represents obstacles that stand in the way of fulfilling human desires with regard to participation in urban life. Thus, if *O* were as large as *D*, *A* would be zero. If *D* were very large and *O* were nil, or near nil, then *A* would be largest.

Now let us apply this equation to the heart of the city. In the typical case —and of course there are marked gradations—*O*, the obstacles, has grown constantly. That means it has become more difficult to get to the city core area, to get around in it, and to avoid inconveniences when participating in core activities.

Simultaneously, *D*, the desire to live in or travel to the city core area, has steadily decreased as economic, physical and social deterioration has spread.

A, the attractive power, under the influence of these two developments, has decreased sharply.

Theoretically, one could increase the size of *A* by changing just one of the other two factors of the equation. One could, for example, leave *D* unchanged but concentrate on minimizing *O* by improving public and private transportation media. Or one could increase the size of *D* by improving the environmental qualities of the core area to such a degree that even after deducting an unchanged factor *O*, the attractive power, *A*, would still markedly increase.

In practice, however, it will be necessary to work simultaneously on both factors on the right side of the equation. This is necessary because factor *O* (obstacles) cannot be reduced practically beyond a certain limit. Some obstacles will always remain. This is inherent in the distance between metropolitan region and city core, and in the technological difficulty of transporting large numbers of persons from many points in the region to one single comparatively small area. Even under the most ideal conditions there will be some time loss, some inconvenience, some discomfort.

Though it is essential to make every effort to decrease *O* to the point where it is as small as practicably possible, full success will be achieved only if factor D is simultaneously enlarged. Toward this end we have to direct the activities that one can summarize under the term "urban design" with all its tools: the creation of improved urban esthetics; improvements in economic and social conditions; the creation of order, convenience and beauty.

In order to be effective, then, our over-all efforts must be shaped as a two-pronged attack, with the aim of, on the one hand, creating environmental qualities that will help fulfill the human heart's desire in the city's heart, and on the other hand, making it possible to reach that central location of the region, the core, with the highest achievable speed and convenience.

Our problem in tackling this dual task is that past and still-existing trends are working in the opposite direction. In most cities in the United States desirability of the city core has steadily decreased and difficulties in reaching the core have mounted at an even faster rate. Thus our task is one of *reversing trends.* We have to reverse the trend toward decentralization, which has been spreading urban functions all over the regional countryside, simultaneously robbing these functions of much of their potency. We have to reverse the trend toward residential scatterization by bringing residence population back into the core area of cities or nearby clusterizations. We have to reverse the trend toward decreased use of public mass transportation and increased use of private automobiles for travel to and from the city core because, as discussed earlier, a compact city area cannot be served effectively by automobile transportation alone.

To actually reverse strong and entrenched trends that have been operative over a long period of time and still are, in undiminished force, is of course a much more difficult task than that of just slowing down a process under way. It is a task that cannot even be approached by any single type of measure, however large and costly the execution of such a measure might be. Neither the replacement of old structures by new ones alone, nor the construction of huge parking facilities alone, nor the improvement of public transportation facilities alone, nor a lifting of the esthetics of the environment alone, nor the activating of cultural, civic and entertainment functions alone, nor slum clearance alone will resolve the urban equation, which is a human one.

What makes the heart of the city tick is not its structures, however large and well designed, nor vehicles nor utilitarian services, but people. Without people to pervade the city in manifold ways, its structures become hollow, meaningless shells. The questions before us can thus be boiled down to one basic, overruling sentence: How can we attract people back to the heart of the city?

In a free democratic society this task cannot be accomplished by decree. We cannot force people into any action they don't deeply desire. If they don't wish to use public mass transportation because it is overcrowded, undignified and inconvenient, they just won't do it. If they don't wish to drive bumper to bumper in and out of the city core and then hunt for a parking space, they just won't do it. If they don't wish to come to a place that has little to offer in opportunities, attractiveness and human experience, they will stay away in droves.

Thus, from a practical point, two sets of measures have to be planned and implemented: those that will make movement to and from the city center as convenient, speedy and comfortable as possible, and those that will lift the environmental qualities of the urban core to the highest attainable level. The aim here must be to reshape the heart of the city into a place that offers more than an opportunity for merely one type of activity such as earning one's livelihood; it should be a place where opportunities for self-fulfillment are multiplied a thousandfold.

I have termed this activity "transfiguration" and have discussed in a general way, in earlier chapters, methods by which a superior type of urban order could be achieved, wherein manifold human activities could proceed undisturbed by the frictions presently arising from inferior organizational patterns.

I want now to talk about some practical applications of the theory of "transfiguration," and I believe I can best do so through case studies of a number of undertakings in which I have been intimately involved.

I shall single out one specific project for a detailed discussion, even though it does not concern one of the large cities nor does it encompass work on an entire city core. This is a project comparatively modest as to expenditures and size of area. It doesn't even completely fulfill all the requirements I have set up as necessary for the double-pronged counterattack toward simultaneous increase of attractiveness and decrease of obstacles. But it does contain elements of all the ingredients of transfiguration, and, beyond that, it has one quality that sets it apart as a milestone on the road to urban revitalization: it is no longer on paper, no longer a dream, but has been actually implemented, has been in full operation since the spring of 1962, and is there for everybody to see and experience. Thus, in the case of this undertaking, it is not only possible to conclude that the revitalization effort *can* be executed but it is also possible at this time to measure the effects such an effort has on the heart of the city and on its metropolitan region.

I am talking about the city of Rochester in the state of New York, and about an undertaking resulting from cooperation between private enterprise and governmental agencies, called Midtown Plaza.

Since Midtown Plaza opened its gates in April, 1962, Rochester has become the Mecca for pilgrimages by city officials, merchants, government agencies, architects, planners, visitors from foreign countries. Midtown Plaza has been discussed and commented upon in hundreds of articles in professional magazines, newspapers, periodicals, on television shows and radio broadcasts. The very fact that the healthier pulsating of one city heart in the United States can create a sensation on the news front is of course, in a sense, a sad commentary on how little we have achieved in the way of practical results in this respect. On the other hand, those who visited Rochester and wrote about it were not mere curiosity seekers. They have generated new interest and new courage by pointing out that a task so difficult that many have despaired of its accomplishment can actually succeed.

How did Midtown Plaza come into being? It was in December, 1956, that we were approached by the heads of two of Rochester's leading department stores: Gilbert McCurdy of McCurdy & Company, Inc., and Maurice Forman and the late Fred Forman of the B. Forman Company, who stated their problem in the following terms:

> Though we are competitors in some respects, we have joined together in order to consider what could be done in order to protect the commercial future of our two stores. Though our business up to date is satisfactory, we are watching with alarm the downward trend of business in centers of other American cities; and we have concluded that it would be wise to take counter action before serious trouble starts. Already a number of regional shopping centers have sprung up in the suburban areas of Rochester, and in some of them we are represented by branch stores. But it appears that none of these smaller branch store units can ever give to our customers the completeness of service which they deserve.
>
> The city approached us with an offer to construct a 500-car garage in a location near to our two stores. We are asked to help to decide where this garage should be exactly located, but we somehow feel that this measure in itself would be insufficient. We realize fully that the future of our enterprises is inseparably tied to the well-being of the city as a whole, but quite especially to the well-being of the city's center. We want, therefore, to engage in the shaping of a long term policy; we, therefore, would like you to investigate the possibility of undertaking steps which could effect significant and long-lasting improvement in our downtown area. If you should advise us that it would be

economically inadvisable to engage in any new construction downtown, we would then have to decide to direct our main attention to the construction of new suburban units. We would, however, quite definitely prefer to secure the future of our downtown stores if this is at all feasible.

With the help of the economic consultants, Larry Smith & Company, we started a thorough investigation of physical, economic and transportation conditions. This is what we found. Downtown Rochester was basically a one-street center with most of its major merchandising enterprises and office buildings strung along Main Street, which acted simultaneously as the main traffic artery for private automobiles, buses and trucks. From this fact resulted traffic congestion on Main Street itself and on all roads leading to it.

McCurdy's department store is located at the intersection of Main and Cortland Streets on what, in real estate parlance, would be called "a triple-A location on the hottest corner." The B. Forman store is located on

The Cortland Street area in Rochester, New York, as it appeared before the Midtown Plaza was constructed. A parking lot is visible in the foreground. A workshop building occupied by Weed and Company (which was weeded out) is in the background. A second workshop building adjoins it to the right. These two structures were the most substantial ones that had to be demolished.

Clinton Avenue, one of the broad thoroughfares leading to Main Street and about half a block distant from the Main Street corner. Its goods deliveries were handled from Cortland Street. The corner of Main Street, Clinton Avenue and Cortland Street was occupied by an office building and the Manger Hotel, Rochester's largest hostelry. The remainder of the area west of Main Street and a few steps removed from it constituted an example of urban blight. The land was occupied by parking lots, shacklike structures containing workshops, warehousing and storage facilities and some economically marginal retail enterprises. The largest amount of the land was not occupied by buildings at all. Cortland Street, a comparatively narrow road, moved little traffic but was nevertheless congested by automobiles moving in and out of parking lots, by trucks serving the two department stores and various workshops and storage facilities, by pushcarts, all of which were slowed down in their movements by persons on foot who were shoppers or employees and who wound their way between the wheels of slowly moving or stalled vehicles. A considerable distance away from Main Street there was one major structure, Loew's movie theater, one of those huge movie palaces which, in the heyday of the film industry, had attracted large crowds but now did so only occasionally.

Observing the totality of the heart of Rochester, we found that the phenomenon of commercial blight, starting immediately behind a thin façade of productive buildings along both sides of Main Street, was a general occurrence. The life tissue of the city had been slowly loosened to a dangerous degree by the demolition of buildings that had once contained urban functions, and their replacement by parking lots, garages, used-car lots, widened roads and other automotive facilities. When photographed from the air, the core area of Rochester appeared like a sea of asphalt and automobile tin roofs, from which rose, in islandlike fashion, some structures holding out against the surf of slow but incessantly moving waves of automotive traffic.

But we also found some encouraging factors. The administration of the city of Rochester had engaged for quite some time in measures that generally fall into the category of necessary prerequisites for the revitalization of the heart. Most of these measures had to do with reducing the obstacles about which we talked earlier.

A loop road of the freeway type, quite similar in concept to the one we had projected for Fort Worth (described in the chapter "The Taming of the Motorcar") had been planned, and was partly completed, partly under construction. A number of radial express roads leading from the outlying regions to the loop road and tying in with it had been constructed.

Central area of Rochester, New York. Freeway type loop road (1) is partly completed, partly under construction; (2) indicates the site of the Civic Center, then under construction; (3) indicates municipally operated multi-story parking structures. Just right of the center one can see the Midtown Plaza project.

A secondary core loop ringing the most active central area was in the talking stage. A number of multilevel garages on the fringe of the most active part of the central area had been erected or were then in construction, though none had been built in the general area of the stores of our two clients.

These garages were financed through municipal bonds. Parking charges were held reasonably low but were sufficient to amortize the bond issue satisfactorily.

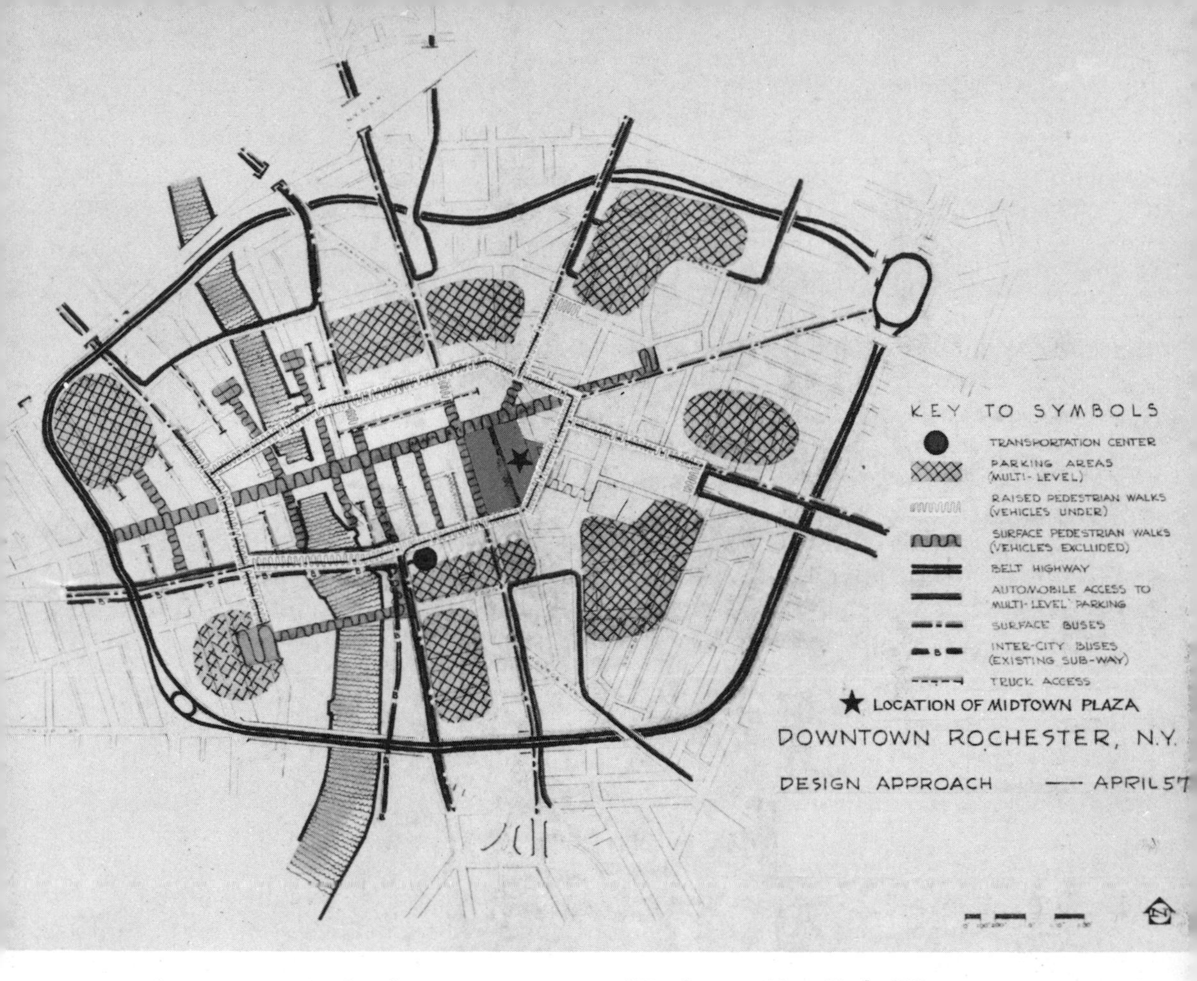

A revitalization concept for the entire core area of Rochester, New York (Victor Gruen Associates). Location of Midtown Plaza as a specific element of the revitalized core is indicated by ★.

The city administration was also actively engaged in work on the other factor of the urban equation: *Desire*. Under way were modernization and enlargement of the civic and cultural center, including the addition of public auditoria. A number of redevelopment projects, which aimed at increasing desirable residential facilities in the areas immediately surrounding the city core, were in planning stages.

The existence of some of the prerequisites for revitalization, and the manifest will of a progressive city administration to continue to take measures in this direction, encouraged us to tell our clients that in our opinion it might very well be feasible to create within the city core of Rochester a development that would make use of the existing and projected potential of greater accessibility, and that might encourage further progress in this direction.

Acting upon our recommendations, our clients entrusted to us the undertaking of studies which, though concentrating on the specific area in which their stores were located, would result in a revitalization concept for the entire core area. From these studies emerged a scheme that established a core loop, which up to then had been a rather hazy concept, as a vital element for an over-all plan. Its construction, we felt, together with improved public transportation through new bus lines and improved bus service, and the construction of some additional parking garages directly accessible from this innermost loop, would make it possible to free the intensely developed heart area from all mechanized traffic, and allow the conversion of Main Street, and its cross streets within the innermost loop, into pedestrian areas, partly covered and partly open. Simultaneously, all unsuitable uses (surface parking lots, warehousing, storage, etc.) could be removed from this compact area, and in their place structures for residences, offices, stores, theaters, and so on could be built.

Within this over-all project for the revitalization of Rochester's core we then outlined an area covering about one-fifth of the land within the projected innermost loop. This specific project area would be bounded by Main Street on one side, Clinton Avenue (where Forman's store was located) on another, by the future first leg of the innermost loop—namely, Broad Street Extension—on the third; two minor streets would limit it on the fourth side.

These were the criteria employed in delimiting this area: that the land area was sufficiently large to develop a strong new core element; that it was so located as to bring about an intimate connection between the two stores of our clients; that the area was for the most part devoid of major buildings so that in its implementation no large-scale demolition would have to take place. Early in 1958 we were authorized to develop a more detailed plan for the approximately nine-acre area indicating tentatively how the land could be utilized.

Larry Smith & Company, on the basis of estimated cost for land acquisition and estimated cost of construction, and of assumed income from rental operations, projected an over-all economic outlook and came to the conclusion that the project would be economically feasible only if some assistance, specifically with regard to the construction of the planned underground garage, were forthcoming from the city. They also made it clear

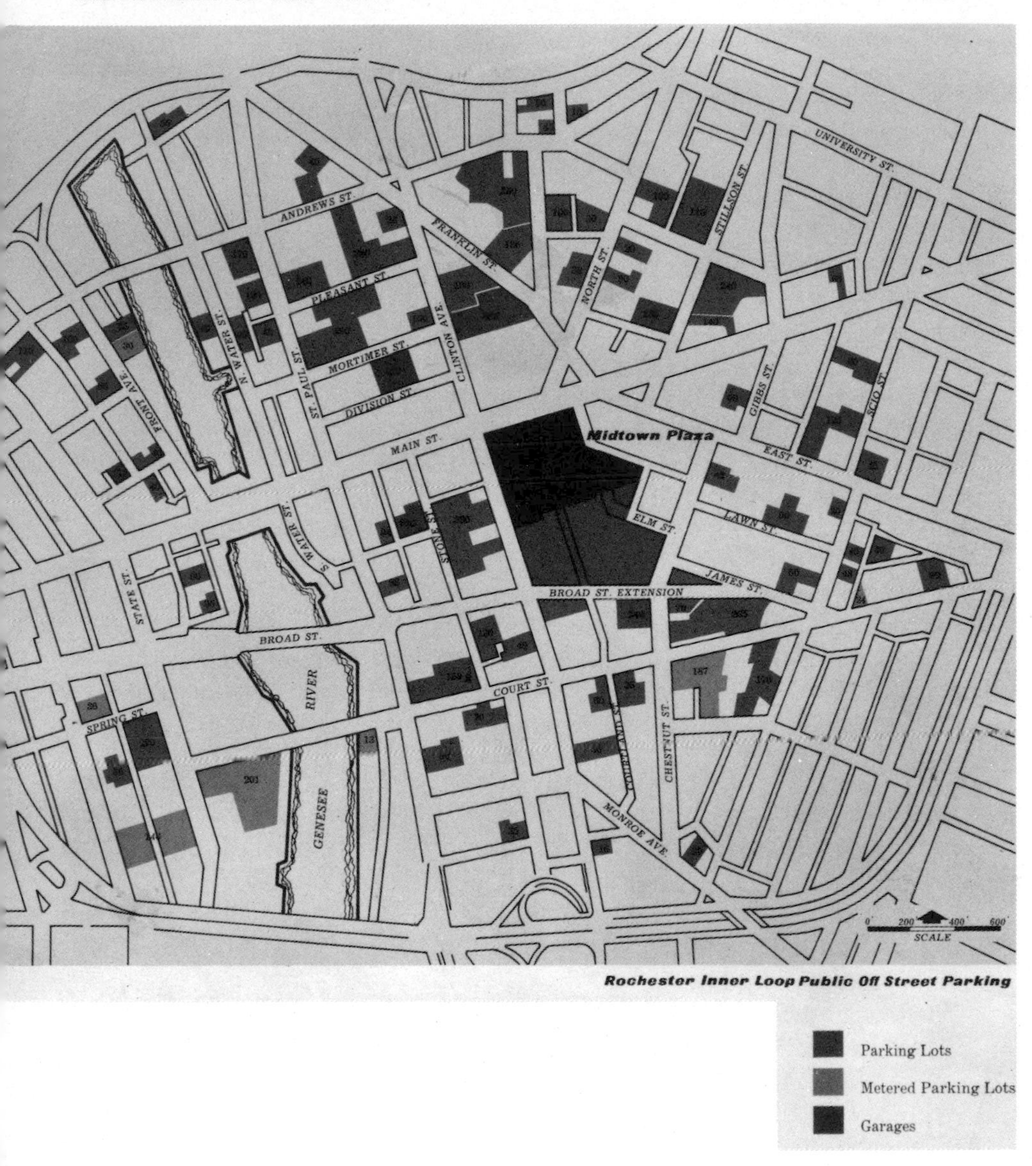

The central area of Rochester, New York, with the Midtown Plaza complex shown in black. Other areas indicated in black and gray are existing parking lots, metered parking lots and garages.

to our clients that the construction of such a large complex in a lethargic core area was fraught with financial risks and that as a pure real estate investment it could not be considered as a profitable venture. Our clients and we became convinced that help from the city with regard to the semipublic provisions for parking would be essential. As far as the financial risk was concerned, our clients declared that their interest in the future of a healthy economic climate for the city of Rochester was great enough so that they were willing to disregard any profit or even possible losses in the real estate venture itself. They were ready to pursue the matter further, but an important tactical decision had to be made. If they were to approach the city officially, news of the plan would necessarily leak out, and in that event it would become extremely difficult to acquire the land for the project area. The McCurdy and Forman department stores decided, therefore, to start with land acquisition. They therefore formed the Midtown Plaza Holdings Corporation, and during many months of negotiations they were able to gain control of all land in the delineated project area.

Around the middle of January, 1958, Mayor Peter Barry and City Manager Robert Aex were unofficially advised of the willingness of our clients to proceed with a project if certain conditions could be met by the city administration. From the beginning, city officials showed intense interest, and after detailed discussions with various officials and with the planning consultant to the city, Ladislas Segoe of Cincinnati, basic agreement was reached, the city agreeing in principle to the following:

Cortland Street and parts of other streets would be closed to all mechanized traffic on the surface, and though these areas would remain public streets, they would, at least on the surface, be open only to pedestrians. Permission would be granted to construct, under land that was partly under public ownership, an underground truck load and service facility, including the necessary ramps leading to and from it, so that all service traffic, loading and unloading, could be located there.

Instead of the originally envisaged 500-car multiple-deck surface garage, a three-level underground garage with a capacity of approximately 2,000 automobiles would be constructed by the city and financed through a public bond issue.

The city would construct as a first link of the core loop a new street, the so-called Broad Street Extension.

The city would make those changes in the utility system which would be essential for the construction and operation of the new core element.

In return for these considerations, the private developers, our clients, would obligate themselves to the following:

They would lease to the city the underground rights below the land they

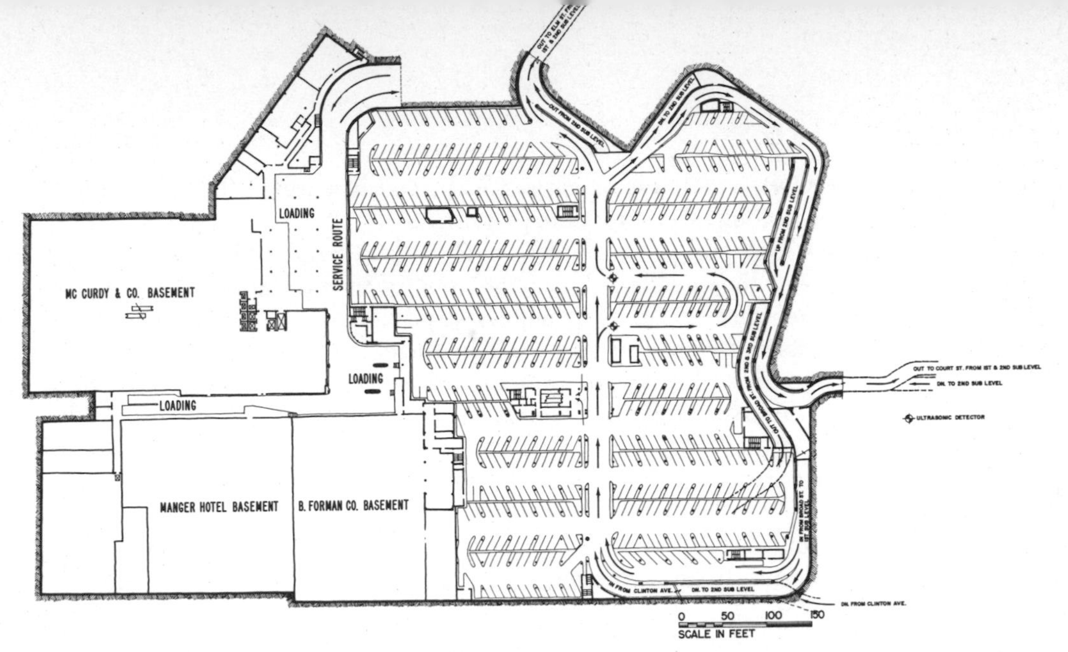

Midtown Plaza, Rochester, New York. Plan of one of the underground levels utilized for garaging and servicing facilities. The two levels below it are similar, but utilized for garaging purposes only. Approximately 2,000 underground parking spaces are provided.

Midtown Plaza, Rochester, New York. Ground-floor plan. Existing structures, some of them considerably enlarged, like the two department stores and the hotel, combined with new structures and grouped around a central pedestrian area known as "the plaza." On the ground floor most of the built-up space is utilized for retailing facilities. The former Cortland Street has been widened into a plaza, approached by pedestrian lanes from the surrounding existing street network. It is still a public thoroughfare but closed to all mechanized traffic.

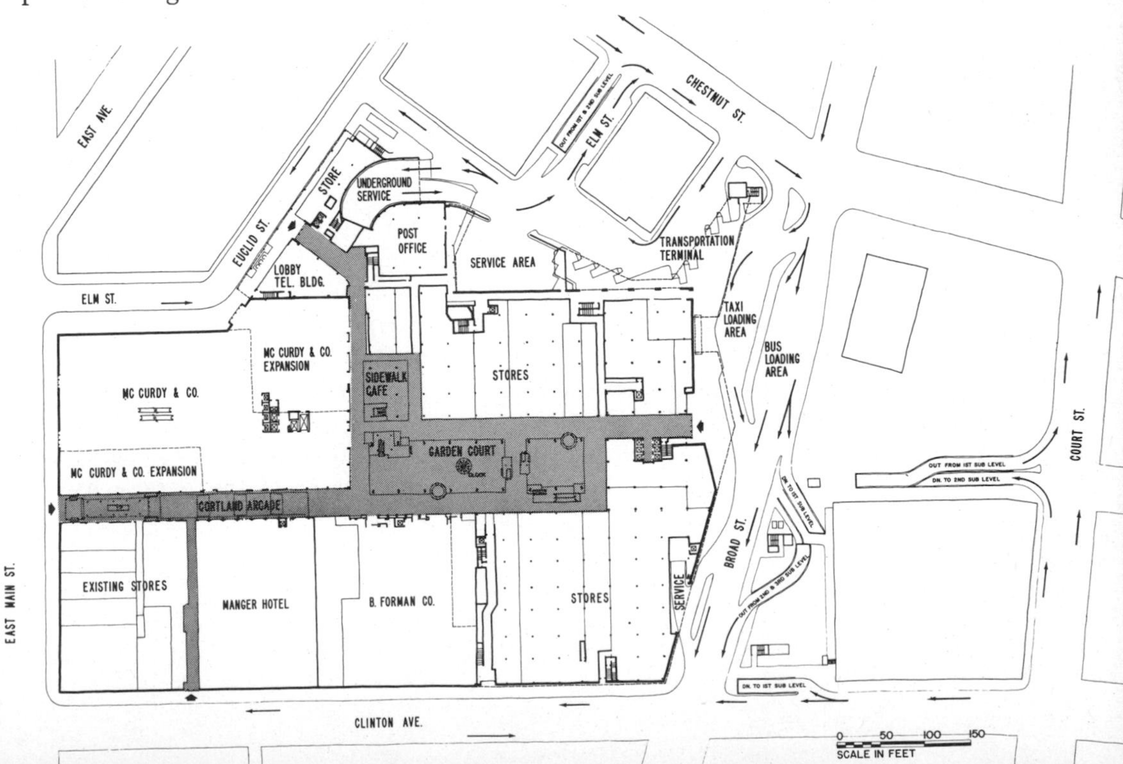

now controlled, which was essential for the construction of the underground garage, for a nominal fee of $1.00 a year.

Immediately upon the completion of the underground garage or any stages thereof, they would start construction of surface buildings of the size and character that had been generally determined.

Economists and engineers employed by the city convinced themselves that although the public works program needed for the project was considerable and costly, the costs could be amortized over a reasonable time span. Added income to the city would result from parking fees and from the additional tax revenue created by the construction of new buildings as well as from the activities that would take place there.

After a number of sometimes quite stormy sessions and after hearing testimony from all sides, the city council approved the project formally in January, 1959.

The problem that had created perhaps the greatest controversy was the increased size of the planned garage and the fact that it had to be created underground, which would, of course, increase construction costs as compared with a multilevel aboveground facility. Yet cost estimates proved that inasmuch as no land acquisition costs had to be incurred (the underground rights were, as already mentioned, leased to the city for $1.00 a year), the combined construction and land cost per car was still approximately the same as what the city had to pay for other multilevel aboveground garages, since in those cases expensive downtown land had to be purchased.

Decisive in the favorable findings of the experts was the fact that, in contrast to the multilevel aboveground garage, which subtracts taxable land from the revenue of the city, in this case not only would there be no subtraction but, on the contrary, additional tax revenues flowing from the structures rising on top of the underground garage.

On the basis of these findings, the city determined to start garage construction and retained us as architects. Thus, we acted as planners and architects for the city in association with Bohacket & Flynn, Rochester architects; for the developer, the Midtown Plaza Holdings Corporation; for McCurdy's department store, as far as the enlargement of their building, remodeling of the old building and furnishing of the total premises were concerned; for Forman's, in connection with their enlargement and their new exterior on the plaza side; and also for some of the tenants of Midtown Plaza.

Inasmuch as the underground garage forms the base structure for all other new buildings, it had to proceed first, and in order not to interrupt operations of existing enterprises, the construction of the garage had to be done in two stages. One of the important accomplishments of this Rochester core revitalization project is that all relocation problems were met without the need for closing any operations for even a single day.

In spite of the complexity of the task, construction proceeded with surprising speed. The first stage of the garage was completed by the end of November, 1960, and shortly after that work on the structures above was started.

The second stage of the garage was completed in November, 1961, at which time construction activities above the top level of the garage began.

The entire project, with some minor exceptions, was completed by April 10, 1962, and on that date opened to the public.

The minor exceptions to the completion were the roofing over of the arcade connecting Main Street with the plaza area of the development and the final installment of the enlargement of the McCurdy store, located on the corner of that arcade and Main Street. Plans for these additions are completed, but the implementation has been held up, to date, because of certain difficulties that have to be resolved before the Midtown Plaza Holdings Corporation on the one hand, and the owners of the Manger Hotel and the office building on the corner of Main Street and the arcade on the other, can reach an agreement.

So much for the history of Midtown Plaza, which, starting with an idea of our two clients in December, 1956, ended five years and four months later with a vigorously functioning new central core area.

What does this project, then, consist of, and in what manner does it carry out the principles for the revitalization of the urban environment which I have discussed in the foregoing chapters?

1. It separates utilitarian functions from human functions, giving human functions the primary, most desirable space; automobile movement and automobile storage, all service traffic, the loading and unloading of goods, all utilities, have been "put in their place," mostly on subterranean levels. Some serving functions, like air-conditioning and heating plants, have been separated carefully from human functions on upper levels of structures. In order to make this separation possible, underground facilities were constructed for the garaging of private automobiles and for the moving of trucks and service vehicles. Up and down ramps were built for these vehicles, and they were located in such a manner as to make entrance and exit possible in the direction of the core loop and the main loop road. In order to assure congestion-free circulation for vehicles, one new road (Broad Street Extension) was constructed and on other surrounding roads traffic improvements were made.

For public transportation, a system of horizonal separation was adopted; a special terminal facility serves long-distance buses, and special boarding facilities for local buses and taxis were provided.

The beneficial effects on utilitarian functions are by now clearly discernible. In spite of the greater automobile, truck and bus traffic, congestion has dwindled.

The surface areas within the development boundaries have been converted into pedestrian reserves on the ground-floor main level and on the balcony level.

Connection between areas reserved for vehicular traffic and those for pedestrian traffic has been made as convenient as possible. Those arriving by public transportation or taxi have to walk only a few steps, without having to cross any traffic, before reaching the pedestrian areas. Those who arrive by private automobile use escalators and stairways, which transport them from all levels of the three-story garage into the pedestrian area.

2. We have improved environmental quality. We have removed "unsuitable uses," which previously existed in the form of a disorderly hodgepodge of parking lots, storage facilities, etc., and replaced them with highly productive facilities. In the open spaces between these new structures we have created an environment that offers the greatest convenience as well as being conducive to the carrying on of business, to relaxation and to enjoyment. Not only have the spaces between the structures been freed of the dangers to life and health which traffic brings in its wake, but additional environmental values have been created as well.

Midtown Plaza's pedestrian areas are fully enclosed, roofed over and air-conditioned in such a manner that year round a springlike climate prevails. Yet the connection with the outside is not lost. Large skylights make it possible to experience within the pedestrian areas the change from day to night and the changes of weather and of season, without having to suffer any of their inconveniences. What was once narrow, overcrowded, disorderly Cortland Street is now a skylighted plaza 300 feet long, 100 feet wide, and three stories high, containing trees, flower beds, fountains, rest benches, sculpture, exhibit spaces, kiosks, an information booth, and so on.

The arcades and lanes connecting the central plaza with the surrounding streets of the core, though they are only one story high, are endowed with similar environmental values.

3. We have striven to create variety and versatility of urban functions. Midtown Plaza is not a shopping center downtown. It does contain two department stores and about 250,000 square feet of other retail establishments, but it also contains a new 18-story structure housing offices of all types and, on the upper floors, a large terrace restaurant, a bar and over

Midtown Plaza, Rochester, New York. In the open spaces between the existing and new structures there was created a superior environment: a three-story-high, 300-foot-long and 100-foot-wide enclosed, skylighted air-conditioned plaza with trees, flower beds, fountains, sculpture and rest benches.

70 hotel rooms. There is a second office building rising above the levels of the stores, containing the headquarters of the Rochester Telephone Corporation. There are a large public auditorium, a number of meeting rooms, a children's play and amusement area, some private technical schools, a bank, a post office, a number of restaurants including a sidewalk café within the plaza, art galleries, travel bureaus, and so on.

4. We have improved accessibility by public and private transportation. As mentioned earlier, a new bus terminal has been provided for regional transportation. It takes the place of terminal facilities that were formerly poorly located and provided unattractive arrival and departure points. It is estimated that the buses are being used, on an average, by 7,000 persons daily.

The special facilities for the loading and unloading of passengers, which Midtown Plaza has provided for a privately operated local bus company, have encouraged this company to inaugurate a number of new bus lines starting and terminating at Midtown Plaza, and to improve operations on other lines.

5. We have succeeded in achieving revitalization in a city core with a minimum of demolition and a maximum of conservation and rehabilitation. Not a single building of significant economic value was destroyed. Old structures like the two department stores and the hotel were harmoniously integrated with the new ones and improved by enlargement, rehabilitation and modernization.

6. Midtown Plaza is the product of close cooperation between government and private enterprise. I want to stress this fact because some reporters felt that the speedy development of Midtown Plaza proved that private enterprise could do a better job by going it alone. From the historic résumé I have just given, it is apparent that governmental action which brought about public improvements—especially with regard to accessibility—preceded to a large degree the planning of Midtown Plaza, and continued during its construction. Without this prior action, private enterprise would not have taken the risk of investment in such a venture, and without the assistance of government it could not have implemented the total plan.

7. Midtown Plaza is a project that meets the challenge to create the highest achievable compactness and density within the core area of a city. It contains approximately 1,600,000 square feet of productive rentable space. Of this, about 715,000 square feet existed previously, the remainder representing a net gain of suitable urban usage area within the same land area. This high usage was achieved in such manner that public spaces could be

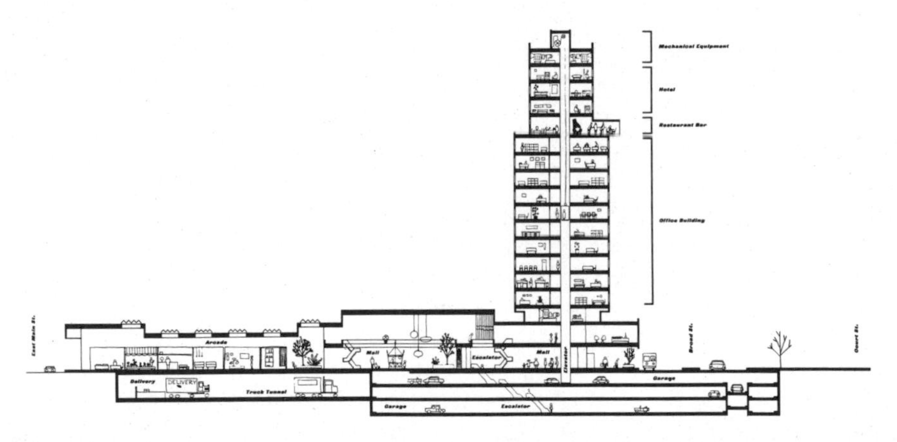

Midtown Plaza, Rochester, New York. Schematic section (longitudinal) shows only one of the two major office buildings. Below ground are the three levels for parking, one level for servicing. On the first and second levels above ground, retail facilities and retail service facilities. On the next eleven floors of the high-rise building are offices. On the fourteenth level, hotel lobby and terrace restaurant. The next three levels are hotel rooms; top level, mechanical equipment.

increased in number and size at the same time. This could be accomplished, of course, only by the method of multiple use of the land. Thus, underground areas on three levels were utilized for car storage and service facilities; the two layers above generally for pedestrian areas, stores, shops, banks, showrooms, auditoria, etc. From this base, then, rise the towerlike structures of the two department stores, two office buildings, and the Midtown Hotel.

8. There was of course a danger that the new facilities provided in Midtown Plaza would trigger the flight of enterprises located in older buildings of Rochester's core area. The management of Midtown Plaza forestalled this by a leasing policy directing all efforts to attract as tenants only those enterprises not already represented in the core area. Thus it can be stated that all the tenants of stores, shops and offices are newcomers to downtown Rochester.

I said before that one of the reasons I wished to discuss Midtown Plaza at considerable length is that it is the only such development in the United States that is actually completed and in operation, presenting therefore the opportunity to observe its results and effects. As these lines are being written, sixteen months have elapsed since its opening in April, 1962. A few days ago, I revisited Rochester in order to get firsthand impressions of Midtown Plaza's operations, of its effects on the central core area, and on the city as a whole. What I have observed encourages me to state that what we have come to regard as the inevitable downward spiral in our city cores can in a short time be converted, even through only *one* well-planned new core element, into an upward spiral—seemingly just as inevitable.

Let me try to prove this. At the time when Midtown Plaza was in the planning stage, twenty years had elapsed since a major private structure had risen in downtown Rochester. The prophets of doom and gloom warned that it would not be possible to rent new office space, and most certainly not store space. As of this date, 95 per cent of all store space is rented and 100 per cent of all new office space.

But beyond that, new building activity all around Midtown Plaza has spurted. A new office building for the Security Trust Company is rising; a new building for the Travelers Insurance Company is under construction; the Rochester Business Institute plans a new structure for its facilities near Midtown Plaza; a new hotel, the Downtowner, has been completed; and in the downtown area as a whole there is unparalleled activity in remodeling, modernizing, repainting and resurfacing of buildings. A number of new downtown structures are in the planning stage.

The most significant and largest structure announced up to now is a new

BEFORE

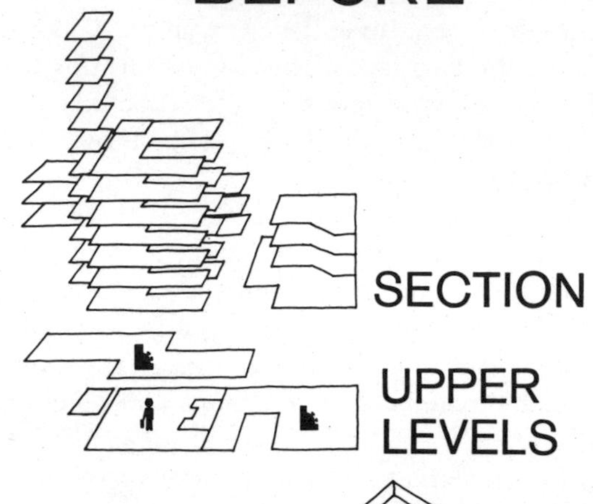

SECTION

UPPER LEVELS

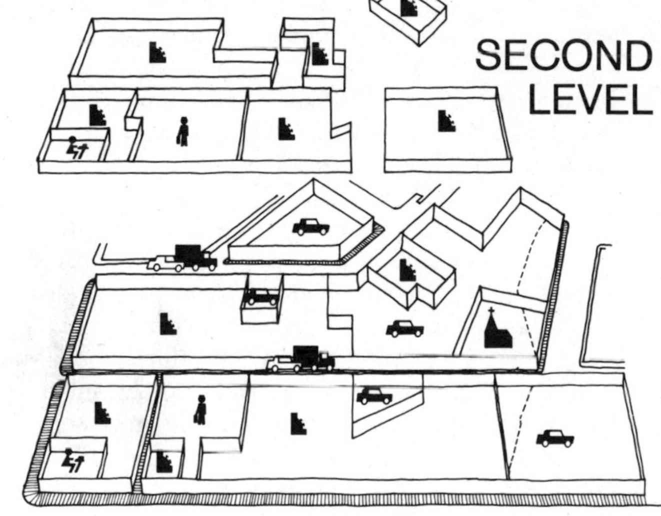

SECOND LEVEL

GROUND LEVEL

RETAIL

OFFICE

HOTEL

PARKING

TRANSPORTATION TERMINAL

CHURCH

SERVICE

AUTO CIRCULATION

MIXED AUTO & TRUCK

PEDESTRIAN

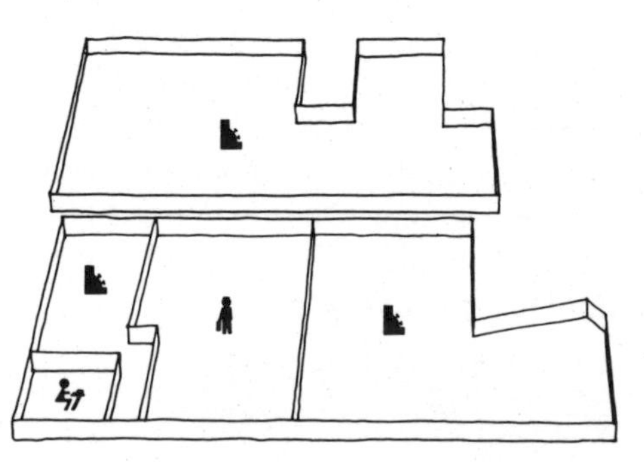

UNDERGROUND

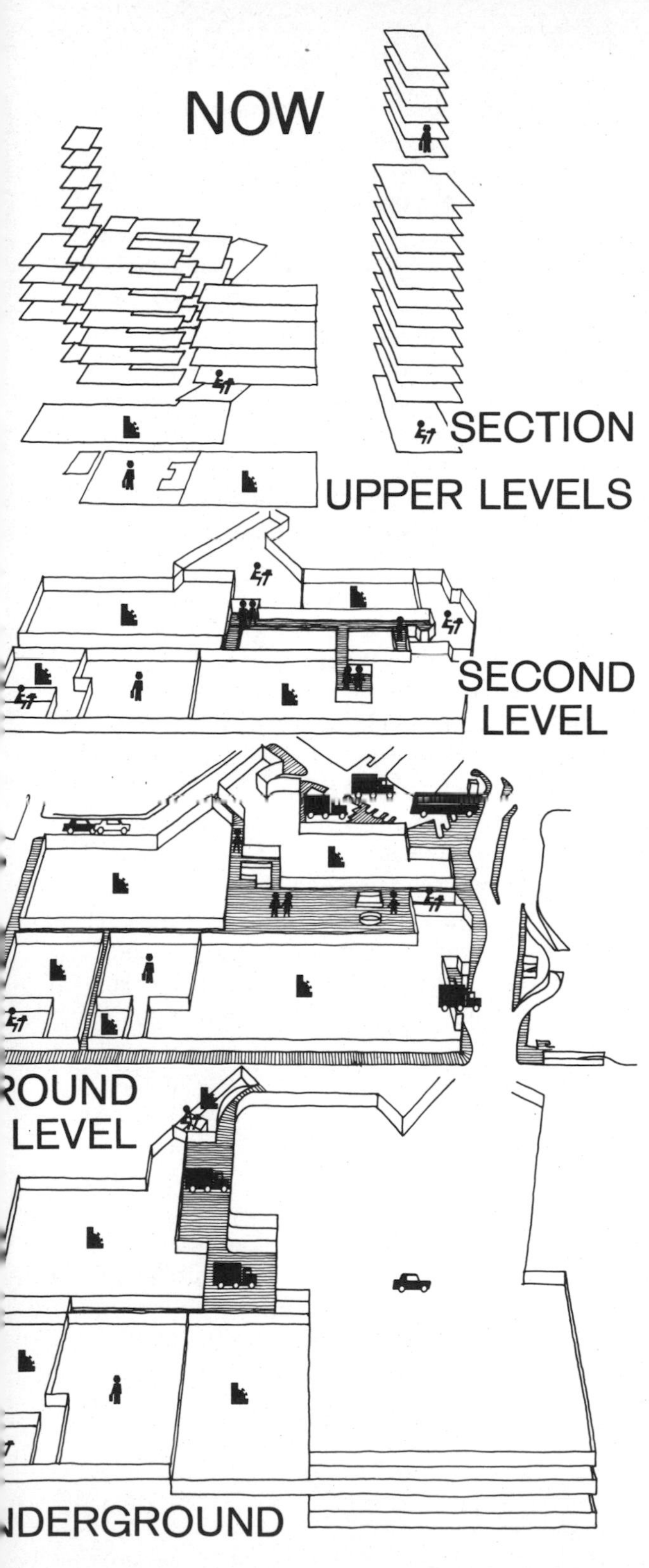

Starting from the bottom of *before* and *now* illustrations, we find:

UNDERGROUND:
Before: only one level, containing storage for retail, hotel and office buildings.
Now: three levels utilized for parking of 2,000 cars, for service and trucking and for retail as well as storage.

GROUND LEVEL:
Before: a confused mixture of parking lots, surface truck and automobile traffic, retailing, warehousing and workshops in shacklike structures.
Now: retailing, hotel and offices grouped around central pedestrian area. In addition, new transportation terminal.

SECOND LEVEL:
Before: small amount of disjointed retailing, some hotel and office use.
Now: markedly increased retailing, office, hotel uses, all connected through balconies, pedestrian ways.

UPPER LEVELS:
Before: only the two department stores and the hotel had upper levels.
Now: department stores are enlarged, two office buildings as high-rise structures were added. One of them contains a hotel on the four top floors.

complex, Xerox Square, which was heralded in all Rochester newspapers on July 16, 1963. This new environmental complex will adjoin Midtown Plaza across Broad Street and will be intimately integrated with it by means of pedestrian bridges. The cost is estimated at $10,000,000. Its major buildings will be two office structures, one of which is projected to be 26 stories high. Xerox, one of the most successful manufacturers of office copy machines, had, by the way, originally intended to construct their office facilities directly adjoining their production plant in Webster, a suburb of Rochester. It appears that the new vigor shown by the core area of Rochester persuaded them to change their original intention and to build in the downtown area. The same change of mind can also be detected in connection with the other new enterprises and structures I mentioned.

The new facilities of Midtown Plaza itself, and of course the new facilities constructed by others, are daily, week in and week out, bringing new urban activity participants into the core area. Their number, however, is much greater than would be explainable if one were to consider just the additional employees and shoppers. This is due to the attracting power the new environment exerts, which has exceeded the fondest hopes of the developers and of ourselves. The enclosed pedestrian spaces and quite especially the large central plaza have proved themselves magnets of the first order. The plaza has taken over the role formerly filled by the old town square. It is not merely a place from which one may reach various offices, hotel facilities and stores, but, beyond that, it has created a climate of new opportunities for which a pent-up desire obviously existed previously. It has become a cause of civic pride, the place where one takes visitors from out of town. There is hardly a day when study committees and delegations from cities all over the United States, and from foreign countries as well, do not arrive there. Rochester has suddenly become a favorite place for conventions, especially for groups concerned with planning, architecture and downtown improvement.

The "Clock of the Nations," which we had visualized as a landmark for the plaza, has not only fulfilled this function but has gone beyond that. At the striking of the hour, hundreds and sometimes thousands congregate around it to admire the puppets, which, through the opening of one of the twelve cylinders, become visible in motion to the accompaniment of folk tunes. When, at certain specific hours, all cylinders open and rotate around the central stem of the clock, the plaza fills up with interested watchers of all ages. The plaza has become a meeting point for individuals who arrange their rendezvous at the Clock or at the sidewalk café, and it also functions as a center for social gatherings. A list of events that took place in the plaza and in the auditorium from May, 1962, to February, 1963, fills sixteen pages

RIGHT Midtown Plaza, Rochester, New York. The Clock of the Nations.

BELOW Midtown Plaza, Rochester, New York. Central Plaza on the occasion of a high school dance.

with remarkable variety. It contains such diverse events as shows of the Rochester Cat Fanciers and of the Mink Breeders Association; receptions for foreign students and an exhibit of the 4-H Club; displays of Tahitian artifacts and of Bibles loaned by the Federation of Churches; a demonstration of Iroquois Indian history; an exhibit of dress and firearms from the Rochester Museum of Arts and Sciences; a Polaris missile display; and a large number of art exhibits. There are listed 70 public musical events of which one, a series of choral concerts given by the St. Joseph School Choir, is reported to have attracted, in all, 24,000 people. Also listed are formal balls of the Junior League of Rochester and the Winter Wonderland Dance of the University of Rochester, as well as a large number of high school and college graduation dances.

Midtown Plaza was also the scene of political meetings of both major parties, each attracting more than 10,000 participants.

What is especially interesting about the pattern of urban participation is that the activities are not concentrated, as in most downtown areas, within the eight-hour working period; cultural, social and recreational functions make the plaza an active, bustling place from early morning to late at night, throughout the week and even on Sundays and holidays.

An interesting sidelight illustrating its impact on the life of the individual is furnished by this story which was published in a local paper. The congregation of a church that had moved to the suburbs decided to institute a program for its senior citizens. The program was announced at a public meeting but had to be shelved when one of the senior citizens in the audience arose and declared, "We don't need a program. We have Midtown Plaza where we can sit, talk, meet people and enjoy ourselves."

The Worcester, Massachusetts, *Gazette* of September 12, 1962, stated, "Midtown Plaza and the heart of Rochester could be described as something like the fairytale King Midas. Everything he touches turns into gold."

The history of Midtown Plaza also highlights one of the weaknesses inherent in the short term of life of our city administrations. The mayor, Peter Barry, who had done most to encourage the construction of Midtown Plaza, came up for re-election at a time when construction activities had not moved aboveground. The election campaign revolved to a large extent about Midtown Plaza, and those who attacked the administration on the basis of "waste of public funds" won the election. Thus it came about that the new mayor, Henry E. Gillette, who officiated at the opening ceremony in April, 1962, was the very one who had forcefully opposed its undertaking. Realizing now the value of the completed structure, he not only praised it but made a generous gesture as well. When it came to the traditional ribbon cutting, he asked the former mayor, to the accompaniment of roaring approval by the citizens crowding the plaza, to assist him. By this gracious act he certainly brought about a more harmonious cooperation between political opponents.

Midtown Plaza has had important effects not only on the city of Rochester; its impact has been nationwide, and its reverberation international. It has given courage to those who plan for and work on the revitalization of other city cores; it has broadened understanding of what is necessary and has eased the way for some of the projected undertakings that I shall now discuss.

If so much could be accomplished with a project like Midtown Plaza, which covers only a small part of a city core, the expectations for the revitalization of the core area of Boston, with its far-reaching integrated approach, should be great. Here, under the leadership of Mayor John F. Collins and development administrator Edward J. Logue, a most comprehensive over-all program for the entire city is taking shape.

In the core, there is already under way the "Government Center" (planned by I. M. Pei, architect), which will contain not only a new city hall and a number of large government buildings but also private office buildings and a variety of other facilities. At this writing, public improvement work underground has been completed, and from the foundations a number of the projected structures have started to rise. There are also under way a number of residential redevelopment projects and rehabilitation projects, some of which are located within the core or in its immediate vicinity.

In Boston, transportation planning is considered an integral part of the redevelopment effort, and improvements in the mass transportation system—including new rapid transit lines, new bus terminals, new subway stations—are significant elements of the entire planning approach. We are presently working on a plan for transfiguration of that part of the core which adjoins Government Center, includes parts of the financial center, all of the retail activities around Washington Street, and reaches around the Common and Public Garden to Arlington Street.

What is especially significant in this undertaking is the pattern of cooperation that has been established between citizenry and government. Mayor Collins describes this pattern as "without parallel in the history of the United States." The cooperation expresses itself as a joint effort undertaken by the Boston Redevelopment Authority and a citizens' committee known as C.C.B.D. (Committee for the Central Business District, Inc.). The committee embraces in its membership retail establishments of all types and sizes, including the Jordan Marsh Company and Wm. Filene's Sons Co., real estate owners, utility companies, banks, newspaper publishers, hotel operators, restaurateurs, movie house operators, and others.

The planning efforts, the mayor announced, would not only be jointly undertaken but jointly supported and financed as well. That this was no idle boast is shown by the fact that our services as planners were retained under two separate contracts: one with the citizens' committee, and one with the Boston Redevelopment Authority.

City government and the citizens' committee have agreed that whatever is planned and implemented must be acceptable to both parties. This of course appears to be the ideal basis to achieve results: not just dictated by the Authority nor purely expressive of motives of private enterprise.

It is of course also the most difficult and time-consuming manner in which to arrive at results, and it will require statesmanlike action to set aside short-term individual interests of the various members of the C.C.B.D. in order to achieve those results which would help the city and its citizens most.

At the time of this writing, some basic planning concepts have been developed and in principle agreed upon by all parties concerned. All of us—the planners, the Boston Redevelopment Authority, the C.C.B.D., economic, transportation and engineering consultants—are now engaged in the task of probing the concepts as to their feasibility from a physical and economic viewpoint.

Though Boston's central area has lost much of its power of attraction because of a rapid spreading out of residential and industrial development, and the inability of public and private transportation media to cope with the increased distances, there are many unique urban features in this old city which we hope not only to conserve but to bring back to full effectiveness. There are, throughout the central core, handsome public structures and churches which could be restored as significant landmarks if they were freed of the blemishes that surface automotive traffic and neglected surroundings have brought upon them.

There is an outstanding urban green and recreational area in the form of the Boston Common and Public Garden. In Boston there still exists a tradition of living in town—in the Beacon Hill area, for example—and with some encouragement, through construction of new residential quarters in a pleasant environment, this tradition of urban living could flourish anew.

There is, finally, an underground rapid transit system which, though it has lost much of its former popularity, is potentially able to act as the main agent of accessibility if some projected new lines are extended, and if general improvement of its station facilities, rolling stock and operations make its use more inviting and convenient.

The basic concept that has been generally accepted is one that organizes the entire core area into a clusterization of pedestrian nuclei, each devoted to a variety of land uses, with an emphasis, however, on those uses which have developed historically. Each of these nuclei would be served by public mass transportation and specifically by the rapid transit system. In order to make each nucleus accessible for automotive transportation (trucks, various types of buses, taxicabs and private automobiles) a system of loop roads surrounding each of the nuclei would be developed and these loop roads would then be connected with the main arterial roads serving the region. Some special-purpose roads for trucks, buses, taxicabs, and for those private automobiles which are entering or leaving garage facilities, would penetrate into each of the pedestrian reserves to a certain depth. They would, however, be designed in such a manner as to permit undisturbed foot traffic in each of the nuclei.

Grade-separated pedestrian connections leading from one nucleus to another will also be provided.

Significant amounts of new residential building within the heart of the city are projected. They will make use of the unparalleled opportunities offered by the inviting vistas over the Common and Public Garden.

It is visualized that the pedestrian areas within each of the nuclei will be provided with the highest obtainable convenience, interest and character. Some of them, especially those within the main retail area, would be covered and air-conditioned; others, such as Old Boston Center, an area richly endowed with historic buildings and located strategically between the Government Center with its tens of thousands of employees and the Washington Street Center, will have open landscaped areas with protected sidewalks in which historic mementoes of Massachusetts' past will be placed.

The basic aim of the Boston core revitalization project is to achieve the goal of better accessibility, mainly by improvement of public transportation; to achieve the aim of compactness by eliminating wasteful and disturbing land usages and replacing them with productive facilities such as new office buildings, stores, theaters and, to a large degree, residential structures; to restrict demolition to those structures which cannot be rehabilitated or are obstacles to the primary planning aims, but in most cases to use the tools of rehabilitation and conservation; to activate urban life in all its expressions in a manner similar to, but on a much grander scale than, that which has been found so successful in Rochester, New York.

I believe that the revitalization of the city core of Boston has a good chance of success if, by our combined efforts, we are able to convince some members of the community that the strong trends of the past twenty years, which brought about deterioration, cannot be reversed by surface measures alone. As everywhere else, there are still those who are firmly convinced that some simple wonder drug can restore health, like any other panacea. There are many such—some originating in the Boston area. Here, as everywhere, there are certain retailers who declare that all they need in

PROJECT AREA NUCLEI		DOMINATING FUNCTION	SUPPORTING FUNCTIONS
Washington Street Center	1	Retail	Office, restaurant, entertainment, parking
Old Boston Center	2	Historic	Retail, tourist, office, restaurant
New England Research Center	3	Office	Retail, hotel, restaurant, parking
Garment Center	4	Fashion display	Retail, restaurant, office, parking
Cultural Center	5	Theater	Retail, restaurant, entertainment, tourist, parking
Park Square	6	Residential Hotel	Retail, entertainment, restaurant, office, parking
Tremont Terrace	7	Residential	Retail, office, cultural, restaurant, parking

EXISTING NUCLEI OUTSIDE PROJECT AREA		DOMINATING FUNCTION	SUPPORTING FUNCTIONS
North Station	I	Transportation	Office, restaurant, retail, residential
Government Center	II	Government Office	Historic, tourist, hotel, restaurant, parking
Fanueil Hall	III	Historic	Service retail, restaurant, waterfront
Waterfront	IV	Residential	Service retail, restaurant, harbor
Financial District	V	Office	Retail, restaurant, parking
South Station	VI	Transportation	Office, restaurant, retail, parking
Tufts New England Medical Research Center	VII	Medical	Restaurant, entertainment, residential
Insurance Center	VIII	Office	Retail, restaurant, residential
Copley Square	IX	Institutional	Hotel, restaurant, retail
Newbury Street Center	X	Retail	Restaurant, office, residential
Prudential Center	XI	Office	Hotel, restaurant, retail, residential

Central area of Boston, Massachusetts. This schematic sketch illustrates the basic concept of organizing the entire core area into a clusterization of pedestrian nuclei, each devoted to a variety of land uses, with emphasis, however, on those which have developed historically. The pedestrian nuclei within the so-called CBD area, for which Victor Gruen Associates is presently developing a plan, are shown with Arabic numerals. The nuclei located in areas outside of this defined project area are shown with Roman numerals.

order to flourish is a huge garage attached to their building. Here, as everywhere, you hear the comment that business might suffer if automobiles are not permitted to stop in front of every shop entrance. And here, as everywhere, you find those who believe that brighter lights, potted plants, and a good paint job could do wonders.

The tendency toward revitalization through cosmetic treatment is well expressed in a project now being considered in Knoxville, Tennessee, where more effective revitalization steps had already been taken in the shaping of historic old Market Square (see page 328). I refer to a project that proudly calls itself "The Gay/Way." A handsome prospectus promises that the measures recommended will prevent "hardening of the arteries," will enable "downtown" to compete effectively with new suburban centers, will bring life back into the city's center. It underscores its promises by juxtaposing two pictures reminiscent of those that used to show a pimply face before the use of a patent cream and a smooth-skinned one allegedly resulting from its use. The recommended measures are: widening of sidewalks, construction of canopies over them for weather protection, modernizing of storefronts, installation of bright lights, placing of flowerpots along curbs.

At first glance the juxtaposed pictures are convincing. The pimply one is a photograph; the smooth one is a nice drawing. In the pimply one, one notices immediately the mass of vehicles congesting Main Street, but in the smooth one, dubbed "The Gay/Way," there are only a few very attractive-looking cars spaced wide apart. Yet there is nothing in the plan to indicate that this would actually happen. Quite the contrary. If the pretty face of "The Gay/Way" would really attract more people, then there would be more traffic confusion, more congestion, more disorder resulting. This trouble would be increased by the fact that the widening of the sidewalks would result in narrower roads. Thus the proclaimed prevention of "hardening of the arteries" would actually not take place; on the contrary, the course of the ailment would be speeded up.

In spite of the fact that all those who sincerely try to bring genuine improvements into the outmoded working pattern of our urban areas have to battle delay because of prejudices, preconceived notions and the desire to get away with surface cosmetics, it can be stated that understanding of the real needs and requirements is slowly spreading. In a number of core revitalization projects, which I shall only briefly mention and which are on a slow but continuous course toward implementation, we have been able to convince government agencies as well as the citizenry of the need for comprehensive and integrated planning.

There is, for example, the revitalization project for the center of Stamford, Connecticut (see pages 230 and 329). This, with a minimum of demoli-

"Gay/Way" project, Knoxville, Tennessee. Though at first glance the juxtaposition of these two pictures seems to imply marked improvement, further analysis reveals that we are dealing here only with "surface cosmetics."

Market Square project in Knoxville, Tennessee. This illustration shows the market square before the project was implemented.

The implemented Market Square project with continuous covered arcades along all buildings around the square, and a market pavilion in the remainder of the center used as a pedestrian area. The two automobiles visible in the picture are there, we hope, only accidentally.

tion, achieves complete separation of utilitarian and human functions. It recreates the heart area as a pedestrian island into which new life is pumped by additional urban functions which will take place in office buildings, public buildings, stores and a considerable number of urban residences. This project has now been fully approved and should come to implementation in the near future.

A similar project for Paterson, New Jersey (see pages 231 and 330)—a revitalization program in the core—has also received approval by Federal, state and local agencies. Here, too, as in Boston, plans were developed with the active participation of the citizens' group know as PLAN (Paterson Looks Ahead Now) and a city administration (under the leadership of Mayor Francis X. Graves, Jr. and urban renewal director William H. Bentele) wide-awake to the needs of their city.

As in Paterson, one of the oldest cities in the United States, so also in Fresno, California (see pages 226, 227 and 228), one of the newer ones, prog-

---

Revitalization project for the core of Stamford, Connecticut. Visualization sketch of Main Street converted into a pedestrian area. In the foreground a residential plaza with a new apartment building on the left. In the middle ground are existing office structures. Behind them on the left side of the picture are a new arcaded store building and a new office building. On the right side of the pedestrian way we see existing stores and a new apartment building with balconies and stores on its first floor. The fact that all disturbances of mechanical transportation are eliminated makes the intimate relationship between office buildings, stores and residential buildings possible.

REVITALIZATION PROJECT FOR THE CORE OF PATERSON, NEW JERSEY

View of Market Street as seen from Paterson Street. Paterson Street becomes a link in the innermost loop road. A bus stop permits visitors to the core to enter the new pedestrian environment.

Main Street shopping promenade. The traffic circulation pattern in this old town was so complex that it was found to be necessary to lead one of the streets over Main Street in order to make automobile circulation feasible. The pedestrian area remains undisturbed by grade crossings. All buildings shown on these drawings are existing ones; no major demolition is necessary.

ress is being made rather swiftly. In Fresno plans were developed in a cooperation between a citizens' group (The Downtown Association of Fresno) and city government (represented by Mayor Arthur L. Selland and redevelopment director Harris O. Hogenson). The work there has proceeded to the stage where our organization, in association with landscape architect Gerald Eckbo, is now preparing working drawings for the conversion of Fulton Street (the main street of Fresno) and its cross streets into landscaped pedestrian areas.

Urbana, Illinois, exemplifies a private revitalization undertaking with municipal cooperation. A Chicago department store, Carson Pirie Scott & Co., was prepared to construct a branch in Urbana provided local interests and government would help to strengthen it by improving the core environment. This led to the formation of a development corporation, which is presently constructing on a strong and significant core element contiguous to the main business area. The buildings of the development surround an enclosed and air-conditioned pedestrian mall; they include the existing Urbana Lincoln Motor Inn, the new Carson Pirie Scott department store, and 165,000 square feet of other retail stores. The city will construct public improvements such as a loop road and multideck parking facilities directly accessible from it (see pages 332 and 333).

In two cities of the United States, so-called pedestrian malls are in full operation. One is Kalamazoo (see page 334), a city for which our office had prepared an over-all redevelopment plan. We had recommended that this plan be executed in various stages, of which the last one was to have been the closing of some of the main streets to automotive traffic. The citizens of Kalamazoo felt that this most dramatic feature should come first, and proceeded accordingly. Thanks to some fortunate circumstances in the over-all existing circulation pattern, the experiment proved rather successful. A number of new stores were built along the new pedestrian way and business has improved.

The second city possessing an operating pedestrian mall is Miami Beach, with its Lincoln Road development. On the basis of last reports, I understand it is reasonably successful. However, Miami Beach is a resort community and therefore atypical, so that its success or failure as a mall experiment could not be regarded as conclusive.

There are many other city projects, presently in work in our offices, which follow generally the same planning principles and methodology. Listed alphabetically, they are:

Buena Park, California
Colton, California
Decatur, Illinois

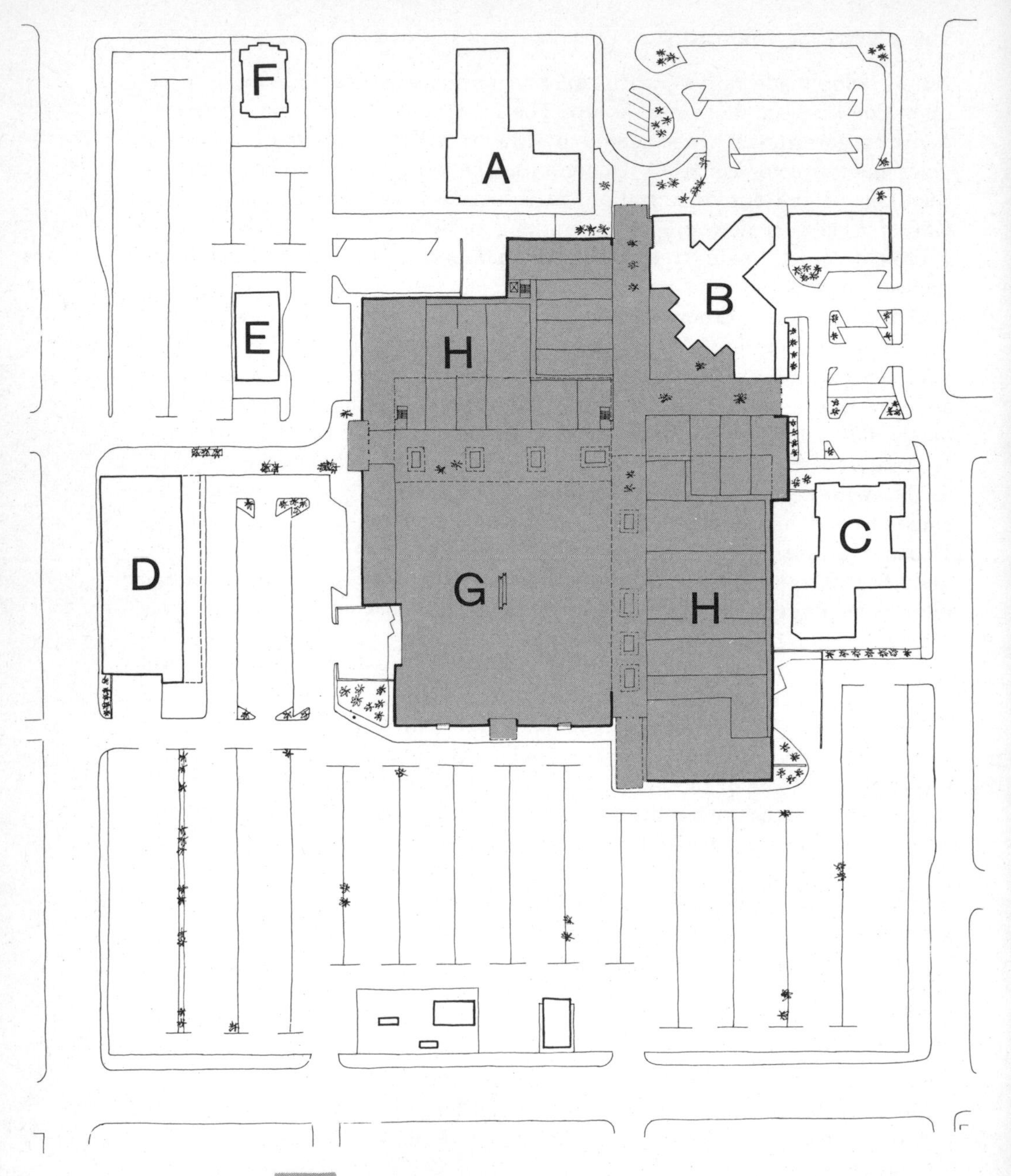

NEW ENCLOSED AIR-CONDITIONED AREA

A	CHURCH	EXISTING AND RETAINED BUILDINGS
B	URBANA LINCOLN HOTEL	
C	POST OFFICE	
D	MARKET	
E	DRUG STORE	
F	APARTMENTS	
G	DEPARTMENT STORE	
H	RETAIL BUILDINGS	

URBANA, ILLINOIS: CORE REVITALIZATION PROJECT

ABOVE *Before Implementation*
The land is under-used; most of it is devoted to streets and surface parking. Most structures are small, disjointed and of low productivity.

BELOW *During Construction (April, 1964)*
Major formerly existing structures (the church, the Urbana-Lincoln Motor Inn, the Post Office) are consolidated through new facilities (department store, retail stores, covered air-conditioned pedestrian areas) into an integrated urban core element. Some internal traffic streets are eliminated; traffic is rerouted over peripheral circulatory road with adjoining parking facilities.

Charles Center, Baltimore, Maryland. In this photograph, the projected new buildings and public squares have been superimposed on an aerial view of the existent city. The complex consisting of some existing buildings and a number of new ones is visible in the center of the photograph. At the time of writing, one structure designed by Mies van der Rohe has been completed and others are under construction.

Kalamazoo, Michigan. Burdick Street converted into a pedestrian area.

HARTFORD, CONNECTICUT ("CONSTITUTION PLAZA")

Core area before development. The characteristic of urban blight is represented by an outmoded street pattern, old structures, destruction of compactness by erosion through parking areas, garages, etc., and many unsuitable uses like warehousing and storage, structures of marginal productivity.

The same area as shown in picture above after partial completion of revitalization program. Note the new circulatory road pattern surrounding large pedestrian areas and the intensified land utilization. The economics of revitalization are illustrated by the fact that the value of taxable properties prior to redevelopment is $2,300,000. The tax values after redevelopment are estimated to be $26,000,000.

Dubuque, Iowa
Green Bay, Wisconsin
Lockport, New York
Newport, Rhode Island
Norfolk, Virginia
Pawtucket, Rhode Island
Redlands, California
Redondo Beach, California
Rockville Center, New York
San Bernardino, California
Santa Monica, California
Stanton, California
Vancouver, B.C.
Waterbury, Connecticut
Woodbridge, New Jersey

There are, of course, a great many significant core revitalization projects on which other planning and architectural offices are engaged. Among these may be found the following:

In New Haven, under the leadership of Mayor Richard Lee, a whole series of improvements—in accessibility, new rehabilitation undertakings, new residential complexes, new industrial centers around the city core—are about to be climaxed with the completion of a major core element on one side of the New Haven green: two major department stores, a number of retail stores, office buildings and hotels adjoining a major parking facility (designed by architect Paul Rudolph and discussed earlier).

Philadelphia was probably the first city to engage actively in efforts toward urban redevelopment (under the guidance of Edmund N. Bacon, executive director of the City Planning Commission). Great strides have been made there toward improvement of public transportation. Commuter traffic especially has literally been put back on the track. Former railroad yards, which cut into the core area and formed what was known for many years as "the Chinese Wall," were removed, and Penn Center, a grouping of office and hotel buildings, rose in their place. Historic monuments were freed from surrounding blight, and Independence Mall is an example of how our historic sites can be lifted to new importance. A number of well-conceived residential developments ring the core. At the moment of writing, the city of Philadelphia is ready to attack the problems of the most intense development within the heart of the city, roughly located along Market Street east of City Hall, and reaching to the new Independence Mall in length, and from Arch Street to Sanson Street in width. On the basis of the concept for this area lie major improvements in public transportation facilities which will find expression in a multipurpose terminal north of Market Street, for commuter trains, long-distance buses, automobiles and trucks.

The city of Bridgeport, Connecticut, stands on the threshold of implementation of a project that would create a strong new core element.

In San Francisco, the comparatively healthy core area will certainly be strengthened by the large new residential development now in construction and known as Golden Gate.

There are, of course, many more, and if I do not mention them all it is partly because I have little personal knowledge of them, and partly because of lack of space.

If we take a look at Europe, we find that there, too, decentralization caused by the growing importance of private automobile transportation has brought about deteriorative effects on the old city centers, and that counter efforts are on the way.

In England there are to my knowledge about sixty-five projects dealing with revitalization of urban centers. I am most familiar with two of them, on which our office has been consulted: one is in Stratford, East London, where an old center, partly damaged by bombing during the war, is to be completely rebuilt; the other is in Wolverhampton, the Midlands, where for reasons of general deterioration similar steps are on the way.

A prime example of reconstruction of an old city center that was destrayed during the war is, of course, Coventry.

A fate similar to Coventry's was experienced by Rotterdam. The rebuilding of this city's major retail area in the form of a pedestrian nucleus, the so-called Lijnbaan (see page 338), has served as a pattern for many projects in Europe.

Stockholm, a highly concentrated city, has embarked on a mammoth project in the very center of town. The completed portions consist of stores, shops, and office buildings arranged around pedestrian areas.

Shopping streets closed to mechanized traffic exist in a number of German cities. A typical example is Stuttgart (see page 338).

Copenhagen converted its major shopping streets, which together are known as Strøget, into a pedestrian way in November, 1962.

In Austria I have seen excellent pedestrian areas functioning to everybody's satisfaction in the provincial towns of Klagenfurt and St. Pölten.

There are in the United States and in Europe undeniable indications that there is still life in the heart of the city. After having gone through an era, starting with the war and culminating in the early 1950s, in which the term "decentralization" was on everybody's lips, and was given more than lip service by residents, merchants, banks and insurance companies alike, we

The Lijnbaan, the new commercial pedestrian nucleus of Rotterdam, Holland.

Pedestrian shopping street, Stuttgart, Germany.

are now living in an era where we are slowly discovering—or rediscovering—the values of centralization and urbanism. Right now, decentralization and recentralization proceed simultaneously. Suburban shopping centers are still being built by the hundreds, sometimes within the influence area of a city core which itself is engaged in a major revitalization program. Such parallel activity of course is a potential threat to the economic success of both enterprises.

There is no doubt, however, that the belief in the suburban region as the only place for expansion has been shattered. Department stores which a few years ago were ready to write off their downtown locations and rely on large suburban units have changed their minds. R. H. Macy, for example, is building a new store in downtown New Haven and has expressed active interest in a number of other locations in city cores for which redevelopment is planned. Even merchandising enterprises that never before had considered central locations as suitable for themselves are now studying a number of such possibilities.

The flight of insurance companies, corporate office buildings, and other major institutions into the suburban regions, if not totally stopped, has slowed down considerably.

The construction of a brand-new city hall in one of our oldest existing city cores (Boston) is certainly symptomatic of the reawakening of interest in urbia.

Another important change in the public mood has taken place within the last ten years. The term "planning," which was looked upon with suspicion as something socialistic if not worse, has become respectable. In all my more recent experiences of exposure to thousands of individuals who, as businessmen or residents, as workers or officials, have discussed and criticized project concepts, an over-all doubt as to the need for planning has never been voiced.

Yet if one considers the hundreds of projects concerned with the revitalization of the heart which either gather dust on shelves or are moving with painful slowness toward implementation over the barriers of lethargy and red tape, one must come to the conclusion that much still remains to be done. The will to establish closer contact with one's fellow men certainly exists. What is preventing us from achieving what we consciously or unconsciously desire is the inadequacy of the legal, intellectual and technical tools at hand. Where these inadequacies lie I shall try to discuss in the following chapter.

20 Are We Equipped?

I HAVE ATTEMPTED TO SHOW, in the preceding chapters, the importance and urgency of the task of transfiguration of our urbanized areas.

The question now arises: Are we equipped to tackle this assignment, and if the answer should not be affirmative, what can we and should we do to improve our equipment and our tools?

The counterattack against the forces of Anti-city will have to be mounted by an efficient and well-organized army. An impressive array of manpower is right now engaged in skirmishes or waiting to be called to duty. One of the handicaps this army seems to suffer under is that while it embraces great numbers of privates, first and second class, and some corporals and sergeants, it has very few, if any, strategists and generals. It is an army of specialists with all types of knowledge and skills within narrowly defined spheres, but, through a faulty training program, it has been carefully shielded from an over-all view of the problem and even kept in ignorance of the interest areas of fellow specialists with whom close cooperation is essential.

To a notable degree, our educational institutions have been training young people with the sole aim of enabling them to earn a living within specific, well-defined fields. Inasmuch as each individual field, in this technological age, has become highly complex, everything that might deflect the interest of a student from his specialty has been protectively removed from the curriculum. Thus, we have trained architects who know how to design an individual structure as far as its visual aspects are concerned but who have to rely blindly on the judgment of other specialists for consideration of utilitarian, economic and sociological aspects. They have also been kept innocent concerning the relationships which the individual structures they design should bear to each other, to cityscape and landscape, or to the community.

We have been training planners solely in a vocational manner, as technicians and administrators, recognizing that most job opportunities in the planning field lie within city planning departments or county or state planning departments. Our planning students have been immersed in knowledge of existing legal tools and administrative techniques but have been discouraged from doing any creative thinking that might interfere with the fulfillment of their prescribed future duties.

In lecturing at various schools of planning in some of our colleges, I have found that the reaction—as far as students were concerned—to a creative planning philosophy was one of utter bewilderment; as to the professors, their reaction was one of obvious distress, caused by the fear that I might be confusing the student mind and deflecting it from its clearly defined itinerary.

We are training traffic engineers by steeping them in that particular "popular science" developed to facilitate movement of the motorcar, filling their heads with traffic counts and systems of automatic signaling, but keeping them quite unaware of the fact that other means of transportation, from pedestrianism to jet planes, even exist.

We are training economists by immersing them in a sea of dollar signs, teaching them the numbers game without giving them an inkling that behind the dollars and behind the numbers are the feelings and thoughts of human beings.

We are training realtors to know everything about real estate values but nothing about real values.

We are training structural, mechanical, electrical and civil engineers, guiding them through the intricacies of their complex fields, but shielding their minds from a true understanding of related fields and the impact of their activities on them.

And we are missing out completely on training men or women who could coordinate the efforts of all these specialists; who could integrate all the specialized knowledge into a meaningful pattern. We are failing to give any of the specialists sufficient awareness of the importance and significance of the role of their co-specialists, and by doing so, we destroy the chance that these technicians, in a spirit of humility, might cooperate with each other.

We are employing, in other words, the techniques of industrial mass production in the field of creating a worthwhile human environment. We have millions of men on the assembly line who perform, day in and day out, one specific little task like the tightening of a screw, but inasmuch as nobody has yet bothered to determine what the end product flowing from the line should look like, the results are more often than not screwy.

The shaping of the human environment cannot be achieved by the assembly line technique. There is an urgent need for the training of a new type of professional man. Lacking a better term, I will call him the environmental architect. He won't need a special title, a special license, or membership in one or another of the professional organizations. But he will have to possess, through a combination of aptitude and training, and as a result of restless seeking for deeper insight into the nature of man, the kind of understanding and convictions that will allow him to view problems and to find their solutions from a high vantage point (not to be confused, however, with an ivory tower).

We cannot hope to train geniuses, but we should attempt to educate men who will at least come close to the universal outlook of the man I paid tribute to in the introduction of this book: Leonardo da Vinci.

We may have to go back to the classic Greek principle of education, "to educate men to know something about everything and everything about something."

That "something about everything" may have to include philosophy, sociology, the arts, literature, economics, politics, science and technology.

We need individuals with a burning interest in and a deep curiosity about all expressions of life, restless seekers after human values. Endowed with a broad background of knowledge in many fields, they will be qualified to act as leaders and coordinators, to select members of their working teams with assurance, to weigh and judge the merits of their advice intelligently; they will be equipped to channel to the best advantage of the whole the individual efforts of the specialists, establishing a sound balance between the primary human goals and the secondary servicing functions.

These men will also have to know "everything about something," and that something will have to be the three-dimensional design of buildings and open spaces.

Thus it appears that the most urgent factor in our task of bringing about an improvement in our equipment is an overhauling of our educational system. Starting in grade school and continuing through high school, we will have to open the eyes of our children to an understanding of the importance of the human environment; and in our higher institutions of learning we will have to expose our youth, whatever their special training may be, to an appreciation of the relationship of their special fields to the whole.

Beyond that, we will have to train those who show sufficient intellectual curiosity and ability to become thoughtful shapers of the human environment.

How imperfectly existing educational facilities serve the task is illuminated by an office memorandum which one of my partners, Ben Southland (who is head of our planning department and an architect by training), circulated to all partners and associates in an appeal for help in recruiting personnel. It read:

> We all agree that nationwide there is a dire shortage of experienced, imaginative people in the planning profession. The natural thing would be to attract outstanding students from planning schools, but we find that these schools are concerned only with administration and planning economics. In the past we have been successful in finding imaginative people only by looking for non-conformists. We have hired people from government posts, but we usually found out to our pain, and I guess to theirs also, that these men, used to regular routine, are emotionally just not fitted to participate in our work which daily and hourly poses new challenges. We have up to now been most successful by transferring people from design and architectural departments into the planning department. Yet these men need additional training and this is always a time consuming process. I therefore urgently appeal for advice and help concerning this problem of recruiting for the planning department.

Even when we are able to resolve the problem of equipping ourselves for the task by mustering the human resources, we will have to furnish the men with the tools for their work—tools such as laws, regulations, administrative techniques, and funds.

Some potent tools have recently been created. Legislation for slum clearance, urban redevelopment, and urban renewal has been enacted by the Federal, state and local governments. In a comparatively short time these laws have been not only created but refined. Yet they still fall far short of being suitable for the task at hand. President Kennedy said, in a message to Congress on housing and urban renewal legislation:

> Urban renewal laws to date have been too narrow to cope effectively with the basic problems facing old cities. We must do more than concern ourselves with bad housing—we must reshape our cities into effective nerve centers for expanding metropolitan areas. Our urban renewal efforts must be substantially reorganized from slum clearance and slum prevention into positive programs for economic and social regeneration. This program, if it is to be effective, must help local communities to go beyond the project and project approach.

This message, I feel, outlines basically the direction in which urban renewal legislation should be shaped. However, in actuality only a few, hesitant steps have been taken in the direction of which the President spoke. Basically, communities still use Federal assistance mainly for the purpose of total clearance of blighted or slum areas, whether they be residential, commercial or industrial, taking advantage of the possibility of assembling individually held properties through the right of eminent domain and, after demolition of existing structures, reselling the land to private entrepreneurs at bargain rates. These bargain rates are achieved by means of using Federal financial assistance for the write-down of land cost. In most cases, small individualized development is then replaced by so-called project development, which, though providing new structures in place of old ones, is not necessarily superior in working pattern and human values to what existed before.

In our free-enterprise society it appears to be perfectly legitimate that the power and financial strength of government should be utilized to create potentials and opportunities for private initiative. But it would appear that government action should be directed to those efforts and tasks which cannot be met by individuals. Only government—Federal, state or city—can effectively create the basic prerequisites for urban organization. Only government can help to create better-functioning urban patterns, improve urban transportation, protect natural resources, create nature reserves and recreational areas.

Relating government action to the specific problem of the revitalization of our established city centers, it is government which can bring about superior accessibility through mass transportation and improved circulation for individualized transportation; it is government which can direct the proper usage of land so that various functions are placed in suitable locations; and on governmental agencies will fall the task of assembling land in those cases where unusable crazy-quilt patterns of individual ownership make meaningful land usage impossible; it is governmental action which is needed to bring about the strict separation of utilitarian and human functions.

However, once the basically sound conditions, opportunities and potentials have been established through such governmental action, then truly enterprising free enterprise can be expected, through individual initiative, to take over.

I believe that there is a clear line of demarcation between the public and the individual spheres of influence. Into the public domain falls the creation of those conditions and prerequisites needed for orderly and meaningful development; into the private domain falls the proper utilization of the opportunities and potentials thus created.

One of the reasons for the comparative lethargy of government in its attitude toward the fate of American cities lies in the composition of the Congress of the United States. Because of the outdated methods by which we elect our representatives, rural interests have a much larger representation in both Houses than actual population distribution would warrant. Thus, measures that would be helpful to the large and growing majority of urbanites usually arouse little interest in Congress and are more often than not defeated. This condition became apparent when the proposal of the Kennedy Administration to create a new Cabinet post for a Secretary of Urban Affairs was voted down. Yet it would appear logical that inasmuch as we have a Cabinet post for a Secretary of Agriculture who represents approximately 20 per cent of the people, it would be only fair if there should be a similar post to afford representation to the 80 per cent of urbanites. A Department of Urban Affairs could be of great significance if within it there could be concentrated the numerous responsibilities now scattered among a large number of departments. A Department of Urban Affairs would, for example, have to be in charge of all problems involving urban transportation—whether by mass media or by individualized means; it would have to handle control of air pollution, water pollution, and all other matters that affect the health, the protection, the convenience and the ability to earn a living, of urbanites.

Another of the tools that will be essential, if cities are to continue to exist, is their power to govern the areas which they are economically supporting. Urban population explosion, combined with urban sprawl and suburbanization, has led to a condition in nearly every metropolitan area in the United States where city boundaries, which usually have been frozen for a long time, no longer coincide even approximately with the influence area of the city. Thus, half—and in many cases even more—of the population depending for its livelihood on the city reside and pay taxes to independent communities spread over the region. To make matters worse, it is usually the economically weakest part of the populace which lives within the city boundaries, requiring the greatest amount of public services but unable to pay the required taxes, and the economically strongest segment which lives outside, enjoying lower tax rates and better services. This absurd situation creates a steady chain of budgetary crises for the central cities; in spite of an endless search for new income sources, they find themselves unable to raise the necessary funds to provide adequate public services, which they have to furnish not only for those living within the boundaries but also for those who visit. Whether this situation should be corrected through legislation—enabling cities to annex areas—or through some form of metropolitan government—which at least would deal with all those problems that affect the entire region—is a much-debated question that will have to be resolved in one form or another.

Of the legal tools that we have on hand, zoning regulations seem to me to be due for a complete overhaul. Zoning was one of the first planning measures adopted in the United States, and when it was introduced it was directed mainly at the protection of residential areas from the annoyances and disturbances of an immature technology. Since the introduction of zoning legislation, technology has grown up, and most of the smoke-belching chimneys and earsplitting noises have disappeared. Zoning today is applied wrongly to promote a compartmentalization of land for various uses, thereby creating unreasonable distances between functions which should be intimately related to each other.

I have put my finger on only some of the soft spots that exist in the arsenal of our equipment for the counterattack. There are many more. But the possibility also exists of inventing and fabricating new tools, if we will use half the ingenuity and money that we are now devoting to the conquest of outer, orbital space for the conquering of inner city space.

In a talk which he gave at the Conference on Metropolitan Transportation and Urban Renewal, sponsored by the University of Southern California, one of my partners, Edgardo Contini, said: "Why should we limit this process solely to the repair of incurable damage, and why not intelligently accept the same degree of community responsibility and participation to anticipate and prevent trouble, to avoid decay and to increase the efficiency, economy, and amenity of urban growth? This extension of the community's control would be far less disruptive of human welfare than urban renewal presently is because nobody would be uprooted except the farmer, who is being uprooted anyway by the increased burden of taxation that accompanies urban sprawl."

Enlarging upon this thought, he pointed to the example of some European countries, specifically Sweden and Holland, and proposed the extension of urban renewal processes from those dealing solely with areas which are already blighted to those which would be in danger of creating new deterioration if unplanned development is permitted.

In similar fashion writes Wolf von Eckhardt, in an article called "New Towns in America" which appeared in the *New Republic* on October 26, 1963. He says: "We have accepted the fact that municipalities, states, and the federal government buy urban land and sell it at discount to private developers. Now we must merely adjust to applying this same principle to open land. Why should slum clearance be O.K. and slum prevention be taboo? Why should we allow the government in urban renewal but not in urban creation?"

The theme of the improvement of our equipment is so broad that a number of books could be written about it—and I hope they will be.

Within the framework of this book, I felt I could not do more than point to the chinks in our armor and state that the answer to the question "Are we equipped?" is, unfortunately, not a satisfactory one.

Does that mean that we have to give up hope and resign ourselves to the idea that the deterioration of urbia is unavoidable? Does it mean that we should abandon all our efforts toward the rebirth of the hearts of our cities? Or does it mean that we should wait, postpone all our efforts, until such time as our equipment is markedly improved? My answer to those questions is:

Though our tools and our equipment are by no means perfect, they have been improved considerably over the past ten years. There is every reason to hope that the future will bring improvement at an accelerating rate.

Until our equipment is further improved, we must work with the tools at hand. This means more sweat, more labor, more time and complications. In some cases it may mean that the solutions will not be ideal, but if they are basically well conceived, they will still result in significant betterment of the urban environment.

I stated at the end of the Introduction that the renaissance of urbia is already under way. The growing number of undertakings, the intensified interest of the citizenry at large in urban problems, and the reawakened interest in public mass transportation prove my contention.

A typical phenomenon throughout the history of the United States is that once the recognition of the urgency of the specific task is recognized by the public, pressures arise that speed up the welding of the tools—legal, educational and otherwise—which are necessary to fulfill it. I believe we now stand at the brink of an epoch during which progress toward the improvement of the urban environment will take place at an ever-accelerating rate.

Some Books

of Special Interest

BURTON, HAL, *The City Fights Back*. New York, Citadel Press, 1954. A useful and rather complete nation-wide survey of what cities are doing to keep pace with traffic, zoning, shifting population, smoke, smog and other problems. From material developed by Urban Land Institute.

Fortune, EDITORS OF, *The Exploding Metropolis*. New York, Doubleday & Company, Inc., 1958. A very readable, well-illustrated series of articles which originally appeared in *Fortune*.

GORDON, MITCHELL, *Sick Cities*. New York, Macmillan, 1963. A devastating catalogue of our urban ills, of interest to professional and layman alike. Points up the gap between urban disease and measures being taken to cure it. Author's expressed purpose: "to light up some of the darker corners of city housekeeping." The book certainly achieves this purpose in a manner which is both enlightening and depressing.

GOTTMAN, JEAN, *Megalopolis*. New York, The Twentieth Century Fund, Inc., 1961. The author appears to take the attitude that inasmuch as we've got Megalopolis we had better like it.

Gutkind, E. A., *The Twilight of Cities.* New York, The Free Press of Glencoe; London and New York, Macmillan, 1962. Discouraged by what has happened to the city Mr. Gutkind obviously once loved —like many of us—the author reacts by giving up completely. He advocates its complete dissolution and a new pattern of centerless regional living.

Handlin, Oscar, *The Newcomers.* Cambridge, Massachusetts, Harvard University Press, 1959. Results of a three-year study of New York's newest immigrants, the Negro and the Puerto Rican, in a changing metropolis. Undertaken by Harvard's Graduate School of Public Administration for Regional Plan Association, Inc., the book will interest those readers who are concerned with the problem of our minorities.

Haworth, Lawrence, *The Good City.* Bloomington, Indiana University Press, 1963. A philosopher's attempt to shape the city of the mind— to give to today's builders an image of the ideal they must seek to foster. The author recognizes complexity and opportunity as underlying conditions of the good city and speaks out in favor of order, duty and community.

Hoover, Edgar M., and Vernon, Raymond, *Anatomy of a Metropolis.* Cambridge, Massachusetts, Harvard University Press, 1959. Comprehensive analysis of the internal structure of a metropolitan area. Part of the New York Metropolitan Region Study undertaken by Harvard's Graduate School of Public Administration for Regional Plan Association, Inc.

Howard, Ebenezer, *Garden Cities of To-Morrow.* Published originally in 1898 under the title *To-morrow: A Peaceful Path to Social Reform.* Republished in 1902 as *Garden Cities of To-Morrow,* S. Sonnenschein & Co., Ltd., London. (Note: The book was republished by Faber & Faber, London, 1945.) One of the classics of urban planning. Although those who follow Howard's teachings are aware of the part which deals with the individual garden city as such, few seem to realize that he also promoted a new kind of metropolitan growth pattern of cellular structure which, at least to this writer, appears to be Ebenezer Howard's most significant and farsighted contribution.

Jacobs, Jane, *The Death and Life of Great American Cities.* New York, Random House, 1961. Mrs. Jacobs' interestingly written and highly personal book has a special value in that it is based on personal experience and observation from the vantage point of her residence located in the Greenwich Village area in New York. Her observations and recommendations are of great validity in areas which are similar in character to Greenwich Village, which can be found in other parts of New York City and in some of the older cities along the eastern seaboard and possibly Chicago. They are, of course, less, if at all, valid for newer cities, for urbanization in metropolitan areas or for the planning of new communities.

JELLICOE, GEOFFREY A., *Motopia.* New York, Praeger, 1961. A study of the evolution of urban landscape which culminates in a proposal for urban living in which structures for human functions are subordinated to the automobile roads located on their roofs.

KEATS, JOHN, *The Crack in the Picture Window.* Boston, Houghton Mifflin Company, 1957; Cambridge, Massachusetts, The Riverside Press, 1957. A "now it can be told" approach to the waning lures of suburbia. Light but by no means frivolous.

LE CORBUSIER, *The City of Tomorrow and Its Planning.* New York, Payson & Clarke, Ltd., 1929. Translated from the 8th French edition of *Urbanisme.* These views, expressed in the beginning of the twentieth century, are surprisingly prophetic as far as the impact of mass transit by automobile is concerned. However, though the proposed solutions have extended and still extend a significant influence on planners and architects, they have rather tended to destroy urbanism by loosening the urban fabric.

MUMFORD, LEWIS, *The City in History.* New York, Harcourt, Brace & World, Inc., 1961. One of the foremost interpreters of urban culture traces the historic growth of the city in an urbane and scholarly fashion. A vital and engrossing book.

MUMFORD, LEWIS, *The Highway and the City.* New York, Harcourt, Brace & World, Inc., 1963. A companion volume to Mr. Mumford's *The City in History,* but may be read for itself alone. Deals with present-day problems of the city. Some of the essays appeared originally in *The New Yorker.*

OWEN, WILFRED, *Cities in the Motor Age.* New York, The Viking Press, 1959. An expert on traffic and transportation realistically appraises the dangers posed by automobile traffic in urban centers. A highly readable book.

REGIONAL PLAN ASSOCIATION BULLETIN No. 100, *Spread City.* New York, Regional Plan Association, 1962. An analysis of the problems of growth of the New York metropolitan area.

SCHNEIDER, WOLF, *Babylon Is Everywhere.* New York, McGraw-Hill Book Co., 1963. A well-illustrated historical and social analysis of the city throughout the ages. One of the author's conclusions: "The city is an invention made by Pedestrians. The parking place cannot supplant the market place." A highly readable book.

TUNNARD, CHRISTOPHER, *The City of Man.* New York, Charles Scribner's Sons, 1963. A backward look at man's efforts to find a satisfactory solution to contemporary social and esthetic needs in urban life. The style is personal and anecdotal.

TUNNARD, CHRISTOPHER, and PUSHKAREV, BORIS, *Man-Made America: Chaos or Control?* New Haven and London, Yale University Press, 1963. An examination of the landscape of mid-century America, the result of five years of intensive research at Yale by a team of experts. Though intended primarily for architects, planners and allied professionals, its ultimately optimistic message is also for the layman concerned with understanding and improving his rapidly changing environment. Well illustrated.

TYRWHITT, J., SERT, J. L., ROGERS, E. N., Editors, *The Heart of the City: Towards the Humanization of Urban Life.* New York, Pellegrini & Cudahy, 1952. A compendium of essays and discussions of internationally renowned architects and planners dealing with the problems of the core of villages, small towns, etc., richly illustrated.

WHITEHILL, WALTER MUIR, *Boston: A Topographical History.* Cambridge, Massachusetts, The Belknap Press of Harvard University Press, 1959. Case history of the physical evolution of a historic city. How its appearance has changed and the reasons for it, amply and charmingly illustrated with old engravings, drawings, lithographs, maps and photographs old and new.

WRIGHT, FRANK LLOYD, *Broadacre City.* The material was first publicly presented as a lecture at Princeton and appears in *When Democracy Builds,* The University of Chicago Press, 1945. Frank Lloyd Wright's Utopia, which takes the form of a spread-out pattern of living that only by the greatest stretch of the imagination can be called a city.

List of Illustrations

Abbreviations: ARCH = Architect
PH = Photographer
S = Source
ART = Artwork

Index